Backroad Mapbook

Welcome
to the fourth edition of
the Backroad Mapbook
for Southwestern BC

The Backroad Mapbooks have had a history of doing substantial changes and updates to the book and we are very confident you will be astounded by the improvements found within this book.

The first part of the book is devoted solely to the reference section. It is easy to see that this section has been expanded. People will find more lakes and streams to fish, more parks to visit, more areas to paddle and even places to look for wildlife.

Despite the additions to the writing, followers of the Backroad Mapbooks will be more impressed with the new look maps. The first thing that will jump out at you is the relief shading. This amazing feature will help people understand the dramatic topography found in Southwestern BC. Another prominent feature is the clarification of paved roads. Now people with RV's and cars will know which roads they will find much smoother to travel on. We have also spent countless hours updating the road and trail systems as well as adding new recreational features such as new provincial parks and wildlife viewing areas.

Southwestern BC is a dynamic area. We cover a large area and offer a lifetime of things to do and see in the outdoors. From Greater Vancouver through to Manning Park and the Fraser Canyon, from Squamish and Whistler past Lillooet and all along the Sunshine Coast, the recreational opportunities are endless.

The Backroad Mapbook is much more than a set of maps; it is an explorer's guide. The maps and writing will let you dream of places not so far away. So sit back and enjoy what we have to offer.

Backroad Mapbooks

DIRECTORS
Russell Mussio
Wesley Mussio
Penny Stainton-Mussio

VICE PRESIDENT
Chris Taylor

COVER DESIGN & LAYOUT
Farnaz Faghihi

PRODUCTION MANAGER
Brett Firth

PRODUCTION
Andrew Allen
Shaan Desai
Shawn Caswell
Farnaz Faghihi
Colin Holdener
Grace Teo
Dale Tober

SALES /MARKETING
Jason Marleau
Chris Taylor

WRITERS
Russell Mussio
Wesley Mussio
Trent Ernst

National Library of Canada Cataloguing in Publication Data

Mussio, Russell, 1969-
Mussio Ventures presents Backroad mapbook with relief maps. -- 4th ed.

Prepared by Russell Mussio, Wesley Mussio and Trent Ernst.
Cover title.
Includes indexes.
Incomplete contents: Vol. 1. Southwestern B.C.
ISBN 1-894556-20-8

1. Recreation areas--British Columbia--Maps. 2. British Columbia--Maps.
I. Mussio, Wesley, 1964- II. Ernst, Trent III. Title. IV. Title: Backroad mapbook.

G1170.B23 2003   912.711   C2003-900142-3

Published by:

Backroad Mapbooks

5811 Beresford Street
Burnaby, BC, V5J 1K1
P. (604) 438-3474   F. (604) 438-3470
E-mail: info@backroadmapbooks.com
www.backroadmapbooks.com
Copyright © 2003 Mussio Ventures Ltd.
Updated 2004, 2005

Acknowledgement

This book could not have been compiled without the relentless effort of Trent Ernst. He headed the research and writing effort and did a fabulous job of digging up new recreational opportunities and describing them in a creative, yet appealing way. We are also indebted to Stuart Kenn for helping us the relief shading to all the maps. Combined with the talented people at Mussio Ventures Ltd., Shawn Caswell, Farnaz Faghihi, Brett Firth, Chris Taylor, Grace Teo, Dale Tober and Heather Yetman, we were able to produce the most comprehensive guidebook for a truly spectacular region of British Columbia. Readers

Books like this are an exercise in research, not only by us, but by the many people who we can turn to for answers and information. Some are paid to know what they know (recreation officers, forest rangers, etc.), some, like us, are just passionate about the outdoors, and have spent their lives learning all they can about their neck of the woods. Some of the people whose knowledge we leaned upon for this update were:

Dan Burnett and all the cubs over at the Beaver Canoe Club, who confirmed what we already knew, and set us straight where we were off our rocker. April Mol, for Wildlife Watching. Inge Wilson at the Hope Chamber of Commerce who helped us find a bunch of new trails in Hope. Lee Lau for verifying accuracy of the North Shore Trails. Brenda Triance at the Squamish Forest District, Holly Meagher at the Chilliwack Forest District, Chris Greenwell at the Sunshine Coast Forest District and the fine folks at Weyerhaeuser for sending us those up to date road maps. We also hassled many other forest service personnel for answers to questions about which sites are currently open, and which ones are closed, knowing that by next year, everything may (and probably will) change. All the BC Parks people who gave us information on new parks, and set us straight on some errors that slipped through the last time. All the people who sent in notes saying that you couldn't catch this species of fish in this lake, or that road had been washed out at that bridge; without input like this, these mapbooks wouldn't be the most accurate, complete and up to date guides in the province. And for all those who helped, but whose names we forgot to write down, thank you.

Finally we would like to thank Allison, Devon, Nancy, Madison and Penny Mussio for their continued support of the Backroad Mapbook Series. As our family grows, it is becoming more and more challenging to break away from it all to explore our beautiful country.

Help Us Help You

A comprehensive resource such as the **Backroad Mapbook for Southwestern BC** could not be put together without a great deal of help and support. Despite our best efforts to ensure that everything is accurate, errors do occur. If you see any errors or omissions, please continue to let us know.

Call (604) 438-FISH (3474)

Toll free 1-877-520-5670

Fax 1-604-438-3470

e-mail updates@backroadmapbooks.com
Mail to: 5811 Beresford Street
            Burnaby, BC, V5J 1K1

All updates will be posted on our web site

www.backroadmapbooks.com

Disclaimer

Table of Contents

Outdoor Recreation Reference Section

Map Section

Foreword

The Backroad Mapbook is truly a unique product. No other source covers Southwestern BC with as much detail or information on all types of outdoor recreation activities.

The Backroad Mapbook is simple to use. There are two sections in the book, the reference section and the maps. If you know the activity you are planning, simply turn to that reference section and find the area that you are interested in. If you are planning a trip to a specific area, you should consult the index to find the appropriate map(s) and look for the various recreational opportunities highlighted in green and red.

The reference section found in the guide includes information on both saltwater and freshwater fishing, hot springs, paddling routes, parks and wilderness camping (recreational sites), multi-use trails (hiking/biking, and off road trails), wildlife viewing and winter recreation. Countless hours have been spent in researching this book, making it the most complete compilation of outdoor recreation information you will find on the region anywhere. This information can be enjoyed by anyone who spends time in the great outdoors.

Our maps have been developed and updated using a wide variety of sources including the current forestry and logging road maps. Therefore, our maps are very detailed as they show a myriad of logging roads in addition to the various trail systems available. We provide a map legend at the start of the maps to illustrate the region we cover as well as how to decipher the various grades of roads and symbols used on the maps.

New to the maps is relief shading. It should be pointed out that this relief is included to give readers a general idea of topography (the accuracy is 25 metres/82 feet with a Sunangle of NW & SW). We have also included UTM Grids (datum NAD 1983; projection Albers Equal Area) and Longitude and Latitude reference points for GPS users. We must emphasize that these are for reference only. We cannot guarantee the accuracy of all sources we use to update the maps.

Although the Backroad Mapbook is the most detailed and up-to-date resource available to recreationists, it must be noted that it is only a planning and access guide. We have gone to great lengths to ensure the accuracy of the book. However, over time, road and trail conditions change. Always be prepared and please respect private property!

Backroad Travel

Generally speaking, Southwestern BC has an excellent backroad system that provides easy access into the backcountry. Cars or RV's can travel many of the secondary roads, most of which are paved or hard packed gravel. The paved roads are shown on the maps as thicker black lines with a white fill. Thicker black lines mark the better gravel or main roads. Branching from the main roads are side roads and trails of all shapes and sizes. These routes, marked by thinner black lines and dashed lines on our maps, should be left to the off-road enthusiasts and trail users.

Although we have done our best to classify the road systems on our maps, road and trail conditions can change very quickly. Weather, the status of road systems and the degree of maintenance can all affect the road systems. During logging hours (6 am to 6 pm) or at times of extreme fire hazard, logging and rural roads may be closed to the public. Other roads may be gated to protect equipment in the area. Further, more and more roads are becoming deactivated. This can result in bridges and culverts being removed, making the road virtually impassable. Be sure to pay attention to road signs and always watch for logging trucks. It is also recommended to contact the nearest Forest District Office for information on specific road conditions.

Unfortunately, it is a period of great upheaval in the provincial recreation system. The Forest Service will no longer be looking after Forest Recreation Sites and many forest service roads (FSR) will not be maintained. This is going to restrict access to many of the sites, and people without access to a four-wheel drive or ATVs may find it more difficult to access the backcountry. On another level, provincial parks are soon going to be looked after by private operators, and some may have services withdrawn. While this is an accurate picture of outdoor recreation in Southwestern BC at the time it was written, we cannot vouch that it will be by the time you read this. If possible, check with someone in the know before you go.

www.backroadmapbooks.com, has updates on access issues, as well as any new or changed information. If you try to go somewhere and find that things have changed from what we've written, please, send us an email and let us know. As always, we encourage comments, stories and pictures from our readers. Please drop us a line.

Russell and Wesley Mussio: Founders of Backroad Mapbook Series

Fishing

(Lake, River and Stream Fishing)

Lake Fishing

With the excellent saltwater and stream fishing available in southwestern BC, no wonder lake fishing receives little interest. If you want to sample some of the local lakes, you will find better luck with the stocked lakes. Unfortunately, many of the fish remain small (usually less than 30 cm/12 in) since most coastal lakes have acidic, nutrient poor waters resulting in small insect populations and slow growing trout.

This is not to discourage you, as there are still a multitude of good lake fishing options ranging from remote walk-in lakes to some fine large trolling lakes. As a general rule of thumb, the lower elevation lakes (lower than 1,200 metres/3,940 feet) offer better fishing beginning in early April until late June. When the low elevation lakes warm, anglers should focus their efforts on higher elevation lakes. These lakes usually open up in early June and remain productive over the summer months. Into the fall, the lower elevation lakes pick up again and by late fall, the higher elevation lakes begin to ice over.

Remember to review the fishing regulations before heading out. Coastal lakes are heavily regulated to ensure that the fish stocks are not significantly depleted and remain healthy for years to come.

If you are looking for more details on the better lakes in the region, why not pick up a copy of **Fishing BC: Lower Mainland**. This book has depth charts, facility and fishing information, hatch and stocking charts and a whole lot more. The lakes marked with a ⊶ symbol are highlighted in the Fishing BC series.

Lower Mainland

Alice Lake Provincial Park (Map 20/D6)
Alice Lake Provincial Park is very popular and receives heavy use throughout the summer months, despite the fact that the fishing is better in the spring and fall. The park is accessed by a short paved road off of Highway 99, and is home to a handful of low elevation lakes. The 11.5 hectare **Alice Lake** has dolly varden, rainbow and cutthroat. In addition to typical spring fly patterns, the trout react favourably to the black ant hatch in May. The stocked fish tend to be small (to 30 cm/12 inches).

> **Edith Lake** is found 1 km (0.6 mile) along an easy trail from the parking lot. Fishing is best in spring and fall for small stocked rainbow and a few wild cutthroat.

> **Fawn lake** is the smallest (1.6 hectare) of four main lakes in Alice Lake Provincial Park. It is also the farthest lake from the parking lot, a 2 km (1 mile) hike in. The lake is stocked with rainbow that average about 20-25 cm (8-10 inches) in size.

> **Stump Lake** is found a short hike from the parking lot and offers stocked rainbow, and splake (a cross between lake trout and eastern brook trout that failed to take). While most of the rainbow fall into the 20-30 cm (8-12 inches) range, there are some here that are up to 50 cm (18 inches).

Allan Lake (Map 3/F2) ⊶
Allan Lake is a small (10 hectare), shallow, low elevation (100 metres/325 feet) lake northeast of Mission in the Hatzic Valley. The lake is surrounded by private property, and contains some rainbow. In summer, the lake is very warm and even less productive than it is in spring or fall.

Alouette Lake (Map 13/C7, 3/C3) ⊶
Alouette Lake is a large (1,650 hectare) lake that is the main feature within Golden Ears Provincial Park. The lake has recently benefited from a fertilization program that aids the intensive stocking program. With the fertilization, the kokanee numbers have picked up and as a result the size of the cutthroat, rainbow, dolly varden and lake trout have shown some improvements. Some of the lake trout can grow to over 10 kg (22 lbs) and are caught by trolling a plug below the 60 feet (18 metre) level. The other species can be found by trolling along the drop-offs at one of the creek estuaries or in one of the many bays. The lake is very deep (up to 130 metres/423 feet deep) and the fish can be scattered.

Alta, Alpha and Nita Lakes (Map 29/G6)
Located in the heart of Whistler, this chain of lakes is found around 620 m (2,035 ft) above sea level. This means May and September are your best times to fish as the water gets pretty warm in summer. Alta Lake, at 100 hectares, is the biggest of the chain. While fishing is not the most popular activity here, the lake does contain rainbow and kokanee that can get up to 1 kg (2.2 lbs), as well as dollies that can get up to 60 cm (24 inches) but are generally a lot smaller. There is a spring/fall speed restriction of 12 km/h (7 mph). To the south is **Alta Lake**, a 15 hectare lake, with substantial development on its shores. The lake still offers some good fly fishing in June and early July, while trolling (electric motors only) can produce a few small kokanee and dolly varden. Further south (and the farthest upstream) **Nita Lake**, is the smallest in the chain at 10 hectares. The lake has an electric motor only restriction and offers small rainbow and some kokanee.

Anderson Lake (Map 40/C2)
This large lake is accessed from D'Arcy or Seton Portage. The lake offers good fishing for rainbow and dollies mainly by trolling. Try a Wedding Ring with worm, Flatfish, Kitamat or Krocodile. There are a number of private residents that line the lake.

Anne Lakes (Map 12/B3)
Located in Pinecone Burke Provincial Park, the 25 hectare **Anne Lake** is reached by a 6 km hike along a logging road and trail. The 10 hectare **Little Anne Lake** is located north of Anne Lake. Given the rough road access, bringing a boat into the lakes is a challenge. Better alternatives include spincasting, fly fishing or bait fishing from the shore or from a float tube. At 900 metres (2,925 feet) above sea level, the lakes (and road) are not ice free until early May. At this time, the small rainbow, which are periodically stocked, are quite aggressive. Fishing should remain steady through the summer and into the fall.

Bear Lake (Map 4/G1)
This tiny (2 hectare) lake is reached by the rough Bear Mountain FSR (4wd access) to the east of Harrison Lake. There are good numbers of small rainbow in the lake. Try a float and bait, small lure or fly for best success any time during the spring or fall.

Belknon Lake (Map 12/B4)
This small lake is the first lake on the trail to Anne and Joseph Lakes. The remote access allows for some good fishing for generally small rainbow, especially after the lake opens up in spring.

Birkenhead Lake (Map 39/E4) ⊶
Birkenhead Lake is home to a provincial park complete with a beach, boat launch and camping facilities. The lake contains fair numbers of rainbow, dollies, kokanee and whitefish. Trolling is the mainstay of the lake with the best time to fish being in the early summer or fall. Try trolling a Flatfish or a gang-troll with a Wedding Ring and worm. For the fly fishermen, sampling the inflow or outflow creeks can prove productive. The water is surprisingly clear, making the fly fishing even more exciting when you see a fish rise. Private cabins are found along the northwest shore of the 410 hectare lake.

Blackwater Lake (Map 39/G4) ⊶
Blackwater Lake is indeed a dark coloured but clear lake located just east of D'Arcy. It is stocked annually with rainbow, which allows

the fishing to remain steady for fairly small fish. Your best bet is to fly fish or spincast from a boat or a float tube during the spring or fall. There is a forest service site with camping on the northeast end of the 15 hectare lake.

Blinch Lake (Map 13/G6)
Blinch Lake is located towards the north end of Stave Lake. This is a high elevation lake, 765 metres (2,487 feet) above sea level, and is accessed only by boat and then a lengthy hike/bike along Roaring Creek. Needless to say, the remote and difficult access ensures that the fishing will be very good when you arrive. You should expect rainbow in the 25-35 cm (10-14 inch) range.

Blue (Fishblue) Lake (Map 24/D1) ◅
Located in the Fraser Canyon, north of Boston Bar, Blue Lake is much more nutrient rich than lakes farther south and west. The fishing starts in late April and tails off in early July for rainbow, which are stocked annually. By September, the fishing picks up again in this low elevation (332 metres/1,090 feet) lake, and continues into November. The lake only covers an area of 6.4 hectares, and is a decent fly fishing lake. There is a resort on the lake.

Botanie Lake (Map 42/C7)
This lake is accessed by the Botanie Valley Road north of Lytton. It provides decent fishing for rainbow, which are best caught by trolling or fly fishing. Access is limited as lake is on Indian Reserve (private property).

Brandywine Falls Lake (20/E1)
A tiny (1 hectare) lake is located at the end of a 300 metre (975 foot) walk from the Brandywine Fall Provincial Park off Highway 99. The lake, which isn't official named or marked on the maps, has a few small rainbow, best taken in the spring or fall.

Brohm Lake (Map 20/D5) ◅
Brohm Lake is located next to Highway 99 and receives heavy fishing pressure throughout the year given its easy access. The lake contains lots of Gammarus shrimp and chironomids, which feed the stocked

rainbow, cutthroat and dollies. You can take advantage of the small hand launch, or it is possible to fish from shore.

Browning Lake (Map 11/B1) ◅
Located in Murrin Provincial Park next to Highway 99, this small (3 hectare) lake is stocked frequently with 20-25 cm (8-10 inch) rainbow. It is not uncommon to see 20-30 fishermen lining the shores. Bait fishing dominates. A day-use area is found next to the lake.

Buntzen Lake (Map 2/A1,12/A7) ◅
Buntzen Lake is a BC Hydro Reservoir, and is subject to dramatic and sudden changes in water level, although at 200 metres (650 feet) deep, you won't have to worry about them draining the lake dry. The lake is easily accessed from loco and is a very popular recreational area. Anglers will find stocked rainbow, cutthroat, dollies and kokanee, all averaging about 30 cm (12 inches) in size. Since there is a powerboat restriction, it is best to bring a float tube or canoe and try spincasting or fly fishing the edges of the lake. The 180 hectare lake has steep drop-offs, and a trail circles the lake making shore fishing quite easy.

Burnaby Lake (Map 1/G2)
Located in central Burnaby, this lake has a few fish to tease ardent anglers. It is not a destination type lake but if you are out paddling with the family, why not bring a fishing rod along.

Butterfly Lake (Map 20/C3)
Difficult access makes this 10 hectares lake a very good fly fishing destination. Rainbow average 25 cm (10 inches) in size and are best caught in the spring and fall.

Burkholder Lake (Map 45/C2)
Located to the west of Yalakom River, this small lake receives light fishing pressure. As a result, it offers some good fly fishing for small rainbow. Casting a small spinner or spoon can also be effective.

Callaghan Lake (Map 29/C4) ◅
Accessed by the Callaghan FSR southwest of Whistler, this large (120 hectare) lake provides decent fishing for rainbow to 1 kg (2.2 lbs). Given the elevation (1,200 m/3,940 ft), the fishing starts in early summer and continues through to the fall. Trolling is the primary method of fishing. The scenic lake is now part of a provincial park complete with a rustic camping area and boat launch.

Campbell Lake (Map 4/F1) ◅
Campbell Lake is a small (3 hectare) lake, found in the mountains west of Harrison Hot Springs. The lake can be accessed by a rough 4wd road, then a short hike in. Alternately, you can access it via a long hike from Harrison Hot Springs. The lake contains a good number of small rainbow best caught in the early spring or late fall by spincasting or fly fishing. The shallow lake is stocked with rainbow.

Carpenter Lake (Map 5, 44, 45)
Carpenter Lake is a long narrow man-made lake, which provides reasonably good fishing for dollies, rainbow and kokanee that reach 2 kg (4 lb) in size. Trolling is the mainstay of the lake although it is possible to spincast or fly fish at the creek mouths. Boaters should be weary of deadheads and draw down on the lake. Large spoons such as a Kitimat, Kamlooper or Krocodile are very effective for the rainbow and dollies. A gang troll with a Wedding Ring and worm or Flatfish works for the kokanee as well as the rainbow.

Cat Lake (Map 20/E5) ◅
A short walk from the Cheekeye River FSR, leads to Cat Lake, a scenic little (5 hectare) lake with good fishing for small rainbow. The low elevation lake provides fishing earlier than others in the area. Fly fishing, bait fishing or spincasting are the preferred methods. The popularity of the lake has resulted in a new development on the rec site and trails in the area. There is a wharf for those who do not have a floatation device.

Cerulean Lake (Map 39/B5)

Nestled below Sun God Mountain east of Birkenhead Provincial Park, Cerulean Lake is seldom fished, as the only access is via helicopter, or bushwhacking up a creek draw from the Birkenhead Lake Forest Service Road. The best fishing is around the northern and western shores where the lake drops off steeply. This is a high elevation (1,709 metres/5,607 feet) lake covering 29 hectares. It is deep and cold and contains a fair number of rainbow in the 15-30 cm (6-12 inch) range.

Chadsey Lake (Map 3/G5)

Chadsey Lake is found within Sumas Mountain Park and is accessed by a trail. It is not particularly great for fishing but does hold some small rainbow averaging around 25 cm (10 inches), which are stocked regularly. Fishing is best in the spring and fall by using a float tube to reach the deeper holes. The lake is 9 hectares in size and is hard to shore fish. Do not be surprised by the large gold fish, which inhabit the lake.

Cheakamus Lake (Map 20/G1–21/A1)

Cheakamus Lake is the easiest lake in Garabaldi Provincial Park to access and the earliest to open up (in May). The lake is accessed by a gentle 3 km (1.8 mile) trail from the end of the Cheakamus Lake Road. It is easy to carry a float tube or canoe along the trail to the 400 hectare lake. The lake contains rainbow in the 20-30 cm (8-12 inch) range, as well as a few larger dollies and lake trout. The lakeshore is heavily forested, limiting access for shore fishing.

Chehalis Lake (Map 14/B6)

North of Harrison Bay on the Chehalis FSR, this 629 hectare lake is 10 km (6 miles) long and provides spotty fishing throughout the year for cutthroat, rainbow or dollies, averaging 30-40 cm (12-16 inches). Trolling is a mainstay of the industry, particularly around where creeks flow into the lake, or the Chehalis River flows out, or at the shallower southern end. Be wary of the sudden strong winds. The lake is deep (up to 150 m/490 ft) and cold, although it is not a high elevation lake (at 227 metres/740 feet). Three forest service sites are scattered along the lake providing camping and boat launch facilities.

Chilliwack Lake (Map 5/F7)

Chilliwack Lake is a big, popular lake that forms the heart of Chilliwack Lake Provincial Park. The 1,200 hectare lake features a number of camping areas and former forest service sites, which have now been consolidated into the one park. Currently, these former forest service sites still have boat launches. The lake contains rainbow, cutthroat, dollies and kokanee, all growing to 2 kg (4.4 lbs). Since the lake is glacier fed, the waters remain cold throughout the summer, while the fishing remains hot. Well, lukewarm, at any rate. The fish here are notoriously difficult to catch, with trolling being your best bet.

Clerf Lake (Map 6/A5)

Clerf Lake is a small high elevation lake located to the south of the Silver Skagit Road. It is reached by a long trail off the Upper Klesilkwa Creek Road. The 8 hectare lake has fairly good numbers of small rainbow easily taken by spincasting or fly fishing in the spring or fall.

Como Lake (Map 2/B2)

An urban lake in the heart of Coquitlam, Como Lake is well stocked with rainbow to offset the heavy fishing pressure. During the spring and fall, the fishing is usually pretty good but in summer, the lake warms up and the fishing slows down. Most people fish spincast or fly fish from shore (there is no fishing on the lake's northern shore) or from the two docks. No motors are allowed on the 4.7 hectare lake.

Crown Lake (Map 47/A5)

Crown Lake is 18 hectares and 855 metres (2,779 feet) in elevation. It has rainbow to 1 kg (2.2 lbs) best caught by fly fishing or casting a small lure throughout the spring or fall. There is a cartop boat launch and camping provided at the Marble Canyon Provincial Park.

Cultus Lake (Map 4/C7)

Cultus Lake is accessed by a paved road south of Chilliwack. The 630 hectare lake is noted more for its boating and jet skiing than fishing, although trolling in the early spring or late fall can produce small rainbow and the odd larger cutthroat and dolly. Provincial parks, stores, resorts, water slides and all manner of tourist traps are available at this popular summer retreat.

Cypress Lake (Map 2/B1)

A gated road off Johnson Street in Port Moody accesses Cypress Lake. It is 5 hectare in size and has small rainbow and cutthroat best taken on a fly, by bait fishing or by spincasting. The lake is quite swampy and should only be fished in the early spring or fall from a float tube or canoe.

Davis Lake (Map 3/F1)

To the east of Stave Lake, Davis Lake is home to a provincial park complete with a campground, beach and boat launch. The 30 hectare lake provides an opportunity to catch small cutthroat (to 30 cm/12 inches) primarily in the spring. This is a low elevation (165 metres/536 feet) lake, and is stocked regularly with cutthroat. The Access Road is gated.

Deeks Lake (Map 11/B4)

Located at the north end of Cypress Provincial Park, the lake is reached along the Howe Sound Crest Trail from the south or the Deeks Lake Trail from the northwest. Either way, it involves a strenuous hike to the lake, which is at 1,000 metres (3,250 feet) in elevation. The 15 hectare lake has small cutthroat, which are caught by spincasting or fly fishing. To save your back hauling a float tube, you can produce by casting from shore at the inflow and outflow creeks. Given the elevation, fishing begins in late spring and extends into the summer.

Deer Lake–Burnaby (Map 1/G3)

Deer Lake isn't a great fishing lake, but it is an easily accessible oasis from the city. The lake is regularly stocked with cutthroat and rainbow, but these fish are muddy and do not make good table fair. The lake can be fished from the shore, or by float tube or canoe/small boat, which are available to rent in summer.

Deer Lake–Sasquatch Park (Map 15/A7)

Located in Sasquatch Provincial Park, Deer Lake has both rainbow and cutthroat in the 20-35 cm (8-14 inch) range. The 55 hectare lake is best fished by boat, although shore fishing along the road is possible. Since the fish are plentiful, they are easily caught using a number of methods.

Dennett Lake (Map 12/D7)

A small (8.2 hectare) lake located in Pinecone Burke Provincial Park. Reports are mixed on this lake. Some say there are no fish; some say you will find cutthroat and brook trout. If you want to find out for yourself, you will have to hike 4 km (2.4 miles) one way to find out.

Devil's Lake (Map 3/C2)

A short trail leading downhill from the 4.9 km (3 mile) mark on the Florence Lake FSR accesses this 46 hectare lake. It is a definite advantage to pack in a canoe or float tube as the western shore is very brushy and the deeper, more productive area is off the northeastern shoreline. Spincasting or fly fishing produces the best for the stocked cutthroats that reach 30 cm (12 inches) in size. The low elevation (106 metre/345 feet) means better fishing in the early spring or fall.

Duffey Lake (Map 40/D7)

This large, beautiful lake is accessed by Highway 99 northeast of Pemberton. The lake has rainbow and dollies (to 2 kg/4.4 lbs), which are best caught by trolling with a gang troll and a Wedding Ring and worm or a Flatfish. There is a campsite and a boat launch at the north end of the lake.

Eaton Lake (Map 5/G2)

Located on a steep trail off the Silver Skagit Road, Eaton Lake holds many small rainbow and cutthroat, averaging 30-35 cm (12-14 inches). The fish rise readily to a fly, but also take to bait or a lure. This is a high mountain lake (1,320 metres/4,300 feet above sea level) and is noted for its cold water. The lake is 45 hectares, and is best fished from a float tube as shore fishing is difficult.

Echo Lake (Map 20/B7)

This mountain lake is located west of Squamish. The difficult access should ensure a peaceful fishing experience for anglers.

Elbow/Echo Lakes (Map 4/D2)

These two lakes are found along the Chehalis FSR north of Harrison Mills. **Echo Lake** is the smaller of the two, at 5 hectares, and contains small cutthroat best caught by spincasting or bait fishing. The 15 hectare **Elbow Lake** is slightly higher (170 metres/ 550 feet) and is stocked regularly with rainbow, which grow to about 20cm (8 inches). Access is restricted due to private property around the lake.

Elsay Lake (Map 11/G6)

This 20 hectare, high elevation lake is found towards the north end of Mount Seymour Park. A long challenging trail passes beneath Mount Seymour and Mount Elsay before reaching the lake. Elsay Lake has good numbers of small rainbow, which take readily to a fly, bait or lure.

Evans Lake (Map 20/C5)

Evans Lake is surrounded by private property limiting access. But ardent anglers can take advantage of the trail system found near Evans Lake Camp. The 6 hectare lake opens up early in the year and is stocked with rainbow to 1 kg (2.2 lbs).

Fire Lake (Map 22/C4)

This long, narrow lake has many small rainbow to 30 cm (12 inches). The remote 155 hectare lake is situated at 1,430 metres (4,648 feet), and is just outside the Garibaldi Provincial Park boundary. The rainbow

here come readily to a fly or lure in the summer through fall. The final kilometre to the lake is along a hiking trail.

Flora Lake (Map 5/F5)

A most difficult hike reaches Flora Lake. You must climb to a summit at 1,770 metres before descending to the lake at 1,356 metres (4,407 feet). Given this, fishing pressure is not heavy. With a float tube, the fishing can be fairly good for rainbow up to 2 kg (4.4 lbs) primarily by fly fishing. It is possible to camp at the 16 hectare lake.

Florence Lake (Map 13/D7)

Florence is a heavily regulated lake with fly fishing only, single barbless hooks and catch-n-release restrictions. Information is mixed about this lake; some reports say that there are a lot of fish, but more recent reports claim the lake is barren. If you go, you go at your own risk. The low elevation lake (390 metres/1,268 feet) covers 32 hectares.

Foley Lake (Map 5/C5)

This 11 hectare lake does not have very good fishing, partly due to the good access and former rec site on the lake. Located at 550 metres (1,788 feet) in a scenic valley, anglers should be wary of the debris in the water, especially near the shore. Persistent anglers can hook into a few rainbow or dollies, which grow to about 35cm (14 inches). There is an electric motor restriction on the lake.

Francis Lake (Map 14/E7)

Accessed by a rough road off the Harrison West FSR, this small (4 hectare) lake is home to stocked rainbow, up to 30 cm (12 inches) in size. These fish are best caught by fly fishing or spincasting in the spring and fall. The lake can be fished from the shore, from a floatation device or from a small boat with an electric motor. The lake is at 365 metres (1,186 feet) and is home to a small forest service site.

Fountain (Kwotlenemo) Lake (Map 41/F1)

Fountain Lake is the most popular of the lakes in the Three Valley Chain. It is 40 hectares in size and home to several popular forest service campsites complete with boat launches. The fishing is fairly good for rainbow to 2 kg (4.4 lbs) by trolling slowly (electric motors only) with a Flatfish or a Wedding Band with a worm. If fishing is slow, nearby **Chilhil** and **Cinquefoil Lakes** may be worth a try.

Galene Lakes (Map 6/D7)

It's a long, tough trail up to the Galene Lakes, which deters all but the most determined of anglers. Expect to take five or six hours climbing 1,250 metres (4,065 feet) over 16 km/9.5 miles to the lakes. The high elevation (1,873 m/6,090 ft) lakes offer decent fishing for rainbow up to 35cm (14 inches) in a great mountain setting.

Gates Lake (Map 39/F6)

Gates Lake is located along the road to D'Arcy and is 65 hectares in size. The lake holds rainbow and dollies to 2 kg (4.4lbs), as well as smaller kokanee and cutthroat. Given the easy access and the private residents that line the lake, this lake receives heavy fishing pressure and is not particularly great for fishing. Trolling or spincasting using a small lure with a worm is the preferred method of fishing the lake. A resort is located at the lake, offering accommodation.

Garibaldi Lakes (Map 20/F2)

Located in Garibaldi Provincial Park, these two spectacular sub-alpine lakes are accessed by the steep but well maintained Black Tusk Trail. The lakes are fairly high in elevation and fishing is possible from June through the summer and fall. Garibaldi Lake provides excellent fishing for small rainbow that can reach the 45-55 cm (18-22 inch) range. Shore fishing is possible using bait, flies or spinners. Lesser Garibaldi Lake holds smaller (25-30 cm/10-12 inches) and fewer rainbow than its bigger brother to the east.

Garrison Lakes (Map 7/E3)

A poorly maintained trail leads off the Sunday Summit FSR to two scenic sub-alpine lakes. The lakes have 45 hectares of open water between the both of them, and produce rainbow to 2 kg (4.4 lbs) by fly fishing.

Given the elevation, fishing is best left to the early summer through fall. The remote access limits fishing pressure.

Glacier Lake (Map 22/B4)

A rough 4wd road leads to this remote lake on the boundary of Garibaldi Provincial Park. The 250 hectare lake is at 415 metres (1,350 feet) in elevation, and is difficult to access. This means that there is fairly good fishing for rainbow trout, kokanee and dolly varden throughout the spring and fall. Trolling is your best bet, although sampling the shoreline with a fly or small lure can be effective.

Grace Lake (Map 4/E1)

Grace Lake is a small (6 hectare), marshy lake that has poor shoreline access. Anglers wishing to chase the stocked rainbow (up to 35 cm/14 inches) are best advised to use a float tube in the spring and fall. Found next to the Harrison West Forest Service Road, the lake and forest service campsite are busy places.

Green Lake (Map 29/G5–30/A5)

Located just north of the Whistler Village Centre, this 205 hectare lake has rainbow to 1 kg (2.2 lbs), dollies to 3 kg (6.6 lbs) and some smaller kokanee. The lake is best trolled although, with patience, bait fishing from the shore can produce.

Greendrop Lake (Map 5/F5)

Greendrop Lake has fair numbers of rainbow to 45 cm (18 inches) best taken on the fly from a float tube. The deep water (to 40 metres/130 feet) ensures that the water temperature remains cold throughout the summer. The lake makes a fine overnight destination.

Gun Lake (Map 44/A4)

Gun Lake is a popular recreational lake to the west of Goldbridge. The 312 hectare lake is lined with cabins, has a resort, a boat launch and even a forest service site on the west side of the lake. The lake offers fair fishing for rainbow to 1 kg (2.2 lb), small kokanee and dollies to 4 kg (9 lbs). Trolling is the mainstay of the lake, which is at 890 m (2,920 ft) in elevation.

Gwyneth Lake (Map 44/A6)

Located next to the Hurley River FSR, Gwyneth Lake is a shallow lake that can be fished using a dry fly (Grizzly King or Royal Coachman) or by spincasting (Flatfish or small spinner with worm).

Hanging Lake (Map 5/E7)

Located high (1,420 metres/4,615 feet) up in the mountains on the border between Canada and the USA, this 25 hectare lake is reached by a steep trail from the south end of Chilliwack Lake. The lake has stocked rainbow that grow over 45 cm (18 inches) in size. Fly fishing and spincasting can be a lot of fun on this lake.

Harrison Lake (Maps 4, 14, 22, 23)

Harrison Lake is a huge (21,780 hectares) lake. It is 55 km (33.5 miles) long, and averages a couple kilometres wide. The best boat access is from Harrison Hot Springs or Green Point. The town also provides full facilities including hotels and camping. Although mainline logging roads run up each side of the lake, there are few access points. You can find cutthroat to 40 cm (16 inches) and rainbow to 1.5 kg (3 lb) by trolling. The best locations to fish near the south end of the lake are at the mouth of Cascade Bay or along the shores north of the Harrison River outflow. The lake is very deep (up to 200 metres/650 feet) and is known for its hostile winds.

Hatzic Lake & Slough (Map 3/F4)

Hatzic can easily be found by travelling 6 km (3.7 mi) east of the town of Mission on Highway 7. Not known as a great fishing lake, **Hatzic Lake** does support rainbow, cutthroat, black crappie, juvenile coho and sturgeon. Rainbow are the most numerous and will reach up to 0.5 kg (1 lb). You might also try your luck in the **Hatzic Slough**, which features similar fishing as the lake.

Hayward Lake (Map 3/C3)

Hayward Lake is a 275 hectare man-made lake easily accessed to the west of Mission. The lake has been extensively stocked with steelhead and rainbow but the fish population has not really grown. The lake is best fished for small rainbow (to 35 cm/14 inches) towards the south end by boat near the Ruskin Dam where there is a 35 metre (114 feet) deep hole. Shore fishing is possible along the western shores or at the north end where the Stave River empties into the lake. There are day-use facilities at the lake together with a concrete boat launch.

Hicks Lake (Map 5/A1-15/A7)

Hicks is the hub of Sasquatch Provincial Park, with its camping, beach and warm water. The lake contains fairly good numbers of rainbow, kokanee and cutthroat, which are larger than those in the other lakes in the park. Better fishing is found around the small island or at the mouth of one of the four bays in the spring or fall. When the water warms in the summer, the sandy beach may be more appealing than the fishing. At this time, it is best to try trolling deep near the centre of the lake. The lake is 150 hectares, and is 300 metres (975 feet) above sea level. The nearby **Beaver Pond** (found to the north) produces surprisingly well. It isn't unusual to catch rainbow or cutthroat up to 40 cm (16 inches). The 2 hectare pond is lined with logs and vegetation, so bringing waders or a float tube is recommended.

Hoover Lake (Map 3/D2)

Although it is found at 440 metres (1,430 feet) into the hills east of Stave Lake, this small (4 hectare) lake tends to warm up in the summer. The lake is accessed by a 3.7 km (2.3 mile) hike from the Dewdney Trunk Road east of Stave Falls Dam. Once you reach the lake, you can expect good fishing from a float tube for rainbow and cutthroat that average 20-30 cm (8-12 inches) in size. Shore fishing is very difficult due to debris except for a few spots along the east shore.

Hut Lake (Map 20/B4)

This small (5 hectare) lake has numerous small (to 30 cm/12 inches) rainbow, which come readily to a fly, bait or small lure. The road up to this lake (at 500 metres/1,625 feet) is very rough and overgrown. It may still be passable by 4wd, but you should probably walk or bike from Levette Lake.

Inkwathia Lake (Map 15/D2)

A high elevation lake northwest of Yale accessed along the Inkawthia FSR. If you have a high clearance 4wd vehicle, you'll only need to walk about 2 km (1.2 miles) to this 14 hectare lake. The lake is home to plenty of rainbow, which can be caught in the summer.

Isabel Lake (Map 12/G4)

Isabel Lake is worth a try if you want a multi-day excursion into rarely visited country. The lake is accessed by an unmarked trail from the shores of Pitt Lake, which, in turn, is only accessed by boat. Once you reach the 25 hectare lake, you will be rewarded with very good fishing for rainbow on a fly or by spincasting. Given the elevation, the fish remain active throughout the summer months.

Ivey Lake (Map 30/C1)

It is catch and release only in this 10 hectare lake, which can be heartbreaking if you happen to land one of the monster rainbow that inhabit this lake. The trout, which grow to 4 kg (8.8 lbs) are cagey. There are also some small cutthroat.

Jane Lakes (Map 29/E7)

The main access route to the Jane Lakes, a series of three mountain lakes, is now blocked by a fence built by BC Rail. You can still trudge in by bike or foot along the old washed out road. The lakes, which are at 930 metres (3,025 feet) in elevation, provide good fishing throughout the spring and fall as they are stocked regularly. There are rumours of rainbow to 50 cm/18 inches (2 kg/4.4 lbs).

Joffre Lakes (Map 31/A1)

Off the Duffey Lake Road near Cayoosh Pass, a trail leads past three sub-alpine lakes. **Upper Joffre Lake** is the highest of these high elevation lakes, at 1,500 metres (4,875 feet), and has the best fishing for small rainbow beginning in July and running to October. **Middle** and **Lower Joffre Lakes** also have small rainbow but the fish are not as plentiful. Rustic camping is possible at each lake.

Jones (Wahleach) Lake (Map 5/C2)

This man-made, high elevation lake (1,655 metres/5,379 feet), is found tucked in at the base of Cheam. The road rises sharply from the valley bottom to the lake where you will find fair fishing for small rainbow and excellent fishing for small kokanee that can reach 1 kg (2.2 lbs) in size. Trolling is the mainstay of the fishery. There is a BC Hydro recreation site at the 500 hectare lake, which provides 30 campsites, a day-use area and a boat launch. Boaters should avoid the dam area at the north end of the lake.

Joseph Lake (Map 12/B3)

Located 950 metres (3,088 feet) above sea level, this 10 hectare lake is reached by a trail leading past Anne and Little Anne Lakes and has fair numbers of small rainbow. The rough logging road network into the lake is not open until late April-early May due to snow accumulation.

Kawkawa Lake (Map 15/G7)

This 80 hectare, low elevation lake (45 metres/146 feet) is found just east of Hope. It is an extremely popular place in the summer for water sports and the park offers picnicking facilities, a boat launch and a beach. Most of the fishing action comes from the kokanee, which can grow to large sizes (to 40 cm/16 inches). Cutthroat and dollies are the other main species, although someone has pulled a 3 kg (6.6 lb) smallmouth bass out of this lake. Shore fishing is limited so it is best to bring a boat and try some trolling. The lake is closed to fishing in the winter.

Kelly Lake (Map 46/F1)

North of Pavilion, this small, windy lake offers fairly good fishing for rainbow to 1 kg (2.2 lbs) on a slow troll using a Flatfish or a Wedding Ring with a worm. The scenic lake is home to Downing Provincial Park, which has camping and day-use facilities.

Kenyon Lake (Map 13/E7)

Kenyon Lake is found on a 4wd road leading northward from Salsbury Lake. The 26 hectare high elevation (700 metres/2,275 feet) lake has a forest service site near its south end. Small rainbow can be caught with reasonable frequency during the spring or fall. The lake is quite deep (up to 40 metres/130 feet), although fly fishing is effective, trolling and spincasting are your best bets.

Killarney Lake (Map 10/G7)

Killarney Lake is a small lake on Bowen Island, about 2 km (1.2 miles) from the Snug Cove Ferry Terminal. This low level lake warms up in summer, so spring and fall are the best times to come here for rainbow and cutthroat.

Kingdom (King) Lake (Map 44/B6)

Access to Kingdom Lake is by way of a 4wd road, which can be driven or hiked. Poor access makes it less popular than nearby lakes, which ultimately means that it is should be offer better fishing. This small (10 hectare) lake is located south of Goldbridge, and contains many small rainbow that can be caught by spincasting or fly fishing throughout the spring and fall. The lake also sports a forest service site.

Klahater Lake (Map 15/F5)

This 10 hectare lake is located alongside the Trans Canada Highway north of Hope. The fishing is spotty for small rainbow and brook trout. There is a cartop boat launch at the lake.

Lafarge Lake (Map 2/C1)

Also known as the Coquitlam Pit, this former gravel pit has been dammed to create an urban fishing hole and picnic site. The small (5 hectare), low elevation (31 metres/102 feet) lake is located between Pinetree Way and Pipeline Road in Port Coquitlam. The lake contains rainbow (the odd one up to 35 cm/14 inches) and catfish. The lake is intensively stocked with rainbow, making this a surprisingly good place to cast a line off the fish way along the western shore.

Lajoie (Little Gun) Lake (Map 44/A5)

Located just south of Gun Lake, this 40 hectare lake provides good fishing for rainbow trout and dollies to 1 kg (2.2 lbs), which can be caught with a fly or with a small lure. There is a cartop boat launch here, but an electric motor only restriction. It is 900 metres (2,925 feet) above sea level, and is best fished in the spring and fall.

Lake Errock (Squakum Lake) (Map 4/B3)

Lake Errock is located alongside Highway 7 and is known more as a recreation lake than a fishing lake. It does have small cutthroat and rainbow best caught in the spring or fall. The lake is 30 hectares in size and 30 metres (98 feet) in elevation.

Lake Lovely Water (Map 20/B6)

To reach this scenic sub-alpine lake, you will have to somehow cross the Squamish River. Then you will have to endure a perilously steep 5 km (3 mile) hike along a poorly maintained trail. Once you reach the lake (some 5-6 hours later), you can camp on the shoreline and sample some of the great fishing for small rainbow (to 0.5 kg/1 km). Shore fishing with bait, a lure or fly is possible.

Lake of the Woods (Schkam Lake) (Map 15/E7)

Off Highway 1 north of Hope, this 20 hectare lake is stocked annually with rainbow, which can grow to 35 cm (14 inches). Fly fishing, trolling and spincasting can produce good results, particularly in the spring or fall. The lake is 350 metres (1,140 feet) above sea level and has an electric motor only restriction. The Lake of the Woods Resort offers accommodation and a boat launch.

Levette Lake (Map 20/C5)

The steep road may deter anglers without a 4wd vehicle, but the number of small rainbow that grow to 30 cm (12 inches) should make the drive worthwhile. The 15 hectare lake is 425 metres (1,381 feet) up into the mountains, and is surrounded by private cabins. At the south end, where the road skirts the lake, there is a steep cartop boat launch. Although bait fishing from the shore is possible, you may wish to bring a float tube or small boat in order to spincast or fly fish away from the trees and debris around the shoreline.

Lewis Lake (Map 20/B3)

An old gated 4wd road leads along Pillchuck Creek up to this small lake. Due to the difficult access, anglers can expect a good fly fishing lake during the spring and fall. The stocked rainbow average 25 cm (10 inches) in size.

Lightning Lake Chain (Map 7/B7)

Lightning Lake is the most popular lake within Manning Provincial Park. The 50 hectare lake is home to a nice campsite, a boat launch and a very good trail system. It is slightly higher in elevation (1,245 m/4,085 ft) than the others in the chain and fishing is steady throughout the summer. The lake contains many small cutthroat and rainbow caught by fly fishing or spincasting. Fly fishermen should note that a caddis fly hatch occurs in early July and a Mayfly hatch occurs in the later part of June.

Flash Lake is southwest of Lightning Lake along the Lightening Lake Chain Trail. It holds a good number of rainbow averaging 30-35 cm (12-14 inches).

Strike Lake is the next lake along the Lightning Lake Chain Trail. It contains many small rainbow (to 20 cm/8 inches) best caught by spincasting, bait fishing or fly fishing.

Thunder Lake is the farthest lake along the Lightning Lake Chain Trail and sees a lot less action than the other lakes in the chain. The 40 hectare lake also contains many small rainbow (to 20 cm/8 inches) best caught by bait or fly fishing.

Lillooet Lakes (Maps 30/G2, 31/A3-A6)

The Lillooet Lakes are not noted for being great fishing lakes since they are extremely murky due to glacier silt. The best time to fish for the rainbow, cutthroat and dollies is in April in the narrows between the two lakes, or at the creek mouths. Using a fly (an attractor type pattern) or bright lure are your best bets. After April, spring run-off causes the lakes to murk up, and the water does not begin to clear until late August when fishing picks up again. Little Lillooet Lake, also called Tenas Lake, is much smaller than Lillooet Lake. There are several forest service sites offering boat launches and camping along the bigger lake.

Lindeman Lake (Map 5/E5)

Lindeman Lake is a cold, emerald green lake that is reached by a fairly gentle 3 km (1.8 mile) trail. The lake has good numbers of rainbow trout that average 30-50 cm (12-20 inches) in size and are best caught on the fly. Although it is possible to fish from shore, a float tube is more effective. The lake is 12 hectares in size and 838 metres (2,724 feet) above sea level.

Ling Lake (Map 5/D3)

It is a long hike from Foley Lake to Ling Lake along a washed-out road, then trail. Once you reach the 14 hectare lake, you will be rewarded with good fishing for rainbow to 1 kg (2.2 lbs). This is a high altitude lake, at 1,370 metres (4,452 feet), so fishing remains good throughout the summer months and into the fall. The lake is best fished using a float tube and casting a fly or small lure.

Liumchen Lake (Map 4/E7)

You will need a 4wd vehicle to access the trail into this small (2 hectare) lake. Due to the difficult access and the high elevation (1,380 metres/4,485 feet), the fishing is quite good for trout into the summer. Some nice trout (to 35 cm/14 inches) are caught here annually.

Liza Lake (Map 44/F3)

Liza Lake is located off the Marshall Lake FSR and offers good fishing for small rainbow that are best caught by fly fishing. Dry flies such as the Royal Coachman or a stonefly pattern can be a lot of fun here.

Lizzie Lake (Map 31/C6)

The road up to this scenic sub-alpine lake is water barred for most its length, requiring a 4wd vehicle. The scenic high elevation area is known more as a staging ground for hikers than for fishing. However, the lake does offers good fishing for small rainbow best caught by fly fishing or spincasting. Despite the trail system, shore fishing is difficult. A small forest service site provides camping.

Loggers Lake (Map 29/F7)

Found in the Whistler Interpretive Forest, Loggers Lake can only be accessed by foot or bike. The scenic lake covers 2 hectares, and is at 750 metres (2,438 feet) in elevation. The fishing remains reasonably good for rainbow that are rumored to grow to 45 cm (18 inches) in size but are usually much smaller. It is best to bait fish or fly fish throughout the spring and fall for the stocked rainbow.

Lookout Lake (Map 14/G6)

This 10 hectare lake is located on the west side of Harrison Lake off the Harrison West FSR. The lake is at 650 metres (2,112 feet) in elevation

and contains a good number of rainbow to 35 cm (14 inches). A 4wd is recommended to access the lake.

Lost Lake (Map 30/A6)

Lost Lake is a tiny lake, once a popular naturalist destination (no, not that kind: the other kind), it is now a popular year round destination. The lake provides a picnic area and beach as well as an excellent trail system, including part of the Valley Trail. The lake is stocked with rainbow that reach 30 cm (12 inches).

Lake Lucille (Map 20/D1)

Lucille Lake is located west of Highway 99 across the Cheakamus River Bridge and requires a short hike when you reach the powerline crossing (the road is blocked by the railway tracks). The 12 hectare lake produces brook trout, and the occasional rainbow in the 30-40 cm (12-16 inch) range with some fish reported to be as large as 2.5 kg (5.5 lbs). The lake has an electric motor only restriction and is found at 395 m (1,295 ft) in elevation.

McDonald Lake (Map 44/B5)

The most effective method of catching the rainbow that inhabit this small lake east of Gold Bridge, is to troll a Wedding Ring with a worm. The difficult access may deter some from bringing in a boat.

Madeley Lake (Map 29/D4)

Found to the northwest of Whistler on the Madeley Lake Road (4wd/bike access), this lake produces very well for small rainbow, up to 30 cm (12 inches). There is a small campground at the north end of the lake with a rough cartop boat launch. It is highly recommended that you bring a float tube or a boat you can pack-in as the lake is difficult to shore fish except at the south end.

Mamquam Lake (Map 21/A5)

Located well inside Garibaldi Provincial Park, this lake is accessed by a 22 km (13.4 mile) hike along the Diamond Head Trail. The lake is seldom fished so it offers very good fishing for rainbow to 50 cm/20 inches (1.5 kg/3.3 lbs). Shore fishing using a small lure, a fly or bait meets with success. This is a high elevation (1,300 metre/4,225 feet) lake and the water doesn't open up until early summer.

Marion/Phyllis Lakes (Map 11/C3) 🐟
To reach these two mountain lakes, you must walk or bike a gated road from Highway 99 just north of Furry Creek. The lakes do not receive heavy fishing pressure and so you can do quite well for small cutthroat and dollies particularly in the spring and fall. It is possible to fish from the shore with bait but it is recommended to bring a float tube and spincast or fly fish.

Marshall Lake (Map 44/G3)
Marshall Lake has good fishing for rainbow to 1 kg (2.2 lbs) primarily by trolling a gang troll with a wedding band and worm. Casting a Krocodile or a Dick Nite also meets with success. There are two forest service sites on the south end of the lake, which is 65 hectares in size and 1,150 metres (3,738 feet) above sea level.

Mead Lake (Map 44/C6)
Just south of Kingdom Lake, this small lake is accessed by a 4wd vehicle or by a hike. It provides good fishing for small rainbow throughout the spring and fall.

Mike Lake (Map 2/G1) 🐟
This lake is located in Golden Ears Park and is accessed by the Mike Lake Road. The 5 hectare lake has stocked rainbow and wild cutthroat that grow to 30 cm (12 inches), best caught in the spring given the elevation (235 metres/764 feet). Fishing from a canoe or float tube is your best bet as the shoreline is shallow and marshy. There is a hand launch at the lake as well as a powerboat restriction.

Mill Lake (Map 3/D7) 🐟
Located in the heart of Abbotsford, next to the Seven Oaks Shopping Centre, this urban lake is heavily stocked, with cutthroat, rainbow and steelhead. The lake also contains crappies and is a popular smallmouth bass fishing hole. Mill lake isn't very big (at 18.5 hectares), and the shores are mostly shallow and swampy but it is still possible to fish the edges (especially in the evening) from shore. You will need a boat (electric motor only) to get to the deepest hole of the lake. The best place to fish from shore is off the dock or from the beach.

Moon Lake (Map 46/A7)
This tiny lake is noted for having large rainbow that reach 2 kg (4.5 lb) in size. The remote lake has poor access and requires hiking or biking in from a 4wd logging road. Fly fishing or spincasting with a small lure or spoon and a worm can be effective.

Morgan Lake (Map 13/D7) 🐟
Morgan Lake is a catch-n-release and fly fishing only lake that sports brook trout and cutthroat to 2 kg (4.4 lbs). For best results, bring a float tube as shore fishing is very difficult and the lake is quite deep in the middle (45 metres/146 feet). The lake, which is reached by trail from the 16.5 km (10 mile) mark on the Florence Lake FSR, is 20 hectares in size and 320 metres (1,040 feet) above sea level.

Morris Lake (Map 4/E1) 🐟
Morris Lake is connected to the Harrison River by a rather large channel. The 90 hectare lake is accessed via a steep road just east of the Weaver Creek spawning channel. The fishing isn't great here, but you might catch a cutthroat (to 50 cm/20 inches) using worms or roe on a spin rod, or a fly rod.

Mosquito Lake (Map 30/D1) 🐟
Located just east of Ivey Lake near Pemberton, Mosquito Lake has a rec site with a picnicking area. The lake has stocked rainbow and cutthroat to 30 cm (12 inches), but the fishing is usually slow. The lake is at 445 metres (1,446 feet) in elevation and is 5 hectares in size.

Moss Lake (Map 15/A7)
If you want to get to Moss Lake, you'll have to hike at least 1.5 km (1 mile), and you'll want to pack a float tube with you. If you don't have a 4wd vehicle, the hike will be longer, but it's these obstacles that has kept this small lake a viable fishing destination in Sasquatch Provincial Park. The lake features cutthroat in the 25-35 cm (10-14 inch) range, and is a great place to go fly fishing.

Mowson Pond (Map 44/C3)
This pond is actually a picturesque lake that can offer very good fishing for stocked rainbow. During the spring and fall some nice sized trout (to 36 cm/14 in) are caught mainly on the fly. Dry fly fishing can be a lot of fun on this lake, which warms significantly in the summer. There is a busy recreation site along with a boat launch on the lake.

Munro / Dennett Lakes (Map 12/D7)
The steep, steep trail will deter most anglers from testing the waters in Munro and Dennett Lakes. **Munro Lake** once covered 25 hectares but the dam let go and with it went the brook trout. A little further up **Dennett Lake** has small cutthroat and brook trout and covers 8 hectares. In fall, when the brook trout are about to spawn, the fishing can be good for aggressive brookies on the fly or by spincasting (Deadly Dick and worm).

Nahatlatch, Hannah & Frances Lakes (Maps 23, 24) 🐟
Strung together like pears on a string by the Nahatlatch River, these three lakes are wonderfully scenic, though the fishing here is not very good. All three lakes hold limited numbers of rainbow, dollies and cutthroat, and, if you're going to make a serious effort to catch something, your best bet is to go trolling in the spring or fall. Several former forest service sites along the Nahatlatch River Road provide camping for the paddlers and fishermen that frequent the area.

Nicomen Lake (Map 7/A3) 🐟
As the crow flies, Nicomen Lake is 10 km from the nearest road, but the hike in is nearly double that, along the Hope Pass Trail/Grainger Creek Trail. A small, scenic tenting site is located at the 10 hectare lake. Given the tough access, you can usually expect some good fishing for rainbow that can grow to 1 kg (2.2 lbs) in size.

Norton Lake (Map 12/B3) 🐟
Norton Lake is noted for having the largest rainbow of all the lakes in the Hixon Creek area, getting up to 2 kg (4.4 lbs). It is also the easiest to find but you will need a 4wd vehicle to drive in. The lake is 715 metres (2,324 feet) in elevation and covers 45 hectares. Fishing is best in the late spring and fall, from a float tube.

Olive Lake (Map 14/A5)
You'll have to bushwhack your way to Olive Lake from the end of the North Statlu FSR, a distance of about 3 km. The lake contains stocked cutthroat to 25 cm (10 inches) as well as some rainbow.

Owl Lake Chain (Map 39/B7)
From the Owl Creek FSR (4wd access), a steep trail leads to Owl Lake as well as several other lakes in the watershed. These lakes have small rainbow (to 30 cm/12 inches) that rarely see a lure. **Owl Lake** sees most of the action and casting from shore is possible. Further north, **Ogre** and **Fowl Lakes** will require some bushwhacking through rugged terrain to access. Due to their remote sub-alpine setting, fishing with most small lures and flies is good through the summer for generally small rainbow. The odd trout can reach 50 cm (20 inches) in size.

One Mile Lake (Map 30/B2)
South of Pemberton and right next to Highway 99, One Mile Lake sees more than its share of anglers. There are a few rainbow and cutthroat (to 30 cm/12 inches) that are best caught by spincasting or fly fishing from a small boat or float tube throughout the spring and fall.

Pavilion Lake (Map 46/G5)
Pavilion Lake-the largest lake in the Marble Canyon Area-has fair fishing for rainbow to 1.5 kg (3.3 lbs), primarily caught by trolling a gang troll with a Wedding Ring and worm or a Flatfish. The lake also offers good ice fishing. A cartop boat launch is available, as is camping and a resort. The lake is 260 hectares and 825 metres (2,681 feet) above sea level.

Pearson Pond (Map 44/C3)

Pearson Pond is a small (8 ha) lake, which is a little more difficult to access and fish than nearby Mowson Pond. Although the fishing is slower, the fish are bigger. In addition to rainbow, there are brook trout that reach 1.5 kg (3.3 lb) in size. A boat is a definite asset here and there is a cartop boat launch and camping at the forest service site. The lake, which is at 825 metres (2,681 feet) in elevation makes a fine ice fishing destination.

Petgill Lake (Map 11/C1)

This lake is accessed by a steep 11.5 km (6 hour) return trail leading from Highway 99. It contains fair numbers of small, stocked rainbow best caught by spincasting or fly fishing from a float tube. Shore fishing is possible but not as productive as using a float tube. The lake is 3 hectare in size and is at 760 metres (2,470 feet) in elevation.

Pierce Lake (Map 5/B7)

This 16 hectare lake is reached by a steep, difficult trail leading from the Chilliwack Lake Road. The hike is worth the effort given the beautiful mountain scenery and excellent fly fishing or spincasting for large, stocked rainbow that can reach 50 cm (20 inches) in size. Dolly varden, a rarity for mountain lakes, can also be found. The lake is quite deep (up to 30 metres/100 feet) and allows for shore fishing.

Pitt Lake (Map 12/G6)

At the south end of Pitt Lake, Grant Narrows Park provides the main boat launch onto this big (5,400 hectare) lake. Anglers will find luck working the creek mouths, deep cliff areas or deeper bays. Brighter presentations help, since the waters are often murky especially in the early spring when the salmon fry are returning to the ocean. The lake contains resident rainbow, dollies, sturgeon and whitefish but the action picks up when the salmon species and steelhead, migrate through the lake. In particular, in the spring (April-May) sea-run cutthroat cruise to the north end of the lake looking for salmon fry returning to the ocean. Try fly fishing (a silver minnow imitation), bait fishing (small minnows) or casting a small silver lure to land one of these prized fish. When boating, watch for the sandbars, deadheads and sudden winds.

Poland Lake (Map 6/G6)

This high elevation lake is accessed by the Poland Lake Trail in Manning Provincial Park. The small lake contains many small rainbow (to 20 cm/8 inches) easily taken by fly fishing or spincasting from the shore or from a float tube. There is a rustic campground next to the lake.

Rainbow Lake (Map 29/E5)

Accessed by trail from the Alta Lake Road, Rainbow Lake is an unproductive lake. But patient anglers can find some large, wild rainbow trout. The few fish that exist are known to grow to good sizes.

Rolley Lake (Map 3/C2)

Rolley Lake is home to a popular provincial park complete with camping, a boat launch and a beach. The 23 hectare lake has stocked rainbow (to 30 cm/12 inches) as well as a few larger dollies and cutthroat. It is best fished near the north end where there is a 30 metre (90 foot) deep hole. A float tube or canoe lets you fish the hole although it is still possible to cast from shore at several places. No powerboats are allowed in this low elevation (221 metre/718 feet) lake.

Ross Lake (Map 6/F7)

At the end of the Silver Skagit Road, Ross Lake sits on the border between Canada and the USA. There is camping, a boat launch and a beach at the provincial park. The lake is best trolled for rainbow and dollies that average 30-45 cm/12-18 inches. The low elevation lake (165 metres/536 feet) covers an area of 200 hectares and is best fished in the spring and fall.

Salsbury Lake (Map 13/F7)

Salsbury Lake is found north of Davis Lake at 425 metres (1,381 feet) in elevation. The 80 hectare lake has small rainbow and kokanee (to 30 cm/12 inches), which are stocked regularly. Fly fishing is slow and shore fishing is difficult due to the debris. Trolling produces better, but

the lake is shallow. Former recreation sites provide access and a gravel boat launch to the lake.

Sasamat Lake (Map 2/A1)

Sasamat Lake is located within Belcarra Regional Park. At 70 metres (228 feet) in elevation, the 45 hectare lake is noted more for its great beach and picnic facilities than its fishing. It is still possible in the early spring and late fall to catch wild cutthroat or stocked rainbow that can grow to 45 cm (18 inches). Powerboats are restricted on the lake from May to September so bring a float tube and spincast or fly fish near the middle of the lake, where there is a 35 metre (114 feet) deep hole, or along the western shoreline. For shore fishermen, a 200 metre (650 foot) long floating dock at the south end of the lake or two docks at the outflow are excellent spots.

Sayres (Cedar) Lake (Map 3/D1)

This low elevation lake is accessed by short trail from the Florence Lake FSR. The 80 hectare lake has a dock where you can launch a small boat or canoe. There is also a fish hatchery and a correction facility next to the lake but no camping facilities. The lake can be fished from shore but it is better to fish with a float tube or small boat in order to cast/troll towards the centre of the lake where the water depth is 80 metres (260 feet). There are rumours of cutthroat up to 7 kg (17 lbs), but the average fish tends to be quite small (30-35 cm/12-14 inches). There are also some small dollies and brook trout. The main catch here, though, is rainbow. There is a bait ban as well as a catch limit and a single barbless hook restriction on the lake.

Seton Lake (Maps 40, 41, 45)

Seton Lake holds large rainbow (to 2 kg/4.4 lbs), lake trout (to 5 kg/11 lbs) and dollies to 6 kg (13 lbs). Trolling a large spoon at the drop-off of one of the creek estuaries such as Madeleine, Tsee or Machute Creeks is particularly effective. Casting a large spoon off the Seton Lake Canal Dock just east of Lillooet can also be very effective. Steelhead anglers will find **Seton Portage**, the short river between Anderson Lake and Seton Lake, fairly productive. Rainbow and dollies (to 2 kg/4.4 lbs) are also found in the river.

Showh Lakes (Map 29/G4)
At 950 metres (3,088 feet) there is good summer angling, which lasts until the late fall, in the main lake. The 4wd/trail access and catch and release fishery limits fishermen so you are likely to be the only one at the lake. The main lake is 10 hectare in size and provides for rainbow in the 30-50 cm (12-18 feet) range.

Silver Lake (Map 5/G1)
This lake is home to a provincial park complete with camping, a boat launch and picnic facilities. The 40 hectare lake has small rainbow, cutthroat and kokanee as well as a few larger dollies (to 2 kg/4.4 lbs). Small steelhead come into the lake in the winter and coho come through in the fall. For best results, you can cast a float with bait from the southern shoreline, fly fish at the creek outflow, or troll the shallow (12 metres/39 feet deep) lake.

Silvermere Lake (Map 3/C3)
This 110 hectare man-made lake next to the Lower Stave River is easily accessed by Highway 7. The lake is very marshy and shallow making it better for water skiing or catching catfish and bullheads than rainbow. The best place to fish for the trout (to 30 cm/12 inches) is near the highway, either from shore or by boat. Private residents line the east side of the lake, making access difficult.

Slollicum Lake (Map 15/A6)
This 25 hectare lake is reached by a 3 kilometre (1.8 mile) trail off a 4wd road on the east side of Harrison Lake. The lake has numerous small rainbow (usually in the 20 cm/8 inch range), which come readily to a fly, bait or lure. Try fishing at the north end of the lake where the fish tend to congregate.

Spruce Lake (Map 43/G1)
This remote backcountry lake is accessed on foot, by bike, by horse or even float plane. It forms the hub of the Spruce Lake Recreation Area and offers camping. The lake is known for its excellent fly fishing for rainbow that can grow to 1.5 kg (3.3 lbs). Working from a float tube or canoe is your best bet since the lake is quite shallow and shore fishing can be difficult. There are private cabins found on the lake.

Stacy Lake (Map 4/E2)
A tiny (2.8 hectare) lake located 803 metres (2,635 feet) up the slopes of Mount Woodside, west of Agassiz. Watch for a spur road to your left after kilometre 7 off the rough Mount Woodside Forest Service Road. The lake is stocked with rainbow, and the fishing here is decent in late spring, and again in fall. The lake is subject to winterkill.

Statlu Lake (Map 14/Ar)
Statlu Lake is located to the north of Chehalis and is reached by a rough 4wd road and then a short hike. Rainbow tend to be small but plentiful in this scenic lake set below some majestic peaks.

Stave Lake (Maps 3, 13)
Stave Lake is a large 4,410 hectare lake, stretching 27 km (16.5 miles) through the mountains north of Mission. Despite its size, access is limited. Most boaters launch near the Stave Falls Dam. There are also a few

places that get to the water from logging roads on either side of the lake. The low elevation lake (82 metres/267 feet) has been damned by BC Hydro resulting in fluctuating water levels and very spotty fishing. There are a few rainbow, cutthroat (to 50 cm/20 inches), kokanee, dollies (to 5 kg/11 lbs) and whitefish in the lake. Trolling is preferred because the fish are scattered but watch for debris and high winds that can make boating treacherous at times.

Starvation Lake (Map 20/B3)
Starvation Lake is a small (1.6 hectare) lake that is reached by an overgrown road leading from the very end of the Paradise Valley Road. The lake produces rainbow as large as 2 kg (4.4 lbs). Rustic camping is available at the lake.

Sunrise Lake (Map 14/D5)
Sunrise Lake is another in a series of small (this one is 5 hectares) lakes found in the hills above Harrison Lake. Sunrise is 396 metres (1,287 feet) above sea level and offers excellent shore fishing and trolling (electric motors only). The lake is quite deep (up to 14 metres/45 feet), and cold. There is a forest service site, and a boat launch that is maintained by the local 4wd club.

Swanee Lake (Map 5/F2)
This small lake is accessed off a long, rough bushwhack from the Silver Skagit Road near where it crosses the Silverhope Creek just south of the Eaton Lake Forest Service Site. The lake has fair fishing for small rainbow from June to early fall.

Tenquille Lake (Map 39/A4)
This scenic sub-alpine lake is found at the 1,645 metre (5,346 foot) level, beneath Tenquille Mountain. It is reached by any one of three trails leading from surrounding logging roads. The lake is a popular hiking and mountaineering destination, but it also has good fishing for rainbow in the 20-30 cm (8-12 inch) range. Fly fishing with a dry fly can be a lot of fun. There is a lakeshore camping area as well as a cabin in the area.

Thomas Lake (Map 13/B3)
Located well and truly back in Golden Ears Provincial Park, Thomas Lake is a fly-in lake (although some creative angler has probably boated up to the end of Stave Lake, biked up the Stave River Forest Service Road, made the perilous crossing over the Stave, and then bushwhacked his or her way into the 182 hectare lake). The fact that few anglers ever make it into this lake, which is stocked with rainbow every few years, means fishing should be excellent.

Trout Lake (Map 14/F6)
Fishing from the bushy, marshy shoreline of this shallow 12 hectare lake is not an appealing proposition. Instead, bring a float tube, or a small boat with an electric motor. The lake is in Sasquatch Provincial Park, and contains many small rainbow that easily take to flies. The lake gets quite warm in summer.

Turquoise Lake (Map 47/A5)
This small (10 hectare) lake has good fishing for stocked rainbow growing to 1 kg (2.2 lbs) primarily by casting a small lure or by fly fishing. The lake is 855 metres (2,779 feet) above sea level and sports a cartop boat launch.

Twenty Minute Lake (Map 7/B7)
This tiny lake is located right along the Gibson Pass Road just east of Lightning Lake. It has the poorest fishing of all the lakes in the park. Rainbow are in the 15-20 cm (6-8 inches) category and are best caught by bait fishing.

Tyaughton Lake (Map 44/C3)
Tyaughton is native for flying fish. On any given evening, you will know why. Trolling a Willow Leaf and Wedding Ring has caught good numbers of dollies and rainbow here. The lake is quite deep and clear making fly fishing difficult, but casting towards shore with a fly or small lure can be effective.

Weaver Lake (Map 14/E7)

Weaver Lake has good numbers of rainbow and cutthroat that reach 50 cm (20 inches). The 81 hectare lake receives heavy pressure during the summer, due in no small part to the scenic forest service site complete with a beach and boat launch. Trolling with a fly or wedding band and worm is popular although the lake, given its numerous bays and undulating shoreline, is well suited to spincasting or fly fishing. Fishing is best on the western side because the water is deeper. The lake is at 260 metres (845 feet) in elevation and has a trail that circles the lake. Better fishing is found in May-June or in Sept-October.

Welcome Lake (Map 2/A2)

This small lake is located in the city of Coquitlam on Gatensbury Street. The lake is stocked with rainbow and cutthroat.

Whonnock Lake (Map 3/B3)

Whonnock Lake is a 50 hectare urban lake located northwest of Mission off of 276th Street. It is a marshy lake that is very shallow and has notably dark but clean water. The lake has cutthroat, crappies and stocked rainbow which all grow to 25 cm (10 inches). The marshy shoreline makes shore fishing very difficult so bring a canoe or float tube (no powerboats). Spincasting and bait fishing are the best methods of fishing usually in the early morning or at dusk. There are day-use facilities at the lake making it a popular summer lake.

Widgeon Lake (Map 12/E6)

Widgeon Lake is a tough lake to access, but it provides very good fishing for stocked rainbow trout to 2 kg (4.4 lbs). For those not willing to pay for a flight in, access to the scenic lake requires canoeing across Pitt Lake and then hike or bike along an old road leading north. Pitt Lake is at sea level, while Widgeon Lake is 770 metres (2,503 feet) above that. The lake is very deep (up to 140 metres/455 feet), and cold. Anyone making the long hike up should carry a float tube, as casting a line from the shore is difficult, if not impossible.

Wilson Lake (Map 14/A6)

Wilson Lake is west of Chehalis Lake along a long series of rough backroads that may need to be walked do to washouts. The lake was stocked with rainbow back in the 80s and trolling seems to be the preferred fishing method. The lake is at 833 metres (2,732 feet) above sea level, and covers an area of 38.5 hectares.

Wolf Lake (Map 4/F1)

This tiny (2 hectare) lake is well stocked with small but plentiful rainbow. It has a small forest service site and is at 105 metres (341 feet) in elevation. The marshy lake is best fished with a float tube.

Wood Lake (Map 14/E5)

Access into Wood Lake is gated when the campsite is not open. This 5 hectare lake contains good numbers of stocked rainbow up to 40 cm (16 inches). Fly fishing or spincasting in the spring or fall is quite effective, especially near the deep hole on the north side.

Wotten Lake (Map 15/B3)

Wotten Lake is a remote lake, containing rainbow. The lake receives very little fishing pressure and can offer exceptional fly fishing and spincasting for rainbow.

Young Lake (Map 12/A3)

Young Lake is a small (5 hectare), remote lake, at 770 metres (2,502 feet) in elevation. The difficult access should mean that the small rainbow will come readily to most flies and small lures, especially after the lake opens up in spring.

Sunshine Coast Lakes

With all the attention on the saltwater and river fishing of the coast, the lakes are often left unnoticed. This is a good thing if you are a lake angler. The native and stocked cutthroat that are found in many of the lakes can grow to some impressive sizes.

Black Lake (Map 25/C4)

This 50 hectare lake is located on West Redonda Island and receives very little fishing pressure. To reach the lake, you must boat to Roscoe Bay Marine Park, and then bushwhack your way in. Once you reach the lake, try trolling or fly fishing for the cutthroat that reach 2 kg (4.4 lbs). There is a tenting site in the marine park.

Bob's Lake (Map 8/E2)

This small (7.6 hectare) lake is home to a recreation site and small rainbow trout. The lake is best fished in the spring and fall as shallow waters warm significantly during summer.

Brown Lake (Map 18/D7)

A small lake found next to the trail leading to Skookumchuck Narrows that has been stocked with cutthroat. Rumour has it that some of these fast growing fish top the scales at 7 kg (17 lbs). That's a big fish for such a small lake.

Carlson / Dragon Lakes (Map 9/F3)

These two lakes are accessed off the Halfmoon FSR (4wd recommended). Both lakes have fair numbers of cutthroat to 30 cm (12 inches) and are about 700 metres (2,275 feet) above sea level. Fishing is certainly better in the early spring or fall. **Carlson Lake** covers 20 hectares, whereas **Dragon Lake** is a mere 1 hectare.

Clowhom Lake (Map 19/E7)

This remote 400 hectare lake is found at the north end of the Salmon Inlet and requires a boat to access. From there, it is advised to pack a canoe into the lake and paddle to the north end where the Clowhom River enters the lake. Because of the difficult access, the lake provides very good fishing during the fall (September-early October) for cutthroat to 2 kg (4.4 lbs) in size as well as a few large dollies. It is possible to fish from shore, although using a floatation device is better.

Cranberry Lake (Map 17/A4)

Cranberry Lake is located just east of Powell River and provides marginal fishing for cutthroat to 40 cm (16 inches) in size throughout the spring and early summer. There is a beach and boat launch at the lake, which is easily accessed by paved road. This low elevation (105 metres/341 feet) lake covers 40 hectares.

Crowston Lake (Map 9/F4)

A rough logging road leads from Highway 101 just south of Trout Lake to this 5 hectare lake. The lake is best fished in the spring and fall as the waters warm significantly in the summer. Since the shore is lined with weeds, fly fishing or spincasting from a small boat or float tube for the stocked cutthroat is your best option. The fish average 20-40 cm (8-16 inches) in size.

Dodd Lake (Map 17/E2)

At 730 hectares in size, Dodd Lake is one of the larger lakes in the Powell Forest Canoe Circuit. The low altitude lake can also be accessed by vehicle along the Weldwood Main. It holds cutthroat that can reach 3 kg (6.6 lbs), and some small kokanee. Trolling is the preferred method of fishing although casting a fly or a lure in one of the small bays can be productive. There are a few forest service campsites on the lake, with the main (Dodd Lake) site sporting a boat launch.

Duck Lake (Map 17/B4)

Duck Lake is a low elevation (155 metre/504 feet) lake, easily accessed on the Duck Lake FSR. It provides fair fishing for cutthroat in the 25-30 cm (10-12 inches) range as well as some small kokanee. Trolling is the preferred method at this 60 hectare lake.

Emily Lake (Maps 16/G6, 17/A6)

Like other lakes on Texada Island, Emily Lake is a very nutrient rich lake, which leads to vibrant insect and aquatic vegetation growth. This means plenty of food for the fast growing cutthroat. The 10 hectare lake is found at the north end of the island by a short trail that leads through private property (permission necessary to access the lake).

Freda Lake (Map 17/G1, 18/A1)
Located on the Stillwater Main (good 2wd access), this 50 hectare lake has a fair number of cutthroat in the 25-35 cm (10-14 inch) range. The lake provides decent trolling throughout the spring and fall.

Garden Bay Lake (Map 9/B1)
Found next to Pender Harbour, Garden Bay Lake sees more attention from paddlers since most of the anglers devote their attention to the saltwater fishery. This is a shame. The pretty lake has stocked cutthroat to 35 cm (14 inches) best caught in the spring or the fall.

Goat Lake (Map 26/F7)
Goat Lake is a low elevation lake containing small kokanee, cutthroat and rainbow. Some cutthroat grow to 2 kg (4.4 lbs). The 410 hectare lake offers excellent fly fishing and spincasting for rainbow when they congregate near the mouth of Eldred River in late April-mid May in preparation for spawning. The rest of the year, rainbow are best caught by trolling, as are the kokanee. There is a pair of rustic campsites along the southeast shore of the lake, which is part of the Powell Forest Canoe Circuit.

Hammil (West) Lake (Map 17/B4)
Hammil Lake is a medium sized (85 hectare) water body found east of Powell River. Given the low elevation, it provides decent fishing for cutthroat in the spring and fall. There is a boat launch as well as a good trail system to provide access for shore fishers.

Haslam Lake (Map 17/B3)
This large (1,190 hectare) lake is easily accessed northeast of Powell River. The lake provides fairly good trolling for cutthroat, rainbow and kokanee that average 30 cm (12 inches) in size. The odd fish can grow to 2 kg (4.4 lbs). Despite its size, the low elevation (150 metres/488 feet) lake has an electric motor only restriction.

Horseshoe Lake (Map 17/E3)
Although a secondary road will bring you to the shore of the 290 hectare Horseshoe Lake, most anglers launch at the forest service site on Nanton Lake. The lake has many small cutthroat, rainbow and kokanee that are best caught by fly fishing or trolling. The cutthroats are known to grow up to 2 kg (4.4 lbs) in size although catching a fish this size is rare. It is best to concentrate your fishing efforts in the channel between Horseshoe Lake and Nanton Lake or in one of the many bays or weed beds that line the western shore of the lake. There are a couple rustic (and quite lovely) camping spots, developed for canoeists on the Powell Forest Canoe Circuit.

Hotel Lake (Map 9/B1)
Hotel Lake has stocked cutthroat to 35 cm (inches) best caught in the spring or fall by fly fishing or spincasting. The low elevation lake covers an area of 25 hectares and is electric motor only.

Inland (Loon) Lake (Map 17/B2)
A popular recreational destination, this 350 hectare lake is located northeast of Powell Lake. Given the low elevation (150 metres/488 feet), it is best to troll in the spring or early summer. The lake provides good fishing for cutthroat up to 50 cm (20 in) in size as well as for a few small kokanee. A well maintained trail circles the lake allowing shore fishing.

Ireland Lake (Map 17/D2)
Ireland Lake is one of the smaller lakes along the Powell Forest Canoe Route, covering 25 hectares. There is no vehicle access to the lake but you can bushwhack from the Goat Lake Main, or hike along either of the portage trails to the lake. The lake offers good fishing for small cutthroat and kokanee throughout the spring and into the early summer. It is best to fish near the creek inlet leading to Dodd Lake or at the outlet to Nanton Lake.

Katherine Lake (Map 9/B1)
Katherine Lake is located in Katherine Lake Park, and offers stocked cutthroat to 35 cm (14 inches) in size. The lake is best fished in April-May and again in the fall. Katherine Lake Park has a beach and camping. The lake is 6 hectares in size and at 25 m in elevation.

Khartoum Lake (Maps 18/A3, 17/G3)
Khartoum Lake is reached from the east end of Lois Lake and, it sees few canoeists since it is out of the way of the main canoe circuit. The lake also does not receive heavy fishing pressure and provides good fishing for cutthroat to 2 kg (4.4 lbs). Concentrate your efforts at the inflow of Lois River or in the channel between Lois and Khartoum Lake. Most anglers access the lake via the Third Lake Road, at the forest service campsite that sports a boat launch.

Klein Lake (Map 18/C7)
Klein Lake is accessed off the North Lake Road, to the east of Earl's Cove. The 14 hectare lake has many small cutthroat easily caught by trolling, fly fishing and spincasting. Its scenic surroundings and good fishing make it a popular destination for locals. A forest service site on the north end of the lake provides camping and cartop boat launch facilities.

Kokomo Lake (Map 18/B7)
Kokomo isn't reached by heading for the tropics (you know, Bermuda, Bahamas, come on pretty mama'), but by portaging a canoe from Sakinaw Lake. Given the difficult access, fishing for small cutthroat can be quite good. The lake is 10 hectares and has an electric motor only restriction.

Lewis Lake (Map 17/D2)
Located off the rough Tin Hat Road, you'll need a 4wd to get to Lewis Lake. The lake provides good fishing for cutthroats to 2 kg (4.4 lbs) in summer and early fall. A small rec site is found on the lake.

Linfoot Lake (Map 10/F4)
Located on Gambier Island, Linfoot Lake is reached by a rough trail. It provides very good fishing for small rainbow throughout the spring or fall. The lake is 5 hectares and sees very little pressure.

Lois Lake (Map 17/F4)

Lois Lake is one of the larger (1,415 hectare) lakes in the Powell River area, second only to Powell Lake. Most people doing the Powell Forest Canoe Circuit start here. The lake is home to cutthroat that can reach 2 kg (4.4 lbs), as well as small kokanee. It is best fished by trolling, but you can also try spincasting or fly fishing at the inflow and outflow of the lake, around the islands or in one of the sheltered bays.

Lyon Lake (Map 9/E1)

Follow the Halfmoon FSR north from Highway 101 north to this 15 hectare lake. The road deteriorates significantly as you approach the lake making a 4wd vehicle a must. There are stocked cutthroat in the 20-40 cm (8-16 inch) range as well as a few larger fish. Fly fishing and spincasting in the spring or fall are your best bets. There is a forest service site at the south end of the lake providing camping.

MacKechnie Lake (Map 18/A7)

Located on Nelson Island, this small (15 hectare) low elevation (25 metres/81 feet) lake provides fairly good fishing for cutthroat to 1 kg (2.2 lbs) in the spring and fall. Old logging roads from Hidden Basin reach the lake.

Mixal Lake (Map 9/B1)

Mixal Lake is 45 hectares in size and offers fishing for small cutthroat mainly in the spring. It is also possible to catch a coho in the fall. The low elevation lake has an electric motor only restriction.

Nanton Lake (Map 17/D3)

Nanton Lake is accessed off the Goat Lake Main and is really an extension of Horseshoe Lake. The 125 hectare lake, has camping on its western shores. In addition to kokanee, the lake has developed a reputation for holding some pretty large cutthroat (to 3kg/6.6 lbs). Try fly fishing or trolling near the channel from Horseshoe Lake or at one of the inflow creeks. The May midge hatch is the most productive time for fly fishermen.

North Lake (Map 18/C7)

North Lake is a well developed lake that is the highest elevation lake (at 330 metres/1073 feet) on the north end of the Sechelt Peninsula. The 15 hectare lake provides slow fishing for cutthroat averaging 25-30 cm (10-12 inches). April-May or October are the best times to fish. The lake has full facilities and has an electric motor only restriction.

Paxton Lake (Map 17/A7)

This small (10 hectare) lake can be accessed by a 4wd vehicle off the Iron Mine Road. The lake contains cutthroat to 2kg (4.4 lbs), which can be caught in the early summer by spincasting or fly fishing.

Powell Lake (Maps 17/A1–26/B2)

Powell Lake is the biggest lake in the Powell River area. At 11,200 hectares, the lake resembles an inlet or a fjord, running narrow and long deep into the heart of the coast mountains. The lake is notoriously difficult to fish, and is subject to strong winds. If you're lucky, you might manage to catch one of the cutthroat or rainbow that can reach up to 4kg (8.8 lbs). Your best bet is trolling around Goat Island, near Olsen's landing, or near Haywire Bay. The lake is only 50 metres (162 feet) above sea level, and has several rustic campsites.

Priest Lake (Map 16/G6)

At 50 hectares, Priest Lake is the biggest lake on Texada Island. As a result, trolling is the preferred method for cutthroats to 2kg (4.4 lbs) in late spring or early summer.

Ruby Lake (Map 18/C7)

Ruby Lake is a popular recreation lake with many summer and permanent residents lining the lake. The 470 hectare lake also has a resort, boat launch and camping. Despite the heavy fishing pressure, the lake produces well for cutthroat, usually to 25-35 cm (10-14 inches), and small kokanee, mainly by trolling. In the summer, the waters in this low elevation lake (35 metres/114 feet) warm up, making water sports more enjoyable than fishing.

Richardson Lake (Map 9/G3)

This picturesque 12 hectare lake is now surrounded by a provincial park. It involves a steep drive to the lake at 760 metres (2470 feet). A former forest service site provides camping at the west end of the lake. The lake is stocked with cutthroat, which grow to 30 cm (12 inches). Trolling is the preferred method of fishing.

Sakinaw Lake (Maps 9/B1-18/C7)

Sakinaw is a large (840 ha), deep lake lined with private residences and summer cottages. The lake is unique since salmon and sea-run cutthroat can be caught in the fall near the channel flowing into the ocean at the southwest end of the lake. With patience, it is also possible to catch large cutthroat (to 60 cm/24 inches) and some small kokanee in the spring. Try using salmon gear in the fall and chironomids in spring.

Sliammon Lake (Map 16/G2)

Found close to Powell River, this 180 hectare lake provides fair fishing for cutthroat to 2.5kg (5.5 lbs) and for small kokanee. Trolling is the preferred method although it is possible to catch fish by fly fishing or spincasting in the many bays.

Tannis Lake (Map 10/B2)

Located along the Mt Steele Backcountry Trail System, this small (10 hectare) lake is one of a series of small mountain lakes in the area. It provides good fishing for rainbow in the 20-30 cm (8-12 inch) range, particularly in the spring or fall by trolling. The lake is 970 metres (3,153 feet) in elevation.

Trout Lake (Map 9/E4)

This small (7 hectare), productive lake is located next to Highway 101 just to the east of Honeymoon Bay. Despite its easy access, the lake has lots of cutthroat up to 2 kg (4.4 lbs). The lake is at 600 metres (1,950 feet) in elevation and is best fished by fly fishing or spincasting towards the weeds on the north end of the lake. An electric motor only restriction is in place.

Unwin Lakes (Map 25/F6)

Unwin Lakes are located in Desolation Sound Marine Park via a short trail. It is possible to portage a canoe or small boat in. The lakes are rarely fished, and provide excellent fishing for cutthroat to 30 cm (12 inches). The lakes total 120 hectares and are best fished in late fall or early summer with bait.

Waugh Lake (Map 18/D7)

Waugh Lake is found on the Egmont Road and is frequently fished for cutthroat and rainbow to 40 cm (16 inches). The cutthroat are a little more abundant as they are stocked regularly. An electric motor only restriction applies at the 55 hectare lake.

West Lake (Map 18/A7)

Located on Nelson Island, West Lake is reached along a network of old logging roads from Hidden Basin. It is a big lake for the island, at 595 hectares and found at a low elevation (25 metres/81 feet). The lake has some surprisingly large cutthroat, growing up to 3 kg (6.6 lbs) as well as rainbow. The lake is best fished in the spring or early summer using a boat. There is a resort on the lake.

Windsor Lake (Map 17/E1)

Windsor Lake can be reached either along the Goat Lake Main or by boat from Dodd Lake (there is a short portage trail). The cutthroat in this lake are very small but the numbers allow fast fishing particularly in the spring. For fly fishermen, the best time to try is in late April-early May during the midge hatch. The 85 hecatare lake is 185 metres (600 feet) above sea level.

Wormy Lake (Map 9/F3)

Wormy Lake is accessed by 4wd road off the Honeymoon FSR. The cutthroat in the lake average 35-45 cm (14-18 inches), and are usually difficult to catch. The best time to fish is during spring when the black ant hatch is occurring. At that time, fly fishing can be a lot of fun.

River Fishing

In Southwestern BC, there is an incredible selection of rivers and creeks, which provide good fishing for the various salmon species as well as sea-run cutthroat and steelhead. However, given the proximity to the province's main population belt, most streams receive heavy fishing pressure. Given that the focus is on migratory game species (salmon, steelhead and sea-run cutthroat), most of the fishing occurs in the fall or over the winter. There is also limited opportunity to fish resident cutthroat, dolly varden and rainbow from the spring through fall.

Please note that the rivers and creeks in the region are heavily regulated to preserve depleting stocks. All streams have a single barbless hook restriction. Further, all wild cutthroat, all wild steelhead, and all wild char (dolly varden, lake trout, bull trout, brook trout) caught south of Jervis Inlet must be released. Steelhead regulations are changing more rapidly than most; if you are steelhead fishing, contact the Lower Mainland office of BC Fisheries at (604) 582-5200 for the most recent information. It is also essential to be aware of the most recent regulations for the most up-to-date information.

Lower Mainland Rivers

The close proximity of many of these streams to Greater Vancouver results in some very busy fishing conditions. If you do not like crowds, be sure avoid those streams mentioned in the local papers fishing reports.

Alouette River (Maps 3/A1-2/E2, 13/C7)

This urban river flows from the Alouette Lake into the Pitt River. It has a small run of steelhead in December through March, cutthroat in the spring and fall and coho in late September–October. Given its easy access, the river has been over fished for years.

American Creek (Map 15/C3)

American Creek is accessed by Highway 1 and the American Creek Road. It has small resident rainbow best caught in July–August after spring runoff. In early summer (June to early July), the odd salmon can be caught near the mouth of the creek.

Anderson River (Maps 24/G6-15/G1)

Anderson River flows into the Fraser River north of Hell's Gate. The river has resident dollies and rainbow, which can be caught by bait fishing or spincasting. There is also a small run of steelhead in the late winter-early summer.

Ashulu River (Maps 28/C7, 19/C1-20/A2)

Most of its length can be accessed by 2wd vehicle except the upper reaches, which are best left to a 4wd vehicle. Due to the falls, the migratory fish are only found in the lower 3 km of the river. Steelhead and dollies can be caught here from March through May. There is also a coho run in October. Resident rainbow and dollies can be caught above the falls by bait fishing or spincasting.

Big Silver Creek (Map 14/F2-23/E6)

This creek flows into Harrison Lake near the Silver Creek Camp. It is easily accessed by an extensive network of logging roads. The creek is only fishable below the falls 7 km (4.3 miles) upstream. Steelhead can be caught in the winter months and resident cutthroat throughout the year.

Birkenhead River (Maps 39/D4-30/D1)

The Birkenhead River flows into the northwest end of Lillooet Lake and is accessed by the Pemberton-D'Arcy Road or the Birkenhead FSR. Sockeye and Chinook Salmon enter the river in good numbers in the fall, as well as some large rainbow trout that follow the salmon upstream. Glacial silt entering the river during spring runoff restricts fishing in May through July. For fly fishermen, use a wet fly such as a Doc Spratley. There is a bait restriction.

Bridge River (Maps 43/A5; 45/F6-46/B4)

This small river flows into the Fraser River to the north of Lillooet. Outside of the upper reaches, good access is found along most of the river.

Steelhead, coho and chinook in the fall as well as resident rainbow offer a good variety of fishing. Float fishing using roe or crayfish is the most effective although using a large spoon (Deadly Dick, Krocodile or Kitimat) can be successful.

Brunette River (Map 2/A2)

The Brunette is a dark river that drains Burnaby Lake. The river has been mistreated in the past, but efforts to clean the river up has seen cutthroat and stocked steelhead taking up residence here again. The green space protecting the river also provides good access for anglers from Cariboo Road and North Road. No fishing is allowed from Cariboo Dam to Cariboo Road, and it is catch and release on all steelhead.

Campbell River (Map 2/C7-G7)

This river flows into Georgia Straight near Mud Bay and, given its urban setting, does not offer great fishing opportunities. There is a very small run of winter steelhead as well as coho and cutthroat entering the river in late fall (October–November). It is possible to catch the cutthroat until the spring as they often winter within the river system to spawn. The **Little Campbell River** has been extensively rehabilitated by the community hatchery and this has helped somewhat in increasing the salmon, trout and steelhead returns. Access to the river is where 16th Ave crosses the river near the Peace Portal and Hazelmere Golf Courses.

Capilano River (Maps 11/C4-1/B1)

The Capilano is perhaps the most popular fishing river on the North Shore. Hundreds of anglers gather here during the prime fishing months. The river has a small summer steelhead run, and a small winter run from December–April. The real action begins in August when the coho start to return to the Capilano Hatchery. The river is heavily regulated, so make sure you check the regulations before heading out.

Cheakamus River (Maps 20/D1-5; 29/E7-G7)

The upper reaches of the Cheakamus River flow beside Highway 99 and provide fishing for small resident rainbow, which are best fished using bait. Beyond the canyon, most of the upper reaches are impassable. Even below the canyon, fishing should be restricted to when the river is not swollen with spring runoff (September–May). The lower Cheakamus offers a fairly good spring steelhead run (April–May). Coho enter the river in October and can be caught in good numbers throughout the winter. A few chinook may be caught in the fall (September–November). Resident dollies and cutthroat are also present year round. The lower Cheakamus River receives heavy fishing pressure especially near Fergie's Lodge and up the Paradise Valley Road. Roe, lures or flies all work for the salmon and steelhead.

Chehalis River (Maps 14/B5-4/C1)

This river flows from Chehalis Lake southward into the Harrison River near Harrison Mills. It is considered one of the best local steelhead rivers. The river provides a good run of winter steelhead beginning in December until March as well as a few steelhead in June and July. Both fisheries are enhanced by hatchery stock. The steelhead are best caught by a float with roe or by fly-fishing using a sinking tip line to ensure that the fly is dragged near the bottom. In addition to steelhead, there are some summer chinook running in July through August as well as a very good coho run (to 7 kg/15 lbs) in October through early December so long as there are fall rains. Since the river is mostly walled in by a steep canyon, most anglers are usually found along the gravel bars near the Morris Road Bridge. Those that make it into the canyon will find it less crowded but difficult to fly fish. Water levels affect the quality of fishing, so check the Vancouver papers fishing reports on this river.

Chilliwack River (Maps 5/E6-4/C6)

This river is known as the Chilliwack River above the Vedder Bridge and the Vedder River below the bridge. The total fishing length is about 36 km (22 miles), all the way to Slesse Creek. The Chilliwack is easily accessed along the Chilliwack Lake Road and therefore receives heavy fishing pressure. The best place to fish the river is above the bridge as there are numerous pools to sample. The river has an excellent steelhead run from December through March as well as a few steelheads in the summer months. Chum and coho fishing can be very good in September to October due to hatchery enhanced coho stock. Cutthroat fishing can be very good beginning in July until October and chinook fishing can be decent in July through September. Fishermen use a multitude of different methods but wool, roe, lures and flies seem to work best for the coho and steelhead whereas flies and small spinners work best for the cutthroat. Because of its popularity, the Chilliwack is a heavily regulated river.

Cogburn Creek (Maps 14/G4-15/A3-C2)
Cogburn Creek flows into the Harrison River just north of the Bear Creek Camp. It has steelhead in January–April as well as some resident cutthroat throughout the year. A set of impassable falls limits fishing to the first 3 km (1.8 mikes) of the creek.

Copper Creek (Map 7/D3)
Copper Creek crosses Highway 3 about 10 km north of the Manning Park East Gate. The creek contains rainbow to 30 cm (12 inches).

Coquihalla River (Map 15/D4)
The Coquihalla River is accessed by Highway 5 and provides a fair run of steelhead in June–September and again in February–March. There are also a few coho in October and November as well as some resident rainbow and dollies. Given the easy access, the river is fished extensively and so you should not expect great fishing.

Coquitlam River (Maps 12/C4-2/C3)
Flowing from Coquitlam Lake into the Pitt River, this shallow, urban river has a small run of steelhead in December–April, coho in November–December and chum in the fall. There are a few small cutthroat and dollies that reside in the river year round. The Coquitlam River Trail provides good access to the various holes.

Elaho River (Maps 37/A5, 28/C1-G7)
The Elaho River flows into the Squamish River and is easily accessed along most of its length by the Elaho Road (2wd access). A few steelhead are found in March–May as well as a few coho in September–October. The river is noted more for its resident dolly varden, which can reach 2 kg (4.4 lbs), as well as smaller rainbow.

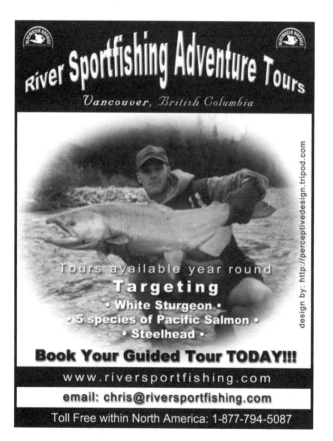

Emory Creek (Map 15/D4)
Emory Creek flows into the Fraser River north of Squeah. The creek is accessed along most of its length by a good logging road. It has small rainbow and dollies best taken after spring runoff. Chinook are available at the mouth of the creek between June–July and there is a small run of fall coho and steelhead in January–March.

Fraser River (Maps 2-5, 15)
The Fraser River, between Coquitlam and American Creek, offers excellent fishing for migratory fish and sturgeon. Most of the fishing occurs off one of the many gravel bars that line the river. Access to many of these bars is limited, making the easily accessible areas, such as Edgewater Bar and Island 22 very busy. Having a boat to access the quieter bars for salmon and the back eddies for sturgeon is helpful. Spring is really the only time of year when fishing is very poor given the high, murky waters and lack of migratory species in the system.

Sockeye (to 7kg/15.4lbs) begin entering the river in mid-July. The main runs occur in late August to late September with hundreds of fishermen lining the gravel bars. Sockeye are caught by bouncing a weight and a piece of fluorescent wool or small green spin-n-glows off the bottom. Fluorescent green out-performs pink in direct contrast to ocean fishing.

Chinook are caught beginning in June after the spring runoff subsides. Initially, float fishing or spincasting near the creek mouths proves most effective since the water is clearer in the estuaries. Later in the summer, the gravel bars begin to appear and the water clears somewhat, fishermen turn to the gravel bars and cast a spin-n-glow or cheater and sinker. As a rule of thumb, use darker colours in the early part of the season and brighter colours later in the season. Although chinook enter the river until mid-October, the best fishing occurs in July. Some chinook can reach 27 kg (60 lbs) but most of them are in the 12-18 kg (26–40 lb) range.

Coho enter the river in late September and provide excellent fishing until December. Bar fishing is the most popular method of catching coho. **Chum salmon** are caught in October and **pink salmon** in August and September. Both species are caught in the same manner as the sockeye except pinks can also be caught by using spoons, spinners or flies. Contrary to popular belief, flies do not have to be hot pink as flies such as a 52 Buick (a small, green shrimp imitation) work. Fly-fishing works best by leaving the fly dead or by a slow steady retrieve.

Sturgeon, which can exceed 450 kg (1000 lbs), are also caught throughout the river system by using a large weight, hook and bait. Although fishing the back eddies can produce a fish of a life time, it is essential to have the right gear. We recommend using a guide. The fishery is now catch-n-release given the recent decline in the population.

Sea-run cutthroat (to 50 cm/20 inches) are caught throughout the fall until early spring by fly-fishing or spincasting. **Steelhead** are available from November–March by float fishing or spincasting.

Gold Creek (Maps 13/C6-3/B1)
This creek is found in the Golden Ears Provincial Park and flows southward into the Alouette Lake. The creek is accessed by a series of trails and can be fished for small cutthroat, rainbow and dollies, which reside in the creek year round. After spring runoff is the best time to fish using bait.

Green River (Map 30/A3)
Green River flows northwest from Green Lake and enters the Lillooet River to the east of Pemberton. Most of the length of the river is easily accessed off Highway 99. Glacial silt entering the river makes it difficult to fish. It is possible to catch a few larger dollies (to 1.5 kg/3.3 lbs) and a few small rainbow.

Harrison River (Map 4/D2-F1)
This is a popular and productive river. At the highway bridge near Harrison Mills, it is not uncommon to see 20–40 fishermen lining the banks

in the late summer and into the fall. In addition to casting from shore, anglers often launch a boat at Kilby Park off Highway 7 and troll a fly or lure in Harrison Bay or near the bridge.

Coho fishing is active between September–November with the best time being in late October. The coho take to roe, wool or lures. Pinks can be fished in late August to October. Spoons, spinners or flies all work. Chum offer an excellent fishery in late October and November and are starting to get more attention from local anglers. Cutthroat fishing can be particularly effective from December through March, although during spring runoff (May–June) the fishing tails off because the waters are quite murky. The cutthroat are in the river in the fall to grab salmon eggs and in the spring to feast on the millions of salmon fry making their journey to the ocean. These fish are best caught by casting a fly, bait (worms, roe or eggs) or small lure. For fly fishermen, stick to a flashy type pattern or a small minnow imitation. The river also offers decent steelhead fishing in December–January.

Hope Slough (Map 4/E3)
Hope Slough is a slow moving meandering waterway just north of Chilliwack. The banks are mostly private property, but the slough can be accessed by a canoe. The slough contains cutthroat, which can be best caught in spring and fall (it gets a little warm in summer). The slough also plays host to a run of coho in fall.

Hunter Creek (Maps 5/C1)
Hunter Creek is a small creek that flows northward into the Fraser River to the west of Hope. Chinook are available at the mouth of the creek in June–July whereas cutthroat and steelhead frequent the estuary in the winter.

Indian River (Maps 11/G2-12/A3-A5)
Indian River flows into the north end of the Indian Arm. The river offers a small spring steelhead run as well as fishing for resident cutthroat and dolly varden. The steelhead enter the river in April when Stawamus-Indian FSR is inaccessible due to snow. Therefore, it is advised to boat up the Indian Arm and access the river that way. The cutthroat and dollies are easiest to catch every second year when the pink salmon fry migrate to the ocean. In fall chum can be found near the estuary.

Kanaka Creek (Maps 3/B2-2/G3)
This is a small urban creek in Maple Ridge which has a few steelhead in January–March, cutthroat in September–April and coho in the fall. Most of the creek can be easily accessed by paved roads and a good trail system.

Lillooet River (Maps 37/B1-30/F2; 31/A7-22/G6)
The **Upper Lillooet River** is a slow meandering stream that is easily accessed from Pemberton via both backroads and logging roads. South of Little Lillooet Lake, the **Lower Lillooet River** is a much faster flowing stream that extends all the way to Harrison Lake. It contains steelhead (March–May), resident dollies, coho (October) and chinook (April–May). However, the river is very silty during spring runoff, and fishing is poor during May through October. Therefore, you should restrict your fishing to the early spring or late fall or try one of the many clear water estuaries such as Rogers Creek. Chinook are closed from July 30 to September 30.

Lynn Creek (Maps 11/E7-1/F1)
Lynn Creek is a difficult river to access, and only has 5 km (3 miles) of fishable waters. There are a couple trails that bring you to some nice holes that hold a small run of winter steelhead in December–April, and small runs of coho and chinook in the fall.

Mamquam River (Map 20/E7)
Mamquam River flows westward into the Squamish River just south of Brackendale. The falls at 6 km (3.7 miles) restrict fish migration to the upper reaches of the river. As a result, the best places to try are at the mouth of the river where it enters the Squamish River or at the estuary of Mashiter Creek. The Mamquam contains fair numbers of steelhead in March–May with April being the best time to fish. Coho and dollies are also present in October through early November.

Maria Slough (Maps 4/D2, 5/A1)
This water body is an extension of the Fraser River near Agassiz. The Seabird Island Road provides access along most of its 10 km (6.1 miles) length. The slough offers some very good fishing for sea-run cutthroat (to 2.5 kg/5 lbs) in October through March along with resident cutthroats and dollies throughout the year. The preferred method of catching the cutthroat and dollies is by bait (worms or eggs), lures or flies. There is also a good run of coho beginning in late October until mid-December (check the regulations for closures). Coho prefer lures (Krocodile or coho lures) or salmon eggs.

Melvin Creek (Map 40/F5)
Melvin Creek is a small creek that flows into Cayoosh Creek. The creek is accessed by trail along its entire length and provides good fishing for small rainbow on a fly or with a small spoon.

Miami River (Map 4/G2)
This stream runs into Harrison Lake at Harrison Hot Springs. The mouth of the creek is the most popular area to fish using bait (salmon roe/eggs and worms) or by casting a small lure. In the summer months, rainbow can be caught with some fish reaching 0.5 kg (1.1 lbs). In late October–November, cutthroat and coho can be caught. Although the mouth of the creek is the most popular spot, some of the larger pools upstream can be particularly good for coho and cutthroat in late November when the waters have risen due to rainfall.

Nahatlach River (Maps 31/F7; 22/F1-24/C1)
The Nahatlach flows into the Fraser River south of Lytton. The fast flowing stream contains resident rainbow and dollies, as well as steelhead in the winter, chinook in the late summer and coho in the fall.

Nathan Creek (Map 3/A5)
Nathan Creek flows into the Fraser just east of Country Line Road and Fort Langley. The river contains cutthroat and coho in the fall, and a small steelhead run in winter.

Nikomekl River (Map 2/B6)
This river flows into Georgia Straight near Mud Bay and, given its urban setting, does not offer great fishing opportunities. There is a very small run of winter steelhead as well as coho and sea-run cutthroat that enter the river in late fall (October–November). It is possible to catch the cutthroat until the spring as they often stay within the river system to spawn in the spring.

Nicomen Slough (Maps 3/D2–4/A2)
This slough attaches to the Fraser, and provides access for coho up into Norrish Creek in October–November. The slough is also a good place to go looking for cutthroat in spring and fall.

Norrish (Suicide) Creek (Map 3/G4)
A falls at 7.5 km (4.6 miles) restricts fishing to the lower reaches. There are steelhead in December–March, cutthroat in the spring and fall and coho in October–November. Small resident rainbow trout are available year round.

Pasayten River (Map 7/D4)
Easily accessed along the Pasayten River FSR, this river is home to small rainbow, which can be caught by fly-fishing or spincasting.

Pitt River (Maps 12/E7-2/C3; 21/C4-12/G3)
While you can lay down a line in the heavily industrialized, lake-like **Lower Pitt River**, you won't want to. At least, not if you can get to the upper reaches. The **Upper Pitt River** offers some of the best fishing in the Lower Mainland and is basically one 65 km long (39.65 mile) fishing hole. The bottom 24 km (14.6 miles) or so of the Upper Pitt is where most of the action takes place. The river is home to rainbow trout, bull trout, steelhead (in spring), sockeye (in August), and coho (in October). However, there is a price to pay for this great fishing. That price is access. There is no way to the Upper Pitt other than boat or plane. Once you get up there, you are on foot, unless you set up transportation and possibly accommodation with the folks at the Pitt River Lodge. The Upper Pitt is catch and release only.

113 Lonsdale Ave.
North Vancouver, BC
V7M 2E7
Phone 604-986-3239

HIGHWATER TACKLE LTD

Fishing Information
Steelheading
Salmon Fishing
Fly & Trout Tackle
Rod & Reel Repairs
Custom Rod Building

Rainy River (Map 10/E3)

Rainy River is accessed by Highway 101 to Port Melon and then along a deteriorating logging road. The river has steelhead in February–March, cutthroat year round and coho in October–November.

Ruby Creek (Map 15/B7)

Ruby Creek flows southward into the Fraser River east of Agassiz. The creek has resident rainbow and cutthroat as well as steelhead in the winter and coho in the fall. Most of the creek can be accessed by gated logging roads that may or may not be drivable.

Scuzzy Creek (Map 24/C5)

Scuzzy Creek flows eastward into the Fraser River south of Boston Bar. An extensive logging road network provides access along most of the creek length. There are small resident cutthroat in the creek that are best caught by bait fishing.

Salmon River (Maps 3/D7-C5)

A slow, meandering river that flows into the Fraser near Fort Langley, the Salmon River is closed to fishing above 232 Street. Resident cutthroat and dolly varden along with a good run of coho in fall, and winter steelhead draw anglers.

Serpentine River (Map 2/C6)

This river flows into Georgia Straight near Mud Bay and, given its urban setting, does not offer great fishing opportunities. There is a very small run of winter steelhead as well as coho and sea-run cutthroat that enter the river in late fall (October–November). It is possible to catch the cutthroat until the spring as they often stay within the river system to spawn.

Seton Portage (Map 40/E1)

The short river between Anderson Lake and Seton Lake called Seton Portage offers steelhead as well as rainbow and dollies (to 2 kg/4.4 lbs). Steelhead fishermen should try near the inflow and outflow using a float and roe. The rainbow and dollies are caught at the mouth of Whitecap Creek using bait (roe or worms) or a variety of spoons.

Seymour River (Maps 11/G4-1/F1)

The Seymour River has a small run of winter steelhead beginning in late December and running until early April. There is also a small summer steelhead run beginning in June until late July. In fall, coho and some chinook head up the river. The Seymour River is the easiest of the North Shore rivers to fish, as it has a trail system (Fisherman's Trail) that extends north along the river to the Seymour Dam. There are numerous pools to fish with the best fishing being in the upper reaches.

Silverhope Creek (Maps 5/G4-15/E7)

This large, fast flowing creek reaches the Fraser River just west of Hope. It has a small steelhead run in the summer (June–August) and again in the winter (January–April). There are also a few salmon that enter the river in the fall and there are some resident cutthroat and dollies. For best success, fish at the mouth of the creek or try some of the deep holes along the creek using bait, spinners or flies. Restrictions include barbless hooks and releasing all fish under 20 cm (8 in) in size.

Skagit River (Maps 7/A5-6/E7)

Along with the Sumallo, to the west, the Skagit River offers the only really good rainbow fishing in Southwestern BC. The Skagit is a slow meandering river that is famous for its good fly fishing for steelhead across the border. On this side, the river is a rainbow river. Fishermen either walk along the Skagit River Trail from Sumallo Grove or float down the river to sample some of the more remote pools. Fishing is restricted until July with the best fishing being towards August–September, after the runoff has subsided. Fly fishermen can do very well using a mayfly imitation (size 16), Grizzly King or Royal Coachman later in the summer. The rainbow in the Skagit River average 20–30 cm (8–12 inches) but can grow as large as 50 cm (20 inches). Dollies enter the Skagit from Ross Lake and can grow as large as 5 kg (10 lbs). These fish are in the river in the fall but some remain year round.

Sloquet Creek (Maps 13/C1-22/C6)

Sloquet Creek flows northeast into the Lillooet River. A deteriorating logging road accesses the lower portions of the creek. There are steelhead in January–April, resident dollies and coho in the fall. While in the area, why not visit the hot springs for a relaxing après fishing soak?

Spuzzum Creek (Maps 24/B7-15/C1)

Spuzzum Creek flows eastward into the Fraser River north of Yale. The creek has steelhead in January–April, Chinook in June–July and resident rainbow. Although the creek is accessed by logging roads along most of its length, the best place to fish is near the creek mouth.

Squamish River (Maps 28/G2-20/C7)

This large river flows southward into Howe Sound at Squamish. It has a total of 60 km (36.6 miles) of fishable water. Due to glacial silt and spring runoff, the Squamish is very difficult to fish from early May to the end of July. Also, the lower reaches of the river below Brackendale are very unproductive. As a result, the best time to fish is in the fall to early spring from below the Cheakamus River to the Ashulu Creek estuary. The river offers steelhead beginning in January with the best time being in late March. A small run of very large chinook to 25 kg (55 lbs) enters the river in July through August. Coho are present in October–November and dollies are available year round.

Statlu Creek (Map 14/A6)

Statlu Creek flows eastward into the Chehalis River and is easily accessed by the Statlu FSR. The creek provides fishing for steelhead in the winter as well for cutthroat year round.

Stave River (Maps 3/B4; 22/A6-13/E5)

The Stave has two distinct sections. The **Lower Stave River** is a short, broad river that flows out of Hayward Lake, which in turn falls out of Stave Lake. The lower section offers the typical migratory species including; summer chinook, fall coho and winter steelhead. The **Upper Stave River** flows into the north end of Stave Lake and can only be reached by boat and then biking or hiking up the Stave River FSR. There are resident cutthroat and dollies in the river. Given the remote access, the river can be very productive, particularly in the late fall.

Stawamus River (Maps 11/D1-20/D7)

Stawamus River is a small stream that flows into Howe Sound at Squamish. It provides slow fishing for steelhead in April–May and coho in the fall. There are also resident cutthroat and dollies.

Stein River (Maps 31/E5-33/A3)

Although the Stein offers very good fishing for steelhead in the winter, chinook and coho in the fall and rainbow year round, few visitors to the valley bring along fishing rods. This makes the fishing all that better. Anglers should try casting a large spoon (Kamlooper, Krocodile or Kitimat) or float fish with roe or crayfish for steelhead.

Sumas River (Maps 3/G6-4/A5)

This river parallels Highway 1 for a good stretch and provides a few cutthroat in the spring and fall, resident dollies year round, coho in the fall (mid-September–December) and steelhead in the winter. A boat launch is available at the Sumas Pumping Station.

Backroad Mapbooks

Sumallo River (Map 6/B2-E3)
The upper reaches of the Sumallo River are easily accessed from the Sumallo River Forest Service Road. The lower reaches parallel Highway 3 east of Sunshine Valley. The river offers good fishing for rainbow and dollies in summer. Although small, the rainbow trout receive most of the attention and can be by fly, bait or small spinner.

Texas Creek (Map 41/D5)
Texas Creek is found south of Lillooet and flows to the northeast into the Fraser River. Texas Creek Road provides access but if you want to reach the upper portion of the creek you will need a 4wd vehicle and a lot of patience (due to water bars). The creek provides excellent fishing for small rainbow using bait, a fly or small lures.

Tingle Creek (Map 13/C5)
This small creek flows into Clearwater Bay on Stave Lake through Mt Judge Howay Recreation Area. The remote creek can only be accessed by boat and then by hiking/biking an old logging road. It provides resident rainbow, dollies and cutthroat fishing.

Vedder River (Map 4/A5-C6)
Below the Vedder Bridge, Chilliwack River is called the Vedder River as it slowly flows into the Vedder Canal. This section of the river is the most popular stream to fish in the Fraser Valley if not the province. It is not uncommon to see hundreds of anglers lined up shoulder to shoulder trying for the winter steelhead, chum and coho fishing in September to October as well as chinook in July through September. Please respect the fish and other people's space and move aside if someone hooks into a fish. Smarter anglers will launch a boat at the Sumas Pumping Station to avoid the crowds. Water levels definitely affect the quality of fishing so be sure to watch the weekly fishing reports in the Vancouver papers. Also be sure to check the current restrictions before heading out.

Weaver Creek (Map 4/E1)
Home to the Weaver Creek Spawning Channel, this small creek has a good run of steelhead in December to March and cutthroat all year. Sections of the creek are closed to fishing.

Whonnock Creek (Map 3/B3)
Whonnock Creek crosses Highway 7 between 272 Street and 280 Street. The river contains cutthroat, has a small run of coho in fall and a small run of winter steelhead.

Widgeon Creek (12/C4)
This creek drains Widgeon Lake southward into Pitt River. It is accessed by canoe from Grant Narrows and cuts through the Pitt-Addington Marsh. The creek has resident cutthroat as well as steelhead in the winter and coho in the fall.

Whipsaw Creek (Map 7/C2-F1)
Just north of Map 7, Whipsaw Creek crosses Highway 3. You can access the northwest banks of the river from the Whipsaw Creek Forest Service Road, or you can access the southeastern shore from the Friday Main. Spincasting or fly fishing from shore produces small rainbow.

Yale Creek (Map 15/C2)
This small creek is off Highway 1 just east of Yale. The creek offers chinook in June through July at the mouth of the Fraser River.

Sunshine Coast Rivers
Brem River (Map 34/F6-G5)
Located far, far away from anything resembling civilization, this remote river is fly or boat in only. Logging roads (which can be hiked or biked) provide access to upper reaches of the river. The river is best known for its winter steelhead but it also has resident cutthroat, a chinook run in summer, and a coho run in fall. Note that there is no fishing area below the falls, 1.5 km (.9 miles) from the mouth of the river.

Brittain River (Maps 27/B7)
Brittain River is a remote river in Jervis Inlet, which is accessed by boat and then by hiking/biking up an old logging road. Due to its limited access, the river is very good for steelhead from November through March as well as resident cutthroat in the spring and fall. The farther you walk/bike up the river the better the fishing becomes.

Chapman Creek (Map 10/B4)
Chapman Creek is located west of Sechelt and flows into the ocean at Wilson Creek. The creek is accessed by the West Road along most of its length and provides fishing for steelhead in February–April, coho in the fall and resident cutthroat year round.

Clowham River (Map 19/F4)
Clowham River is a remote stretch of water that flows southward into the northeast end of Clowham Lake. It provides sea-run cutthroat fishing in the spring and fall as well as coho fishing in the fall. There are also resident cutthroat and dollies available.

Deserted River (Map 28/A6)
Deserted River is a remote river flowing into the Jervis Inlet that can only be reached by boat and then bushwhacking up the river. Given its difficult access, there is a good run of steelhead in the winter as well as coho in the fall.

Gray Creek (Maps 10/A3-9/G3)
Gray Creek flows from a series of mountain lakes into the Sechelt Inlet south of Tuwanek. The creek has cutthroat in the spring and fall and coho in the fall.

Lang Creek (Map 17/C5)
Lang Creek flows from Duck Lake into the ocean just southeast of Powell River. A good logging road and trail system makes access fairly easy. There are steelhead in January–March as well as cutthroat in the spring and fall in the river. However, the best fishing is now in the shallow estuary for hatchery chinook averaging 20 kg (44 lbs). They are fished in mid September to late October by casting a spoon or large fly from the beach. Since the waters are shallow, it is well advised that you use a lure that does not sink too quickly or you will lose a lot of tackle. The occasional coho and chum can also be caught.

McNab/McNair Creeks (Map 10/D4; 10/F2)
These two small creeks flow into the Thornbrough Canal near Port Mellon. McNab Creek, which is accessed by boat, has resident cutthroat, coho in October–November and steelhead in the winter. It is preferable to bring a mountain bike to access the upper reaches of McNab Creek.

McNair Creek, which is accessed by Highway 101 and logging roads, has cutthroat in the spring and fall, coho in October–November and steelhead in the winter.

Potlatch Creek (Maps 10/G1–11/A2)

A boat access only river north of Anvil Island in Howe Sound, Potlatch River is a good cutthroat stream in spring.

Rainy River (Map 10/E3)

The Rainy River is just north of Port Mellon and the end of Highway 101. The river contains cutthroats, which are best caught in spring and fall as well as a fall run of coho and winter steelhead.

Roberts Creek (Map 10/B6-C5)

Roberts Creek is found west of Gibson and contains steelhead and cutthroat. Those fish are best caught near the estuary.

Sechelt Creek (Map 10/D1-F1)

Sechelt Creek is a remote creek located towards the north end of the Salmon Inlet. The creek is accessed by boat and then following a logging road, preferably with a bike. Anglers will find resident cutthroat as well as coho in the fall and steelhead in the winter.

Skwanka River (Map 27/B3)

The Skwanka is another remote river with a logging road that follows the river valley. The river contains cutthroats, chinook, coho and a small run of winter steelhead.

Theodosia River (Maps 26/A5-25/F6)

This remote river flows into the Theodosia Inlet near Desolation Sound Provincial Marine Park. The river is accessed by boat and then by following the Theodosia Main logging road up the river. Therefore, it is best to bring a bike if you want to try the upper reaches of the river. The river provides steelhead and cutthroat in the spring and fall as well as coho in September–October.

Tzoonie River (Map 19/A4)

Tzoonie River is a remote river flowing southward into Narrows Inlet. It is accessed by boat and then by following the Tzoonie River Road preferably by mountain bike. The river provides steelhead fishing in December–March as well as coho fishing in the fall. There are also resident dolly varden and cutthroat in the river system.

Vancouver River (Maps 19/A12-18/G2)

The Vancouver River is yet another remote river that flows into Jervis Inlet. A mountain bike can be used to access the length of the river along an old rail line/road from Vancouver Bay. The river has steelhead in January–May, cutthroat in October–November and coho in the fall. There are also resident dollies available. Given the remote access, the fishing is usually very good.

Saltwater Fishing

The regulations guiding recreational fishing in Southwestern BC are always in a state of flux. Conservation measures to protect fish stocks (from ground fish to shell fish to coho and sockeye) are a lot more stringent these days. Fish responsibly. This means protecting the environment and the resource, and practicing safe fishing habits and respect towards others. Handle fish with care, and limit your catch to ensure fish for the future. Remember: barbless hooks are to be used at all times for salmon fishing along the Pacific Coast.

The information provided here is as accurate as we can make it, but fishing regulations and openings change every year, sometimes every day. In addition to reading the regulations, it is advised to check with a local bait shop or with the Department of Fisheries and Oceans for the most recent openings, regulation changes and size limits. DFO's website is www.pac.dfo-mpo.gc.ca.

Howe Sound/Vancouver Area

Fishing in the proximity of Vancouver does not measure up to other coastal locations. But with some patience and some luck, good salmon fishing is possible. The real advantage of the Howe Sound and Burrard Inlet is the easy access from Vancouver. This is also its Achilles Heel, as this area is notoriously over fished. Even with tighter regulations, this area will always see more pressure than other areas because of the sheer population in the area.

Boat launches are available near the entrance to False Creek, at Ambleside Beach in West Vancouver, at Horseshoe Bay, at Sewell's Marina, at MacDonald Park in Richmond and several locations along the Fraser River. Most launches charge a hefty fee, around $10. It is also possible to access the Howe Sound from the Sunshine Coast. The closest boat launches are at Langdale and Gibsons.

Bowen Island (Maps 10/G7-11/A6)

Due to its close proximity to Vancouver, Bowen Island is a popular fishing destination. Although the southern end of the island gets most of the attention, there are many areas to drop a line in:

Collingwood Channel: This location often produces very well for winter chinook in December–April. Trolling along the west side of Bowen Island can produce at that time. Mooching near the reef off Tunstall Bay is also very effective.

Cowan Point to Cape Roger Curtis: This area stretches along the southern end of Bowen Island. It is a good area for wintering chinook in December to April. Most fishermen troll deep 25–35 metres (80–120 feet) along the first tide line using hoochies or bait (strip or whole) with a flasher. Cowan Point also produces well for chinook in May through July, coho in late August to October, pinks in late August to September (odd years) and sockeye in September with trolling being your best bet. Mooching live herring or strip casting off Cowan Point also works for chinook throughout the year. The area is very popular because of its consistent fishing success but weather can be a real concern as the point is exposed.

Grafton /Galbrath Bays: Located on the northwest corner of the island and sheltered by Hutt Island, this area holds chinook most of the year (except August-September). Actually catching a fish here is a hit-and-miss proposition. Mooching with live or strip herring in the middle of the channel between Hutt Island and Bowen Island or in the centre of Grafton and Galbrath Bay is most productive. Trollers circle the north end of Hutt Island or troll the two bays. Coho can be found here in July or October. Pinks can be caught in late August and September in odd years.

Hutt Island: Located off the Northwest corner of Bowen Island, the small Hutt Island (and the smaller Hutt Rock) are spotty producers of winter (feeder) chinook from October to April, with larger fish rolling into the area in May thru August.

Queen Charlotte Channel: This passage is best known for its pinks, which move through here in July.

Seymour Landing: Located on the east side of Bowen Island just north of Cowan Point, Seymour Landing has some reasonable fishing for chinook in May. Troll deep 25–35 metres (80–120 feet) for best success.

Snug Cove: This cove is often trolled southward to the Copper Mine for chinook from December to March and from June to August. Coho can be found from July to September. Watch out for heavy traffic in the area, especially ferries.

Tunstall Bay: Located just north of Cape Roger Curtis, this is an area to try in December to April for wintering chinook. A deep troll using herring (whole or cut) or hoochies is most effective.

Capilano River (Map 1/D1)

The mouth of the Capilano is an incredibly popular area to fish, especially for the coho that congregate at the river mouth. If you are fishing from shore for the coho beginning in June until November, casting any one of a number of lures works (Krocodile, Stingzildas, Buzz-Bombs, No. 4 Colorado or Chrome Flatfish). For boaters, it is best to anchor 20–30 metres off the lighthouse and mooch with live herring, herring strips or small cut-plug herring on a tide change. A number of chinook in the 10–15 kg (30–40 lb) range also come into the area in late summer until mid-October. These fish are best caught by trolling (watch the boating traffic) during flood tides with bait. In December through April, winter chinooks frequent the mouth and can be caught by mooching 60–80 metres offshore.

Fishermen's Cove/Eagle Harbour (Map 11/A7)

Fishermen's Cove is located south of Horseshoe Bay, and has a hit-and-miss fishery. It can be excellent for short stretches, and then not a single fish will be caught for weeks. Winter chinook, from December through April, are found off the south end of **Eagle Island**. There are also chinook and coho from June to October. It is best to mooch with live or cut herring rather than troll. Some fishermen also try jigging although with less success than mooching. To the north, **Whytecliff Point** offers a good place to troll for winter chinook in March and April. The tides off the point make mooching undesirable.

Fraser River Estuary (Map 1/A2-C7)

The Fraser River is the pathway for millions of migrating salmon. It is no wonder the river mouth can provide some of the best fishing anywhere. To fish the Fraser, you have a number of boat launches to choice from: McDonald Park (on Sea Bird Island), False Creek (behind the Planetarium), and Dyke Road at Gilbert Beach. Each of the launches involves a 20–30 minute boat ride to the estuary. Once you reach the estuary, simply look for the boats and you will have a good idea where to fish. Between Point Grey Bell Buoy and the QA marker off the North Arm, the T-10 marker off the Middle Arm, around the Sand Heads off the end of the Steveston Jetty in the tide lines and from Roberts Bank to the Tsawwassen Ferry Terminal all seem to produce at particular times.

The sockeye fishery beginning in mid June and lasting until the end of September gets most of the attention. There are a number of different runs including the unproductive Stuart River as well as the better Horsefly River and Adams River runs. The waters of the Fraser are murky making it difficult for the fish to see your lure easily. If possible, stack the lines so that you have a number of flashers off each downrigger, some of which have no lure so there is plenty of movement to attract the fish.

Other salmon species do not draw as much attention as the sockeye. Pinks are in abundance in odd years at the mouth in August. The same set-up for sockeye catches pinks. Chinook and coho can be caught in August to October by trolling a flasher with a hoochie or bait (herring or anchovy). In the last few years, the chinook fishery has really picked up. Some large fish 20 kg (50+ lbs) have been caught around the Point Grey Bell Buoy, T-10 marker and the Sand Heads. The best time for the coho is October when the 6 kg (13 lb) northerns begin to appear but watch for the fishing closures that are usually in effect. The occasional fisherman mooches for the coho near the QA Marker or off the Sand Heads. Chum, which seem to like a flasher with a dark hoochie (Army

Truck, green, or purple), are present in October to November.

Gambier Island (Maps 10/G4-11/A5)

This island is north of Bowen Island in Howe Sound. Except for the southern end, the waters around Gambier Island, at the time of writing this book, are now closed to fishing between May 31 and September 27. The open areas, unfortunately, are usually quite spotty. Your best bests are Grace Islands, Halkett and Hope Points, which are described below. West Bay also has some good fishing

Grace (Twin) Islands: This area can be good, on occasion, for winter springs in December to February and for coho and mature chinook in July through October. Trolling around the south end of the islands are the best areas. The coho are fished in 10–20 metres of water whereas the chinook tend to be deeper.

Halkett Point: This point is found off the east shores of Gambier Island. It occasionally produces winter chinook in November–March, mature chinook in May–July and some coho in September–October. Trolling is the best method of fishing as the fish concentration is low. Mooching off the western tip can produce on occasion.

Hope Point: This point is found at the southeastern most tip of Gambier Island. Trolling around the point at 25 metres (80 feet) using a dodger/ flasher and Apex, hoochie or herring (whole or cut), produces chinook and coho in July–September.

Hole in the Wall (Map 11/B7)

This is a very popular fishing spot just north of Horseshoe Bay, and is so named because of a mining test hole on the granite cliff rising above the ocean. The area is notoriously fickle. Mooching with live, whole or strip herring near the bottom is the most productive fishing method for chinook in November through March and again in July through September. It is best to stay near the cliffs where you will find a 150 metre ledge. Trollers also work the area in the winter months at 25–35 metres (80–120 feet) using a flasher with a hoochie or whole or strip herring. The occasional coho is caught in the area between July through September. The preferred time to fish the area is in the morning during

high water. Further north, **Sunset Beach** also provides the opportunity to cruise for chinook.

Howe Sound (North) (Maps 10, 11)

This region is closed to fishing from March 31 to September 27 from the south end of Gambier Island northward. As a result, fishing is restricted to winter springs (chinook) with the best locations being trolling 30 m (100 feet) off McNab Creek, the log booms at Port Mellon and the south end of Anvil Island. Port Mellon and McNab Creek are usually better in December through February whereas Anvil Island is better in March through April. Mooching off the Woodfibre Mill is effective in January through March particularly if you stay close to the pilings off the ferry wharf. Current is light in the area so a small weight (1-2 oz) works. Other options include mooching off Furry Creek, mooching herring off the booms in front of Shannon Falls and trolling off Porteau Cove. Please note that winter mooching is limited by the lack of available live bait.

Indian Arm (Map 12/A6)

Indian Arm produces an excellent fishery for pinks in late August–early September, during odd numbered years (2003, 2005, etc.). These fish congregate just south of the Vancouver Yacht Club against the rock cliff. It is best to drift fish while casting a red and white wobbler or similar lure into the school of fish. It is easy to locate where the fish are congregated, as you will see the males jumping. Another good fishery occurs in late October when chum enter the arm.

Keats Island (Map 10/E7)

This small island to the west of Bowen Island is best fished for wintering chinook in November through April off Cotton Point. Mooching and trolling both work. Trolling around the point at 25–40 metres (80–140 feet) with plugs or whole herring in a teaser head is best. Moochers usually anchor off the point in water up to 180 metres (600 feet) deep. Cotton Point can also produce well for chinook and coho in June–October.

At the south end of Keats Island is **Home Island**, a small rock outcrop also known as Salmon Rock. This area receives heavy fishing pressure because it is a constant producer for chinook in March and April and chinook and coho in June–September. Mooching with live or strip herring within 15 metres (50 feet) of the southwestern corner of the island is the best spot because the bait accumulates in that area due to tide action. Jigging lures are also effective. Trollers circle around the southern end of the island using flashers or dodgers with a wide variety of lures or bait.

Gibson Gap is a very good producer of chinook and coho in June–September. The Gap is a shallow rock shelf (4–15 metres/12–50 feet) that extends from the south end of Keats Island to Cape Byng on the Sunshine Coast. The water on either side of the shelf drops off rapidly to 45 metres (150 feet) and it is at the drop-off where the fish hold. Trolling with herring (cut-plug or whole) with a flasher or mooching with live or strip herring works. The chinook tend to be in the deeper waters.

Pasley/Worlcombe Islands (Map 10/E7)

Near the southwestern end of Bowen Island, these islands offer good fishing for winter chinook in December–April. Try trolling deep off the south end of either island. **Worlcombe Island** is also a very popular coho area in July–October with trolling along the southern end being the most productive. A silver bucktail or a dodger with most coho type lures works as does cut or whole herring. Mooching or strip casting can also produce if you focus on the outside edge of the island.

Passage Island (Map 1/A1)

A small island located between the south end of Bowen Island and the Grebe Islets. Anglers can find chinook and coho in September and October on the west side of the island. Pinks and sockeyes are also found in this area in September.

Point Atkinson (Map 1/A1)

The lighthouse in Lighthouse Park marks Point Atkinson. A rock shelf extends off the point to the 18–25 metres (60–90 feet) level before dropping off to 60 metres or more. It is at this drop-off that trolling is most effective for chinook in the winter and July to September as well as for a few coho and pinks in August through September. Due to strong currents, it is best to troll a flasher with a hoochie, anchovy or herring in a circular manner around the point and into **Caulfield Cove**.

Also in the area is **Grebe Islets**, which are also known as Seal Rocks. They are best trolled on the outside edge as there is an underwater reef leading from Erwin Point to the island making trolling in the inside a very expensive proposition as you are sure to lose your tackle.

The Shipping Lanes and the QB marker (Map 1/B1)

The QB marker is found in the middle of Burrard Inlet and offers some marginal fishing primarily for winter chinooks between December and April. The area has a sandy bottom and is best to fish off the bottom by trolling a flasher with a hoochie (white preferable), Apex or herring strip.

If fishing is slow, why not try off **Jericho Beach**. Work the area off the drop-off with a flasher and hoochie, whole herring or Apex. Coho can also be found in both areas from July through September.

West Vancouver Waterfront (Map 1/B1-C1)

This region sports an active trolling fishery for chinook in the winter and early spring and for coho in August through September. The best place to try is 300 metres (1,000 feet) offshore where fish tend to congregate around the notable underwater bench. No one particular area along the West Vancouver Waterfront is more productive than another, although fishermen tend to stay in West Bay or off Navy Jack Point. Trolling to the Ambleside boat launch from Navy Jack Point can prove effective. The typical coho and chinook gear (flasher with hoochie or herring strip) seem to produce the best. Some fishermen mooch in the area but it is certainly not as productive as trolling because the fish are not focused in one area and the currents make mooching difficult. The winter chinook average 4–5 kg (10+ lbs) and are best caught by using a small herring or anchovy in a teaser head. A deep troll (35–55 metres/120–180 feet) is preferred.

Sunshine Coast/Powell River Areas

The fishing on the Sunshine Coast is similar to what is found on the East Coast of Vancouver Island. As a general rule, fishing is better here than around Vancouver, but not as good as places farther north or west. Of course, that's just a general observation, and there are lots of good places to fish along the coast, from the crowded Pender Harbour to the remote corners of Jervis Inlet.

Bargain Bay (Map 9/B2)

Bargain Bay is a good place to try in the evening between July–September for coho. Trolling during March–April for bluebacks as well as trolling for wintering chinook from November to early June can produce. Moochers or strip casters do very well by anchoring off of **Whitestone Islands,** by fishing in 15–20 metres (50–70 feet) of water in front of the waterfall or working Bjerre Shoals, which extend from Harness Island south to **McNaughton Point.** Live herring is by far the most common bait. Trollers tend to stick around Whitestone Islands.

Copeland Islands (Maps 16/C1-25/C7)

The Copeland Islands are north of Lund and offer some good fishing for chinook and coho. The best location to fish is on the inside passage either by trolling a plug at 15–25m (60–90 feet) or by fishing from shore. Chinook begin to appear in mid April and can be caught until July. Coho tend to be near the islands in July and August.

Desolation Sound (Map 25/F6)

An early chinook run begins in April and peaks in May. Mooching at one of the points (Zephine Head, Price Point, or the tip of Melville Island) or trolling along one of the many islands meets with success.

Earls Cove (Map 18/C6)

From May to August, Earls Cove is a good destination for coho and chinook. It is sheltered from the winds of Jervis Inlet so it makes a good place for smaller crafts. If you are fishing for chinook, it is best to try a deep mooch (20–45 metres/65–100 feet) with strip or live herring or try trolling a plug or whole herring in deep water. For coho, the bluebacks come into the area in May and then you can catch mature coho until August. These fish are taken by trolling or mooching.

Egmont Area (Map 18/D6)

In order to get into the Sechelt Inlet, fish must first pass **Egmont Point.** Fishing can be quite good throughout the year. As a result, the area is very popular. For chinook, a deep mooch is most effective although mooching with live herring in 15–45m (50–150 feet) of water can also be effective. Coho tend to take lighter gear and can be caught near the surface trolling a variety of coho lures, by mooching with live herring or by strip casting. Moochers tend to stay closer to Earls Cove than the point, whereas the trollers tend to troll toward Egmont.

>   **Egmont Harbour** is not a popular fishing location but there is a nice 25 metre (80 foot) hole on the west side of the island at the entrance to the harbour.

>   **Silvey's Bay** is located across from Egmont, and offers good fishing for both chinook and coho near a group of small islands (Sutton Islands). Fishing is good both inside and outside the islands. As a rule of thumb, you should fish closer to the shoreline and move out over the course of the day. The area is best trolled due to the heavy currents of the Skookumchuck Narrows. Both coho and chinook can be taken throughout the summer months and the occasional chinook can be taken during the winter.

Foley Head (Map 18/C5)

This point provides good fishing for bluebacks beginning in May, as well as mature coho until September. The best location is on the Prince of Whales Reach side of the point.

Gibsons Harbour (Map 10/E7)

There is a popular fishing hole found just east of the piers off at the drop-off. The area is best fished from December–May for wintering chinook although there are chinook and coho in the summer, too. Mooching live herring is the preferred method although it is possible to troll or cast a

jigging lure. Nearby **Keats Island** (see Howe Sound section above) is a good area to try.

Gower Point (Map 10/D7)

Gower Point is considered one of the premier coho areas on the Sunshine Coast as the fish must pass by the point on their way to the Fraser River or other rivers of the Burrard Inlet. If you are fishing the area for the first time, trolling with a whole herring or hoochie and a flasher at 15–25 metres (60–80 feet) is your best bet. Locals fishing the area usually anchor near the drop-off at the south end of the point and try mooching or strip casting. Jigging also works on occasion. Coho are caught from July–September with the evening being the best time of day to try. There are also good numbers of pinks caught during late July and early August in odd years and the occasional chinook is caught here in May–September.

Halfmoon Bay (Map 9/D4)

This bay is one of the best fishing areas on the Sunshine Coast, producing chinook from November through to March as well as in June and July and again in September. Coho are present in July through September. Both species are best caught by trolling around the points leading into the bay.

Harmony Island / Granville Bay (Map 18/B4)

This area is popular for chinook in April through early June as well as coho fishermen later in summer (July and August). The best place to fish is at the north end of the islands or near the estuary of Freil Lake. Mooching is by far the method of choice using live herring with one ounce of weight. Trollers should stay near the drop-off and use a combination of a plug or flasher with a hoochie or herring (cut or whole).

Harwood/Vivian Islands (Map 16/F3)

To the east of Powell River, **Harwood Island** marks a good area for salmon fishing. The best spots to fish for coho and chinook are off the east and southwestern sides of the island using a deep troll. Nearby **Vivian Island** offers chinook in July and August primarily by trolling. There are also coho in June through August caught by casting or mooching.

Lasqueti Island (Map 8/E5)

By far the best location to fish around Lasqueti Island is off **Young Point,** which attracts many moochers. The moochers use live or strip herring and anchor 5–25 metres (30–150 feet) off the point fishing for coho that are found in 10–15 metres (30–50 feet) of water. Casting lures can also meet with success if the coho are feeding near the surface. Trollers can circle the point or work their way up to **Bull Passage** with reasonable success. Coho are the most common fish here, with July being the best month to catch them. Off the northeastern end of Lasqueti Island from Fegen Islets to False Bay, fishing produces coho and a few chinook primarily by a shallow troll. Mooching with live or cut herring or casting jigging lures also produces. At the south end of **Jenkins Island** is a good spot to troll for coho in June through October with the bigger northerns coming through in September to October. The occasional chinook can be caught in July and August.

Lund (Map 16/D1)

Lund is known as a saltwater fishing community and has full facilities to support the fishery. Right off the waterfront, it is possible to catch wintering chinook in December to April and mature chinook in May through June. Most fishermen troll along the waterfront all the way to the south end of Copeland Island. Others try off of Hurtado Point just south of Lund. Sockeye can also be found here in July and August.

Mystery Reef/Grant Reefs (Map 16/C3-E3)

Mystery Reef is situated to the northwest of Harwood Island. It is known to produce good numbers of coho in May through June as well as a few chinook in July and August. If the bait is near the reefs, anchor off the north or south end of the reef and try some mooching or jigging. Otherwise, try trolling around the reef as the fish are likely scattered. Finding **Grant Reefs** is half the fun as they are submerged but marked by a series of kelp beds. The reefs provide good fishing for coho from May to July and chinook in July and August.

Nelson Island (Maps 8-9, 17-18)

Nelson Island is the large island that is found at the northwest end of Sechelt Peninsula. Scattered around the island are several good fishing holes.

Ackland Reef (Map 9/A1), which is several hundred yards off the mouth of Quarry Bay, provides one of the best fisheries for coho throughout July and August. The area is difficult to find but once you do, it is best to anchor at the edge of the reef in 15–30 metres (50–100 feet) of water and try jigging or mooching. Chinook are around in May through August.

Fearney Point (Map 9/A1) provides a popular fishery for chinook, pink and coho. Most fishermen troll around the point using anything from bucktails for the coho to a flasher and hoochie for the chinook. Moochers can anchor near the point.

Green Bay (Map 18/A7) is located in Agamemnon Channel on the southeastern side of the island. This area offers good fishing for chinook as well as coho and bluebacks. Moochers do well by concentrating in the inlet to the bay or on the point to the north of the bay where there is a nice tide rip caused by the point. For trollers, it is best to troll around the point.

Quarry Bay (Map 9/A1) is a good area to troll a bucktail for coho in July–August or a hoochie or herring (strip or whole) for chinook in April–July and November. It also provides good mooching for both coho and chinook using live herring.

Telescope Pass (Map 17/G7) extends between Nelson Island and Hardy Island and is a seldom-fished area that can be very productive for chinook and coho. Most fishermen anchor near the entrance to the pass and mooch with live herring at varying depths. Trollers can circle the entrance to the pass.

Pender Harbour (Map 9/B1)

The shear number of resorts and guides in the immediate area is proof of the fine fishing around Pender Harbour. The following are some of the hotspots.

Daniel Point: Best trolled or mooched in deep water for chinook from November to May. The area is hit and miss.

Francis Point: On the southern tip of Francis Peninsula, Francis Point is a good location for trolling for both chinook and coho. The chinook are most prominent in May through June and are best fished deep. The bluebacks are fairly abundant in May–June and the mature coho appear in September. Coho like bucktails or flashtails trolled near the surface.

The "Gap": Leading into Pender Harbour, the area is extremely popular with fishermen. It offers a good place to mooch with live herring for chinook throughout the year. The occasional coho will also be caught. It is possible to troll through the area but the confined space and the busy traffic makes trolling difficult.

Hodgson Islets: The area on the east side of Hodgson Island is best mooched with live or cut herring or jigging near the bottom. The area does not receive the same fishing pressure as other spots near Pender Harbour despite it being a consistent producer of chinook from November–May. It is best to fish during the outflow tide.

Lee's Bay: Located between Daniel Point and Irvines Landing, the bay offers one of the most popular mooching areas for chinook throughout the year. The occasional coho can also be caught. Fishermen almost exclusively use live herring on a one oz weight at varying depths depending on the season (deeper for summer and winter and shallower for spring time). The area is also trolled using live herring, plugs or hoochies. The bay is often crowded with 50–75 boats on a summer evening.

Sakinaw Estuary: Also known as the A-Frame, this area is best trolled or mooched near the point south of the actual estuary. The best fishing for the chinook is in December through March although it is possible to catch chinook year round. Occasionally, coho come into the area in the summer (July–August) and can be caught in good numbers.

Porpoise Bay (Map 9/G4)

Porpoise Bay is located at the south end of Sechelt Inlet, and is mainly fished by locals given its close proximity to Sechelt and difficult access from anywhere else. Mooching off the pier for chinook starting in March is surprisingly effective although it is best to bring a boat and fish farther out, near the drop-off. Moochers tend to use live bait. It is also possible to troll the bay out to Angus Creek. Mooching is the preferred method as there are a few strong currents and it is a sheltered bay. In the late fall (September–October), jigging produces chum and coho.

Powell River (Map 17/A4)

The old boat breakwater, known as **The Hulks**, marks the location of some good chinook fishing in May through August. Most fishermen begin trolling near the Hulks at dawn and then work their way outward throughout the morning. The opposite is true for the evening fish. Mooching or jigging is also worth a try especially when the chinook run is at its peak.

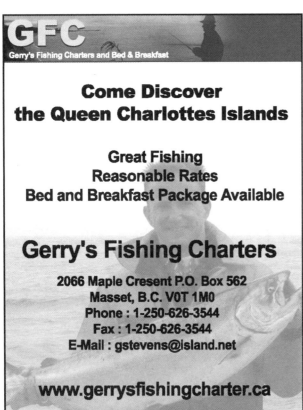

Another area to try is the **Westview Waterfront**. The occasional wintering chinook can be caught in December to April on a deep (25–40 metre/80–130 feet) troll. The better fishing, however, is in May through July for chinook and coho.

> **Grief Point** is located south of Powell River and can be good year round. The focus, however, is in May to August when the chinook are found off the point in good numbers. Trolling or mooching are the primary fishing methods.

> **Myrtle Point/Rocks** are found between Powell River and Brew Bay and offer good fishing for chinook from May to July and for coho in July. Trolling along the shoreline from Myrtle Rock all the way to the point is the most common method of catching fish.

Roberts Creek Area (Map 10/B6)

The shoreline extending from Wilson Creek all the way to Gower Point can be a very productive trolling area for coho from June to October and for chinook in June and again in September–October. It is also possible to catch wintering chinook in December to March. Moochers tend to focus their efforts approximately 200 metres (650 feet) from the wharf at **Roberts Creek** where there is a noticeable drop-off. The area is subject to large swells.

> **Camp Byng** is marked by the Camp Byng sign to the northwest of Gower Point. It is a popular area given that coho can be caught in fair numbers from July–September and chinook can be caught throughout the year from May–September. A large shallow area extends from the beach off Camp Byng some 200 metres (750 feet) offshore. It is at the drop-off where moochers, strip casters and trollers focus their efforts.

> **White Islets** are two small reefs found to the south of Wilson Creek. The odd coho is caught during the summer months off the west and south ends of the islands on a deep troll or by mooching. Since the islets are several kilometres south of the shoreline, the area can be quite exposed.

Saint Vincent Bay (Map 18/A4)

Saint Vincent Bay has a number of fishing holes all the way out to Elephant Point and Culloden Point. Both points are best for coho (bluebacks beginning in April until May and then mature coho throughout the summer) whereas Saint Vincent Bay is best for chinook. This area can be extremely busy during the summer months with both moochers and trollers.

Sangster Island/Seal Reef (Map 8/G6)

Sangster Island is located off the southern tip of Lasqueti Island. Due to its exposure, it is best to fish the area with a larger boat. If you do venture out to the island, it can be extremely productive for coho throughout the summer months. Fishermen concentrate their efforts off the kelp beds off the southern end of the island. Jigging for chinook and coho as well as trolling anything from a bucktail to a flasher with a hoochie, plug or bait can be effective. Off the northwestern tip of Sangster Island is another good area that holds coho during the summer months. It is best to anchor near the drop-off and mooch or cast lures. Trolling is also possible as long as you stick to the outside.

Nearby **Seal Reef** is another exposed area that offers coho and the occasional chinook. Most fishermen mooch with live or cut herring but it is also possible to catch fish by trolling or by casting a lure on the outside edge of the reef.

Sarah Point (Map 25/C7)

Sarah Point marks the northern tip of Malaspina Peninsula. It is a good spot for fishing because fish entering Desolation Sound must pass by the point. There are some wintering chinook but the main fishery is from May and June for chinook and late August to early September for coho. Trolling around the point seems to work the best, although mooching or jigging at the drop-off should not be ruled out.

Sargeant Bay/Trail Islands (Map 9/E4)

Sargeant Bay is found west of Sechelt and offers fishing for chinook and coho. The chinook are in the bay in the highest concentration from

December to early June whereas the coho are present in July–September. Trolling along the drop-off of the southwestern side of the bay is the best area to try. Moocher's focus on the southwestern point where a series of back eddies and a sharp drop-off exists. Jigging can also produce at times.

Trolling a half kilometre off shore towards **Trail Islands** is also worth a try. These four islands are not very productive, but they do offer anglers the opportunity to catch coho and the odd chinook in the summer. Trolling at the drop-off on the outside or at the ends of the islands with plugs, hoochies or bucktails is the most efficient method. Moochers prefer the inside passage where water depths range from 18–40m (60–140 feet) deep using both live and cut herring. The outside fishing grounds are subject to strong winds and adverse weather.

Savary Island (Map 16/B2)

In July and August, the south side of Savary Island can be trolled using a bucktail/ flashtail or a typical coho lure. The coho can be found in good numbers all the way along the south side of the island and northward to Hernando Island. Jigging or casting along the kelp beds on the south side of the island can also be effective.

Scotch Fir Point (Map 17/E6)

This point marks the beginning of Jervis Inlet and migratory salmon must pass here to get into the Inlet and its system of creeks and rivers. As a result, it offers good fishing throughout the summer months for coho and in December–March and May for chinook. Trollers try all the way from Frolander Bay to Thunder Bay but generally focus around the point. Moochers and jiggers focus off the point.

Sechelt Inlet (Maps 9/F1-G5; 18/E7)

This long narrow inlet leads all the way from Egmont south to Sechelt. **Porpoise Bay** (see above) sees the most pressure, as it butts up against Sechelt, but there are a number of other places to fish the sheltered inlet. Coho start running through this area in July, and chinook in August. In odd years the inlet sees a good fishery for pinks, too. Some areas to try include **Snake Bay**, **Tillicum Bay**, **Carlson Point** and **Highland Point**.

Secret Cove (Map 9/C3)

This area provides some excellent fishing for chinook when the fish are in the cove. Mooching with live herring near the piers or on the outside is the most popular method of fishing. Trollers are limited to the outside using a flasher with a plug or bait. Chinook season runs from September–June, and coho can be caught in October.

Skookumchuck Narrows (Sechelt Rapids) (Map 18/E7)

These rapids are located at the estuary of Earle Creek. The area is best left to larger boats because the currents can reach up to 15-20 knots. Because of the strong tides, fishing on the slack is highly recommended as is going with an experienced fisherman who knows the waters. Otherwise, the fishing hole is extremely dangerous. If you do wish to venture out, fishing around the islands at the mouth of Earle Creek or on the opposite shoreline during slack tide is your best bet. Mooching with live bait and 1-2 oz of weight or jigging a lure are effective. Trolling is not an option.

To the south of **Earle Creek** is a bay that forms behind a granite point. In the bay is a strong back eddy, which often produces coho and chinook by mooching with live herring or using jigging lures.

Skookumchuck Bay is situated away from the strong tides of the narrows. For this reason, the area receives heavy fishing pressure with most anglers trolling for chinook early in the morning or in the evening. Early in the morning, the fish tend to be near the surface whereas over the course of the day, they drop to the 15-35 m (50-120 feet) level. Coho are also found in the area and are taken near the surface using bucktails or any one of a number or coho lures. Mooching during the tide flow often meets with success.

Texada Island (Maps 8, 9, 16, 17)
Texada Island is a popular destination for residents of the Sunshine Coast and beyond. Larger boats can cross Malaspina Strait, while smaller boats usually base their activities from one of the scenic campsites around the big island.

Anderson Bay: Located on the southeast side of Texada Island (Map 9/A4), the mouth of the bay offers some good trolling and mooching for chinook in April to July and coho beginning in May until August.

Blubber Bay to Davis Bay: The eastern most part of Texada Island (Map 16/F5-7) provides a good trolling area for coho and chinook in May through September. The coho tend to be in the tide lines and can be caught by trolling a bucktail or flashtail. The chinook congregate in Crescent and Blubber Bay or off Favada Point. Mooching, trolling or jigging all work.

Coho Point (Grilse Point): Located at the northern tip of Texada Island (Map 16/G5), this point is a premier coho area. The best time to fish is in August. The area is deep with many shoals and so it is easy to troll. The occasional chinook is caught off the point towards Cyril Rock.

Mouat Bay: Primarily a trolling area for coho, anglers can try anywhere from Gilles Bay to Mouat Islets (Map 8/A1). If you wish to mooch, it is best to focus your efforts around Mouat or Dick Islands

in the shallows using cut or live herring. The area is quite exposed to winds and should be left to a calm day.

Northeast Point: This point (Map 17/D7) is a good area to fish for coho in July and August. Trolling in the tide lines using a flasher with a hoochie, herring or flashtail is fairly good as is bucktailing. Mooching or jigging at the drop-off can also work. Northeast Bay may be worth a try if the point is not producing.

Rebecca Rock: Situated a couple kilometres (about a mile) off the north end of Texada Island (Map 16/F5), coho and chinook are present in good numbers from July to September.

Sturt Bay: Found near Vananda (Map 16/G6), this is a holding area for chinook in the summer months when bait is present in the bay. Given the confined area, mooching and jigging are your better choices. Outside the bay, coho can be caught from July to September by trolling in the tide lines.

Texada Island Pilings: Just north of Anderson Bay, on the southeast side of Texada Island (Map 8/G3), are a series of pilings from an old logging operation. This is a good mooching area for chinook throughout the year using live or cut herring. The best place is between 30–60 metres (100–200 feet) out from the pilings. The area is also trolled using live herring, plugs or hoochies. There are coho that can be caught in May through August.

Upwood Point: The southernmost point of land on Texada Island (Map 9/A4) is Upwood Point. Coho can be found from July to October whereas chinook cruise the area year round. The area is best trolled using typical salmon gear.

Thormanby Islands (Map 9/C5)
Epson Point is the westernmost tip on North Thormanby Island. Like other areas around Thormanby Island, coho can be taken in good numbers from May to October and chinook from December to April and again in July to September. The best place to troll is southwest of the point where a prominent drop-off is located. Moochers and strip casters congregate near the drop-off and along the kelp beds. At the north end of the island is a bell buoy, which marks a good location to catch bluebacks and coho in May as well as the odd chinook. Trollers usually circle the fringe to the south of the bell buoy near the sharp drop-off. A shallow troll using weights seems to work the best.

Pirate Rock/Bertha Island are found at the south end of South Thormanby Island. The exposed rocks, which may be submerged during high tides, are best left to calm days. Look for bluebacks in April and coho throughout the summer months (late June–September) by trolling around the rock using the typical coho gear. Stay at least 30 metres (100 feet) off shore to avoid hook-ups. Jigging and strip casting is also very effective particularly if anchoring off the southern tip in 15–21 metres (50-70 feet) of water. The odd chinook is caught in June through September. Bertha Island offers one of the best locations for coho in the strait. Coho are taken from May to October with trolling on the outside of rocks being the most popular method of fishing. Moochers and jiggers tend to do well in the shallow water extending towards South Thormanby Island.

Merry Island is found south of Welcome Beach and offers good trolling for chinook from May–September, bluebacks in April and coho from August–September. The best places to focus your effort are at the south and north ends of the island in deeper water (over 25 metres/80 feet). Mooching with herring or casting a jigging lure can also produce. Big swells are common to the area.

Vancouver Bay (Map 18/E3)
Located in the Prince of Whales Reach, this small bay is the estuary of Vancouver River. The bay offers a variety of fish including coho, sea-run cutthroat and chinook. The chinook, however, are the main attraction. For best success, troll along the drop-off of the river estuary in 15–45 metres (50–150 feet) of water. Cutthroats are best caught by fly-fishing or by trolling a small lure.

Hot Springs

There is no better time to experience one of the natural hot springs that can be found in Southwestern BC than when a gray, rainy Vancouver spring (or fall or winter) day is getting you down. Most of these springs take a bit of work to get to, but the joys of having one of nature's great delights all to yourself is worth it. Sunny summer days are also fine times to visit these springs, but they are often packed with backcountry explorers.

Most of these hot springs are clothing optional, so if you are in the area, and really want a soak but forgot the suit at home, that doesn't necessarily have to stop you. Hot Springs etiquette dictates that, if there are people present in bathing suits, it is best to at least ask before jumping in starkers. Some people just don't understand this sort of behaviour, especially if it is a family with kids.

Unfortunately, some hot springs have suffered from abuse at the hands of stupid people. Broken bottles, garbage, and other crap make the experience less than pleasant. Please help keep the areas clean!

Clear Creek Hot Springs (Map 23/G7)
Clear Creek Hot Springs (sometimes called Ruth Larson Hot Springs, though less frequently these days) are found beneath a steep rocky mountain face high above Harrison Lake. The soaking pools are located just off the Clear Creek Main, about 12.9 km (7.9 miles) from its junction with the Harrison East FSR. The main road, which was deactivated a while back, has recently been reactivated, and the gate at the bottom of the road is usually locked. How this will change access to the hot springs once they are done logging is anyone's guess. For now, it means an extra 7.4 km (4.5 mile) hike/bike up the road from the gate. The easiest way to get up (and especially down) the road is by mountain bike. Avoid this one during active logging periods.

There are four soaking pools, the hottest of which is 43°C (109°F). These are wild springs, but there has been a lot of work put in here. Pipes carry the hot water to the main pool, an old cedar-box. There is also a porcelain bathtub, an old hot tub, and a fiberglass tub. Alternatively, there is an old cedar swimming pool nearby that is rarely used. While there are other hot springs closer, Clear Creek is the quickest one for Vancouverites to get to, and is often packed, especially on summer weekends.

Keyhole (Pebble Creek) Hot Springs (Map 37/F1)
These wild hot springs are located about a 1.5 km (.9 mile) scramble along the banks of the Lillooet River, and are inaccessible in times of high water. The springs bubble out onto the sand about 15 metres (40 feet) above the river on the north bank, and there are several vents to choose from, or to share if you brought a group. Chances are you will have to dig your own soaking pool, as there has been no development here. To get to the springs, park in the pullout about 5.4 km (3.3 miles) past the Meager Creek Forest Service Road, just before the Lillooet Forest Service Road leaves the river and climbs steeply east.

Meager Creek Hot Springs (Map 37/E4)
Meager Creek Hot Springs are found in a deep valley on the eastern edge of the glacier-covered Coast Mountains. They sit in a region of past volcanic activity and present geologic activity. It is spectacular, remote and sometimes dangerous. Steep terrain of volcanic ash and river gravel makes this an area of landslides, floods, and avalanches. (Four people have died here since 1975.) The hot springs are located near the bottom of an open field that has a number of hot streams running through it. The main pool is about three feet deep, and there are a couple smaller pools. The site, once popular with a more bohemian crowd, is now highly regulated, and the BC Forest Service is charging a $5 fee for day use. Because the sites are now being publicized at visitor info centres in the area, the pools are often three people deep in tourists. Most locals have given up on the site, but during mid-week shoulder season, it is sometimes possible to have the site to yourself. There is an enforced no camping ban, and a manned gate at the Lillooet River Bridge Crossing to keep track of visitors. The closest camping is an undeveloped site at km 38 of the Lillooet River Road. The hot springs are open from mid-June to mid-November. They are about 45 minutes down the Lillooet Forest Service Road, then south on the Meager Creek Road. These roads are rough, but passable by two-wheel drives, when they are passable at all. (The Meager Creek Road is often closed due to washouts, mudslides, etc. Call the Squamish Forest District (604-898-2100) for current conditions.) From the parking lot, it is an easy 300 metres (1,000 feet) to the bathing pools.

Pitt River Hot Springs (Map 21/D7)
Tucked into a nook between the cliffs of the Pitt River Canyon and the Pitt River, the Pitt River Hot Springs are one of the most scenic hot spring destinations in Southwestern BC. Despite the scenery and the fact that they are the closest hot springs to Vancouver, they are also the least visited. Why? Well, the 30 km (18.3 mile) paddle/boat ride (watch out for the sand bars!) up Pitt Lake puts some off. Others don't like the idea of a 22 km (13.4 mile) bike along a fairly level, but active, logging roads. For some, it might be the thought of the precarious scramble down to the pool from the top of the cliff (ropes are provided). Whatever the reason; if you do go, chances are you'll have the place to yourself, give or take the occasional local logger dropping in for a dip. To get to the springs from the docks at the north end of Pitt Lake, follow the main road along the Pitt River for just over 21 km (12.81 miles). Just past the 21 km sign, a road leads left (west). Follow it down to the bridge over the Pitt. The difficult 300 metre (1,000 foot) trail to the hot springs heads north (right) just after you cross the bridge. For the less adventurous, there are also tour operators that will run you up to the hot springs.

Sloquet Hot Springs (Map 22/D7)
Due to the popularity of this site, it is now home to a fee based forest service campsite. From its source, the springs flows over a 10 metre (30 foot) cliff into several progressively cooler pools built out of stones before emptying into the frigid waters of Sloquet Creek. People might be tempted to take a shower in the hot waterfall, but be warned, at its source, the water is an extremely hot 68°C (154°F). The water has a fairly strong sulphurous odour, but not enough to detract from the pleasure of soaking in wild springs.

It is a long, somewhat challenging drive from the nearest highway. The Harrison West Mainline Logging road runs north from Hwy 7, and has a 20 km (12.5 miles) section of rough 4wd road to negotiate before the access road on the north side of Sloquet Creek. Most visitors come from the north, off Hwy 99 along the Pemberton-Douglas Forest Service Road. Follow the access road about 8.6 km to the parking area. From here is a short jaunt down an old road to the meadow above the springs, where it is possible to pitch a tent. The trail down to the springs from the meadows may be hard to find. Simply follow your nose and the faint smell of sulphur will lead you down to the springs.

St Agnes Well (Skookumchuck) Hot Springs (Map 22/B2)
In Chinook Indian jargon, the name Skookumchuck means "good water," which is a great description of the soaking to be found here. Today, these hot springs are more commonly known as St Agnes Well Hot Springs. Located on private land owned by the Tretheway family, (who have graciously opened up the springs to the public) the St Agnes Well springs are more developed than others in the area. An A-Frame bathhouse covers the main soaking pool (half a fiberglass septic tank, which will hold about six people), and there are several other soaking tubs outside the bathhouse. The water is hot, 54°C (130°F), but a second pipe brings in cold water, so bathers can adjust the temperature to their liking. There is camping here, by donation ($10 recommended). The springs are located below the Pemberton-Douglas Forest Service Road, near BC Hydro tower #682, next to the rushing Lillooet River. The hot springs are open year round.

Paddling Routes
(River, Ocean and Lake Paddling)

From the rush of whitewater rafting and kayaking to the serenity of sea kayak touring, to just plain cruising around on a lake in a canoe, Southwestern BC provides an endless array of water-based recreational fun. In fact, you will find many of these activities within an easy drive from Greater Vancouver. Of course, accessibility often means many other people will be out enjoying themselves. It's true, some of these routes are often busy, but it's not as bad as you might expect. Besides, if you truly want to get away from the crowds, there are places covered by this mapbook where few people ever go. If you really want to be alone with your paddle, you only need to travel a little further a field.

River Paddling

From lazy rivers that meander though the Fraser Valley lowlands to raging whitewater streams, there are routes to satisfy every paddler. For each route we have listed where the best place(s) are to put-in, as well as take-out. We have also included the length of each run, and some general comments.

We use a modified version of the international scale to grade rivers. The grade of a run tells you how difficult the overall stretch of river is while individual rapids, chutes and other features are rated by class. A run might be rated grade II overall, but one section might feature a class IV drop. Most of the challenging features have portages to help less experienced paddlers negotiate the route more safely.

Water flow also effects how difficult a run is. For this reason we have provided the difficulty of grade and class at both low water and high water. If a run is rated grade II/III, it means that at low flows the run is grade II, while at high flows it is grade III.

Alouette River (Maps 3/A2-2/E2)
The Alouette River (or South Alouette River) flows 23 km from the BC Hydro Dam on Alouette Lake to its confluence with the Pitt River. While the upper reaches are the most interesting and provide some whitewater, it is also very shallow, and obstructed. This section of river is impassable to all but the most determined of paddlers. On the other hand, the lower section is a perfect family style (grade 1) paddle. Some folks put-in at the 206 Street Bridge, but it is better to put-in 2.5 km (1.5 miles) below, at the Neaves Road Bridge. By this point in time, the river has left the mountains and is constrained by dykes. The paddling is easy, and it is possible to paddle upstream as well as down. For people looking to do an out-and-back trip, it is recommended that they start at the Harris Road Bridge, and paddle the 5 km (3 miles) upstream to the Neaves Road Bridge while they are still fresh before paddling back down with the (ever so slight) current. The last stretch of river is 1.6 km (1 mile) from the Harris Road Bridge to the plodding Pitt River.

Big Silver Creek (Map 14/F2)
An easy river, with a couple class II features, Big Silver Creek is a great place for novices to learn their whitewater chops. Access to the put-in is west from the junction of the Harrison East/Clear Creek roads, along a difficult, but mercifully short (ten minute) trail. The take-out is just south of the Silver River Logging Camp on Harrison Lake; watch for a small road leading down to the lake off the Harrison East FSR.

Birkenhead River (Map 30/D1)
From the put-in where the D'Arcy Road crosses the river north of the Owl Creek Rec Site, to the take-out north of Mount Currie, this is a 5 km (3 mile) Grade III/IV romp along the turquoise waters of the Birkenhead. The river is quite shallow and moves quickly through almost continuous rapids. By late July, the water volume has fallen significantly, and it can be a fairly bumpy ride through even shallower water.

Capilano River (Maps 11/D7-1/D1)
At high water levels, the Capilano is a beast, rated up to Grade V, and sometimes (at very high water levels), unrunable. At low water, it is Grade III run, with some Class IV drops. The Capilano is one of the most popular rivers in the entire province. Partly due to the location, and partly due to the fact it is rarely too cold to kayak. The Cap is a dam controlled drop-and-pool river that flows through North Vancouver in a surprisingly wild valley. From the fish hatchery just below Cleveland Dam to Ambleside Park, it is 5.6 km (3.4 miles), but there are a number of other take-out points, including Park Royal Mall and Klahanie Park. Watch for people fishing from the riverbanks.

Cayoosh Creek (Map 41/A4-A2)
Like most small volume rivers, the character of the Cayoosh changes tremendously with water. As the water level rises, the difficulty increases; taking it from a grade II run up to grade IV at higher water levels. The Cayoosh runs alongside the Duffey Lake Road from Cayoosh Pass to the small town of Lillooet. The most common section for paddlers to run is a 5.8 km (3.8 mile) section between Boulder and Copper Creek. There are two put-ins; one about 2 km (1 mile) south of Boulder Creek and the other about 1 km south of the Cottonwood Rec Site. The take-out is found at a logging road bridge just before Copper Creek.

Cheakamus River (Maps 20, 29)
This glacier-fed river has many, many possible put-ins and take-outs, and is never more than a few hundred metres from a road. Easy access makes this a popular river. Please note that the canyon stretch below Daisy Lake is not navigatable.

Put-in: Westside Main/Black Tusk Road (Map 29/F7)

Take-out: Highway 99 Bridge at Function Junction (Map 29/F7)

A fast, technical 1.5 km (1 mile) section of river that is popular with the play boaters (there are rodeo holes all over the place). The river is rated grade III/IV, with some class V features at high water levels.

Put-in: Highway 99 Bridge south of Daisy Lake (Map 20/D1)

Take-out: Highway 99 salt sheds (Map 20/D3)

This is a 4 km (2.4 mile) section of grade III/III+ whitewater, with a class IV drop near the mid-point of the run. Despite the fact that this section is below the Daisy Lake Dam, it still acts very much like a wild river; there is just so much water coming down during spring run-off, that BC Hydro usually keeps the gates fairly wide open.

Put-in: 11 km (6.6 miles) north of the Sun Wolf Outdoor Centre on Paradise Valley Road. The first few kilometres are paved; the last requires 4wd. (Map 20/C3)

Take-out: Sun Wolf Outdoor Centre (Map 20/B5), or continue onto the Squamish (River)

Normally a grade II/III route that runs 12 km (7.3 miles) through the forests north of Squamish. There are a number of alternate take-out (or put-in) spots along the way to shorten the run. At higher water, eddies can disappear and more of the run is Grade III making this river appropriate for intermediate kayakers and experienced open boaters. There are plenty of play spots including a great surfing hole right at the put in, and an exciting drop at Culliton Creek. As with all rivers in this region, watch for logjams and sweepers.

Chehalis River (Maps 14/B7-Map 4/D1)
The put-in for this grade III+ river is at the 17.3 km (10.6 mile) mark of the Chehalis FSR along an overgrown road; you will have to hike about 20 minutes to the put-in. More advanced paddlers can put-in at about 1.7 km past the Statlu Creek Bridge but be prepared for one continuous boulder garden. The Chehalis has lively and almost continual drops with rodeo holes and surfing waves to make this a fun river to run. When you have a chance to breathe and look around, you will notice that the scenery is pretty spectacular, too. Due to challenging canyons and few places to escape, this river is rarely run.

Chilliwack River (Maps 4, 5)

The Chilliwack River Valley offers good fishing, abundant camping sites, easy access and phenomenal scenery. Paddlers looking for an excellent place to get away for the afternoon, for the day or for the weekend will find three routes ranging from an easy grade II run to a difficult grade IV route.

Put-in: Camp Foley (Map 5/B6)

Take-out: West of Slesse Creek (Map 5/A6)

This section of the Chilliwack is 9 km (5.4 miles) of steep, demanding, and nonstop whitewater action. Rated grade IV, with some even higher features (and one mandatory portage around Fish Hatchery Drop; a class VI manmade feature). Expect to take about four hours to complete this exhilarating stretch.

Put-in: Slesse Creek Bridge (Map 5/A6)

Take-out: Chilliwack River Provincial Park (Map 4/E6)

An 18 km (11 mile) stretch of up to grade III water (with some class IV drops), and a 1 km (0.6 mile) stretch that features some of the most challenging features on the river—the Tamihi, Campground and Sawmill Rapids. Many people choose to portage the rapids, especially in high water, but for expert paddlers, this section is one of the highlights of the four hour-plus trip.

Put-in: Chilliwack River Provincial Park (Map 4/E6)

Take-out: Vedder Crossing (Map 4/C6)

Like many rivers, the Chilliwack starts to calm down as it gets closer to its final destination, the mighty Fraser. By the time it reaches Vedder Crossing, the Chilliwack has basically run out of steam. From Chilliwack Provincial Park to Vedder Crossing, this is a 6.5 km (4 mile) run along relatively easy grade II waters. A great testing ground for novices, or as a warm up before tackling some of the bigger water upstream. The river is medium flow, with lots of braiding and gravel bars, and is runable from spring to fall. Allow about two hours to run it. Longer if you wish to continue on the Vedder River (see below).

Cogburn Creek (Map 14/G3)

From the Harrison East FSR Bridge to the Bear Creek Logging Camp, it is a mere 3 km (1.8 miles), but they are a wild 3 km, indeed. Rated grade III/IV with lots of boulder gardens and technical maneuvering, during spring runoff, it is almost continual whitewater from the put-in until you hit Harrison Lake. It is a short but peaceful paddle south on the lake to the camp.

Coquitlam River (Map 2/C1-C3)

The Coquitlam is more of a winter run than a summer run, when the river all but disappears. It offers an 8 km (4.9 mile) route through grade III water during high and medium water levels. This is a great place for intermediate paddlers to practice their skills, as there are lots of places to bail. The put-in is off of Pipeline Road, while the take-out is off Shaughnessy Street.

Elaho River (Maps 28/E6-G7; 37/C7)

This fast, silty and cold river begins its source in the giant Elaho Glacier, well removed from any signs of civilization. The Upper Elaho is a difficult, rarely run river, while, to our knowledge, the far upper reaches of the Elaho has only been run once. Most trips on the Elaho start about 3.5 km (2.1 miles) upstream from its confluence with the Squamish River, and finish their run after the canyon section of the Squamish. The Elaho is grade III/IV, and has some really great surfing waves at moderate water flow. This scenic stretch of river offers some great cliff jumping opportunities and is very popular with the rafting companies. The Elaho is subject to flash flooding, especially during spring rains.

Fraser River (Maps 1, 2, 3, 4, 5, 15, 24, 33, 41, 42, 46)

Whew. And that's just the bottom half of this 1,600 km (976 mile) historic river. Southwest BC captures the mighty Fraser's two extremes. The Fraser Canyon, which begins north of Hope, is a class IV water body that should only be attempted by commercial rafters. On the other hand the lower reaches, from Hope to Vancouver, offer a more placid river. Although this stretch does not have any whitewater, it can still be dangerous (up to grade III) due to the speed and volume of water. In particular, watch out for boils and standing waves between Hope and the Highway 9 Bridge at Bridal Falls. As you get closer to the mouth, watch out for the Pitt River confluence, and the commercial traffic (fishing boats, tug boats, barges, etc.) plying these waters.

Harrison River (Map 4/F1-D2)

An easy grade I paddle takes you from Harrision Hot Springs to the Highway 7 Bridge, just before the Harrison flows into the Fraser. While this 15 km (9.1 mile) trip is scenic and enjoyable (except when the wind picks up on the broad river), the best time to go is in the fall, when the salmon are spawning. Eagles. Fish. Fishermen. Fall leaves. What more could you ask for?

Kanaka Creek (Maps 3/A3-2/G3)

Kanaka Creek is a mostly slow moving river—hardly more than grade I, with a couple really slow grade II sections. For the most part, Kanaka Creek is perfect for an idyllic family float close to Maple Ridge. There are a handful of places to put-in or take-out along the sprawling Kanaka Creek Park, or the more adventurous can head out onto the Fraser, and cross to Derby Reach Park. If you don't want to shuttle, you can put-in at the Highway 7 bridge, and paddle upstream for as far as you want, then return. Be careful not to venture above 112 Ave, as there are a pair of waterfalls a few hundred metres upstream.

Lillooet River (Maps 22, 30, 37, 38, 39)

A long, large, windy and cold river that starts deep in the heart of the Coast Mountains before eventually spilling into Harrison Lake. It is faster in its upper reaches. Traveling the Lillooet often feels remote, although in truth the river is paralleled by logging roads for its entire runable length. As an added bonus, there is a number of hot springs near the river, a great way to end a hard day's paddle.

Put-in: 2.9 km past the Pebble Creek Bridge (Map 37/G2)

Take-out: Meager Creek Bridge (Map 37/G2)

This section is a short (5 km/3 mile) stretch of Grade III/IV whitewater, about the toughest stuff you will find on the Lillooet. It features lots of

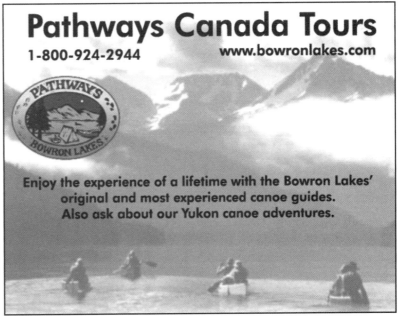

great scenery and easy access, the Mamquam is a great river to practice on, and short enough to run two or three times in a day. From the upper put-in on the Mamquam FSR, to the Government Road Bridge (just west of Highway 99), this is a 5.8 km (3.3 mile) stretch.

Nahatlatch River (Map 24)

The Nahatlatch is a small, challenging river that flows through a series of canyons on its way from Hannah Lake to the Fraser River. Access is from the Nahatlatch Forest Service Road on the north bank of the river. Although it sees little use from kayakers, those who have done it consider it one of the premier whitewater rivers in North America. Not surprisingly, the river is a popular commercial rafting destination. There's good paddling from April to October, with the best time coming mid-summer, when the river has passed its peak flow, but hasn't slowed to a trickle yet.

Put-in: Old Ranger Station on Hannah Lake (Map 24/A1)

Take-out: West end of Francis Lake (Map 24/A1)

A short, warm up route between Hannah and Francis Lake, this shallow 1.5 km (.9 mile) section is rated grade II/III, with steady rapids.

Put-in: East end of Francis Lake (Map 24/A1)

Take-out: Apocynum Campground (Map 24/B1)

This is an 8 km (4.9 mile) section of grade III whitewater, with a number of class IV features, including some of the most storied rapids in the province. Some of the names include the Rose Garden, Meat Grinder and Head Wall. This last one is worth noting; if you do not execute a sharp turn, you and your boat will get stuffed under an overhanging ledge. Needless to say, this is not a route for the faint of heart.

Put-in: Apocynum Campground (Map 24/C1)

Take-out: Bridge on Nahatlatch FSR (Map 24/D1)

Grade III+/IV, with a number of class IV and V features makes this last stretch of river, if anything, even more exhilarating than the last section. In all, it is a 5.3 km (3.3 mile) epic section of whitewater that is equal to anything, anywhere. This is not a place you want to go if you don't know what you're doing. But for those with adequate skill, this is a riot. The best time to go is as spring runoff is just starting to drop (high water, but not too high).

Nicomekl River (Map 2/ F5-A7)

From Old Yale Road to Crescent Beach, the Nicomekl travels 25 lazy km (15.3 miles). While the trip is all flat water, the river itself is small, narrow, and often blocked by obstructions, making this a tough trip to complete in a day. Portaging around obstacles is difficult; the banks are steep, and often overgrown. A trio of pipes cross the river. Two of you will have to carry it around, one of you may be able to squeak under. There is also a flood control dam to portage around. While parts of this river are pretty, it has seen a lot of abuse over the years, especially on the lower sections. This river provides an accurate picture of the state of urban rivers in the Lower Mainland.

North Alouette River (Maps 2/ D1-E2)

While the North Alouette River begins at Jacobs Lake in the UBC Research Forest, it isn't until the 232 Street Bridge in Maple Ridge that it is even feasible to put-in, and even then, from 232 Street to Neaves Road, the river is shallow and congested with rocks, logs and vegetation. Lining, and sometimes carrying, the canoe is a must. From 232 Street to Neaves Road is 7 km (4.3 miles); from Neaves Road to Harris Road is a much nicer 7.1 km (4.3 miles). Those that do travel the river will find a tranquil setting with abundant waterfowl to enjoy.

Pitt River (Maps 12/F7-2/C2)

Although this is a flat water paddle, the Pitt moves a lot of water and sees a fair bit of boat traffic, making it a sometimes dangerous place to be. The Pitt is also a tidal river so it is advised to consult tide charts so you won't have to fight against the current paddling downstream. From Grant Narrows to the Port Mann Bridge on the Fraser is a 23.8 km (14.5 mile) paddle through a farmland type setting.

rock gardens and standing waves, and one really nice hole to play in. Expect to take the better part of two hours to do this section, which can be done on its own, or as the start to a longer expedition down the tamer sections of the Lillooet.

Put-in: Meager Creek Bridge (Map 37/G2)

Take-out: Bridge on Upper Lillooet River Road (Map 38/G5)

After the Meager Creek confluence, the Lillooet meanders along a broad, flat floodplain with lots of braided channels. While this is an easy grade II route, picking the right route can be tricky due to the many false channels. Expect to take at least 8 hours to do this 35 km (21.4 mile) section of the river.

Put-in: Bridge on Upper Lillooet River Road (Map 38/G5)

Take-out: Highway 99 bridge east of Pemberton (Map 30/C1)

As the Lillooet approaches Pemberton, the river widens and slows down. This 23 km (14 mile) section is little more than a scenic float, which usually takes about 6 hours to complete.

Put-in: Little Lillooet Lake (Map 30/G7)

Take-out: Last bridge before Harrison Lake (Map 22/F6)

South of Pemberton, the Lillooet turns into a long, narrow lake, or rather, two lakes, separated by a short section of moving water. Most kayakers skip this section, though folks (usually canoeists) who are doing a multi-day trip from beginning to end do float this section as well. Below Little Lillooet Lake, is a 33.9 km (21.1 miles) float to the final take-out before Harrison Lake. Most of this section is grade II, but there are some class III features, just to make it interesting. The hot springs at St. Agnes Well is a popular and relaxing alternate take-out spot about halfway down this run. Although most trippers take-out at the last bridge before Harrison Lake, long distance canoeists/kayakers can continue on into Harrison Lake. From the big (and often windy) lake it is possible to continue down to the Fraser and even out to the Pacific Ocean.

Mamquam River (20/G7-D7)

A short, challenging grade III route is found just south of Squamish. With

River of Golden Dreams (Map 29/D6)

Flowing through the heart of Whistler, from Alta Lake to Green Lake, this is a great river for a lazy summer day float. There are two parks on Alta Lake, Wayside and Lakeside, where you can launch your boat. The river winds its way though a marshy area between the two lakes. This is also a popular float trip on inner-tubes/air mattresses.

Salmon River (Map 2/G5)

Like many Fraser Delta Rivers, the Salmon is difficult to paddle in its upper reaches. Not because of whitewater, but because it is narrow and overgrown. The first good launch point comes at McMillian Park on Glover Road near Fort Langley. At low water, the Salmon looks more like a flooded ditch than a river, but don't despair, it gets bigger. Most people take-out at the 96 Avenue Bridge about 8 km (4.9 miles) downstream where there is a pump station/flood box blocking the river.

Serpentine River (Map 2/C5-A6)

176 Street is the most practical launch site on this 27 km (16.5 mile) river. Above this point, the river is blocked by vegetation. The Serpentine winds its way through the lowlands of Surrey, down to Mud Bay. It is 18 km (11 miles) from 176 Street to the Sea Dam just past the King George Highway in White Rock. It is possible to portage around the dam, and continue into Mud Bay.

Seymour River (Maps 11/G7-1/F1)

The Seymour is a great challenge for novices looking to hone their skills, or for experts looking to get in a bit of paddling during winter. In August, the Seymour is a little too shallow to paddle, but it is fine the rest of the year. The Seymour is a grade II/III river, with boulder gardens at low water and lots of play holes at high. The river is certainly not wild, but it does flow through a pleasant suburban paradise. From Seymour Park on Riverside Road to Burrard Inlet it is 4 km (2.4 miles). In summer, contact the GVRD regarding keys for the gate on Riverside Drive.

Skagit River (Map 6/E7-E3)

A grade III/IV route through a scenic valley at the base of sheer mountain faces, the Skagit is a beautiful river to run. The river is best run after spring runoff, from July to October. Most people put-in at Ross Lake near the US border. From here to Silvertip Park, the river follows the Silver Skagit Road. But for the last 12 km, to the confluence with the Sumallo River, the Skagit flows through a wild valley. You can take-out at the Sumallo confluence. Watch out for log jams.

Squamish River (Maps 20, 28)

The Squamish River is a cold, murky, big volume river that makes its way from the Pemberton Icefield south to Howe Sound at the city of Squamish. The river is never too far from a road but for the most part, it feels like you are in another world, far from civilization. In late fall along with salmon, the area is home to thousands of bald eagles.

Put-in: Bridge near 37 km marking (Map 28/G7)

Take-out: Log sorting area near 29 km marking (Map 20/A1)

An 8.2 km (5 mile) run through the scenic Squamish Canyon, a grade III/IV section that features some great big standing waves. The Steamroller Rapid can get as big as 3 metres (10 feet) during high water levels. While this is a river for rafting and advanced kayakers in peak season, at lower levels (April or October), it is a great run for advanced open boaters. Watch for logjams and sweepers.

Put-in: Log sorting area near 29 km marking (Map 20/A1)

Take-out: 21 mile bridge (Map 20/A3)

An easy float through the broad valley of the lower Squamish to the forestry campsite near the bridge. This section avoids all the really challenging features on the river, and is rated grade I/II. This is a 12 km (8 mile) section of the river, and can easily be done in conjunction with the next segment of river.

Put-in: Powerhouse (Map 20/A4)

Take-out: Brackendale (Map 20/C6)

This section is a 32 km grade II route with three Class V sections below the Ashlu Creek junction. The Begining of this section is better left to commercial rafting companies or people with experience on the big river. Closer to Brackendale many people like to run the river in January to get an up close view of the Bald Eagles. Be wary of obstacles such as deadheads and logjams as well as braiding channels.

Still Creek (Map 1/G2)

Not the first place people think of when they think of canoeing, and, in truth, there are some pretty areas to be found on this urban creek, especially the section from Burnaby Lake Park to Willingdon Avenue, a one way trip covering 3.8 km (2.3 miles). For a truly urban experience, canoe under Willingdon, and stop for lunch at McDonalds. While points further upstream are scared, it might be worth a trip, just to see the damage that has been done to this creek.

Sumas River (Map 3/F7–4/A5)

From just about the US border (Vye Road Bridge) to Hougan Park (13 km/7.9 miles from Vye Road), the Sumas is a slow moving river. By the time you reach Hougan Park, almost all forward momentum has stopped, and you will have to paddle the remaining 10 km (6.1 miles) to the Sea Dam, just upstream from the confluence with the Vedder Canal. The Sumas is a nice easy paddle, but a little too close to Highway 1 for some people's tastes.

Vedder River (Map 4/C6–A5)

From Vedder Crossing to Number Three Road, the Vedder River is a spicy grade II/III. Not as challenging as the Chilliwack upstream, but still enough to provide lots of fun, especially for open boat canoeists. This section is 8 km (4.9 miles) long. Beyond Number 3 Road, the Vedder becomes an easy float down to the Sumas confluence along the slow moving Vedder Canal. Not particularly difficult, but a nice family outing, with great views of Sumas Mountain.

Ocean Paddling

An endless coast with numerous sheltered inlets makes ocean paddling a peaceful and scenic way to explore Southwestern BC. We have included a number of popular routes, though it is just a fraction of the places you can go by sea kayak or, sometimes, canoe.

Boundary Bay (Map 1/G7)

Extensive tidal flats make this a difficult place to explore by boat at low tide. From Boundary Bay Regional Park to Crescent Beach, it is 22 km (13.4 miles) one-way. It is often windy here, sometimes too windy to safely paddle. The best time is early in the morning.

Copeland Islands Marine Park (Maps 16/C1, 25/C7)

Known locally as the Ragged Islands, the Copeland Islands are a fairly easy 8 km (5 miles) paddle north of the boat launch at Lund. The islands are home to colonies of seals and a diverse array of tidal life. The marine park also offers campsites. An easy circuit route for novice kayakers would be to paddle to the Copeland Islands, then around the tip of Malaspina Peninsula, and down Okeover Inlet.

The Curme Islands (Map 25/D6)

A handful of small islands, just off the east coast of Mink Island in Desolation Sound, the Curme Islands lure kayakers looking for a less populated wilderness experience.

Desolation Sound Provincial Marine Park (Map 25)

Desolation Sound is BC's largest and most popular marine park. It has warm, sheltered waters, spectacular scenery, and lots of nooks and crannies to explore. Marine life flourishes in these waters, which can reach temperatures of 26° Celsius (79°F) in summer. The park is rich in native history as well as natural beauty. Birders will find this area a delight, with loons, kingfishers, eagles, gulls, plovers, murrelets, grebes, herons, oyster catchers and more. It is also possible to explore past the park, and all the way into the emerald green Toba Inlet. En route you can visit Homfray Channel, which features the second deepest waters off the coast at 730 metres (2,394 feet).

You can launch from two locations. From Lund, the paddle is more exposed but it takes you past the Copeland Islands Marine Park. If you choose the more sheltered Okeover Inlet route, be prepared for tidal currents up to 2 knots. It can take anywhere for three days to two weeks to explore this area, and even then, you will feel like you've only scratched the surface.

False Creek (Map 1/D2)

An extremely protected inlet, False Creek is slowly outgrowing its commercial roots and becoming an urban playground. The most prominent feature here is the Science World Globe, but on the water you will see sea kayaks, dragon boats, canoes, paddle cycles, row boats and even Hawaiian Outriggers.

Hotham Sound (Map 18/B3)

Located off Jervis Inlet, Hotham Sound is a peaceful destination, easily accessed from Saltery Bay. The Sound offers sheltered paddling, with many coves and bays to explore. On the way from Saltery Bay, you will pass through St. Vincent's Bay, then round Elephant Point, where the sound opens up before you. In addition to the majestic Coast Mountains as a backdrop, one of the highlights of this trip is the 444 metre (1,456 foot) Freil Falls, which are across from Elephant Point. There is a marine park on Harmony Islands where you can camp.

Howe Sound (Map 11)

Howe Sound stretches north from Horseshoe Bay to Squamish and is framed by the rugged, towering peaks that have always tormented the road builders on the Sea to Sky Highway. Before that road went in, the only way to Squamish was by boat. Even today, some would argue it's still the only way to get to Squamish. There are a number of great destinations in the Sound, including Gambier Island, which can be circumnavigated in about two days, and Anvil Island, a good one-day trip. The most popular places to launch are Porteau Cove, on Highway 99, followed by Port Mellon, on the Sunshine Coast.

Indian Arm (Maps 1/G1, 2/A1, 12/A6)

The northernmost reaches of Indian Arm are protected inside the boundaries of the Indian Arm Marine Park. This is a gorgeous place to paddle that is well protected from the winds but sees a lot of small boat traffic that can kick up some chop. Regardless, this is the domain of the recreationist, with many sites to see (Silver and Granite Falls), places to camp (Twin Islands, Bishop Creek), and places to just stop and enjoy the stillness of nature. It's 23 km (14 miles) up the west side of Indian Arm, from Deep Cove to the Indian River. Add another kilometre if you travel the east side from Belcarra Park.

Jervis Inlet (Maps 17, 18, 27)

There are three good launching points into this undeveloped fjord, which stretches deep into the rugged Coast Mountains, and neatly divides the Sunshine Coast into two. Edgemont is one, Earls Cove is the second, and Saltery Bay the third. Highlights include the Princess Louisa Inlet and Chatterbox Falls near the head of Jervis Inlet and of course the endless views of the majestic mountains. The inlet can be a dangerous place to be caught if the weather blows up, as the steep cliffs that plunge into the water for long stretches at a time offer no place to take shelter. It will take one to two weeks to explore the inlet.

Jedediah Island (Map 8/F4)

Sheltered from all but the most persistent winds by Texada to the north and east and Lasqueti Island to the south and southwest, this 64-acre island is a favorite of kayakers. The archipelago of islands is often referred to as a string of pearls. This is BC kayaking at its best. Jedediah Island is accessible either from Secret Cove on the Sunshine Coast, or Texada Island. There is no water available on Jedediah.

Pender Harbour (Map 9/B1)

Pender Harbour is a well-sheltered harbour, with many small islands and bays to explore. There is no formal camping here, but there are some places that a tent can be pitched.

Port Moody (Map 2/A1)

A large, sheltered finger poking into the Lower Mainland from Burrard Inlet. This is a working harbour, so there is lots of traffic and not many places to land or launch a boat from.

Redonda Islands (Map 25)

Warm water, secluded coves, the BC's tallest island mountain (outside of Vancouver Island) and excellent fishing make West and East Redonda Islands great paddling destinations. These islands are very large, and it will take the better part of a week to circumnavigate even one. You can launch from Lund or Okeover Inlet and paddle up Desolation Sound before crossing over. Maybe it is time needed or the exposed crossings, but the islands are not popular paddling destinations.

Savary Island (Map 16/B1)

Savary Island has long, curving and dazzling white beaches. It is a summer Shangri-la, attracting kayakers from around the world. This is also where the great tidal currents from the north and south meet, creating a unique environment of warm water, unlike anywhere else on the Coast. If you don't feel comfortable with the 3 km (1.8 mile) crossing, a water taxi at Lund will transport you across. Be warned: there is no fresh water on Savary, so pack what you will need.

Sechelt Inlet (Map 9, 18)

A popular sheltered inlet that is almost a lake, making this a great place for novice kayakers to get their sea legs. From Porpoise Bay you can travel a few hours or a few weeks into the inlet, exploring its many marine parks and sheltered bays. You can do a round trip, or start at Porpoise Bay and arrange for a shuttle at Egmont. This area is home to many marine birds and animals; there is even the occasional killer whale spotted by fortunate sea kayakers.

Skookumchuck Narrows (Map 18/E6)

Some people do silly things. Like surfing the waves that set up in this narrow bore, which has been clocked at up to 16 knots, creating standing waves over 2 metres (6 feet) high.

Circuit Routes

While there are few circuit routes of note in BC, the Sunshine Coast has been blessed with three circuits; two short, and one long. Two of the circuits involve a mixture of ocean and lake paddling.

Pender Harbour Route (Map 9/B1)

While Pender Harbour is a popular destination for sea kayakers, some (mostly canoeists) choose to do a 13 km (7.9 miles) circuit that includes three portages. The portages are: 200 metres from Agamemnon Channel to Sakinaw Lake (please ask for permission to cross the Indian Reserve), 800 metres between Sakinaw Lake and Mixal Lake, and 700 metres from Garden Bay Lake to Pender Harbour. It is also possible to tag the Mixal Lake/Garden Bay leg of this route to the Agamemnon Channel Route above.

Powell Forest Canoe Route (Maps 17, 26)

Easily one of the best canoe circuits in the province, the Powell Lake Canoe Route can be done in as few as three days. Most take up to a week or more to paddle the 90.4 km (54.8 mile) route. Paddle is a bit of a misnomer; 10.7 km (6.5 miles) of the route is spent carrying your canoe, including one 2.4 km (1.5 mile) hump from Windsor Lake down to Goat Lake. Down being the operative word, losing over 100 metres (300 feet) in elevation isn't all that easy when you're packing a canoe. Only suicidal folks would want to carry up this hill. Which is why most travel this route counterclockwise: from Lois Lake, through Horseshoe, Nanton, Ireland, Dodd, Windsor, Goat and finally, Powell Lake. This route features great canoeing, and some sweet spots to camp, including the Horseshoe Lake Rec Site and the Beaver Lake Rec Site. Lois Lake and Powell Lake are both big lakes, and can be very windy. It's best to travel these lakes early in the morning.

For folks who don't want to canoe the entire circuit, it is possible to double back on your route from Dodd Lake, via the tiny Beaver and Little Horseshoe Lakes. Other options include travelling north on Goat Lake to the Eldred River estuary or cut across from Powell Lake to Inland Lake (many make this trip merely to camp on Anthony Island). It is even possible to circumnavigate Goat Island on Powell Lake. Be forewarned, there are no campsites if you go this way, although there is a trail to Frogpond Lake. There is road access to most of the lakes on the circuit, so people can just do parts of this circuit without committing to the whole thing.

Ruby Lake Circuit (Maps 9/B1, 18/C7)

This is a 31 km (18.9 mile) circuit route that starts and ends at Earls Cove. Expect to take two or three days to finish the route. Starting in Ruby Lake, paddle to the south end, where there is a 750 metre portage to Sakinaw Lake. Between Sakinaw Lake and the Agamemnon Channel is a 200 metre portage that crosses Sechelt Indian Band land. Please ask for permission to cross before you set out. Dangers en route include high winds on Sakinaw Lake, and strong tidal currents out in the channel. It's best to travel with the tide so check the tide charts. Near the south end of Sakinaw Lake you may see Indian pictographs painted on the rocks. When you get back to Earls Cove, you're only about a kilometre from the starting point. Smart people will have left their car at the cove.

Lake Paddling

There are hundreds of lakes and sloughs scattered throughout Southwestern BC and many if not all make a fine place for a day or overnight paddling venture. Below, we have provided some of the most popular destinations for canoeists. As an added convenience, we have indicated which lakes have rentals available nearby.

As a general rule, big mountain lakes tend to attract wild weather patterns and wind, which funnels down through the narrow valleys. Although you can expect wind at any time, it is often calmer in the morning. Always stay close to shore.

Alice Lake (Map 20/D6) rentals

Alice Lake is a small lake, north of Squamish, and the namesake of Alice Lake Provincial Park. This is a popular vacation spot for families. Because there are no motorized boats permitted, the lake is a haven for canoeists.

Alouette Lake (Maps 3/C3, Map 13/C7) rentals

A fjord-like lake that runs 17 km (10.4 miles) into the Coast Mountains, Alouette Lake is an extremely popular cruising lake. There are a number of destinations to aim for from the boat launch near the south end of the lake: Campers Beach (4.5 km/2.7 miles) away, Moyer Creek Campground 9 km (5.5 miles) along, and the Narrows at 10.5 km (6.4 miles). All these are found on the western shore.

Alta Lake (Map 29/G6) rentals

A small, motor-free lake in Whistler, a few minutes southwest of the village. Some people beetle about the lake, but most continue along the River of Golden Dreams to Green Lake (see rivers, above). Launches are at Wayside and Lakeside parks.

Birkenhead Lake (Map 39/E4)

Nestled in the mountains north of Pemberton, Birkenhead Lake is a great place to paddle. There is a nice wilderness campsite at the mouth of Sockeye Creek as well as good fishing for kokanee, dolly varden and rainbow trout. The lake is open to powerboats, and can be windy, especially in the afternoon.

Buntzen Lake (Map 2/A1,12/A7)

It's 9 km (5 miles) around Buntzen Lake, making this a nice afternoon canoe trip. The long, narrow lake provides the illusion of paddling on the ocean since it is surrounded by mountains to the east and west. If you ever do run into trouble, you can put to shore almost anywhere and walk back to your car along the trail that circumnavigates the lake. With a powerboat restriction in place, Buntzen Lake is a peaceful place to ply the paddle.

Burnaby Lake (Maps 1/G2, 2/A3)

A return trip from the Still Creek Footbridge at the west end to Cariboo Dam at the east end is 10.8 km (6.6 miles). This urban lake provides a recluse for a wide variety of wildlife including; beavers, muskrats, coyotes, geese, ducks, herons and ospreys. There are three access points: at the Burnaby Lake Pavilion, from the bridge over Still Creek on the Cottonwood Trail and the Piper Avenue Spit.

Callaghan Lake (Map 29/C4)

A high mountain lake west of Whistler, Callaghan Lake is a great fishing lake. Few people come here just to paddle, but it is not unheard of. It's a pretty lake, with an ugly rec site (the access point) on its southern shore. If you plan to camp, rumour has it there may be some nicer places accessible by canoe. The lake is subject to squalls and some high wind, so it's best to stick close to shore.

Chehalis Lake (Map 14/B6)

Chehalis Lake is the smallest of the long, narrow lakes that run generally north and south along the North Shore/Fraser Valley (a series that includes Harrison, Stave, Alouette and Pitt Lakes). There are three rec sites on the lake that provide possible access to the lake. We recommend launching from the Chehalis Lake South Rec Site and circumnavigating the lake. Alternatively, follow the western shore to the rocky beach at Skwellepil Creek.

Chilliwack Lake (Map 5/F7)

A big mountain lake, located near the BC/Washington State border at the end the scenic Chilliwack Lake Road, which is paved to the park campsite. Chilliwack Lake is deep, cold and often windy, but it is fairly remote and quite scenic. The wilderness feel makes this a popular destination with canoeists, most of whom are prepared to spend more than a day here. Watch out for high winds, and don't get too close to the Chilliwack River outflow, lest you get sucked downstream.

Cultus Lake (Map 4/C7) rentals

This lake is one of the most popular destinations in the area. In addition to powerboats, the lake is famous for the high percentage of yahoos on jet skis. Besides boaters, canoeists and kayakers must watch out for the wind, which can blow up quickly.

Davis Lake (Map 3/F1)

A small lake that is not even a kilometre long, Davis is a small, pretty, and warm lake, which makes it a great place to head in summer. The logging road access and short walk into the lake does deter some, while the garbage and half-burned campfires kicking around the campsites will offend all. If you do plan to take advantage of the rustic campsites at both the north and south ends of the lake, please help remove the unsightly mess of the inconsiderate visitors of the past.

Deer Lake-Burnaby (Map 1/G3) rentals

Deer Lake is a small lake in Burnaby. It is a pretty urban lake, though sometimes hard to get to, with all the traffic controls in the area. Your best bet to get to the lake is off Canada Way.

Goat Lake (Map 26/F7)

Part of the Powell Lake Canoe Route, Goat Lake can be accessed by a 2.4 km portage down from Windsor Lake, a long, long paddle down Powell Lake, or, with a bit of work, from the Goat Lake Forest Service Road. There are two backcountry rec sites on the narrow lake, which is a lot more sheltered than the giant Powell Lake.

Green Lake (Map 29/G5, 30/A5)

The biggest of the lakes to be found in Whistler, Highway 99 follows the northwest shores of the lake on its way to Pemberton. There is a boat launch (powerboats are allowed), and some great views of Blackcomb and Whistler Mountains.

Harrison Lake (Maps 4, 14, 22, 23)

Harrison Lake is a big, big lake. At 60 km (36.6 miles) long and 9 km (5.5 miles) wide in places, it is a big, windy, exposed lake. It's not a lake to be taken lightly, especially by canoeists. Still, it is a lovely lake, and, as long as you paddle in groups, stay close to shore, and keep an eye on the weather, you shouldn't have any problems. There are a number of landing and camping sites on the west side of the lake, but on the northeast side camping is unorganized, and landing and shelter can be hard to come by.

Haslam Lake (Map 17/B3)

A fair sized lake, Haslam Lake is much less paddled that the lakes of the Powell Forest Canoe Route that surround it. Which is not necessarily a bad thing, especially if you're looking to do something different. If you don't mind carrying a canoe, you can do a mini-circuit. There is a short portage from Haslam to the tiny Giavanno Lake, and from there, a rather long portage down to Powell Lake.

Hatzic Lake (Map 3/F4)

Hatzic Lake is a doughnut-shaped lake with an island in the middle. It doesn't seem like a big lake, but you will travel 9.5 km (5.8 miles) around the outer shore, or 5 km (3 miles) around the island. If that's not enough paddling, you can head into Hatzic Slough (at the northern end of the lake), or into nearby Chilqua Slough, both of which attach to the lake. At low water, the sloughs, and even the lake itself, can be too shallow to paddle effectively.

Hayward Lake (Map 3/C3)

Although Hayward Lake is only 4.3 km (2.6 miles) long and 1 km (0.6 miles) wide, you will cover more than 12 km if you paddle along the shoreline. This is a lake with lots of nooks and coves to explore. Be warned that the dams at both ends of the lake are off limits.

Hope Slough (Map 4/D3)

It is 17.9 km (10.9 mile) from the Chapman Road Bridge to the main body of the Fraser River. Much of this paddle is through farm area, and you will probably see signs of this (like cows) as you make your way down the slough. There is a current for the first 9.6 km (5.9 miles), and it will be difficult to paddle back upstream. There is an alternate put-in at the Hope River Road/Camp River Road/Kitchen Road Intersection, as well as at the Hope River Kiwanis Park, on Camp River Road.

Horseshoe Lake (Map 17/E3)

Horseshoe Lake looks a bit more like a boot rather than a horseshoe, but that's what it's called. Access to the lake is via a 1.7 km (1 mile) portage from Lois Lake to the south, or via a channel from Nanton Lake to the northwest. All in all, this latter option is much easier. The campsite at the south end of Horseshoe Lake is one of the nicest in the area, and if you're planning on canoeing, why not spend a day or two here.

Inland (Loon) Lake (Map 17/B2)

Although found in the recreational paradise of the Powell Forest, this popular lake is not a part of the canoe route itself. It is only a short carry from Powell Lake, and some people do choose to carry to Inland Lake and end their trip here. Most people just drive to the Inland Lake Rec Site and launch from there. There is a popular hiking trail around the lake and several boat/trail access campsites. The Anthony Island site is by far the most beautiful of the bunch.

Jones (Wahleach) Lake (Map 5/C2)

Tucked in behind Cheam Peak and Four Brothers Mountain, Jones Lake is a pretty lake, one of the first real mountain lakes when you're heading east out of the Fraser Valley. Alas, it is also a manmade lake, trapped behind a BC Hydro Dam. And, with a water fluctuation of up to 20 metres (60 feet), the shoreline is not pretty. But, oh, the mountains that surround this lake! You could not ask for a prettier spot to launch a canoe.

Kawkawa Lake (Map 15/G7)

A small lake, tucked in between Hope and the big mountains beyond. There is a day-use provincial park, as well as three resorts that appeal to the summer crowds. Although the lake can be busy, there are secluded coves for paddlers to explore. Kawkawa Lake is also famous for its giant kokanee, which can be found up to 1.5 km (3 lbs).

Khartoum Lake (Maps 17/G3, 18\A3)

Khartoum used to be the Third Lake of the Third Lake Road, which you will have to follow to get to the Khartoum Rec Site. The rec site is the main access point onto the lake but people who stray from the main Powell River Canoe Route will find a portage trail between Khartoum and Lois Lake. Depending on water levels on Lois Lake, which are controlled by a BC Hydro Dam, it may be possible to paddle between the two lakes.

Lightning Lakes (Map 7/B7)
A chain of four lakes—Thunder, Strike, Flask and Lightning Lakes—threaded together by Lightning Creek. Only the last three, Strike, Flask and Lightening, are reasonably canoeable. There is a 15 minute portage between Lightning and Flash lakes and a 30 minute portage between Flash and Strike Lakes.

Lillooet Lakes (Maps 30/G2–G7, 31/A3–A6)
The Lillooet River slows down past Pemberton, and finally stops for a rest in the long, narrow, cold Lillooet Lake. There are a number of camping spots, both developed and random, along the length of this lake. To the south, Little Lillooet Lake is not much wider than the actual Lillooet River, and the current is only slightly slower, too. Little Lillooet isn't usually canoed by itself, but rather as a part of a longer trip from Lillooet Lake down the river.

Lois Lake (Map 17/F4)
Lois Lake is one of the larger lakes on the Powell Forest Canoe Route. When it is windy, Lois Lake can get choppy, but there are some sheltered places, especially on the northwest side of the lake (this area is home to a ghost stand of bleached trees thrusting from the water). Watch out for logs and snags just under water.

Nahatlatch Lakes (Map 23/G1)
The most common paddlers out on Nahatlatch Lake are rafters, practicing their strokes before heading down the wild and wooly Nahatlatch River. However, there's nothing to say that canoes or kayaks can't explore the long narrow lake as well. There are three rec sites on the lake, and two more on Hannah Lake, which is a short stretch of grade II/III whitewater away.

Nicomen Slough (Maps 3/G4–4/A4)
From the Deroche Bridge to Dewdney Nature Park is 14 km (8.5 miles) of shallow, slough that separates Nicomen Island from the Mainland. At low water, parts of this slough are too shallow to canoe, especially around Norrish Creek. As a result, it is best to go early in the year, when the weather warms up, but before water levels are too low.

Pitt Lake (Maps 12/G6, 13\A5)
Pitt Lake is the second largest lake in the region, second only to the monstrous Harrison Lake. The end of the Pitt Valley opens up to the Fraser Valley, and all the way to the open ocean, so the lake can get pretty windy, especially in the afternoon. It is a couple kilometres longer up the eastern shore (30 km/18.3 miles in total), but it has more places that a canoe/kayak can pull into if the wind blows up. The western shore has long stretches where there is nothing but a cliff face plunging straight into the water. Zealous paddlers have been known to bring along bikes to cycle the 15 additional kilometres to the oh so beautiful Pitt River Hot Springs.

Pitt Polder (Map 2/F1)
Once a flood plain, dykes were constructed back in the 1950s to keep the lower Pitt River flooding under control. A polder is actually the land reclaimed from underwater, so you're not actually canoeing on it, but on the parts still under water. The water levels rise and fall with the tides.

Powell Lake (Maps 16, 17, 26)
Powell Lake is a big lake, with lots of floating cabins and powerboat traffic, which can kick up an awful wake. There is also some commercial traffic, such as tugboats carrying log booms, but your biggest worry will be the wind. It can get blowing something fierce down the lake and many unsuspecting paddlers have been swamped when rounding a point. Fortunately, there are a lot of places to take shelter, including, if you are desperate, behind a log boom/wave suppressor that surround the floating cabins.

Sakinaw Lake (Maps 9\B1, 18/C7)
A long, narrow lake, Sakinaw is a popular getaway from Vancouver for a lot of people, many who own cabins on or around the lake. There is no formal camping on the lake, which is part of two canoe circuit routes described above.

Sasamat Lake (Map 2/A1)
Sasamat is an extremely popular lake in the summer. So popular that, during the peak hours the parking lot for the beach is always packed and usually gated. Wiley canoeists have been known to find other places along Bedwell Bay Road to launch from. It's a small lake, which means two things. The first is that it is usually unaffected by wind. The second is that it is one of the warmest lakes in the Lower Mainland.

Sasquatch Park Lakes (Map 5/A1, 15/A7) rentals
The three small lakes in Sasquatch Lake Provincial Park are all fine places to paddle. Deer and Hicks Lake are also open to powerboats but most boaters are the ones trolling for the abundant trout in the lakes. Trout Lake is the smallest of them all and can be circumnavigated, without much effort, in a very short time.

Stave Lake (Maps 3, 13)
The third-largest lake in the area, you would travel over 70 km (42.7 miles) circumnavigating the whole lake. To put that in perspective, the Powell Forest Canoe Route is only about 10 more kilometres (6 more miles) of actual paddling and takes up to a week to explore. The big lake does not see as much boat traffic as nearby lakes but the wind can still kick up without warning.

Widgeon Slough (Map 12/F7)
This is one of the most popular places for canoeists in the Lower Mainland, and for good reason. It is a spectacular trip, canoeing from the open floodplains of the Upper Fraser Valley into a mountain valley, with Burke Mountain towering on your left hand side. The scenery is phenomenal, the wildlife plentiful (part of the slough is one of only five National Wildlife Areas in the country), the canoeing easy, and the options of exploring the other channels and nearby trails are endless. Crossing the narrow channel of open water from Grant Narrows Park past Siwash Island to the entrance of the channel, can be difficult when it is windy. From Grant Narrows to the Widgeon Creek Campground is 4.5 km (2.8 miles).

Parks
(Regional and Provincial)

Regional and City Parks

There is nothing more appealing than a beautiful green space to help you get away from the hustle and bustle of the city. Vancouverites are blessed with one of the nicest park systems in the word. Further from the city, the parks become more remote and less crowded. Although camping is rarely offered at the regional and city parks, there are usually well developed trail systems, lovely picnic areas and plenty of nature to appreciate. Since listing all the city parks would be too lengthy, we have described the destination type parks in the area.

Aldergrove Lake Regional Park (Map 3/A4)

This regional park is centred around the man-made Aldergrove Lake, tucked away in the rolling hills beside the US border. The park is 280 ha, and contains both the lake and the surrounding forests and fields. There are 9.5 km (5.8 miles) worth of trails, most of which are open to horseback riding and biking. During the hot summers, most people come here to swim in the warm waters or lay back on the white sand beach that surrounds the lake.

Belcarra Regional Park (Map 2/A1)

Protecting the eastern flanks of the entrance to Indian arm, this 1,116 Regional Park is the second largest of the GVRD parks, second in size only to Lynn Headwaters. Belcarra is a popular recreation destination in summer, with 22 km (13.4 miles) of trails (only 6 km/3.7 miles open to horseback riding and 9.5 km/5.8 miles open to mountain bikers). There are two main recreation areas in the park. The first is Sasamat Lake, a popular swimming lake, looped by a trail. The second area is down at the docks. The two areas are connected by the Cod Rock Trail.

Boundary Bay Regional Park (Map 1/F7)

The biggest draw to this 182 ha regional park are the sandy beaches and the warm waters of Boundary Bay. When the tide goes out, almost all the water in the bay disappears, leaving a magical intertidal world to explore. The shallow pools fill with marine life, and you can walk for miles on the mud flats. The park is also the start of the multi-use 16 km (9.8 mile) Boundary Bay Regional Trail.

Burnaby Fraser Foreshore Park (Map 1/E3)

This picturesque riverside park is located south of Marine Way tucked between an industrial park and the river. The park is long and narrow, and, once you get away from the manicured lawns of the picnic area (off Bryne Road), there are some interesting sites to see and many side trails to explore.

Burnaby Mountain Park (Maps 1/G2, 2/A2)

Most people know this park because of the manicured gardens, Japanese sculpture and high-class restaurant at the top of the mountain. Further east, there is a large, wild swatch of mountain captured within the park boundaries, too. There are great views over both the city and Burrard Inlet from the top and an established trail system cutting through the forested slopes of the hill.

Burnaby Lake Regional Park (Maps 1/G2, 2/A3)

The majority of this 311 ha regional park is Burnaby Lake itself, but the really interesting part of the park is where the marshy area water meets the land. It is here where birds and small mammals tend to hang out. You can explore this area from shore, along the 19 km (11.6 miles) of trails, or from the water in a canoe or kayak.

Campbell Valley Regional Park (Map 2/E7)

There are 20 km (12.2 miles) of trails in this 549 ha regional park, 14 km (8.5 miles) of which are open to horseback riders. The trails are the most prominent feature in the park, winding their way through forest and field, marsh and meadow. Campbell Valley is also home to a number of historical sites. The park is accessed at the end of 208th St south of Langley.

Capilano River Regional Park (Map 11/D7)

The Capilano River cuts deep into the North Shore. The steep canyon walls, the view from the Cleveland Dam and the few pockets of old growth trees are just some of the highlights of this spectacular area. There are 14 km (8.5 miles) worth of multi-use trails to help you explore. In the fall, the Capilano Fish Hatchery becomes the centre of attention, as people flock to watch the returning salmon spawn up the river. Anglers also line the banks of the river and more than a few have landed more than a giant fish. The Cap is a great whitewater river and the odd kayaker has been hooked by errant lures.

Cascade Falls Regional Park (Map 3/F2)

This 9.5 ha site is one of the three nature parks in the Fraser Valley Regional District. The park's main feature is a series of waterfalls on Cascade Creek. The largest of which, the upper falls, plunge 28 metres (90 feet) to a large pool. Below the pool a series of smaller falls, in a deep, narrow gorge, drop the remaining 18 metres to the valley floor.

Central Park (Map 1/F3)

Central Park is a patch of green space near the ever-expanding glass and concrete of Metrotown. If you can't get out of the city, this is a good place to go to relax. Only in the heart of the park will the noise of the city fade, but it is easy to ignore the traffic whizzing by on Boundary Road as you relax on the grass beneath the shade of a Douglas fir. The park also hosts 8.5 km of multi-use trails winding their way through a small urban forest.

Cheam Lake Wetlands Regional Park (Map 4/G4)

Located just east of Highway 9, this 93 ha park is mostly lake and wetlands. This is a BC Wildlife Watch site, and there are plenty of birds and small mammals in the area. There are a number of trails in the park to explore, some of which are under water in spring and early summer.

Cliff Gilker Regional Park (Map 10/B6)

This small regional park is easily accessed off Highway 101 adjacent to the Sunshine Coast Golf & Country Club. It provides a series of popular hiking trails through a forested setting with little elevation gain. Wooden bridges cross several small streams and Roberts Creek in amongst some large second growth timber. There are four well-maintained and easily followed trails within the park.

Colony Farm Regional Park (Map 2/C2)

This is a recently developed 262 ha parcel of land near the Fraser/Coquitlam River confluence. There are a series of dyke trails to walk or bike and viewing platforms for the nature lover. From Highway 7, turn south onto Colony Farm Road and continue to the parking area at the end of the road.

Crippen Regional Park (Map 10/G7)

Bowen Island has been a popular getaway for people from the Vancouver area since the early 1900s. People come here to get away from the city and spend a few hours living on island time. The most prominent feature in this 242 ha park is Killarney Lake. It is possible to walk off the ferry, walk around the lake, and return to the ferry in an easy afternoon stroll. There are 11 km (6.7 miles) of trail here.

Cypress Falls Park (Map 11/B7) 🚶 ⚐

The main features of this park, a little known gem of a park near Horseshoe Bay, are a series of waterfalls on Cypress Creek. There are a number of trails in the park, and the most popular destination is, of course, the falls.

Deas Island Regional Park (Map 1/E5)
🏕 🚶 🐎 🛶 🐟 ⚐

A small (72 ha) park on the Fraser River, Deas Island isn't actually an island, but a peninsula, jutting out into the Fraser. While thousands of commuters pass by here every day, fighting back the road rage that threatens to envelop them, most have no idea that just a few metres away lies a peaceful riverside park. There are 9 km (5.7 miles) of trails through the park, taking you along Deas Slough, along the banks of the Fraser, and past the heritage buildings. The picnic area is a fine place to enjoy a sunset from.

Deer Lake Park (Map 1/G3)
🏕 🛶 🚶 🚵 🛶 🛶 ⚐

An urban park, protecting Deer Lake—an oasis of calm in the midst of the city—Deer Lake is home to arts, culture and history, as well as the natural beauty of the park itself. There are canoe rentals for folks who want to get out on the lake for a lazy paddle, as well as well developed trails, a beach, and a surprising amount of wildlife for a park surrounded by city. To get to the park from Highway 1, take the Kensington South turnoff. Turn west on Canada Way and follow the signs to Deer Lake Park.

Derby Reach Regional Park (Map 2/F3)
⚠ 🏕 🚶 🚵 🐎 🐟 ⚐

Edgewater Bar, located in this park, is considered by many to be one of the best, if not the best, fishing bars on the Fraser River. In August and September, this section of the riverbank is choc-a-block with anglers, while the channel just off shore is stuffed with salmon. Besides fishing, this is one of just two regional parks with public camping. There are 37 camping spots, all of which have access to the river. There are two trails—the 1 km (0.6 mile) Edge Trail, and the 4 km Houston Loop trail that skirts Derby Bog. Derby Reach was the original site of Fort Langley. Although the fort is no more, there are a few historical buildings.

Dewdney Nature Regional Park (Map 3/G5) 🛶 🚶 🐟 ⚐
This nature park is located outside the dyke on the east side of the south end of River Road South in Dewdney. This is a popular spot for bar fishing along the Fraser River. There is also a boat launch.

Don Bosch Regional Park (Map 18/D7)
🏕 🛶 🛶 🚶 🚵 🛶 ⚐

Ruby Lake is a beautiful roadside lake the entices many people to stop at this small park. In addition to the nice beach, there is boat launch for paddlers and anglers to enjoy.

Glen Valley Regional Park (Map 3/B4) 🏕 🚶 🛶 🐟 ⚐
This park is a thin strip of land along the Fraser River to give access to Two Bit, Poplar and Duncan Bars. Anglers frequent the area and there is a canoe launch, a couple picnic tables and even some short walking trails to enjoy.

Everett Crowley Park (Map 1/E3) 🚶 🚵 ⚐
A former landfill that, despite lots of reclamation work still shows its roots. This is not a pretty place to hike, but mountain bikers may find the trail system enjoyable. They're not technically challenging, but you don't want to make a mistake and fall, as nasty blackberry bushes encroach on the trails.

Fraser Foreshore Park (Map 1/F3) 🏕 🚶 🚵 ⚐
The ever expanding park and trail system in South Burnaby makes a fine year round destination. During summer, the picnic area is very busy while the trails see sporadic use. The main trail is the 4 km (2.4 miles) long stretch alongside the Fraser River between Boundary Road and the picnic area off Bryne Road. New development has created more options for people wishing to explore the marshlands around Bryne Road and further east.

Grant Narrows Regional Park (Map 12/F7) 🛶 🚶 🚵 🛶 ⚐
While Grant Narrows Park is a mere 6 ha, with little to offer other than a boat launch, it bounds on a number of interesting ecological areas and low-lying wetlands. The 1,500 ha Pitt Wildlife Management Area lies to the south of Grant Narrows, to the east is the UBC research forest, and across the narrows is the Widgeon Slough. All of these areas are prime wildlife habitat and home to a wide variety of birds and other creatures. From the park, there are almost 14 km (8.5 miles) worth of dykes that can be walked or biked, as well as the 4 km (2.4 mile) Mountainside Trail. In addition to viewing platforms, there are canoe rentals available for folks who want to canoe across to Widgeon Creek.

Iona Beach Regional Park (Map 1/B3) 🏕 🛶 🚶 🚵 🛶 ⚐
While the park is built around the beach, the most noticeable feature here is the 4 km (2.4 mile) long jetty, jutting far into the Strait of Georgia. For many years, this out-of-the-way corner of the Lower Mainland was the sewer of the Strait, and it was a nasty, disgusting, unpleasant place. But in the late 1980s, pipes were added to carry the sewage farther out into the strait, well away from this area. Now it is quite a pleasant place to be, and a testament to the recovery powers of nature. It is an isolated green space, and home to many birds and small mammals. There are tidal flats to explore, as well as marshes, grasslands, and the beach, for which this park gets its name. The beach is a great place for a picnic or to go sunbathing, and some people even go swimming.

Kanaka Creek Regional Park (Maps 2/G3, 3/B3)
🏕 🚶 🚵 🐎 🛶 🐟 ⚐

Kanaka Creek Regional Park follows the valley of Kanaka Creek for 11 km (6.8 miles). This is not a popular recreation park, but it does see its fair share of picnickers, trail users, canoeists and nature lovers. There are a couple picnic sites, one just above Cliff Falls, and one at the Bell-Irving Fish Hatchery. The hatchery is a fine place to see spawning salmon in fall, while the mouth of the creek is another nice place to watch for wildlife. There are also several walking trails in the 413 ha park, totaling 10 km (6 miles) but these do not all connect.

Katherine Lake Regional Park (Map 9/B1) 🏕 🛶
This small lake, with its nice, family-friendly beach, is a great place to spend a hot afternoon. The park is found off Garden Bay Road.

Symbols Used for Parks and Trails

🏕	Campsite /Trailer Park
🅰	Road Access Recreation Site
⚠	Trail or Boat Access Recreation Site
🏕	Day-use, Picnic Site
🛶	Beach
🛶	Boat Launch
🚶	Hiking Trail
🚵	Mountain Biking Trail
🐎	Horseback Riding
⛷	Cross Country Skiing
🛷	Snowmobiling
🧗	Mountaineering /Rock Climbing
🛶	Paddling (Canoe /Kayak)
🏍	Motorbiking /ATV
🏊	Swimming
🏠	Cabin /Hut /Resort
🔋	Interpretive Brochure
🐟	Fishing
⚐	Viewpoint
♿	Wheel Chair Accessible
⛷	Downhill Skiing
🏂	Snowshoeing
🤿	Diving
🕐	Resevations

Lower Seymour Conservation Reserve (Map 11/G7)

Formerly known as the Seymour Demonstration Forest, this 5,200-ha site was renamed in 1999. This valley is sandwiched between the ridges of Lynn Headwaters Regional Park and Mount Seymour Provincial Park. The main recreational feature of the park is the new trail that parallels the service road from the parking lot to Seymour Dam. This paved trail leads 10 km (6 mile road) one-way and is a popular walking/biking/roller blading path. But there are many other trails in the park, some official, others not, leading to various spots in the park. Most of the official trails are in the southern corner of the park, including the Fisherman's Trail. This trail runs along the Seymour River providing access for hikers, mountain bikers and, of course, anglers. Another popular but unofficial trail, is the Temple of Time, which leads to some of the largest old growth trees still standing in the Lower Mainland. No dogs are allowed in the park.

Lynn Canyon Park (Map 1/F1)

The majority of visitors to this park are here for one thing: the suspension bridge. It's like a mini version of the Capilano Suspension Bridge, and you don't have to pay to come here. Some continue on, but most admire the view into the deep gorge below, then leave. After crossing the suspension bridge, the majority of foot traffic heads north, to a rocky area just below a waterfall through a narrow canyon. In summer, this is a popular destination for families, and bolder individuals cliff dive in the pool at the base of the falls (not a recommended activity). To the south, a trail follows the canyon for a few kilometres, then crosses over Lynn Creek, and returns on the other side, above the canyon.

Lynn Headwaters Regional Park (Map 11/F6)

Lynn Headwaters is the biggest of the regional parks in the Lower Mainland and it helps protect parts of the famed North Shore Mountains. One of the nice things for visitors is that buses stop just a few hundred metres outside the park, making it accessible to everyone. You only have to walk a short way into the park along the access road to have the sounds, smells and sights of the city fade away, to be replaced with the sensations of this verdant park. There are a number of fabulous hiking trails including the Headwater Trail (15.5 km/9.5 miles return), and the Hanes Valley Loop, which takes you over to Grouse Mountain and back on the Baden Powell Trail (15 km/9 miles). The trails in Lynn Headwaters also hook up with trails in the Lower Seymour Conservation Reserve to the east. In winter, when there is snow, the trails are taken over by backcountry skiers.

Matsqui Trail Regional Park (Map 3/D5-E5)

Located along the Fraser River beneath the Mission/Abbotsford Bridge, this 117 ha park is thin and long, stretching 10 km (6 miles) along the south bank of the Fraser. The park is threaded together by a dyke trail, which runs the length of the park. There are six formal camping spots, a popular picnic area and plenty of space for bar fishing. But the main feature of the area is the scenic Matsqui Trail. Part of the Trans Canada Trail, this broad multi-use trail can be stretched into a multi-day (or week or month) adventure.

Minnekhada Regional Park (Map 2/E1)

Minnekhada occupies an interesting parcel of land. Part of the park is in the mountains, and is forested and rocky. Part of the park is in the lowlands, and is marshy, with dykes providing access to the Addington Lookout. In fall, when the wild berries are ripe, it is not surprising to see black bears around the Minnekhada Farm area. There are over 12 km (7.3 miles) of trails through the park, from easy dyke walks to fairly stiff climbs up to the rocky knolls.

Mundy Park (Map 2/B2)

This is a suburban park with 12 km (7.5 miles) of multi-use trails weaving their way through cool, lush forest of the 180 ha park. The heart of the park is Mundy Lake, but the smaller Lost Lake is also a popular destination. The park is found off Como Lake Road and makes

a pleasant year round destination.

Neilson Regional Park (Map 3/E4)

A ten-acre park on the west side of Hatzic Lake, provides public access to the lake. There has been some development, including a cookhouse, picnic tables, improved beach area, and approximately 2 km (1.2 miles) of walking trails. The park looks out across the Fraser Valley, with Mt. Cheam in the distance. There is also a private campsite on the lake.

Pacific Spirit Regional Park (Map 1/B2)

This park actually surrounds the University of British Columbia, although the main bulk of the park is located just east of the university. Pacific Spirit has the proud distinction of being the only clothing optional park in the Lower Mainland, and while most of the naturalists hang around Wreck Beach, the entire foreshore area, around the point to Acadia Beach, is clothing optional. It is possible to walk the 6 km (3.6 miles) foreshore at low tide (although there are some dangerous areas, especially to the southwest) where you will find a lot more than old men sans shorts. The biggest part of this park is the southeast corner, which has become a haven for mountain bikers. There are over 90 km (54.9 miles) of trails in the park, of which 60 km (36.6 miles) are open to mountain bikers and horseback riders.

Richmond Nature Park (Map 1/E4)

The Richmond Nature Park protects a relic example of the raised peat bogs that once covered more than 25 per cent of Richmond. In addition to the bog flora, bog creatures like snakes, turtles, coyotes and deer are often seen. A 5 km (3 mile) network of trails allows you to explore the park.

Shelter Point Regional Park (Map 8/B1)

On Texada Island, this regional park is easily accessed south of Gillies Bay on the 'Texada Island Highway'. Within the park is a scenic 2 km trail that leads along the ocean through some large windswept Douglas-fir.

Stanley Park (Map 1/D1)

Stanley Park is the life and love of the city of Vancouver whose reputation is built on the beauty of its natural surroundings. Stanley Park is wilderness light, an introduction to some of the magic of nature without ever having to leave the city. With many developed areas like Lost Lagoon, the Aquarium, the Zoo, the totem poles… it is easy to forget that there are still fragments of the wilderness here. It is impossible to name all the recreational activities—from roller blading the Sea Wall to playing pitch and putt to relaxing on one of the beaches to hiking the trails on the west side of the park, to splashing in the kids water park, to watching the marine life in the Aquarium. Stanley Park is one of the great urban parks in North America, and, despite its' popularity on a sunny summer Saturday, it is still a wonderful and worthwhile place to visit.

Sumas Mountain Regional Park (Map 3/G5, 4/A5)

Sumas Mountain is an upside down bowl shaped monolith that dominates the eastern part of the Fraser Valley. The park once sat as an undeveloped provincial park, but has now been taken over by the Fraser Valley Regional District. Hikers will enjoy the trail to the top and the tremendous viewpoints while anglers often try their luck fishing in tiny Chadsey Lake.

Surrey Bend Regional Park (Map 2/D3)

This new park captures a unique section of relatively untouched, flood plains on the Fraser River. There are a few trails here, used mostly by anglers to access the river. Across the waters of Parsons Channel, on Barnston Island, is the **Roberts Point Rest Area**, which has washrooms and a picnic area. Cyclists often cycle counterclockwise around the island road, stopping at the scenic point for a picnic lunch. From the ferry to Roberts Point is 2 km (1.2 miles) if you head west, and 8 km (4.8 miles) if you head east (counterclockwise).

Tynehead Regional Park (Map 2/D4)

Located just off Highway 1, Tynehead is a 260 ha park consisting of rolling meadows and forest in the centre of North Surrey. The park contains the headwaters for the Serpentine River, and is a popular place to watch salmon spawning in fall. The park is also home to the unique Butterfly Garden. They have grown plants here that attract butterflies, and have even provided viewing platforms.

Provincial Parks & Recreation Areas

In the early 1990s, there was a serious push to preserve 12% of the provincial land base as parks. As a result, there were dozens of new provincial parks created, many of which fall inside the scope of this mapbook. While some of these parks are nearing a decade old, they still have little in the way of developed facilities. While this is attractive for the hardcore outdoors person, who lives for adventure, there are few recreational facilities for the car-based adventurers. Still, there are many older parks that will meet the needs of these folks.

At this time, there is a great deal of change happening in the provincial park system. Campground fees are being raised and daily parking fees are being added to popular parks. Further, things like free firewood and the ever-popular interpretive programs are no longer. What other changes will we see over the next few years? Only time will tell.

Regardless, the many provincial parks and recreation areas are our frontline to the outdoors. Whether it is a car access campsite to a remote wilderness retreat, provincial parks provide the best places to experience the Great Outdoors. Since many of the sites are so close to the largest population base of the province, most campgrounds fill up quickly. It is recommended to make reservations well ahead of time (look for the ❶ for those sites that accept reservations). Call **1-800-689-9025** or visit www.discovercamping.com to learn more about fees and additional information.

Alexandra Bridge Provincial Park (Map 24/F7)

A small (55 hectare) day-use park is located high above the Fraser River. The original Alexandra Bridge dates back to 1926, and you can walk across to the other side of the river. A short distance downstream, highway traffic uses a more modern crossing. In addition to walking back and forth across the steel grate bridge and throwing stones into the water, there is a picnic area just off the highway.

Alice Lake Provincial Park (Map 20/D6)

Alice Lake is a popular provincial park, 13 km (7.9 miles) north of Squamish. There are 108 campsites here, which is usually full all summer. Alice Lake is one of four lakes that dominate this park, and water sports like swimming, fishing and canoeing are the most popular activities here. There are a number of trails in the park, ranging from a stroll around Alice Lake, to the 6 km (3.6 mile) Four Lakes Trail. The park covers 396 ha and now charges a daily parking fee.

Apodaca Provincial Marine Park (Map 10/G7)

Apodaca is an 8 ha marine park located on the eastern shore of Bowen Island. There are no developed facilities, but it is a good place to moor your boat and explore the shore. The park protects the shoreline, which consists of scenic cliffs and rocky knolls.

Arrowstone Provincial Protected Area (Map 47/G4)

A new 6,203 ha protected area, located in the foothills northeast of Cache Creek. The park is accessed off the Arrowstone Forest Service Road and Highway 1. The park protects the Arrowstone Creek Drainage as well as the Cache Creek Hills. There are no developed facilities in the park, but is fairly accessible for hikers, hunters and nature lovers to explore.

Bedard Aspen Provincial Park (Map 42/C2)

A small 173 ha park, with no developed facilities, surrounds Bedard Lake. It is an interesting area of high biological diversity. The area is accessed by trail from logging roads to the east and the west of the park. There is random backcountry camping wherever you can find a spot to pitch a tent.

Birkenhead Lake Provincial Park (Map 39/D3)

This recently expanded park encompasses the turquoise-coloured Birkenhead Lake, as well as the rugged mountains that surround the lake. This is truly a beautiful spot, located 55 km (34 mi) northeast of Pemberton via the Blackwater Lake Road. In addition to a popular campground, there is a daily parking fee. There is also a boat launch, a beach, and hiking/biking trails (one of which follows the western shore of the lake, and is part of the Sea to Sky Trail). The park is home to many animals, including bobcat, moose, deer and black bear.

Blue Earth Lake Provincial Park (Map 42/D3)

Blue Earth Lake Park is located in a deep valley and offers fishing and camping at the main lake. There are a few small areas of old-growth Douglas fir and mature aspen, while spawning trout may be seen in the shallow channel between the lakes in early summer. The 705 ha park is bisected by a rough logging road to the east.

Brandywine Falls Provincial Park (Map 29/D7)

There are 15 campsites at this roadside park, situated 47 km (28.7 miles) north of Squamish. The 70-metre (227 foot) high Brandywine Falls are located just a few minutes from the day-use area, and are one of the most photogenic falls in the area. There are a number of trails in the area, including a section of the Sea to Sky Trail that links up with a suspension bridge.

Brackendale Eagles Provincial Park (Map 20/C6)

Brackendale Eagles Provincial Park lies in the Squamish River watershed, a large low lying valley through the Coast Mountains. This valley has long been recognized as one of the most significant areas of wintering bald eagles in North America. These majestic birds can be seen feasting on the spawned out remains of Chum Salmon from November to February each year. A new 755 ha provincial park was developed to protect habitat for the eagles. There are no developed facilities in the park, and it is recommended that people view the eagles from outside the park boundaries. The park is located on the west side of the Squamish River, but one of the best viewing locations is across the river at the municipal dyke on Government Road in Brackendale.

Bridal Veil Falls Provincial Park (Map 4/G4)

Bridal Veil Falls Park is a 32 ha day-use area located just off Highway 1 east of Chilliwack. The landscape encompassing the park is characterized by low elevation valleys and lush, rounded mountains. The falls tumble 60 metres (195 feet) over a smooth rock face and make a fine hiking destination. Zealous hikers can continue up, the steep trail to the impressive peak of Mt. Cheam.

Buccaneer Bay Provincial Marine Park (Map 9/C4)

Buccanneer Bay is a tiny 1 ha park with a broad sandy beach at the southern tip of North Thormanby Island. The large sheltered bay provides safe anchorage in most summer conditions for small boats or kayaks. This is also a popular scuba diving location. There is random beach camping (with space for about 8 groups) allowed.

Callaghan Lake Provincial Park (Map 29/C4)

Callaghan Lake is a high mountain lake at the end of a rough two-wheel drive road. In addition to ten rustic campsites, the lake and nearby Cirque Lake offer fishing for rainbow and lake trout. There are also numerous small wetlands and small lakes, especially in the southern and eastern areas of the park, and in the upper headwaters of Callaghan Creek. Callaghan Country Wilderness Adventures operates a commercial cross-country ski operation, which includes 4 km (2.4 miles) of groomed trails within the park (part of a total of 38 km/23.2 miles in its operating area), and a mountain cabin west of the park. A zone has also been designated for snowmobile use, providing an access corridor to the bowls north of the park.

Cascade Recreation Area (Maps 6, 7)

This is big (11,858 ha) recreation area that is bounded by both the Skagit Valley Recreation Area and Manning Provincial Park. One can access the area from either the Cascade Recreation Area Parking Area, or along the Whipsaw Creek Road. This pristine backcountry wilderness area has seen very little development over the years. In summer, the area is accessed on foot or by horse, while in winter the northeast corner of the Granite Mountain area is open to snowmobiling.

Chilliwack Lake Provincial Park (Map 5/F4-F7)

Chilliwack Lake Provincial Park has recently been expanded to 9,122 ha. The expansion includes the east side of the lake, and unfortunately the old Forestry campsites at Depot Creek, Post Creek, Sappers Park and Paleface Creek have been deactivated. The park is centred around the large mountain lake, but also includes some old-growth forest on the mountain slopes, and spectacular sub-alpine and alpine ridges. Chilliwack Lake is ideal for boating, canoeing, kayaking, swimming (although it doesn't get very warm), and fishing. There are 40 km (24.4 miles) of trails, including parts of the recently established Trans Canada Trail and the historic Centennial Trail. Campers will find 146 drive-in campsites, and backcountry campsites at Greendrop, Lindeman, Flora, and Radium Lakes. The park is located 64 km (39 miles) southeast of Chilliwack.

Chilliwack River Prov Park (Map 4/E6)

A popular spot for both anglers and kayakers, this day-use site is also a nice place for a picnic.

Clendinning Provincial Park (Maps 28, 36, 37)

This remote, wilderness park is not accessible by road nor trail. It was developed to protect the old-growth forests, alpine areas and glaciers surrounding Clendinning Creek to the southwest of the proposed Stoltman Wilderness Park.

Copeland Islands Marine Park (Maps 16/C1, 25/C7)

Located northwest of Lind, this provincial park encompasses the scenic Copeland Islands. The area is a sanctuary for birds, as well as an excellent spot for scuba diving. The park is often used as a stopover point by sea kayakers heading into Desolation Sound, but the islands also make a nice two or three-day destination themselves.

Coquihalla Canyon Provincial Park (Map 15/G7)

This park is situated around the Othello Tunnels built in the early 1900s as part of the historic Kettle Valley Railway. The tunnels are impressive, as are the great views of the canyon, a 93 metre (300 foot) deep gorge of near-vertical granite. The old rail bed is part of the Trans Canada Trail. A daily parking fee applies.

Cornwall Hill Provincial Park (Map 42/E1)

This is a 1,188 ha day-use site, with few developed facilities. Still, it is popular with recreationists, who do anything from hiking to hang-gliding here. The park contains the only active Forest Service Lookout Tower in the Kamloops District.

Cultus Lake Provincial Park (Map 4/B7)

This 656 ha park, located 13 km (7.9 miles) south of Chilliwack, sees a lot of water-based activity. There are four campgrounds in the park: Clear Creek (80 sites), Delta Grove (58 sites), Entrance Bay (52 sites) and Maple Bay (106 sites). In summer the beaches are often packed, and the lake is positively abuzz with powerboats and jet skis. There are canoe rentals, but the lake can be a dangerous place to be in an open craft, as winds can pick up at any time. There are five main trails in the park, ranging from the interpretive stroll along the Maple Bay Trail to a 5 hour hike along the Edmeston Road to Road 918 Trail. The trails also hook up with trails outside the park. A daily parking fee applies.

Cypress Provincial Park (Map 11/B4–B7)

Cypress has the distinction of being the most popular provincial park in the province. Most of the visitors to the park come in winter, as Cypress is home to a popular ski hill, just 15 minutes from downtown Vancouver. On a clear day the views from the top of Mt. Strachen (pronounced Stawn) are spectacular! To the south is the sprawling metropolitan area of Vancouver, while to the southeast is snow clad Mount Baker in the Cascade Mountain chain. To the west and southwest lie the Gulf Islands and Vancouver Island with Georgia Strait in the foreground. But the park is much more than just the ski area, and covers nearly 3,000 ha. There are many trails in the park, including the strenuous but rewarding Howe Sound Crest Trail. A daily parking fee applies.

Davis Lake Provincial Park (Map 3/F1)

Davis Lake Provincial Park is located 19 km (11.6 miles) north of Mission. Continue from Sylvester Road past the park boundary and look for a side road that descends south, down the slope to the short trail into Davis Lake. The 192 ha park surrounds the small, warm water lake with pretty beaches, a scenic waterfall and good fishing. While it is primarily a day-use park, walk-in camping is permitted.

Desolation Sound Provincial Marine Park (Map 25/F3)

Desolation Sound is one of the most popular yachting and sea kayaking destinations in the world. It is also BC's largest marine provincial park encompassing Gifford Peninsula and several small islands. Despite its remoteness at the end of the Sunshine Coast, with no access other than by water, it can be busy in the summer. Boat cruisers, sea kayakers and anglers all flock here from Lund or Okeover Inlet. There are several developed camping areas throughout, and the shallow bays are famous for warm waters and oysters. For more information, consult the fishing and paddling sections of the book.

Downing Provincial Park (Map 46/F1)

This 100 ha park is often used by folks travelling the Clinton-Pavilion Road, a steep but scenic mountain road. It is a small but popular park that all but encircles Kelly Lake. The park is at the base of a dramatic mountain ridge, which creates an impression of remoteness, despite the proximity to Clinton.

Duffey Lake Provincial Park (Map 40/D7)

Located about 35 km (21.4 miles) east of Pemberton, Duffey Lake is nearly halfway to Lillooet along the Duffey Lake Road (Highway 99). Duffy Lake is a beautiful lake, and is a popular place for boaters.

Elephant Hill Provincial Park (Map 47/G7)

This park protects a pair of prominent hills in a naturally dry grassland area, which are home to rattlesnakes. The grasslands are closed to vehicle traffic, and no camping or day-use facilities are provided. There is random hiking in the 979 ha park, which is a popular destination with wildlife watchers. The park is easily accessed off Highway 97C south of Cache Creek.

Emory Creek Provincial Park (Map 15/F4)

Emory Creek is a roadside park next to the Fraser River, 18 km (11 miles) north of Hope. There are 34 campsites in this 15 ha park. This is a popular spot with anglers.

Epson Provincial Park (Map 42\G3)

A 102 ha park on the west bank of the Thompson River, north of Spences Bridge. The park provides access to the river and includes both river and upland habitat.

F.H. Barber Provincial Park (Map 5/B1)

This is a small day-use area between Highway 1 and the Fraser River.

Garden Bay Provincial Marine Park (Map 9/C1)

Located around Mount Daniels, this small marine park has a dock, a picnic area, and hiking trails. It can be accessed by water, or by land, off Garden Bay Road. On the rock bluffs next to the ocean is a stand of juniper trees, a rare site on the Sunshine Coast.

Garibaldi Provincial Park (Maps 20, 21, 22, 29, 30)

A huge 194,650 ha wilderness park located next to Squamish and Whistler, Garibaldi is a popular destination with outdoor enthusiasts. Day trips are possible (a parking fee applies), but most people who visit plan on spending a few days, or even a few weeks, exploring this alpine paradise. The main access points into the park from south to north are, the Diamond Head Trail, The Black Tusk Trail, The Cheakamus Lake Trail, the Singing Pass Trail, and the Wedgemount Lake Trail. The park has an interesting geological background; volcanic action formed many of the park's peaks. Lava from Clinker Peak created The Barrier, a natural dam that created the 300 metre deep Garibaldi Lake. The Barrier has been declared a Civil Defense Zone, and there is no camping or stopping while travelling through the Zone. There are many popular, developed backcountry camping areas, like Garibaldi Lake, Taylor Meadows, Diamond Head, Singing Pass and Wedgemount Lake. In summer and fall, this is the domain of backpackers; mountain bikes are only allowed as far as Elfin Lakes on the Diamond Head Trail. In the winter, snowshoers and backcountry skiers take over.

There are a number of popular backcountry ski touring routes in Garibaldi (see Winter Recreation for more information). No dogs are allowed in the park.

Golden Ears Provincial Park (Maps 2, 3, 11, 13, 21, 22)

🏂 ⛺ 🏕 ✈ 🚶 🚴 🐴 🛶 🚤 🎣 🐟 🚻 ♿ ☾ windsurf

Although less than a third of the size of the massive Garibaldi Provincial Park to the north, Golden Ears, at 55,590 ha, is still one of the largest parks in the province. Most of the recreational usage happens in the southern portion of the park, around Alouette Lake. There is swimming, windsurfing, water skiing, canoeing, boating, fishing, or just lazing about the beach. There are two vehicle accessible campgrounds in this park, Alouette (205 sites) and Gold Creek (138 sites). Another popular spot is North Beach, which features random beach camping, located a short hike in from the parking lot. Backcountry or walk-in camping is allowed at Alder Flats on the West Canyon Trail and Lake Beautiful on the Alouette Mountain Trail, but there are no facilities provided. A number of trails push farther back into the park, the longest being the Hector Ferguson Trail, but even this trail extends only about a third of the way to the north boundary of the park. There are a number of other trails, including one to the park's namesake, the Golden Ears themselves. The Golden Ears are not the prominent peaks that tower above Maple Ridge; that's Alouette Mountain. A daily parking fee applies.

Goldpan Provincial Park (Map 33/F1) 🏂

A 5 ha provincial park sandwiched between Highway 1 and the Fraser River. There are 14 campsites here, but, with Highway 1 and the railway so close, it is not a peaceful place. It is recommended to pick Shihist Park to the south if you want a nicer place to visit.

Ha'thayim (Van Donop) Provincial Marine Parks (Map 25/A7) 🚶 🚤 🛶 ⚓ 🐟

Von Donop Inlet is a popular anchorage for recreational boaters. This inlet is at the southern terminus of the Inside Passage, a mostly sheltered route for boaters. Visitors to the park can follow an old road to connect with Squirrel Cove.

Halkett Bay Provincial Park (Map 10/D3, 11/A5)

🏕 🚤 🚶 ✈ 🚤 ⚓ 🐟 ◿

Located on Gambier Island, this park is only accessible by boat. There are ten picnic sites, and a trail leaves from here and up to Mount Artaban. There are mooring buoys and dingy floats for boaters.

Harmony Islands Provincial Marine Park (Map 18/C4) ⛺ ✈ 🚤 🐟 🚻

These small, sheltered islands are just north of the towering Freil Falls in the sheltered Hotham Sound. Swim, go snorkeling, fish, or just appreciate nature.

Harry Lake Aspen Provincial Park (Map 47/B6) 🚻

This park, created in the last decade, is located west of Cache Creek off Highway 99. There are no developed facilities in the park.

Indian Arm Provincial Marine Park (Maps 12/A6) ⛺ ✈ 🚤 🐟 ◿

To the south of the much larger Indian Arm Provincial Park is a small marine access park that protects Raccoon and the Twin Islands. These small islands are rocky, sparsely covered islands. There is rustic camping on Twin Islands, which are connected by a narrow, sandy isthmus that is exposed at low tide. Please respect the parcels of private land on the Twin Islands.

Indian Arm Provincial Park (Maps 2\A1, 12/A6) ⛺ 🏕 ✈ 🚶 🚤 🚤 🐟 🚻

Indian Arm is a long, narrow fjord that extends north from Burrard Inlet. The 6,821 ha park protects the upper portion of the inlet and is primarily accessed by water, although there is logging road access from Squamish. The landscape is spectacular, with rugged, forested mountains, alpine lakes, and numerous creeks and waterfalls, including

the 50-metre high Granite Falls. The Arm is ideal for motor boating, kayaking, canoeing, and scuba diving, while the Indian River and the lower reaches of some of the creeks are great for fishing. The flat beach areas along the shorelines of Bishop Creek provide a good area for rustic camping or even picnicking. Granite Falls is another popular area for camping and picnics. There is a day-use area on the north side, near a small dock, while tenders will often set up on the south side of the falls.

Inland Lake Provincial Park (Map 17/B2)

🏂 ⛺ 🏕 🚤 🚶 🚤 🐟 ♿

This park has taken over the former, very popular Forest Service Recreation Site and trail north of Powell River. There is a 13 km (7.9 mile) wheelchair accessible trail around Inland Lake, along with less developed connecting trails to nearby Powell Lake. The main campsite offers 16 campsites with picnic tables, cabins for disabled people as well as a wharf. Tenting only sites spread around the lake, including the scenic boat access only sites on Anthony Island.

International Ridge Provincial Park (Map 4/C7) 🚶 🚻

Just east of Cultus Lake, this park encompasses the slopes of Mount Amadis. The main attraction to this park is the scenic International Ridge Trail.

Jedediah Island Provincial Park (Map 8/F4) ⛺ 🚤 🐟

Jedediah Island has long been the destination of boaters and kayakers. It is the largest and most diverse island of a chain of over thirty islands and islets located north and west of Lasqueti Island.

Joffre Lakes Provincial Park (Map 31/A1) ⛺ 🚶 🛶 🐟 🚻

This 1,460 ha wilderness park contains the lovely Joffre Lakes and the towering (2,701 metres/8,778 feet) Joffre Peak. The trail leading past the three lakes is a fairly rough 5 km (3 mile) mountain route. Beyond the rustic campsite at Upper Joffre Lake is only recommended for mountaineers prepared for travelling on glaciers and snowfields.

Kawkawa Provincial Park (Map 15/G7) 🏕 🚤 ✈ 🚤 🐟

Just east of Hope, off the Kawkawa Lake Road, there is a day-use area on the west side of the warm Kawkawa Lake. In addition to the popular beach, anglers will find excellent fishing for kokanee.

Kilby Provincial Park (Map 4/C2) 🏂 🏕 🚤 🚶 🐟 🚻

Tucked away in a rural pastoral setting, Kilby Provincial Park is located just past the historical Kilby General Store. This provincial park is a great place to watch wintering bald eagles, trumpeter swans, geese, and small songbirds. This scenic riverfront park has 38 camping units as well as the main boat launch onto the Harrison River.

Manning Provincial Park (Maps 6, 7)

🏂 ⛺ 🏕 🚶 🚴 🐴 🚡 🚤 🚤 🐟 🚻 ♿ ⛷ 🎿 ☾

Situated in the Cascade Mountains of southwestern BC, E.C. Manning Provincial Park encompasses over 66,500 ha of rugged mountains, valleys, meadows, lakes and rivers. Manning is a four season recreational paradise. Trails, ranging from a few hours to a few days (or months since the Windy Joe Trailhead marks the northern terminus for the Pacific Crest Trail leading all the way to Mexico), lakes for canoeing and fishing, wildlife for viewing, and downhill and cross-country skiing in winter. Highway 3 runs through the park providing good access to campgrounds, picnic sites and several trailheads.

Campers will find four campgrounds in the park. Lightning Lake Campground is the most popular site in the park with 143 reservable sites. It is open for winter camping but the last to open in the spring. There are several hiking trails starting at this campground as well as popular beach and good fishing in the area. Coldspring Campground has 64 sites, all of which are first come first serve, sandwiched between the highway and the Similkameen River. The Canyon Nature Trail starts at this campground. Hampton Campground has 99 first come, first serve sites. Finally, the Mule Deer Campground has 49 first come, first serve sites. This is the first campground to open in the spring and early campers will find some pretty sites on the Similkameen River. Trail users will also find designated areas for backcountry camping. In winter, tenters can camp at the Lone Duck Group Camping area.

Marble Canyon Provincial Park (Maps 46/G5, 47/A5)

A small provincial park just east of Pavilion on Highway 99, Marble Canyon is set at the base of 1,000 metre (3,250 feet) high limestone cliffs. The 335 ha park contains a trio of lakes, Crown, Pavilion and Turquoise Lakes, with a 34 unit campsite at the south end of Pavilion Lake.

Mehatl Creek Provincial Park (Maps 23, 31, 32)

As one of British Columbia's newest protected areas, the 23,860 ha Mehatl Creek is a wilderness getaway for backcountry adventurers. During the summer, visitors can trek 3 km (1.8 miles) up the park's only established trail to Mehatl Falls, which is nestled in a sub-alpine bowl. Parking is available adjacent to the 48 km bridge of the Nahatlatch River Forest Service Road in a vacant dry land log sort area. Other activities include fishing in the lower creek, and wildlife viewing.

Mount Elphinstone Provincial Park (Map 10/D5)

This park preserves three postage stamp-size remnants of old-growth forest on Mount Elphinstone, totaling about 140 ha. These areas contain some of the oldest trees in the province. Mount Elphinstone is also home to a prolific number of mushrooms, some of which have yet to be properly identified. Tread carefully and take only photographs.

Mount Richardson Provincial Park (Map 9/G2)

A new provincial park, just east of the Sechelt Inlet, is accessed off the rough Sechelt FSR. In addition to established trails up the mountain, there is a former Forest Recreation Site and fishing at Richardson Lake.

Mount Seymour Provincial Park (Maps 1\G1, 11\G7, 12\A6)

The 3,508 ha Mount Seymour Provincial Park is located 30 minutes northeast of downtown Vancouver. The park is notorious for winter recreation. The downhill ski area is popular with snowboarders and family skiers, while backcountry skiers and snowshoers have endless areas to play in. During summer, Mount Seymour, Mount Elsay and

Mount Bishop all make great hiking or backpacking destinations (wilderness camping is permitted in the sub-alpine north of Brockton Point). Alternatively, the extensive trail system on the lower flanks of Mount Seymour is riddled with mountain biking trails. The park is easily accessed off the Mount Seymour Parkway. A daily parking fee applies.

Murrin Provincial Park (Maps 11/C1)

This small park surrounds tiny Browning Lake and is a very popluar stop for travellers on the Sea to Sky Highway. In addition to picnic tables and a good fishing hole, rock climbers can be seen testing their skilss on the bluffs rising above the parking lot. A daily parking fee applies.

Nahatlatch Provincial Park (Maps 22, 23, 24, 31)

Nahatlatch Provincial Park is a long and narrow 1,695 ha park, abutting Mehatl Provincial Park in the west. The natural beauty of this spot, nestled in the glacier covered mountains, with old growth forest and a lake and river system like no other in the Lower Mainland. A series of small streams flow into, out of, and between the three lakes in the park. Their waters drain into the Nahatlach River, one of the best whitewater rivers in the province. For those not interested in these high adrenaline antics, they can canoe in and between the lakes. There are six former Forest Service Recreation Sites that provide camping in the park. From east to west they are, Frances Lake, Hannah Lake, Old Ranger Station, Nahatlatch Lake, Salmon Beach and Squakum. The park entrance is located on the Nahatlach FSR (an active logging road) approximately 25 km (15.3 miles) northwest of Boston Bar. It is identified with a park information shelter.

Nairn Falls Prov Park (Map 30/B2)

The waterfall for which this park is named plummets 60 metres (195 feet) into the valley below. They are accessible by a short, easy trail. The scenic park is not as busy as some of the others in the area. There are 88 campsites next to the Green River, a good fishing river for dolly varden and rainbow trout.

Okeover Provincial Park (Map 16/E1)

On the east side of the Malaspina Peninsula, this 4 ha park is used as a launching point for sea kayakers heading out into Desolation Sound. There are 14 vehicle/tent sites open seasonally and four small, sites open all year. These sites are usually full, and are located close together so there is not much privacy. There is also an undeveloped boat launch and a government wharf here.

Oregon Jack Provincial Park (Map 42/D2)

This undeveloped 222 ha park protects a spectacular limestone canyon and falls (called The Notch) on Oregon Jack Creek.

Peace Arch Provincial Park (Map 2/C7)

The Peace Arch sits on the International Boundary, where BC's Highway 99 and Washington States' Interstate 5 meet at the Canada/United States border. There are 41 picnic tables throughout the day-use park. This is not a wilderness park, but is pretty nonetheless, an elegant, well-manicured park with lovely flower gardens.

Pinecone-Burke Provincial Park (Maps 2, 12, 21)

A large, still undeveloped park is tucked in between (and behind) Pitt Lake and the Coquitlam Lake Watershed (and Indian Arm Park, and Golden Ears...). It's a big 38,000 ha park, capturing some of the rugged territory to the west of Pitt Lake, and Upper Pitt River Valley. The park protects a number of sites that have been historically popular, but unprotected, like Burke Mountain in Coquitlam, Widgeon Slough and Widgeon Valley (which are accessible only by canoe or kayak from Grant Narrows). Most visitors make Widgeon Lake, a pretty lake in a hanging valley, their ultimate destination. But if you keep right instead of heading left to Widgeon Lake, you will follow the Fool's Gold Route north and west to hook up with the Mamquam River FSR southeast of Squamish. This route is infrequently travelled (and possibly hasn't been hiked in about five years).

Plumper Cove Provincial Marine Park (Map 10/E7)

A small marine park on the northwestern shores of Keats Island, this park is accessible by canoe/kayak, boat, or by the infrequent foot ferry from Gibsons (the Dogwood Princess). From Keats Landing, it is 2 km (1 mile) to the park. The park offers a snug anchorage for boaters, and a good overnight destination for sea kayakers out of Gibsons. The park has a developed area with forested walk-in campsites, fire rings, and water. Marine facilities include a wharf and mooring buoys, while the pebble beach is great for swimming and picnicking.

Porpoise Bay Provincial Park (Map 9/G4)

Located on the shores of Porpoise Bay in Sechelt, this small provincial park has space for 84 campers. The large sandy beach is the main feature in the park, but there are trails that lead to the estuary of Angus Creek, offering great views over the inlet. In the fall, this is a good place to watch spawning salmon. Reservations are recommended for camping and a daily parking fee applies.

Porteau Cove Provincial Park (Map 11/B3)

Howe Sound is the southern most fjord in North America. Porteau Cove offers 59 scenic camping spots stretched out along the shores of the sound, plus a popular walk-in beach area just south of the main campground. An old ship has been sunk to attract marine life for scuba divers, making this one of the most popular diving spots in BC. The park is sandwiched between the BC Rail Line and the ocean, and many campers have awoken to the rumbling of trains passing by. Be careful around the tracks. Reservations are recommended for camping and a daily parking fee applies.

Princess Louisa Provincial Marine Park (Map 27/G4)

Princess Louisa Inlet is located far inland, accessed by way of Jervis Inlet. The 8 km (5 mile) long inlet is in a magnificent granite-walls gorge; mountains rise sharply from the water's edge to heights in excess of 2,100 metres (7,000 feet). Up to mid-June, the warm sun melting the mountain snow pack creates more than sixty waterfalls that cascade down the steep granite cliffs, straight into the ocean. The most famous of these, Chatterbox Falls, tumbles 40 metres (120 feet). Beyond the seven to ten knot Malibu Rapids at the entrance, the inlet is as placid as a mountain lake. Wilderness campsites are provided with toilets and picnic shelters nearby. Mooring buoys and docks are provided, while walking trails provide access to nearby scenic features.

Roberts Creek Provincial Park (Map 10/A6)

Located off Highway 101 west of Gibsons, this 14 ha park is built around a cobblestone beach. Swimming is possible for the tough of foot (swimming shoes are a good idea), and from the beach you may see orca (killer) whales or harbour seals. At low tides, the intertidal area exposes an interesting display of marine life.

Rolley Lake Provincial Park (Map 3/C3)

Less than an hour's drive from Vancouver, Rolley Lake Provincial Park is a quick escape from urban life. The small, warm water lake provides opportunities for swimming, fishing, and canoeing. For campers, there are popular 64 sites nestled in the trees, just minutes from the lakeshore. There is a trail that circles the lake and leads down to Rolley Falls. Reservations are recommended for camping and a daily parking fee applies.

Roscoe Bay Prov Park (Map 25/D5)

Encompassing a small fjord on West Redonda Island, this is a popular sea kayaking destination. There are rustic tenting sites and it is possible to hike up to Black Lake, which is a great fishing lake.

Sabine Channel Marine Park (Map 8/G4)

Sabine Channel is the channel between Texada and Lasqueti Island. This new park protects a chain of small islands and islets that are popular with kayakers and boaters.

Saltery Bay Provincial Park (Map 17/G6)

This provincial park is found just west of the Saltery Bay Ferry Terminal. There are 42 campsites at the east end of the park. There are also two day-use areas, one adjacent to the camping area, and one 2 km (1 mile) west. There is great scuba diving in Saltery Bay, with the famous Emerald Mermaid, a 3 metre (9 foot) bronze statue at 10 fathoms in front of Mermaid Cove and a disabled access ramp. From the shore, visitors can sometimes see killer whales and sea lions in the distance. Mounds of seashells, called middens, indicate that this was a traditional gathering area for First Nations.

Sargeant Bay Provincial Park (Map 9/E4)

This tiny park is known for its abundance of intertidal and marine life. In fall, this is a great place to watch fish spawning up a fish ladder. In addition to the picnic area and beach next to the sheltered, undeveloped cove, there is a good trail system. One trail leads through a cedar forest to the tidalpools, another trail leads inland past Triangle Lake and the many swamp creatures found there.

Sasquatch Provincial Park (Maps 4\G1, 5/A1, 15/A7)

Sasquatch Provincial Park is located north of Harrison Hot Springs, close to Harrison Lake. There are over 175 camping sites available in three popular campgrounds. The park is home to a series of pocket lakes. Hicks and Deer Lakes are ideal for small motorboats and canoeing while Trout Lake provides a more tranquil fishing experience. Reservations are recommended for camping and a daily parking fee applies.

Sechelt Inlet Provincial Marine Park (Map 9/D2-10/B1, 18/D4)

This park is actually made up of nine different marine access sites scattered throughout Sechelt, Salmon and Narrows Inlets. From south to north to east the sites are: Piper Point, Tuwanek Point, Oyster Bay, Skaiakos Point, Nine Mile Point, Halfway Islet, Kunechin Point, Thornhill and Tzoonie Narrows. The inlets are a popular sea kayaking destination and the HMCS Chaudiere was sunk off Kunechin Point to create a wonderful artificial reef for scuba divers. All of the sites, with the exception of Skaiakos, have some development such as tent pads.

Shannon Falls Provincial Park (Map 11/D1)

Shannon Falls are the third highest falls in the province, at 335 metres (1,089 feet) and are truly an amazing site as they cascade down a steep mountainside. The park offers a small day-use area that allows highway travellers a place to picnic beneath the falls. Many people also explore the trails that lead up and behind Shannon Falls, or to the top of nearby Stawamus Chief. Climbers, looking to get to the top of The Chief by a slightly more direct route, also use the park. A daily parking fee applies.

Silver Lake Provincial Park (Map 5/G1)

Situated in the scenic Fraser Valley, just down the Silver Skagit Road, Silver Lake Provincial Park is a small, largely undeveloped lakefront area 12 km (6.7 miles) southwest of Hope. There is a gravel boat launch and plenty of scenic beauty. This area is renowned for it's fly-fishing. There is a 50-unit campground next to the lake.

Simson Provincial Marine Park (Map 9/C4) ▲ 🖼 🖼 ⚓

South Thormanby Island is a fairly dry island with a rocky shore and number of small bays. Rising above the ocean is Spyglass Hill. This park is accessed by small boat or kayak, as there are no docking facilities. A trail traverses the island starting at Farm Bay, on the southeast corner of the island.

Skagit Valley Recreation Area (Map 6/D6)
🎿 ▲ 🏕 🖼 🚶 🚴 🐎 🛶 🖼 🖼 ⚓ 🏕

The Skagit Valley Provincial Recreation Area is part of a larger protected area complex that includes the US North Cascades National Park and the Ross Lake and Lake Chelan National Recreation Areas. This is a large protected area, at 32,577 ha, in a valley that was carved by glaciers. The valley is an excellent outdoor recreation destination with 50 km (30.5 miles) of trails, great fishing and 131 campsites (between the Silvertip and Ross Lake Campgrounds and the less known Whitworth Meadows Horse Camp). There is also backcountry camping throughout the area, including more developed sites at Delacey Camp, Large Cedar Camp, and Galene Lakes.

Skihist Provincial Park (Map 33/D3)
🎿 🏕 🚶 🖼 🖼 ⚓ 🏕 ♿

Used primarily as a stopover by travellers on the Trans Canada Highway (Hwy 1), there are 56 campsites set back into the ponderosa pine forest above the Fraser River. The park is also a popular base camp for visitors enjoying river rafting, fishing, and exploring the Thompson River area. From the newly established loop trail, there are great views of the Thompson Canyon, and a chance to see mountain goats or elk in the surrounding hills.

Skookumchuck Narrows Provincial Park (Map 18/E7)
🏕 🖼 ⚓ 🏕

Skookumchuck Narrows are an impressive site during tide changes. The water is so constricted that standing waves up to 2 metres (6 feet) high and currents up to 30 km per hour are the result. Several unwary vessels have been lost in the whirlpools, yet you often see extreme kayakers surfing the waves. This 123 ha park is found south of Egmont along an easy 4 km (2.4 mile) trail. Check the tide tables for best viewing times.

Smuggler's Cove Provincial Marine Park (Map 9/C4)
▲ 🚶 🖼 🖼 ⚓ 🛶

The name of the cove comes from rumrunners, who in days gone by used this bay as a staging area for trips down into the US. You can still visit the area by boat or kayak but many people come overland, which requires a 1.3 km (0.8 mile) hike from Brooks Road to the ocean. Along the forested shoreline, you will find five tent pads, and a hiking trail along the shoreline.

South Texada Island Provincial Park (Maps 8/G4, 9/A4)
🚶 🖼 ⚓ ⚓ 🏕

Essentially a boat access park, the shoreline is steep and rocky with few places boaters can land. Visitors can enjoy the fine hiking, kayaking and fishing in the area. A separate parcel of the park is located at Anderson Bay, on the island's southeastern shore. Anderson Bay is a much more protected anchorage for boats.

Spipiyus Provincial Park (Maps 9/E1, 18\D7) 🖼 🏕

Only a tiny bit of the old growth forest remains in this area, but this new provincial park protects the area. The park has many small streams, and some narrow, high waterfalls that few people ever visit. There are no facilities.

Spruce Lake Recreation Area (Maps 43, 44)
▲ 🚶 🚴 🐎 🛶 ⚓ 🏕 🏕

The Spruce Lake area is an outdoor recreationists heaven. It offers world-class hiking and backpacking, horse packing, mountaineering, fishing, cross-country skiing and mountain biking. There are 164 km (100 miles) of wilderness trails in the area, which traverse over gentle mountain passes and meander through lush alpine grasslands and flowers to destination trout lakes. Most of the area remains as

pristine wilderness except at the southern and eastern perimeters where extensive logging is being carried out. The main access points into the area are the Gun Creek Road, Mud Creek-Taylor Creek FSR and the Slim Creek FSR. Or if you prefer, you can always charter a floatplane into Spruce Lake itself.

Squitty Bay Provincial Marine Park (Map 8/G5)
🖼 ⚓ ⚓ 🏕

A rocky point encloses Squitty Bay, a small bay near the southeast tip of Lasqueti Island north of Young Point. This bay can be a welcome refuge from the windy and open waters of Georgia Strait.

Stawamus Chief Provincial Park (Map 11/D1)
🎿 ▲ 🏕 🚶 🏕 🏕

The Chief is Canada's rock climbing mecca. After years of climbers sleeping in their VW Vans in the parking lot, BC parks finally developed an actual campground at the base of The Chief. There are 15 vehicle access sites, and more than twice that in tenting pads. There are trails in the park, leading up and around the backside of the large granite monolith.

Stein Valley Nlaka'pamux Heritage Park (Maps 31, 32, 33, 40, 41) ▲ 🚶 🖼 🖼 ♦ ⚓ 🏕

The Stein Valley area has for centuries had a very special and spiritual meaning to the aboriginal people in this region. This is clearly shown by the many unique pictographs and petroglyphs on the rock faces of the valley. As a result, the valley is protected and the provincial government and the Lytton Indian Band jointly manage the park. It is a spectacular 107,191 ha wilderness park, with 150 km (91.5 miles) of hiking trails, cable crossings, cabins and established backcountry campsites. Although a day hike is possible, most people who visit the area spend a few days. The Stein River is a hardcore white water rafting/kayaking river. These folks hike in from the west side (off Horlick Creek Road), and arrange for a shuttle on the other side.

Teakerne Arm Provincial Park (Map 25/C3)
🚶 🖼 🖼 ⚓ 🏕

A 30-metre high (95 feet) waterfall that cascades from Cassel Lake directly into the ocean is the main feature of this 128 ha park. There is a protected anchorage, and a trail to the warm Cassel Lake, which makes a great wilderness lake to swim in.

Tantalus Provincial Park (Maps 19\G3, 20/B5)
▲ 🚶 🖼 🏕 ♦ 🏕

This new park is built around the former Lake Lovely Water Recreation Area. The 11,351 ha park now includes the Tantalus Range, a popular mountaineering area. Hikers and backcountry skiers frequent the area and the ACC Cabin, which can be reserved, makes the stay that much more enjoyable.

Tetrahedron Provincial Park (Map 10/C2)
🚶 🚴 🖼 🏕 🏕 ⛷ ⛷

Tetrahedron is the largest provincial park on the Sunshine Coast. The park is foot access only and boasts an extensive trail network in addition to some terrific backcountry huts. The area makes a great rock climbing or backcountry skiing destination.

Two Springs Provincial Park (Map 47/A5) 🏕
A new, undeveloped park located just north of Highway 99.

Upper Lillooet Provincial Park (Map 37/C2) 🏕
This remote 19,996 ha park is not accessible by road nor trail. It was developed to protect the old-growth forests, wetlands and high alpine ridges and glaciers around Lillooet River. Salmon spawn in the many tributaries and wildlife such as black-tailed deer, moose, grizzly and black bears, mountain goat and wolverine are abundant.

Walsh Cove Provincial Park (Map 25/C2) ▲ 🖼 ⚓ 🏕
This is a small provincial park found on Walsh Cove on West Redonda Island. The park is rarely visited but offers an undeveloped anchorage with some pictographs on the rock faces.

Multi-Use Trails
(Hiking, biking, ATV's and much more)

The thickly forested Coast Mountains are an outdoor recreation-ists paradise. Trails lead up, down, over and around these rugged mountains. Options range from short interpretive trails to epic treks through places that few people have ever visited. Many of the trails are destination oriented, leading to fishing lakes, mountain vistas, waterfalls and more. Because the mountains, for the most part, start at or near sea level, much of the hiking happens through lush rain-forest. It is a testament to the serious height of these mountains that so many of them break out into sub-alpine and alpine territory. The farther away from the Coast and Fraser Valley you get, the higher your starting point and the easier it is to break out of the trees.

Higher elevation trails and routes (over 1,000 metres/3,000 feet) may have a limited season due to late season snow. Trail users should leave these trails for late summer and early fall (July until October). If you are travelling on unmarked trails, we recommend that you have mountaineering knowledge and are equipped with a topographic map and a compass. A GPS could also be invaluable to help mark the trail you have taken.

Finding the trailhead is sometimes the toughest part of the adventure. Refer to the appropriate map in this book to determine where the trail begins. In urban and rural areas, trails often start off small side roads, too small to mark on our maps. In these areas you might want to have a city map on hand to help locate the trailhead.

To help you select the trail that best suites your abilities, we have included information on elevation gain, return distance and special features wherever possible. Also included in each description is a symbol to indicate what the trail is used for—hiking, mountain biking, horseback riding, ATV, etc. Unless otherwise noted, distances and times are for round trip hikes.

Despite the wealth of trails listed below, it still only represents a fraction of the outdoor opportunities for adventurers, who can follow old game trails, or logging roads to places that few people know about. If you are planning on getting off the beaten path, be careful. The Coast Range is very rugged terrain, and each year people die because they underestimate the land.

For Your Information

Trails are usually tagged with one of the following descriptors: An **easy** trail has gentle grades, and is suitable for family excursions. A **moderate** trail can involve a long, steep hill, some technical sections (roots, boulders, etc.), and is probably enough to tax most users. Just because they're not considered difficult, doesn't mean that they aren't challenging. Don't overestimate your ability, or underestimate the dif-ficulty of the trail. Only experienced trail users should consider **difficult** trails or routes. These trails are often rough and/or unmarked.

Trails are grouped into the following categories:

- Greater Vancouver/Fraser Valley - Hope/Fraser Canyon

- Island Trails - Lillooet/Goldbridge - Manning Park

- North Shore/Howe Sound - Powell River - Squamish

- Sunshine Coast - Whister/Pemberton

Please Note: Our maps are designed only as a general access guide and are not intended to navigate you through a hidden mountain pass or across an expansive ridge network.

Greater Vancouver / Fraser Valley Trails

Vancouver is world renowned for its natural beauty. The dynamic trail systems in the region allow visitors and locals to get upclose and personal with this beautiful part of the province. For other options be sure to visit our Regional and City Parks section found earlier in the book.

Agassiz Trails (Map 4/G2) 🚶 🚴 ℹ️

The Agassiz Dykes provide a series of gated access roads that run along the Fraser River to the south of Agassiz. These routes can be accessed off of Highway 7 below Mount Woodside, south of Maria Slough or from several of the intersecting rural roads. These peaceful trails are bordered by farmland and offer views along the Fraser River.

Also in the area, is Green Mountain, a moderate series of mountain biking trails found off the Agassiz bypass, just north of the railway tracks (on the west side). A tough climb takes you 455 metres (1,479 feet) up the access road to the network of trails at the top of Green Mountain. The access road eventually turns into a single-track trail and will take you down to the farmer's field on the other side. You can ride back up or return to the start along the Highway.

BC Parkway (Map 1/D1-G3) 🚶 🚴

A 40 km (25 mile) recreation corridor, stretching from False Creek in Vancouver to Westminster Quay in New Westminster, the BC Parkway follows the Skytrain corridor for the most part. In most places, there are two sets of trails, a paved cycling path and a gravel walking path, although nobody really pays attention to this distinction. This is an urban trail, rarely removed from the hustle and bustle of the city.

Bear Lake Trail (Map 4/G1-5/A1) 🚶 🚴 🏇 🚴 🐟 ℹ️

Follow a series of old logging roads up Bear Mountain to Bear Lake. The trip is 24 km return to the tiny lake tucked in a pretty valley.

Belcarra Regional Park Trails (Map 2/A1) 🚶 ℹ️

Accessed by the Bedwell Bay Road off loco Road, this regional park encompasses Bedwell Bay and Burns Point, which juts out into Indian Arm. A 5.5 km (2 hour) round trip follows the shoreline past Burns Point to Jug Island. There is a pleasant secluded bay at the end of the trail. Views of Mount Seymour and Second Narrows Bridge are provided along the trail. Another pleasant walk circles around Sasamat Lake. This easy, one-hour hike offers a cool, refreshing stroll through the heavy forest around the lake. Other trails include the 5 km (3 mile) Admiralty Point Trail and the 7 km (4.1 mile) Cod Rock Trail.

Blue Mountain Trails (Map 3/A2)

Unfortunately access into this fine off-road network has been closed (the main access road is gated and is signed as a private property.

Boundary Bay Dyke Trail (Maps 1/E7–2/A6) 🚶 🚴

This dyke trail starts from 17A Ave in Tsawwassen and skirts Boundary Bay all the way to the southern railway tracks (junction of Highway 99 & 91) in Surrey. Along the 25 km (15.3 mile) route, you pass Boundary Bay Airport, Delta Air Park and several access points, which can shorten the route.

Bridal Trails (Map 4/G1) 🚶 🚴 🏇

Just east of Harrison Hot Springs, a pair of easy trails can be explored. The **Bridal Trail** is 3.5 km (2.1 mile) and marked with green markers, while the **Mount Streetsidehill Trail** is 4 km (2.4 mile) and marked with Red Markers.

Buntzen Lake Trails (Map 2/A1–12/A7) ⛵ 🚶 🚴 🏇 🏕

Lake Beautiful, as it was originally known, is a popular recreation area that is easily accessed by Sunnyside Road to the north of Port Moody. Within the forest next to Buntzen Lake are a series of multi-use trails that range from gentle family strolls to difficult hikes. Most of these trails interconnect, meaning you can create your own adventure. An on site map will help you pick your route.

Academy Trail: This is mostly a horse trail, although it sees a fair number of pedestrians as well. The trail leads from the Alpine Riding Academy at the park entrance all the way to the north end of Buntzen Lake. About halfway along it joins up with the Pumphouse Road. The trail is 10 km/6 miles (2 hours) return with minimal elevation gain.

Buntzen Lake Trail: This popular route is an 8 km/4.8 mile (3 hour) route that circles Buntzen Lake. The best place to start is the South Beach Picnic Area, and hike in a counterclockwise direction around the lake. At the north end there is suspension bridge, while at the south end there is a floating bridge to cross. This is an easy, well-maintained trail with minimal elevation gain.

Diez Vista Trail: This is a moderate 14 km/8.5 mile (5 hour) return hike with 455 metres (1,479 feet) elevation gain. The trail goes up and down a lot, and is quite steep and challenging in places. Ultimately, you reach the summit at 600 metres (1,950 feet) and will be rewarded with an excellent view of Indian Arm and Buntzen Lake. Or rather, with a series of views, as the name means "ten lookout trail." Although the trail leads from the Pumphouse Road to the north end of the lake, it is recommended to do this trail north to south.

Dilly-Dally Trail: You can't Dilly-Dally if you expect to finish this trail in a day. It is a long, steep, difficult 25 km/15.2 miles (10+ hour) trail leading from the South Beach Parking Lot gaining 1,100 metres (3,575 feet) to the summit of Dilly-Dally Peak. From the summit, you can continue south on to Eagle Peak by following the ridge. The trail is best tackled in July to October.

Eagle Peak Trails: A steep, difficult 15 km/9.1 miles (6 hour) hike, which leads past Eagle Mountain to Lindsay Lake. The 1,020 metres (3,315 feet) in elevation gain is a small payment for the amazing view. From tiny Lindsay Lake, you can continue on to Eagle Peak, which is another 5 km (3.1 miles) return. An alternative route is to traverse down the slope to the north end of Buntzen Lake. The difficult hike is accessed off the gated Powerline Road.

Halvor Lunden (Eagle Ridge) Trail: Call this a route, instead of a trail, as it incorporates parts of the Lindsay Lake Loop, Swan Falls Loop and Dilly Dally. It deserves mention because Halvor Lunden is the father of trail building in the Lower Mainland, and he built a number of classic trails (High Falls, Deeks Bluffs, Three Chop) in this book. This route takes you up the ridge and past ten tiny lakes. How far you walk depends on how you string the trails together.

Lakeview Trail: This rough, steep, 5.8 km/3.5 mile (2 hour) trail extends along the eastern slopes of Buntzen Ridge on the west side of Buntzen Lake. The hiking/biking/equestrian trail is accessed just north of the Pumphouse Road from the south or from the suspension bridge at the north end of the lake.

Lindsay Lake Loop: The trail to Lindsay Lake gains 1,020 metres (3,315 feet) as it makes a 15 km (9.1 mile) loop to Lindsay Lake, as well as to several viewpoints over Vancouver. Take a left at El Paso Junction and up to the small lake. This is where the loop begins and ends.

Nature & Energy Trails: Two short, 1 km (0.6 mile) trails that circle a wooded knoll south of the boat launch. The Nature Trail is a self-guided trail that follows the shores of Buntzen Lake before leading through a forested area to the South Beach Picnic Area. The Energy Trail is another short loop trail with attractive views of Buntzen Lake.

Swan Falls Loop: A difficult 20 km (12.2 mile) loop gaining 1,150 metres (3,738 feet) up through the so-called lakes district (home to ten tarns) of Eagles Ridge. The route continues on to Eagle Peak (Mount Beautiful), then down to Swan Falls and the Powerhouse Road.

Burke Mountain Trails (Map 2/D1) 🚶 🚴 🏕

Located at the south end of the new Pinecone Burke Provincial Park, most of the trails are reached by the parking lot near the entrance to the Gun Club off Harper Road.

Burke Ridge Trail: The Burke Ridge trail begins on the gated old road before breaking off onto a well-marked trail, which climbs steadily uphill to the ridge. The trail is 20 km/12.4 miles (8 hours) return gaining 880 metres (2,860 feet) to the 1,225 metre (3,981 foot) ridge. From the top, you can see into the rarely seen Coquitlam Watershed, as well as the surrounding area.

Coquitlam Lake View Trail: This is a 9.4 km/5.7 mile (5 hour) hike gaining 200 metres (650 feet).

Galloway Trail: Part of the Burke Mountain maze of trails, the Galloway has the distinction of being one of the best intermediate rides in the area. Which is saying a lot, as most trails around here are either über-hardcore or ultra-easy. This 12 km (7.5 mile) trail is a fast, fun ride with some technical sections.

Munroe-Dennett Loop (see below):

Sawblade: This is the most popular (but misused) mountain biking trail in the area. The trail starts north (left) from the main road. This 11.5 km (7 mile) trail features a difficult crank up 400 metres (1,300 feet) and eventually meets up with the Coquitlam River Trail. An easier option is to continue along the main road past the second gate and follow the trail heading south.

South Slope Trail: This is an 18km/11 mile (6-7 hour) trail climbing 880 metres (2,860 feet).

Triple Crown: This is a great moderate ride, which combines three shorter trails into an epic 15 km (9.1 mile) journey, climbing 550 metres (1,787 feet). The trail ultimately takes you down to Galloway Road (south of Harper Road).

Village Lake Trail: A 15 km/9.1 mile (7 hour) hike gaining 680 metres (2,210 feet). Mountain bikers should expect difficult, rocky trails and a lot of climbing.

CENTRAL VALLEY GREENWAY

Although not yet a reality, Better Environmentally Sound Transportation (BEST) are working hard to create the Central Valley Greenway. The greenway will stretch along a relatively flat, direct route through Vancouver, Burnaby, New Westminster and finally Coquitlam. The trail will be open to hikers, bikers, wheelchairs and rollerblades. When finished, the 25 km long recreation corridor will link Science World on Vancouver's False Creek with the confluence of the Brunette and Fraser Rivers in New Westminster. But the completion date for the Central Valley Greenway is set for 2004, although the folks at BEST are optimistic that the corridor will be moderately functional this year. For more information on the proposed greenway, as well as current maps of the route, visit the BEST website at www.best.bc.ca.

Woodland Walk: An easy trail that bisects the second growth forest at the base of Burke Ridge. This trail, with little elevation gain (200 metre/650 feet), is 7 km/4.3 miles (3 hours) taking you past some spectacular waterfalls, over a moss covered bridge and through remnants of logging from the turn of the century.

Burnaby Lake Regional Park (Maps 1/G2, 2\A3) 🚶 🐎 👫

You can explore the shores of Burnaby Lake along the 19 km (11.6 miles) of trails that surround the lake. There is an extra 4 km (2.4 miles) of horse trails, but these run close to the freeway and are not the most pleasant to walk on. It is possible to stitch the Cottonwood Trail, the Pavilion Trail, the Southshore Trail, the Avlon Trail and the Brunette Headwaters Trail together to circumnavigate the lake.

Burnaby Mountain Area (Map 2/A1) 🚶 🚲 🐎 👫

The west side of the mountain is now part of an ecological reserve and, outside of the Trans Canada Trail, the trails are only open to hiking. The more popular east side trails are now officially designated as multi-use trails, much to the pleasure of local mountain bikers. Although the trails on top do offer the odd vantage point, most of the trails cut through a thickly forested area. You can access these trails from the SFU Campus, Gaglardi Way or North Road.

Burns Bog (Delta Nature Reserve) (Maps 1, 2/G5) 🚶 🚲

A trio of easy looping trails, ranging from a few hundred metres to 1.3 km (0.9 miles) in length, lead through the ancient Burns Bog. The main trail is a gated service road that can be used by cyclists to join up with the Delta Watershed Trails (see below). From this road, the loop trails take you through the unique fauna and eerie woods of the nature area. Although boardwalks are being added, be prepared for wet trail conditions, especially in winter. Access is from the parking lot of Great Pacific Forum off Nordel Way or from River Road in Delta.

Burrard Thermal Trails (Map 2/A1) 🚶 🚲 🏍 👫

This is a popular mountain biking area. In winter, this area is well drained, and usually doesn't see snow; therefore, bikers tend to flock here when the mountain trails are not rideable. The trail network starts near White Pine Beach at Sasamat Lake. Most of the biking trails are accessed off the 3 km (1.8 mile) BC Hydro access road, which climbs a bit, then descends 165 m towards Bedwell Bay. Hikers will enjoy this short, easy trail, with its views over Burrard Inlet, but mountain bikers tend to get off the main road and onto the more challenging motor bike trails, which range from moderate to extreme.

Campbell Lake Trail (Map 4/F1) 🚶 👫

The Campbell Lake Trail is a rugged trail that climbs from the sign on Highway 9 across from Balsam Ave., south of Harrison Hot Springs, to a remote mountain lake. The average grade of the trail is a steep 16%, climbing 630 metres (2,047 feet) over 4.8 km (2.9 miles). Expect to take about three hours to the lake, with good viewpoints of the Harrison Lake and the Cheam Range along the way. It is possible to arrange for a pick up at the top, via the rough 4wd Mount Woodside FSR.

Caswell (Red Mountain) Trail (Map 3/C4) 🚶 🚲

This is a 9.8 km/6 mile loop, climbing 310 metres (1,007 feet). This trail heads west from the Mill Pond and combines old roads with single-track trails.

Centennial Trail (Maps 3-6) 🚶 🚲

At the time it was built back in the mid 1960s, the Centennial Trail was one of the most ambitious trail building projects in BC. These days, the trail has fallen out of favour, and most of the really interesting sections have been incorporated into other trails, including the most recent mega-trail project, the Trans Canada Trail. Technically, the Centennial Trail extends 420 km (256.2 miles) from The Plaza of Nations in Vancouver to Joe Lake near Keremeos, but in truth, the only sections that still survives on it's own is the section from Chilliwack Lake (Map 5/C3) to the Skyline Trail in Manning Park (Map 6/D4), although some sections are seriously overgrown.

Cheam Peak Trail (Map 5/A4) 🚶 🚲 👫

Found at the end of the rough (lots of cross ditching) Chilliwack-Chipmunk FSR, the Mount Cheam Trail is a beautiful alpine hike. You climb 632 metres (2,054 feet) over 9.5 km/5.8 miles (4 hours). The sheer peak offers amazing views of the Fraser Valley. Along the way you'll pass Spoon Lake, rolling sub-alpine meadows dotted with wildflowers in July-August and a steep trail down to Bridal Falls. The trail is best hiked from July to September since the area is prone to avalanches in the winter. You can also hike up from Bridal Falls along a forest service road (parts are still active) but this trail is 30 km/18 miles (at least a day) and climbs 2,080 metres (6,760 feet) to the top. This latter route misses the meadows but is good for cyclists, although you'll probably want to do the last section on foot.

Cheam Wetlands (Map 4/G3) 🚶 👫

It was only a few years back that Cheam Lake had been drained to harvest lime. Now, an easy network of trails (totaling about 6 km/3.7 miles) meanders around the eastern edge of Cheam Lake. The highlight here is the abundance of waterfowl and small animals.

Coquitlam River Trail (Map 2/C3–C1) 🚶 🚲 👫

This scenic river trail makes up a good portion of the historic PoCo Trail. From the Mary Hill Bypass to the Orr Creek Falls this trail stretches 13.5 km (8.2 miles) along the Coquitlam River. In fall, spawning salmon can be seen in the waterway. Several roads (Pitt River Road, Lougheed Highway, Shaughnessy Road) provide alternate access points. All levels of mountain bikers and hikers can enjoy this gentle trail. Beyond the falls, the trail narrows and gets more difficult as it climbs to meet up with the Burke Mountain Trails.

Cresent Beach (Map 2/A7) 🚶 👫

An extremely popular 4 km (2.4 mile) oceanfront walk. This trail system follows a wide, packed trail along the waterfront.

Davis Lake Park (Map 3/F1) 🚶 🐟

Reached by the Lost Creek FSR off Sylvester Road, this small provincial park offers a 5 km/3.1 mile (1.5 hour) easy, flat walk which circles the pretty lake.

Delta Millennium Trail (Map 1/F5) 🚶 🚲 👫

This trail was built to link an existing hiking/biking trail in Ladner with the Deas Island Trails. Eventually, there will be a bridge over Green Slough, which will link Vasey Road and Deas Island.

Delta Watershed (Map 2/A5) 🚶 🚲 🐎

The watershed has certainly seen some development over the last few years. While the city has been developing the trails and making them more appealing to walkers and horseback riders, creative cyclists have been constructing some impressive structures that rival those found on the famed North Shore. The watershed remains one of the most popular mountain biking destinations in the Lower Mainland. It is one of those great riding areas that has easy access and can be enjoyed by all levels of cyclists. There are several access points including 64th Ave to the north and Highway 10 to the south. As a rule of thumb, the trails to the north of the service road are short and follow well developed trails. To the south, less developed trails offer more of a challenge.

Denham's Trail (Map 14/E7) 🚶 🐟

From the Weaver Lake Recreation Site, a 6.2 km (3.8 mile) trail loops around this picturesque fishing lake. Relatively flat, the trail makes for an easy three-hour hike with a number of side trails from which to access the lake.

Elk-Thurston Trail (Map 4/G5) 🚶 👫

A grueling 14.6 km/8.9 miles (7 hour) hike starts on the Chilliwack Bench FSR at a small gravel pit. You climb over 1,000 metres/3,250 feet (mostly at the beginning) to the summit of Mount Thurston and breathtaking panoramic views of the Chilliwack Valley and the border peaks. The trail begins in a forested setting before entering the wildflower carpeted sub-alpine meadows near the base of Elk Mountain. The trail then continues to Mount Thurston through the meadows then onto an exposed ridge, which can be windy.

Flora Lake Trail (Map 5/F5)

It is only a 7 km hike to the lake, but because of the stiff climb and rugged trail, it is best done as a two-day trip. The trail climbs 1,130 metres (3,672 feet) in elevation to the ridge before dropping 430 metres (1,397 feet) to the beautiful lake. This is a difficult hike, with two very steep sections, but your reward is breathtaking views of the Chilliwack Valley, old mining trails around the lake and fairly good fishing. It is possible to follow a rough, undeveloped trail past the Flora Creek Falls to Greendrop Lake.

Fool's Gold Route (Map 12/C7-B1)

Heavy lobbying for conservation of the extensive untouched forest to the west of Pitt Lake resulted in the creation of the Pinecone Burke Provincial Park. Within the park is the rugged and difficult to follow Fool's Gold Route. The route runs some 50 km (30.5 miles) and will take most backpackers at least a week to complete. While there are popular day/overnight hikes from both trailheads, only a very few have ever done this route from tip to tail. This route is an excellent choice if you desire a challenging, remote wilderness experience. It is best left to experienced backpackers equipped with compasses, topographic maps and mountaineering knowledge.

From south to north, the route follows the Widgeon Lake Trail, from Widgeon Creek. Rather than branching left to the lake, the Fools Gold Route continues along an old road and trail to Pitt Pass. From here on, the route involves a lot of bushwhacking and route finding skills are absolutely necessary. After reaching the pass at 720 metres (2,340 feet), the route descends into the DeBeck Creek drainage, which offers some of the nicest, untouched sub-alpine forests around. Eventually, you will pass through Bull Pass at 1,060 metres (3,445 feet) on your way to the Cedar Spirit Grove, a stand of 1000-year-old cedar trees. From here, the route leads to the west and becomes easier to follow. It is even marked by pink flagging. The trail culminates on a spur road off the Mamquam River FSR.

Ford Mountain Trail (Map 5/C5)

From the sign at the end of the Ford Mountain FSR (4wd access), a short 1.7 km/1 mile (1.5 hour) one-way hike follows the treed ridge to an old forestry lookout with panoramic views. The moderate trail leads sharply uphill for the first 30 minutes before easing up. The trail gains 400 metres (1,300 feet) in elevation. Experienced hikers can continue along the bare ridge to the base of Williams Peak, which adds an additional 6 km/3.6 miles (2 hours), climbing 460 metres (1,495 feet) along the way. If you do not have a 4wd vehicle, it is possible to hike the road but this requires an additional climb of 620 metres (2,015 feet) over 4.5 km/2.7 miles (2.5 hours) one-way.

Golden Ears Provincial Park Trails (Maps 2, 3, 12, 13)

The most prominent peak in this park are actually the peaks of the Blanshard Needle, which are often mistaken as the Golden Ears. They're not. The twin knolls of Golden Ears are farther north, and are not as noticeable as the needle. There are a number of trails in this wilderness park, some multi-use, some hiking only. The highlights include an abundance of wildlife and the scenic Alouette Lake.

Alouette Mountain Trail: This difficult 22 km/13.4 mile (9 hour) return trip climbs 1,100 metres (3,575 feet) to the summit. Along the way, you will pass some scenic meadows and ponds. There are a couple variations on how to start this trail, either along the Incline Trail, Mike Lake Trail, or the old fire access road. The latter is the easiest (but longest), and is open to mountain bikers and equestrians, who are able to follow the fire access road to the hitching post at Lake Beautiful.

East Canyon Trail: This rocky, 11 km (6.7 mile) trail follows the banks of Gold Creek north to the Lower Falls. This trail is open to mountain bikers but expect a difficult trail with rough sections and a 320 metre (1,040 feet) elevation gain. Past here, the Hector Ferguson Trail continues deep into the heart of the park.

Golden Ears Trail: This popular 24 km/14.6 mile (10 hour/overnight) trip gains 1,500 metres (4,875 feet) to the popular peak. The hike begins at the West Canyon Parking Lot and follows Gold Creek and the West Canyon Trail to Alder Flats. Most people heading for the peak set up camp here and hike the remaining distance to the peak without a pack. This is a good idea, as most of the elevation gain happens in the last few kilometres. At this point, the trail heads steeply up the ridge past a rustic mountain shelter to the summit of Panorama Ridge. You will break out of the trees, and into the high, rocky alpine. Enjoy the views of Pitt Lake and the surrounding area as you climb to the top.

Hector Ferguson Trail: A 22 km (13.4 mile) hike along the east side of Gold Creek. The trail leads to a tiny lake that forms the headwaters of the creek, deep in the heart of Golden Ears. This is the farthest north you can hike into the park by land (there are a couple lake access routes that head farther in). Expect to take at least a day to get to the lake and back.

Mike Lake Trail: An easy 8 km/4.9 mile (2-3 hour) hike gaining 100 metres (325 feet) from the trailhead on Fern Crescent.

Menzies Trail: An easy 18 km/11 mile (5–6 hour) return hike leading from the Fern Crescent Trailhead to the West Canyon parking lot. Horseback riders frequent this trail.

West Canyon Trail: Beginning at the West Canyon parking lot, this trail heads north, following the western banks of Gold Creek. A bridge over the creek at Lower Falls allows you to cross the creek and head down the East Canyon Trail back to the parking lot. This makes for a nice 9 km/ 5.5 mile (3 hour) return hike with minimal elevation gain.

Hanging Lake Trail (Map 5/F7)

This is a moderate 8 km/4.9 mile (4 hour) round trip hike to a gorgeous lake, at the base of Mount Lindeman. Hanging Lake provides good fishing and Lindeman is a fine rock-climbing destination.

Harrison Lookout Trail (Map 14/E5)

Located off the Harrison West FSR, this short but steep 4 km/2.4 miles (one hour) trail leads to an old forest service lookout on a hill above Harrison Lake. You hike along an old road to a beautifully wooded trail past mossy knolls to the vantage point from the lookout some 350 metres (1,138 feet) later. The panoramic views of Harrison Lake and the Chehalis Mountains can be rewarding on clear days.

Hayward Lake Trails (Map 3/C3)

The Pond Interpretative Trail: A short easy stroll around a small beaver pond. The 1.5 km/0.9 mile walk takes you about 30 minutes to complete. There are educational signs displaying different stages

of the forest canopy's life cycle. The trails have little elevation gain and can be hiked or biked year-round.

The Railway Trail: This trail can be accessed either near Ruskin Dam from Wilson Road or off of the parking lot just south of the Dewdney Trunk Road. This easy trail leads 12 km (7.3 miles) return along an old rail bed, which was used in the early part of the century while building Stave Falls Dam. The trail can be quite muddy at times and is set through a forest offering a view of the lake. This trail should take hikers about three hours.

The Reservoir Trail: A new 9 km (5.5 mile) hiking trail that follows the east shores of the reservoir over very fragile soils. Along this trail there are spectacular views of Steelhead Falls, a floating bridge over the Hairsine Inlet, old growth and second growth forests, picnic benches and tables, numerous bridge crossings over small creeks, and interpretive information signs.

Hoover Lake Trail (Map 3/D2)

Give yourself about an hour to reach the lake as you hike through a heavy forest, east of Stave Falls Dam. This trail starts out along an old road, then a trail as it climbs steadily to the lake. The trail is 7.4 km (4.5 miles) return with an elevation gain of 250 metres (812 feet).

International Ridge Trail (Map 4/D7)

Accessed off Vance Road within the International Ridge Provincial Park, this 18 km (11 mile) ridge route leads to the 1,525 metre (4,956 foot) high summit of Mount Amadis. You will climb 1,325 metres (4,306 feet) over about 8 hours. From the summit, you get a good view of the Fraser Valley and over the border into Washington State.

Ling Lake Trail (Map 5/D3)

The trailhead for the Ling Lake Trail is found at the end of Foley Creek Road. Unfortunately, there is a gate located near the Foley Creek Rec Site so you will have to hike or bike up the logging road before actually starting the trail. From the gate, the trail is about 18 km/11 miles (give yourself at least a day) to the alpine lake. The principle users of the trail are fishermen.

Liumchen Lake Trail (Map 4/E7)

This is a beautiful alpine hike that starts at the end of the very rough Liumchen East FSR (about 9.5 km/5.8 miles along this 4wd road). From the trailhead you climb sharply uphill, through a mix of forest and meadows to a ridge, which offers great views of the Chilliwack Valley. From the ridge, the trail drops 280 metres (910 feet) into the lovely Liumchen Lake bowl. It will take about five hours to hike 9.4 km (5.7 miles) return, but if you're in the area already, why not set up camp at the lake and spend a day or two exploring the trails to the surrounding peaks. Church Mountain is an additional 1.5 km (0.9 miles) along the ridge. Liumchen Mountain is south from the alpine meadows. You will climb 457 metres (1,485 feet) over 2.5 km (1.5 miles) one-way to this great vantage point that overlooks Washington State. The hike is best done in late summer (for the flowers) or in early autumn.

Matsqui Trail (Map 3/D5–F5)

Since this dyke system is part of the Trans Canada Trail, you can virtually walk, bike or horseback ride as long as you like. Most visitors start from the picnic area in this popular Regional Park (found at the end of Riverside Road below the Mission Bridge), and walk towards the Page Road trailhead. This portion of the dyke is about 17 km (10.4 miles) return and offers several vantage points of the Fraser River.

Minnekhada Park Trails (Map 2/E1)

This regional park is located on Quarry Road northeast of Port Coquitlam. Within the park, there are 12 km (7.3 miles) of interconnecting trails through a thick canopy of second growth forest. All the trails are well maintained with little elevation gain. The main trail leads from the large parking lot on the west side of the park past a marshy lake to a picnic site. Eventually, you reach a viewpoint overlooking the Addington Marsh next to Pitt River. Another trail circles the perimeter of the park in a clockwise

direction. This trail leads the hiker through some wet, boggy sections, and several brooks. A further option is to cross the floating bridge in the middle of the marshy lake and head west to the viewpoint. If you are interested in a dyke walk, then take Oliver Drive off the Quarry Road and park at a convenient point after the gates. From there, you can explore the Addington Marsh for a return distance of up to 14 km (5 hours).

Mount Crickmer Trail (Map 3/C1)

From the Florence Lake FSR, the difficult 20 km/12.2 mile (8 hour) hike follows an old gated road, and then a trail to the top of Mount Crickmer. The route gains 1,190 metres (3,867 feet) as you cross several gullies and creeks on your way to the open meadows below the rocky summit. From the top, there are fantastic views of Stave Lake, Mount Blanshard and Mount Robbie Reid to the north.

Mount Klaudt Trail (Map 14/D7)

Mount Klaudt is one of the two mountains that frame Hemlock Valley. In summer, a trail climbs to the saddle below Mount Klaudt, before switchbacking its way up to a viewpoint over Harrison Lake. This moderate trail is 11.5 km (7 miles) return. While it doesn't climb to the top, it gets close enough.

Mount Laughington Trail (Map 5/B5)

The spur road from the Chilliwack-Foley FSR leading to the base of Mount Laughington is usually gated. This makes the hike fairly strenuous 19 km/11.6 miles (8 hours) to the summit, gaining 1,340 metres (4,355 feet) in elevation along the way. If the road is not gated, then the hike is reduced to 5 km/3.1 miles (3 hours) return, gaining 200m (650 feet).

Mount Slesse Memorial Trail (Map 5/C7)

This trail climbs about 300 metres (1,000 feet) along the old Nesakwatch Creek FSR to a monument built to acknowledge a plane crash. The hike takes about 1.5 hours and has spectacular views of the mountains all around. Please respect the memorial site and do not pick up any debris of the plane crash. Beyond the monument, where the road forks, a trail to the right leads to an old glacier bed. From the old logging landing, turn left uphill through the blueberry bushes to a ridge and then follow the trail and ribbons to the old glacier. A propeller in a crevasse indicates the end of the hike, but mountain climbers can continue from this point. The trail has been officially sponsored by the Valley Outdoor Association, who has also flagged the beginning of the trail to Mount Rexford.

Mount St Benedict Trail (Map 3/C1)

The trail leads from the Davis Lake Provincial Park and is 15 km (7 hours) return gaining 1,000 metres (3,250 feet) to the summit. The hike involves traversing a mixture of old road and trails along Mundro Creek past tiny McKay Lake to the summit. Good views of Mount Judge Howay and Robbie Reid are offered from the top, but the hike up is unremarkable (unless you like clear cuts). Snow limits the hiking season to July through October.

Munro-Dennett Lake Trail (Map 2/E1-12/E7)

From the signed trailhead on Quarry Road, the hike begins along an old road for a few hundred metres before the trail climbs relentlessly straight up the hillside through a thick, mature Douglas-fir forest. Eventually, the trail levels as you approach the beautiful marshy area around Munro Lake. Since Dennett Lake requires another short but steep grunt up an ill-defined trail, many people stop at Munro Lake. To Dennett, the hike is 10 km (6 hours) return gaining 860m but route finders can join up with the Burke Ridge Trail (see above). Due to snow and wet trail conditions (on top), this hike is best left until late June through October.

Nicomen Island (Maps 3/G5, 4\A4)

Nicomen is a quiet little island that has a 5 km (3 mile) scenic riverside dyke trail. From December to February, Bald Eagles are common in the area.

Pacific Spirit Park (UBC Endowment Lands) (Map 1/A2) 👣 🚵 🐎

This large urban park offers an enjoyable place to walk, jog, horseback ride or mountain bike. There are over 90 km (54.9 miles) of trails in the park, of which 60 km (36.6 miles) are open to mountain bikers and horseback riders. Please obey the signs. With easy access from a variety of locations (4th Avenue, 16th Avenue or SW Marine Drive), these trails are popular year round as they dissect the lush vegetation and old growth forests of Pacific Spirit Park. Mountain bikers will find the trails north of 4th Avenue more challenging.

Pierce Lake/Mt McFarlane Trail (Map 5/B7) ⛺ 👣 🐟 ⛑

A rough, steep trail climbs steadily from the Pierce Creek Recreation Site to the south end of Mt McFarlane. It begins by rising sharply through a second growth forest before breaking out onto a scree slope. From here, the trail crosses Pierce Creek and begins to deteriorate before reaching the lake. On the way, you will pass two lakes, alpine meadows and some spectacular viewpoints. Plan on doing this difficult trail as an overnight trip since you climb 1,780 metres (5,785 feet) on this 7 km (4.3 mile) one-way trail. If you don't want to commit to an overnight trip, a good destination is Pierce Lake, which is a good fishing lake. Pierce Lake is only a 4.3 km/2.6 mile (3 hour) one-way hike, although you will still climb 1,080 metres (3,510 feet).

Pioneer (Bear Mountain) Trail (Map 3/E3) 👣 🚵 ⛑

Found to the east of the Dewdney Trunk Road, are a series of trails that are best accessed from Saunders Road (off Richards Ave.) to the south. **Saunders Trail** is a short interpretive 0.6 km (0.3 miles) trail at the foot of Bear Mountain. The **Pioneer Trail** follows an old forestry road to the top of the hill, where the Bear Mountain Challenge Downhill Mountain Bike Race is held. From the top, you descend along single-track to the Mill Pond, some 3.2 km (2 miles) later. Also in the area is the Carral Loop.

Pitt Polder Wildlife Area (Map 12/G7-2/F1) 👣 🚵 🐎 ⛑

The extensive dyke network begins at the end of Rannie Road in Grant Narrows Park. The dykes are flat, wide cart paths perfect for mountain biking, horseback riding and hiking. The distance of the route really depends on how far you want to travel, as there are 20 km (12.2 miles) of interconnected dykes and side trails in the area. Waterfowl is abundant in the marshy wetland.

Pitt River Dyke Trail (Map 2/D2) 👣 🚵 🐎 ⛑

As part of the Trans Canada Trail and the historic PoCo Trail, this series of interconnected dyke trails has seen some recent improvements. Still sections remain overgrown, mostly with nasty brambles. The main dyke trail runs from the end of Kingsway north to the Debouville Slough Lookout Trail in Port Coquitlam. This is an 11 km (6.7 mile) trip, and leads to a wildlife viewing tower. Beyond the tower, the trail hooks up with other trails in Minnekhada Park.

Point Grey Foreshore (Map 1/A2) 👣 ⛑

This is a great place for a hike on a blustery day. The land and ocean have a character that is one part tempest, one part romance. Even better, the beaches, which are usually crawling with people, are yours and yours alone. There are places along here that—if it wasn't for West Vancouver across the water—you could almost fool yourself into thinking you were hundreds of miles away from the nearest human. Access can be found from the steep trail down to Wreck Beach (the famous nude beach) along SW Marine Drive at gate 3 in UBC.

Post-Greendrop Trail (Map 5/E5) ⛺ 👣 🐟

The popular trail starts at the Post Creek Recreation Site and climbs 370 metres (1,202 feet) over 5.2 km to the south end of Greendrop Lake, taking you past Lindeman Lake. This moderate trail leads along the steep valley that has some rough rocky sections. There is rustic camping at Greendrop Lake and good fishing in both lakes. The Centennial Trail continues along a logging road, but most people just spend the night at Greendrop Lake, then return. For the more adventurous, an unmarked route runs northeast to Flora Lake.

Radium Lake Trail (Map 5/E7) ⛺ 👣 📷 🐟 ⛑

From the end of Paulsen Road, a suspension bridge crosses the Chilliwack River to the start of this moderate trail. The climb is steady as you gain 880 metres (2,860 feet) over this 12 km/7.3 mile (6 hour) return trek. Tiny Radium Lake is nestled below two towering peaks and is home to a forestry cabin that can be used as a base to explore nearby peaks. The routes to MacDonald Peak or Mount Webb should only be explored by experienced hikers/scramblers.

Richmond Dyke Trails (Map 1/C5) 👣 🚵 ⛑

This is an extremely popular place for hikers, bikers, joggers, and families looking for an easy walk together. The gravel trails are broad and exposed to the ocean breeze. The open flats along the dyke are a great place to watch the sun set. The most popular section is the West Dyke Path, which runs 10 km (6 miles) from north of Westminster Highway to Steveston. The wide gravel path takes you past radio receivers as you peer out on the Straight of Georgia, and there are a couple of really nice fish and chip shops at the end of the trail. The South Dyke is found between Gilbert Road and No. 5 Road.

Roberts Bank Dyke Trail (Map 1/C7) 👣 🚵 ⛑

This 9.5 km (5.8 miles) dyke trail leads from River Road and 34th Street to the Ferry Causeway in Tsawwassen.

Rolley Falls Trail (Map 3/C2) 👣 ⛑

Accessed from the Rolley Lake Provincial Park or the Florence Lake FSR, this short, 2 km (1.2 mile) loop leads past two sets of falls providing a great view of Stave Lake along the way. The well-developed trail climbs 130 metres (422 feet) as it meanders through a thick second-growth forest. Allow 1 hour to do the loop, or continue around the Lakeside Trail, which circumnavigates Rolley Lake, and adds another 1.5 km (.9 miles) and 45 minutes to your trip.

> ### TRANS CANADA TRAIL(TCT)
>
> The Trans Canada trail weaves its way from Horseshoe Bay to Hope, and into the Okanagan as it ultimately makes its way across the province and the country. While there are a couple extended sections in this region that cannot be easily hiked in less than a day (most notably between Chilliwack and Hope), this section of the TCT is designed for day hiking. In fact, many people have hiked on the TCT without knowing it, as the trail incorporates many pre-existing trails into the route. Included in the TCT are parts of the Centennial Trail, the Baden Powell Trail, Burnaby Mountain Trails, the Pitt River Dykes, the Matsqui Trail, Tamahi Trail, the Kettle Valley Railway and more. Some sections of trail still have yet to be built, and the trail is routed onto interim routes, either roads or trails. For a complete step-by-step description of the route, check out **Trans Canada Trail: The British Columbia Route**, produced in cooperation with Trails BC.

Ruby Creek Trail (Map 15/B7) 🚶 🚵 🐎 🏕️

The Deer Lake FSR continues past Deer Lake as a four-wheel drive road. This route is a fairly easy 14 km (8.5 mile) return trip to a viewpoint over the Fraser River. While the road connects to Highway 7, it crosses private property, so turn around at the viewpoint, about halfway down into the valley.

Sasquatch Provincial Park Trails (Map 4/G1, 5/A1, 15\A7) 🚶 🚵 🐎 🐟 🏕️

The roads into and around Sasquatch Park offer enjoyable mountain biking or hiking in a wilderness setting. These trails are easy, and perfect for the family. The more popular routes start from the various gated access roads.

Deer Lake Trail: An easy trail, which leads along the north side of Deer Lake.

Hicks Lake Trail: This relatively easy trail circles Hicks Lake. The route starts from the gated access road on the north side of the lake. At the south end of the lake it is possible to follow an old logging road along the Seabird Island Overlook Trail.

Moss Lake Trail: This is the most difficult route in Sasquatch Provincial Park. It follows the steep and rocky access road past Moss Lake to several unnamed lakes.

Serpentine Fen and Dyke Road (Map 2/A6) 🚶 🚵

Located just north of White Rock, this trail is found on 44th Avenue off of King George Highway. It is an enjoyable trek through a Wildlife Management Area that is home to several species of birds.

Stanley Park (Map 1/C1) 🚶 🚵 🏕️

We dare you to find another trail in Southwestern BC that sees as much traffic (foot, bike and inline skating) as the Stanley Park Seawall. This 8.8 km (5.5 mile) seawall is part of a much longer (20 km/12.2 mile) seawall system that helps form part of the Trans Canada Trail. Besides the Seawall, there are 35 km (22 miles) of trails in the park, although only one other (a combo of Bridle Path, Lake Trail and part of Beaver Lake Trail) is open to bikers. The trails are mostly short, interconnected trails that can be joined together into a number of combinations. The trails on the western side of the park are, in general, longer and wider than the trails on the eastern side of the park.

Statlu Lake Trail (Map 14/A4) 🚶 📷 🐟 🏕️

This trip starts near the 40 km sign on the Chehalis FSR. It is an 8 km/4.9 mile (4 hour) hike, which follows the creek draw past Statlu Lake and into the headwaters of Chehalis River. The main trail ends at a waterfall, gaining 610 metres (1,983 feet) along the way. From here, there are further routes (mostly rough access trails for mountain climbers) along the north side of Statlu Lake up the Brotherhood Trail to the Upper Lake or on to the Mount Ratney climbing area.

Stave Dam Interpretive Trail (Map 3/D3) 🚶 🚵 🏕️

Just east of Stave Falls Dam are a series of short trails. The **Stave Dam Interpretive Trail** is a short (1.7 km/1 mile) trail that cuts through a second growth forest with an elevation gain of 150 metres (488 feet). Further east, the **Steelhead Mountain Trail** is a short (2 km/1.2 mile) trail that climbs from the south end of Campbell Street (off Johnson, off Cardinal) along an old forest service road.

Sumas Mountain Trails (Maps 3/G5–4/A5) ⛺ 🚶 🚵 🐟 🏕️

With the recent development of the Trans Canada Trail, there are a few alternatives up this scenic mountain. From the west the original trail begins off the Sumas Mountain Road (at the tiny sign marked Centennial Trail), while the new trailhead is found at the end of Carlyle Road. Expect to hike through thick underbrush and cross Wades Creek along the way past Chadsey Lake to the summit. From the east side, start at the Sumas Dam beneath a rock bluff off Quadling Road. From there, the trail leads uphill through an old cut block before reaching Chadsey Lake and eventually the summit. Regardless of which route you take, the hike is about 12

km/7.3 miles (5 hours) return gaining about 700 metres (2,275 feet) in elevation. From the top are great views of Sumas Prairie and Vedder Mountain. Some hikers prefer to forgo the last 280 metre climb to the summit, and instead stop at the peaceful Chadsey Lake.

Teapot Hill Trail (Map 4/C7) 🚶 🏕️

It is only 2.5 km (1.5 miles) and 250 metres (813 feet) to the top of Teapot Hill. Compared to other epic hikes in the area, you do not get great views from the top. But they are better than you would expect, and this is a good place to stretch the legs after a long, wet winter

U.B.C. Research Forest (Maps 2/G1—12/G7) 🚶 🏕️

There are a number of trails and old roads in this large research forest, just north of Maple Ridge. The routes range from easy saunters around interpretive trails, to some fairly stiff hikes, with elevation gains of up to 610 metres (1,983 feet). The trails weave their way through a mixed second growth forest and some of the high points offer good views over the Fraser Valley. Take 232nd Street north of Haney and park at the gate near the forestry headquarters. You must register at the office before heading out. No mountain bikes are allowed.

Upper Chilliwack River Trail (Map 5/G7) 🚶

From Depot Creek at the south end of Chilliwack Lake, the trail starts along the shores of the lake to the estuary of the Chilliwack River. Where the trail splits, follow the right branch leading south to the US border along the east side of Chilliwack River. This is a rewarding trail that meanders among an ecological reserve with old growth cedar, majestic Douglas-fir and amabilis fir next to the Upper Chilliwack River. It is also an easy trail covering 5.4 km/3.3 miles (3 hours) return. The more adventurous can continue on into Washington State, along a difficult two-day trail, which ultimately leads to Mount Baker.

Vedder Mountain Trails (Map 4/B7–C7) 🚶 🚵 🐎 🏕️

An excellent hiking trail is found off an old spur road on the Vedder Mountain FSR. This is a well-developed, moderate 11.5 km/7 mile (6 hour) trail gaining 375 metres/1,219 feet (mostly at the start) to the summit. Once you break out of the dense hemlock forest you will be rewarded with views of Sumas Prairie, Vedder Canal and area. Spring flowers brighten the way. Once on the summit, you can follow an old trail down to return along the road. Alternatively, you can use the old trail from the Yarrow side to access the top.

For mountain bikers, this is *the* place to ride in the Chilliwack area. The main route follows the FSR from Parmenter Road, 21.5 km (13.1 miles) around the ridge. This moderate ride offers great views of the surrounding valley while climbing 490 metres (1,592 feet). Several side trails in the area have been developed by motorcyclists, and provide experienced mountain bikers with fast and twisty thrills. A popular option follows the Vedder Mountain Classic Route. This route heads south (left) from the FSR and follows several trails and old roads back to the main road and the start (some 17 km/10.4 miles and 340 metres/1,105 feet later).

Vedder River Trail (Map 4/A5–C6)

[icons]

The scenic dyke system along the north side of the Vedder River has benefited from extensive work by the Chilliwack Rotary Club. This trail is open to hikers, bikers and horseback riders and is part of the Trans Canada Trail. The main access points are the Keith Wilson Bridge to the west and Vedder Crossing to the east.

Widgeon Bowl Lookout Trail (Map 12/E7) [icons]

This is a stiff, stiff climb up 700 metres over a mere 2 km (2,275 feet in 2.4 miles); that's just about one metre up for every two metres you hike. Overall the trail gains just over 900 metres in 5 km (2 hours). The trailhead is difficult to find from the water accessible Widgeon Lake Rec Site, or from Burke Mountain along a poorly marked trail. Although the views of Pitt Lake from the bowl below Widgeon Peak are spectacular, the stiff climb is only for folks in really good shape.

Widgeon Falls Trail (Map 12/E7) [icons]

A popular boat access hike found across from Grant Narrows Park at the south end of Pitt Lake. From the end of the slough at the Widgeon Lake Rec Site, an easy 2.7 km (1.6 miles) walk leads along the west bank of Widgeon Creek. Allow one hour to reach the falls gaining 40 metres (130 feet) along the way. The trail runs parallel to an old logging road, and there are a couple places where the two connect.

Widgeon Lake Trail (Map 12/E6) [icons]

The first part of this trail from the Widgeon Lake Rec Site is along an old logging road. It is possible (some would even argue preferable) to bring a mountain bike along in your canoe, and cycle the first leg of the trail. The second stretch of this 18.5 km (11.3 mile) trail is not for mountain bikes. This last section climbs steeply up into the cirque where Widgeon Lake is located, getting progressively steeper the closer you get. The lake is at found at the 815 metre (2,673 foot) mark and most of that is gained in the last couple kilometres.

Williams Lake Trail (Map 5/C5) [icons]

Beginning at the Foley Lake Recreation Site, the trail is a difficult 13 km/7.9 mile (7 hour) hike gaining 1,200 metres (3,900 feet) to the lake. Not only will you feel like a mountain goat as you scramble up (and up), you might actually see one. The trail begins by crossing Foley Creek and then it rises sharply along the ridge above Williams Creek to the lake. In spring, runoff makes creek crossings difficult, and, if there is snow left, there is a good chance that there will be an avalanche. Leave this one until late summer and early fall.

Whippoorwill Point/Sandy Cove Trail (Map 4/G1) [icons]

Most visitors to Harrison Hot Springs enjoy the easy stroll to the source of the hot springs. However, few take in the scenic trail that leads to Whippoorwill Point. This 5 km (2.4 mile) trail climbs quickly from the hot springs to its high point, which is only about 40 metres (130 feet) above the lake. From here it descends to Sandy Cove, which is a great place for a picnic, and on to Whippoorwill Point. Although the trail is regarded as easy, there are tricky sections to negotiate.

Williams Ridge Trail (Map 5/D5) [icons]

A grueling 11 km/6.7 mile (6 hour) trail is found near the 32 km mark of the Chilliwack Lake Road. Orange markers indicate the steep, undeveloped trail as it rises through a second growth forest past a clearing with a good view of the valley. From here, the trail continues along a forested ridge to connect with the Ford Mountain Trail (see above). This is a tough hike, gaining 1,440 metres (4,680 feet) including a lung-busting 900 metres (2,925 feet) in the first 1.5 km to the ridge that runs between the lookout and Williams Peak. It is also possible to scramble up to the prominent Williams Peak.

Hope/Fraser Canyon Trails

Botanie Mountain Trail (Map 33/B1) [icons]

The length of the hike really depends on how far you can drive along the old lookout road leading from the Botanie Valley Road. If you do not have a 4wd vehicle then you'll have to hike about 17.5 km (10.7 miles) over 8 hours, climbing 1,425 metres (4,631 feet) to the lookout. Along the way you will pass open meadows with wildflowers (in July) along with great views of the Stein Valley, Thompson River and Fraser River. The hiking season runs from June to October.

Clerf Lake (Map 6/A6) [icons]

This hike is about a 9 km (5.5 miles) round trip, depending on how far you can drive up the logging road. The majority of this hike is on old logging roads. Only the last 1.5 km (0.9 miles) is on a rough trail. A similar route leads to an unnamed lake just south of Clerf.

Dewdney Trail (Map 6/E2–7/E1) [icons]

Originally constructed in 1860 by Edgar Dewdney, this was one of the first trade routes linking the coast with the interior. These days, most of the route is either grown over or has been covered by roads, but there are some places where the historic route still survives as a trail. The longest surviving section is found in the Cascade Recreation Area, beginning at the parking lot on Highway 3. The trail extends 36 km/22 miles (2 days) to the pass, gaining 1,131 metres (3,676 feet) along the way. It is possible to trek over the divide into the Whipsaw Creek FSR. The trail is a popular horseback destination with its panoramic views of the valleys and mountains. There are several side trails and overnight facilities along the well developed trail system.

Eaton Lake Trail (Map 5/G2) [icons]

This trail begins at the Eaton Creek Recreation Site on the Silver Skagit Road, south of Hope. The trail leads 4.1 km (3 hours) one way to Eaton Lake, a popular fishing lake. Along the way, you will gain 915 metres (2,974 feet) in elevation, which is a fairly stiff climb. The rewarding trail begins by approaching Eaton Creek before descending rapidly to a log bridge, where there are great views of the falls and rapids. From here, the hike heads upward towards the lake. It is possible to camp at the south end of the lake or continue on to Eaton Peak.

Galene Lakes Route (Map 6/D7) [icons]

This route begins off 55 km down the Silver Skagit Road, at the Chittenden Bridge parking area. It takes you 32 km/19.5 miles (11 hours) return to the Galene Lake, climbing 1,250 metres (4,063 feet) along the way. The trail crosses a footbridge, then proceeds through meadows along the Skagit River before following Galene Creek up to the lake. The lake offers a rustic campsite, some decent fishing opportunities and great views. The trail is best hiked from July to October.

Gate Mountain Trail (Map 24/F7) [icons]

The Gate Mountain Trail is a steep, difficult trail that climbs 1,200 m (3,900 feet) along a 16 km/9.8 mile (7 hours) old pack trail. The trailhead is found just south of the Coopers Corner Rest Area (watch for a pullout on the west side of the road). The hike follows a mixture of logging roads, old pack trails (including the Hudson Bay and First Brigade Trails) and new hiking trails. Eventually, you will pass through a meadow with wild flowers before reaching the Notch and then finally the summit of Gate Mountain. Both the Notch and the summit both provide excellent views over the Fraser Canyon.

Ghost Pass Trail (Map 6/D2) [icons]

This trail begins at the West Gate of Manning Park and leads along an old engineering road to a signed trailhead. You must climb to Ghost Pass, which is 11 km (6.7 miles) one-way from the trailhead, before reaching Ghost Pass Lake. Beyond the lake, the trail is overgrown and difficult to follow but it eventually connects with the Hope Brigade Trail and the Rice Trail.

Hope Mountain Trail (Map 15/F7) 🚶 🎣

The trailhead is found opposite Nicolum Park on Highway 3 along a 4wd road. The road climbs 8 km (4.8 miles) over many waterbars to the parking lot. The difficult trail leading to the right (left leads to Wells Peak) will take about 5 hours to climb Hope Mountain. After climbing 800 m (2,600 ft), you will be rewarded with panoramic views (on clear days).

Hope Lookout and Loop Trail (Map 15/F7) 🚶 🎣

The Hope Loop is an easy 2 km (1.2 mile) trail in the shadow of Hope Mountain. From the end of the loop, the trail to the lookout climbs steeply up the talus slopes of the mountain to the viewpoint at 500 metres (1,625 feet).

Hope Pass Trail (Maps 6/E3-G3, 7/A2) ⛺ 🚶 🐎 🎣

Although this trail begins inside Manning Park, most of the trail actually lies in the Cascade Recreation Area. This trail leads from Cayuse Flats on Highway 3, 26 km/15.9 miles (7–9 hours) one-way to a branch road off the Whipsaw Creek FSR. The first 4 km (2.4 miles) of the trail follow an old fire access road before the trail heads in a northeastern direction along the banks of the Skagit River. At around the two hour mark, watch for the Grainger Creek Trail, which departs to the right. As an alternate, you could loop back along this route and camp at Nicomen Lake. The trail reaches Hope Pass at the 21 km mark (12.8 miles) before descending to the Whipsaw Creek FSR. Some people turn around at the pass, and hoof it back to Cayuse Flats for a very long (12–14 hour) day hike. From Highway 3 to Hope Pass, there is an elevation gain of 1,050 metres (3,413 feet). There is an interesting side route to Dick's Cabin on top of Skaist Mountain.

Kwoiek Valley Trail (Map 32/E6) 🚶 📷 🐟 🎣

From the end of the logging road, an 11km/6.7 miles (5 hour) hike leads past Kokwaski to Chechiwa Lake. The Trail is outgrown and disappears completely beyond the second lake making for a very challenging trail. Along the way, you pass by several waterfalls gaining 600 metres (1,950 feet) to the height of land at 2,000 metres (6,500 feet). An unmarked route accesses Chachiwa Glacier.

Landstrom Ridge (Map 15/E7) 🚶 🎣

A short, stiff trail that climbs 150 metres (488 feet) in about 1.5 km (0.9 miles) as it makes its way up to a series of four lookouts on Landstrom Ridge. Expect to take about two hours to complete the easy 3 km (1.8 mile) round trip.

Lucky Four Mine Trail (Map 5/C4) 🚶 🎣

This moderate trail climbs 650 metres in 4 km (2,113 feet in 2.4 miles) one-way as it makes its way along an old access road to the site of an old mine. From the mine, a difficult route heads up and onto the glacier below Foley Peak, an additional 2.5 km and 400 metres up.

Mount Lincoln Trail (Map 15/F3) 🚶 🎣

Mount Lincoln towers east of Highway 1 just east of Yale. A rough, sometimes sketchy 5 km (3 mile) trail leads up to the 655 metre (2,129 foot) summit, gaining 580 metres (1,885 feet) along the way. This difficult climb sometimes resembles rock climbing more than hiking, and indeed, there are a few spots where there are fixed ropes to help you ascend. Although not as tall as other mountains in the area, there are still some great views of the Fraser Canyon.

Mount Outram Trail (Map 6/C2) 🚶 🎣

This trail begins at the West Gate of Manning Park and leads along the old engineering road to a signed trailhead marking the route to Mount Outram. This moderate trail is 18 km (9 hours) return and is best hiked from July to September. The total elevation gain is 1,760 metres (5,720 feet). The trail begins in a forested setting before crossing the creek and then continuing through a series of meadows to a steep, rocky ridge and eventually up to the summit of the mountain. You get a spectacular view of the surrounding mountain peaks from the top.

Ogilvie Peak Trails (Map 15/G7) 🚶 🎣

This trail climbs steeply from the Kawkawa Lake Road for about 4 km (2.4 miles), until it breaks out into the sub-alpine of Ogilvie Peak. From here you can pick your route to a series of peaks and ridges.

Onion Lk/Monkey Wrench Riding Area (Map 42/B6) 🏍

This popular off road biking area offers a series of trails/old roads in the hills around Onion and Turnip Lake. The trails are best left to motor bikes and ATV's.

Othello Tunnels (Coquihalla Canyon) Trail (Map 15/G7) 🚶 🚲 🐎 🎣

This popular trail is part of the Kettle Valley Railway, which is in turn a part of the Trans Canada Trail. Most people only hike though the canyon itself, an easy walk through a dramatic gorge and the equally impressive Othello (Quintette) Tunnels. This short trail is less than a kilometre return but it is possible to stretch this into a 12 km/7.3 mile trek along the north side of the Coquihalla River all the way to the Hope Cemetery. Yet another option is to follow the Nicola Valley Trail from the railgrade up and over the mountain and back to the parking lot. This last option makes a nice 8 km (4.8 miles) loop.

Silver Daisy Mountain Trail (Map 6/E4) 🚶 🎣

It is possible to do this 20 km (12.2 mile) trail up to the summit of Silver Daisy Mountain in about 9 hours. The trail starts at the Sumallo Grove Picnic Area off Highway 3, crosses the Skagit River, and switchbacks its way up a steep hill to a saddle, which offers great views of the Skagit Valley. From here, the trail continues through a meadow to the 2,040 metre (6,630 foot) summit, gaining 1,435 metre (4,664 feet) along the way. Part of the trail follows an old mining tram. The trail is best left for late summer/early fall.

Skagit River Trail (Map 6/D6–E3) ⛺ 🚶 🚲 🐎 🎣

This trail begins at the Sumallo Grove Picnic Area and leads 13 km/7.9 miles (6 hours) one-way along the east side of the Skagit River. Along the route, you pass through an ecological reserve, which has a nice grove of old growth cedar, fir and cottonwood. The trail is best hiked in mid-June when the wild Rhododendrons start blooming at Sumallo Grove. The adventurous can hike all the way to the 26 Mile Bridge on the Silver Skagit Road but the last part covers a poor, often indistinct trail. It is 20 km (12.2 miles) one-way to the road.

Skyline Trail (West) (Maps 6/E7, 1\B7) ⛺ 🚶 🎣

The western trailhead to the Skyline Trail is accessed off the Silver Skagit Road at the parking lot north of Ross Lake. The trail leads 26 km/15.9 miles (10 hours) from the valley bottom to an alpine ridge at Camp Mowich. Along the way, the trail climbs steeply, gaining 1,310 metres (4,258 feet) to the ridge. The hike initially begins in a forest and then crosses several creeks before proceeding into some sub-alpine meadows and then along the ridge. As part of the historic Centennial Trail, it is possible to continue on to Lightening Lake.

Spirit Caves Trail (Map 15/E3) 🚶 🎣

The trailhead is located off Highway 1, across from the Pioneer Cemetery at the south end of Yale. This 5 km/3 mile (3 hour) trail gains 500 metres (1,625 feet) to the caves and several vantage points.

Stein Valley Trails (Maps 31–33 and 40–41) ⛺ 🚶 🔺 🎣

In the late 1980s, environmentalists fought long and hard to see the Stein Valley preserved in a park. This provincial park boasts a number of impressive hiking and backpacking trails, many of which are multi-day treks. It is possible, utilizing a shuttle system, to create some interesting one-way trips, although most of the roads leading to the park are very rough. The main access is from the Westside Road, just north of Lytton.

Blowdown Pass to Cottonwood Creek (see Whistler Trails) is an alternative route into the Stein River Trail.

Brimful Lake (Map 41/C7): Brimful Lake was the spectacular site of the music festivals, back when this area was not a park. From the Texas Creek Trailhead, Brimful Lake is about 6.5 km (4 miles) in. This trail is not marked, but is fairly easy to follow. At last report, the Texas Creek FSR had been deactivated, and has 103 water bars to cross in the last 14 km (8.5 miles).

Elton Lake Route (Map 31/G5): This is a route with no defined trail that leads to the spectacular Elton Lake. The trail is only 4 km (2.4 miles) long, but climbs steeply to a cobalt-coloured lake at the foot of a glacier.

Stein River Trail (Maps 33/A3–31/F5): This 58 km/35.4 mile backpacking route leads through the heart of this magnificent wilderness. To reach the trailhead, cross the Fraser River north of Lytton, and proceed 4.5 km north along the Westside Road to the short side road leading to the trailhead. From here, the trail follows the Stein River through the heart of the park to the park boundary at Tundra Lake. The trail begins as a moderate riverside route that takes you from the dry terrain typical of the Fraser Canyon area to some cool, lush old-growth forests and eventually the spectacular alpine ridges. In addition to 8 campsites, there are cable car crossings and also numerous Indian Pictograph sites along the trail. Beyond Cottonwood Creek (30 km in) the terrain becomes more difficult and is subject to severe weather changes. The section between Stein Lake and Tundra Lake is a steep, challenging section that climbs about 1,100 m (3,600 ft). Beyond Tundra, it is an additional 12 km of alpine travel (losing 700 m/2,200 ft) to make it to Lizzie Lake, where wise travellers have arranged for a shuttle pick up. Many people allow a week to explore the area, but it is possible to do an overnight trip to the first river crossing. This is a wilderness trail; in addition to many fallen trees, bears are common and snow is a definite possibility in the alpine.

Stryen Creek (Map 33/A3-32/G4): From the main trailhead on West Side Road, there is a 6.5 km (4 mile) access trail to "The Forks." From here, you can head east for 8 km (4.9 miles) or west 5 km (3 miles). The main attraction is the pictographs at the forks. The trail can be difficult to follow at first, but the route gets easier farther along. There is backcountry camping along the eastern fork.

Texas Creek Trail (Maps 41/C7-32/C1) The Texas Creek Trail is a 10 km (6 mile) long trail (or rather, a pair of trails, one of which swings around Brimful Lake), which provides alternate access into the heart of the Stein. The difficult hike leads through some expansive alpine area providing great views of the surrounding valleys.

Thacker Mountain Trail (Map 15/F7) 🚶 🚲 ⛺
In the heart of Hope, this trail leads 5 km/3 miles (1.5 hours) along an old road to the summit of Thacker. You gain 160 metres (520 feet) and are rewarded with a good view of the Fraser Valley and Hope.

Wells Peak Loop Trail (Map 5/G1) 🚶 ⛺
The access road is found opposite Nicomen Park on Highway 3 and is marked by the Hope Mountain Trail sign. Once up the rough waterbared road, the trail to the left leads to Wells Peak some 8 km (4.8 miles) later. Allow 5 hours as the hike is strenuous as it climbs 700 m (2,275 ft) to the summit.

Whatcom Trail (Map 6/F2–G1) ⛰ 🚶 🐎 ⛺
From the Cascade Recreation Area parking lot off of Highway 3, this trail follows the Dewdney Trail for 2.5 km before splitting off to the right. From there, the trail climbs steeply through second growth forest to the sub-alpine meadows of Whatcom Pass and the Punch Bowl. The trail then descends into the Paradise Valley and the Tulameen River (north of our maps). You will gain 650 metres (2,113 feet) over 17 km (10.4 miles) one-way to the ridge. Unless you are on horseback, you will probably want to arrange for a shuttle at the far end. The hike is best done in late summer or early fall.

Island Trails (Bowen, Gambier, Texada...)
Cornell Trail (Map 16/G6) 🚶 🚲 🐟
An easy walk along an old mining trail past Emily Lake on Texada Island. The trail leads from Vananda at Prospect Road and can be extended as long as you like along the gas pipeline.

Dorman Point Trail (Maps 10/G7-11/A7) 🚶 ⛺
From the picnic grounds at the ferry in Snug Cove on Bowen Island, this trail leads 4 km (2.4 miles) one-way to a small lookout near Dorman Point. The hike involves a steady uphill climb where you will be rewarded with excellent views of Whytecliff Park and Vancouver.

Gambier Lake Trail (Map 10/G4) 🚶 🚲 🐟 ⛺
On Gambier Island, this 17 km/10.4 mile (6 hour) trail leads from the ferry terminal past the general store and continues up the hill. After crossing Mannion Creek, the trail follows an old road eventually leading to Gambier Lake. The trail gains 475 metres (1,544 feet). It is possible to take a side trip to Mount Liddle, which involves a 900 metre (2,925 foot) climb over 14 km/8.5 miles (7 hours). This second trail follows an overgrown road past Muskeg Lake and along a ridge with some excellent views of the ocean.

Keats Island (Map 10/E7) 🚶 🚲 ⛺
Keats Island is a small island accessed by foot ferry from Gibsons. From the landing, it is a 2 km (1.2 mile) jaunt to Plumper Cove Marine Park. At the park, a handful of trails weave their way through the woods, taking you to viewpoints, and along oceanfront trails.

Killarney Creek/Lake Trail (Map 10/G7) ⛺ 🚶 🚲 ⛺
On Bowen Island, the Killarney Creek Trail follows the north side of Killarney Creek past the small set of falls at the head of the lagoon. You also pass a fish spawning channel before circling lovely Killarney Lake. The best place to find the trailhead is at the Union Steamship Co. Store in Snug Cove or at St. Gerard's Catholic Church. The trail is about an 8 km (2.5 hour) hike from the ferry landing around the lake.

Mount Artaban Trail (Map 10/G5) 🚶 ⛺
The trailhead to this Gambier Island hike is accessed by boat to the south end of Halkett Bay Park (near the scout camp). The hike involves a 600 metre (1,950 foot) elevation gain beginning on an old road before passing by a couple of streams and continuing uphill through the forest and some open meadows. As a rule of thumb, stay to your right along the rough trail until you reach the summit, about 17 km/10.4 miles (7 hours return) from where you started.

Mount Gardner Trails (Map 10/G7) 🚶 🚲 🐎 ⛺
The trailhead to this popular network of multi-trails is found on the road between poles 490 and 491 off the Mount Gardner Road. From the end of the road, a series of trails begins. The main trail climbs 725 metres (2,356 feet) to the summit along paved, gravel and forested paths. From the top, you will be rewarded with a great view of Bowen Island and Howe Sound. The main trail is 10 km (6.1 miles) long, but there are many side trails (mostly old logging roads) to explore. Most of the exploring is by mountain bikers, not hikers. From the ferry landing it is a long 17.5 km/10.7 mile (7 hour) hike/bike.

Shelter Point Regional Park (Map 8/B1) 🚶 ⛺
Shelter Point Regional Park is easily accessed off the Texada Island Highway. Within the park is a scenic 2 km (1.2 mile) easy trail that leads along the ocean through some large windswept Douglas-fir.

Texada Island Loop (Maps 8,16,17) ⛰ 🚶 🚲 🐟 ⛺
From the Blubber Bay Ferry Terminal, this is a long, moderate 73 km (44.5 mile) return bike ride that should take a day to complete. Cycling in a clockwise direction from Vananda, you follow Central (High) Road, to Bell Road and down to the hydro lines. Here a steep downhill will bring you to the Davie Bay Road, where you head north to Gillies Bay and back to Vananda and the ferry. It is possible to take side trips to both Bob's Lake Rec Site or Shingle Beach Rec Site to camp.

Lillooet/Goldbridge Trails

The farther away from the coast you get, the further the rain clouds have to travel overland. As a result, the mountains around Goldbridge and Lillooet are a lot dryer than the mountains around Vancouver and Squamish. This beautiful area of the province remains a hidden gem to outdoor recreationists. Below, we have only touched on a fraction of the endless multi-use trails in the area.

Brett-Hog Creek Trails (Map 45/A4)
Accessed off of Marshall Lake Road, you will find a series of 35 km of trails taking you around Carol Lake along Hog and Brett Creeks and beyond. There really is no limit to the distance you can travel.

Burkholder Lake Trail (Map 45/C2)
From Lake La Mare Recreation Site off the Yalakom FSR, this 10 km/6 mile (4 hour) trail takes you to Burkholder Lake. From Burkholder, you can continue west to the Shulaps Range, which are over 20 km away.

Hogback Trail (Map 45/D1–46/A1)
Beginning near the end of the Leon Creek FSR, this 6 km/3.7 mile (3 hour) hike leads to the alpine meadows of Hog Mountain.

Kwotlenemo (Fountain) Trail (Map 41/F1)
This popular recreation lake is home to a series of multi-use trails. In winter the 12 km (6.7 miles) system is used by cross-country skiers, while in the spring through fall, mountain bikers and hikers frequent the trails. The lake is accessed by the Fountain Valley Road.

Marshall Lake Trail (Map 44/G3)
A 10 km/6.1 mile (4 hour) scenic trail takes you up the hill from the east side of Marshall Lake down to Carpenter Lake. From here, you can arrange for a pick up, or retrace your path.

McGillivray Pass Trail (Maps 39/G1–40/A2)
A scenic but challenging route takes you up and over the pass between Bralorne and Anderson Lake. The trail begins from the Kingdom Lake FSR, and leads 15km one-way along McGillivray Creek. You will eventually spill out on an old road on the west side of Anderson Lake. The area is a popular backcountry skiing area in the winter.

Melvin Creek Trail (Map 40/F5)
From the Cayoose Creek Rec Site on Duffey Lake Road, this 6 km (3 hour) one-way trail crosses Cayoosh Creek and accesses a large alpine basin containing several small lakes. The trail was built by hunting guides but hikers and horseback riders can enjoy the route in the spring and summer.

Marriott Basin Trail (Map 40/A7)
From the Duffy Lake Road, this trail heads high into the sub-alpine at the foot of Mount Marriott along an old road. Keep left as you hike up the road and left again where the trail splits (the right trail heads to Rohr Lake). Marriott Basin is an explorer's paradise; once you get up to the basin, you can wander almost anywhere you want to. But please avoid treading on the fragile plant life. You will hike about 16 km (9.8 miles) and climb 370 metres (1,210 feet).

Moon Lake Trail (Map 46/A7)
Located off Bridge River Road, this is an 8 km (4.8 mile) 3 hour hike along an old four-wheel drive road/trail to Moon Lake. Extreme cyclists can continue onto Mount McLean.

Mount McLean Trails (Map 46/A7)
Picture yourself descending from a high alpine meadow 2,100 vertical metres (6,825 feet) down to the sagebrush in the valley below. En route you will cover 14 km (8.5 miles) of spectacular single-track trail. Now, keep that image in mind as you grunt 14 km and 2,100 vertical metres up to the top of Mount McLean from Moon Lake. Luckier (and richer) folks have been known to catch a helicopter to the top.

Rohr Lake Trail (Map 40/B7)
If you hang a right about a kilometre after the old Cayoosh Creek FSR turns into a trail, you will climb up and into the Rohr Lake Basin. While the majority of this hike is along the old logging road, the trail climbs quickly into a lovely sub-alpine meadow. You can enjoy a relaxing day at Rohr Lake, or make an adventure of it and head for the peak of Mount Rohr. The joy of this area is there are so many options that you will want to spend a few days exploring. The lake is only 9 km (5.5 miles) return from where you parked your car, climbing 430 metres (1,410 feet) along the way.

Seaton Highline Road (Map 40/A3–D1)
A scenic but grueling four hour mountain bike ride follows the road next to the hydro lines high above Anderson Lake. The roller coaster route stretches 32 km (18.8 miles) from D'Arcy (and the end of the Sea to Sky Trail) to Seton Portage.

Seton Ridge Trail (Maps 41/A1, 40/F2)
From a switchback on the Seton Ridge Logging Road, this is an 11 km/6.7 mile (5 hour) route taking you along the ridge between Cayoosh Creek and Seton Lake. Once you are in the alpine, you can access the surrounding mountains for even better views or explore the endless alpine meadows.

Spruce Lake Trails (Maps 43, 44)
The Spruce Lake area offers world-class hiking and backpacking, horse packing, mountaineering, fishing, cross-country skiing and mountain biking. There are 164 km (100 miles) of wilderness trails in the area, which traverse over gentle mountain passes and meander through lush alpine grasslands and flowers to destination trout lakes. The main access points into the area are the Gun Creek Road, Mud Creek-Taylor Creek FSR and the Slim Creek FSR. The Forest Service offers an informative topographic map detailing the area. Most of the trails have few or no signs, so you will have to keep an eye on your map as you travel. In addition to the trails listed below, there are a number of rough routes that are only for experienced route finders, including routes to Eldorado Mountain, Upper Slim Creek, Leckie Creek, and Mount Sheba.

Deer Pass Trail: From the packers cabin near Trigger Lake, this trail climbs 800 metres (2,600 feet) in 4.5 km (2.7 miles) to Deer Pass. The trail continues north of our maps as it loses 600 metres (1,950 feet) in the next 5.5 km (3.3 miles) to Tyaughton Creek, where it joins the Tyaughton Creek Trail.

Gun Creek Trail: A 22.5 km (13.7 mile) return trail that climbs 650 metres (2,113 feet) along Gun Creek to the junction with the Deer Pass and Warner Pass Trails.

High Trail: The trailhead for this 13 km (7.9 mile) trail is near the south end of Tyaughton Lake. The first 5 km (3 miles) of the trail is an old, 4wd accessible mining road. The trail crosses the Taylor-Pearson Trail, then climbs up and over a steep hill (your highest point is 1,000 metres/3,250 feet higher than the trailhead). Beyond the hill, the trail drops into the Eldorado Basin, and climbs 400 metres/1,300 feet up to Windy Pass. Beyond Windy Pass, the trail drops to the Potato Patch Trailhead. The High Trail is 20 km (12 miles) long.

Lower Gun Creek: From the signed trailhead off Slim Creek FSR, this is the main trail into the heart of the Spruce Lake area. The trail crosses a footbridge (Jewel Bridge) and follows the north side of Gun Creek eventually breaking from the pine forest to the open grasslands and aspen trees. The mountain views are tremendous. After a couple hours, the trail forks (at Cowboy Camp). The right trail climbs 200 metres (650 feet) on its way to Spruce Lake, where campsites and a beach are found. The lake is an excellent fishing lake producing large rainbow trout. It is also possible to follow the Gun Creek Trail and a variety of shorter trails further into the wilderness area.

Open Heart Trail: This short 5 km (3 mile) trail begins at the north end of Spruce Lake and takes you to the Gun Creek grasslands.

Spruce Lake Creek Trail: A 4 km (2.4 mile) trail along Spruce Lake Creek connecting the lake with Tyaughton Creek. The trail is in poor condition.

Taylor Basin Trail: This is one of the gentlest mountain routes you will ever encounter. Depending on how far you can drive up the Mud Creek-Taylor Creek FSR, it may take you a few hours to walk to the cabin at Taylor Basin. The route follows an old road beyond the footbridge as it slowly climbs through a scenic valley with wildflowers, wildlife and fantastic mountain views. The route is extremely popular with mountain bikers and snowmobilers.

Taylor-Pearson Trail: A steep, difficult trail between upper Taylor Creek and Upper Pearson Creek.

Tyaughton Creek Trail: A pair of trailheads off the Paradise Creek FSR leads onto another one of the main access trails. The 31 km (18.9 miles) trail follows Tyaughton Creek to near its headwaters in Elbow Pass (and north of our maps).

Tyaughton Lake Trails: From Tyax Mountain Resort, a series of trails lead around the north end of the beautiful lake. These trails are used by guests on foot, horseback and in winter cross-country skis or snowshoes. To the south, an easy 2 km (1.2 mile) trail starts across from the Friburg Recreation Site and joins up with the High Trail.

Upper Eldorado Trail: This old mining road starts at the cabin in Taylor Basin and clings steeply (300 metres in 1 km/ 975 feet in 0.6 miles) to a pass overlooking the Upper Eldorado Basin. The trail then drops into the basin and joins the High Trail. From the trailhead to the junction is 4 km (2.4 miles).

Upper, Mid and Lower Grasslands Trails: A trio of trails in the high grasslands that are one of the main features of this area. The trails are found near the campsite at the junctions of Gun Creek and Spruce Lake Trails.

W.D. Trail: This trail starts at Spruce Lake and heads north for 5 km (3 miles) to join up with the Tyaughton Creek Trail.

Warner Pass Trail: This trail starts just past the packers cabin northwest of Trigger Lake and climbs along Warner Creek to Warner Lake. Past the lake, the trail climbs to the pass, then down to the end of the mining road at Battlement Creek (off our maps). From the cabin to Battlement Lake is 21.5 km (13 miles). The high point of the trail is the 750 metre (2,438 foot) Warner Pass, at the 10 km (6 mile) mark.

Texas Creek Trail (Maps 32/C1)

From the end of the deactivated Texas Creek Road, the trail leads south 10 km/6.1 miles (4 hours) one-way to the Stein Valley. The difficult hike leads through some expansive alpine areas providing great views of the surrounding valleys. A side trail swings around Brimful Lake.

Tommy Creek Trail (Map 44/G5)

This 10km (6.1 mile) hike leads along an old mining exploration road and then along an overgrown trail to the sub-alpine. The trailhead is accessed by boat to the south side of Carpenter Lake. This is Grizzly Bear country so come prepared with bells and bear spray.

Viera Creek Trail (Map 45/E6)

This is an 8 km/4.8 mile (3 hour) trail along a series of mining exploration tote roads and old hunting trails. The trailhead begins a few kilometres west of Mission Dam off the Carpenter Lake Road.

Manning Park Trails

The high elevation park has an extensive network of trails ranging from short, easy valley walks to week long expeditions. Some of the trails even hook up with trails outside the park, in the Skagit Valley and Cascade Recreation Areas as well as down into Washington State. The hiking season is limited from June through October.

Bonnevier Trail (Map 7/E5)

Originally built as a packhorse route in the early 1900s, this is a difficult trail that is best hiked from west to east. You will lose more elevation than you gain in this direction (about 950 metres/3,088 feet). The trail starts 7 km (4.3 miles) along the Heather Trail, head east and follow the trail downhill to McDiarmid Meadows. The total distance hiked is 25 km (15.3 miles) one-way, and can be done as a shuttle trip in a long day. Water is available at the 9 km (5.5 mile) mark.

Dry Ridge Trail (Map 7/D6)

From the Cascade Lookout along the road to the Blackwell Meadows, you will find a 3 km (1.8 mile) out and back trail. The trail begins in a lush forest of fir and pine before opening up onto the sub-alpine meadows of Dry Ridge. There are great views south overlooking Lightning Lake and Mount Frosty.

Frosty Mountain Trail (Map 7/B7)

Frosty Mountain is the highest peak in the park. A pair of difficult trails lead to the peak just below the actual summit. From the Windy Joe Trailhead it is a 29 km (17.7 mile) return trek, while from Lightning Lakes it is a 22.2 km (13.5 mile) route. It is possible to combine the two into a 27.5 km (16.8 mile) loop. The Lightning Lakes route is shorter, and has slightly less elevation change (1,150 metres/3,738 feet). Although this trip can be done in a long, strenuous day, there are campsites on either route. The best times to visit Frosty Mountain are in late July/early August when the meadows are full of wildflowers, or mid-September when the Larch trees turn a brilliant gold colour. The high elevation and north-facing slope means this is one of the last trails to be free of snow. For folks not wanting to make the entire trip, Larch Plateau at 9 km (5.5 miles) is a worthy destination. Do not be fooled by their size, these trees are estimated to be 2,000 years old.

Grainger Creek Trail (Maps 6/G2, 7\A3)

In order to reach the Grainger Creek trailhead, you have to hike 6 km (3.7 miles) along the Hope Pass Trail. At the junction of Grainger Creek and the Skaist River, the Grainger Creek Trail swings east up the valley climbing steadily for 11 km (6.7 miles) to the western end of Nicomen Lake. The trail gains 800 metres (2,600 metres) to the lake, which has a lovely camping area at it's northern end. This trail can also be reached by hiking the Heather Trail to Nicomen Lake.

Heather / Three Brothers Trail (Map 7/B2–C6)

This is the main trail through Manning Park's vast sub-alpine meadows. In mid-July to August, the sub-alpine are notorious for their amazing display of colourful wildflowers. To get here, you will have to drive up to the trailhead. Fortunately, the road leads all the way up to the sub-alpine, meaning you will only gain 292 metres (949 feet) to the Nicomen Ridge overlooking Nicomen Lake. The trail is 21 km/12.8 mile (7 hours) one-way but it is possible to add the steep, 1 km (0.6 mile) side trail up to the top of the First Brother to the venture. Please remember that these sub-alpine meadows are extremely fragile.

Lightning Lakes Chain Trail (Map 7/A7–B6)

This trail begins at the Spruce Bay or the day-use area and leads 12 km/7.3 miles (4 hours) one-way past a series of good fishing lakes. This is an easy walk through a pleasant forest. Wilderness camping is offered at Stake Lake and fishing can be excellent.

Lightning Lake Loop (Map 7/A7)

An easy 9 km (5.5 mile) loop takes you around Lightning Lake, the first of four lakes in the Lightening Lake chain. Beavers are a common sight along the trail.

Monument 78 (Castle Creek) Trail (Map 7/C7–D7)

This is one of several trails that offers a chance to hike into Washington State. From the Monument 78/83 parking lot, it's a 12 km/6.7 mile (3.5 hour) one-way hike. The trail follows Castle Creek to the USA border and the monument that marks the border between the two countries. Along the trail, you will pass through several meadows climbing about 200 metres (650 feet) along the way. From the monument, it is possible to connect with the Windy Joe Trail via the Pacific Crest Trail. It is also possible to hike to Monument 83, through Washington State. Wilderness camping is available 0.5 km south of the monument.

Monument 83 Trail (Map 7/E7)

From the Monument 78/83 parking lot, this is a 16 km/9.8 mile (5 hour) one-way hike along an old fire access road to the US Forest Service tower. Along the trail, you will pass by an old cabin built in the 1920s by the US Forest Service as well as Pasayten Pete's grave. It is possible to head east out of the park on the **Pasayten River Trail,** which is part of the historic Centennial Trail. You will gain 850 metres (2,763 feet) to the tower.

North and South Gibson Trails (Map 7/A6)

In the winter, this trail (or pair of trails) is part of the cross-country area. In summer, it is possible to follow the 7.6 km (4.6 mile) trail on foot or mountain bike. There is only 125 metres (650 feet) in elevation change, although most of that comes in one hill. The trail parallels the Gibson Pass Road between Strawberry Flats and the Lightning Lake Campground.

Pacific Crest Trail (Map 7/C7)

Dreaming of Mexico? Well if you have 6 months of spare time, the first leg of the famous trail that cuts through the backcountry of USA to Mexico starts from Manning Park. This section is only the first 26 km (15.9 miles) of the 4,000 km (2,440 mile) trail, but think of the bragging rights you will have! This moderate hike will take about 8 hours and you will gain 200 metres (650 feet) in elevation along the way.

Poland Lake Route (Maps 7/A6-6/G6)

This trail is an easy 8 km/4.9 mile (3 hour) one-way hike from the gate at Strawberry Flats to Poland Lake. Although the climb is gradual, you will still gain 435 metres (1,414 feet) in elevation along the way. The area is a popular cross-country ski area, and the backcountry campsite sees a lot of use in the summer. From the lake, it is possible to hike 9 km/5.5 miles (3-4 hours) one-way to Allison Pass on Highway 3 rather than return to Strawberry Flats. If you choose this alternate route, the hike will lead you along an unmaintained trail (Memaloose Trail). It is a good idea to have a vehicle waiting for you.

Self Guided Nature Trails (Maps 6, 7)

Within Manning Park are five short nature trails idea for the elderly or for families with small children. These trails also offer highway travellers a nice break and a chance to stretch their legs.

Beaver Pond Trail (Map 7/C7): A short (0.5 km/0.3 mile) trail that starts from the Visitor Centre and loops around a small pond. In May and June the pond is usually full of waterfowl.

Canyon Nature Walk (Map 7/B6): An easy 2 km (1.2 mile) trail that begins at the Coldspring Campground and leads 2 km (45 minutes) along both sides of the Similkameen River.

Paintbrush Nature Trail (Map 7/C6): This trail starts at the Naturalist Hut at Blackwell Peak, which is reached via the Cascade Lookout Road. The trail takes you through a sub-alpine meadow full of wildflowers in mid-July to early August.

Rein Orchid Trail (Map 7/A6): This is a 0.5 km (15 minute) long trail beginning at the parking lot on Gibson Pass Road. The trail leads through a bog, which is full of flowering orchids in June through July.

Sumallo Grove Trail (Map 6/E3): From the Sumallo Grove Picnic

Area, this is a short, easy (30 minute) trail past some old growth cedar and Douglas-fir. The blooming Rhododendrons (in June) are spectacular.

Skagit Bluffs (Map 6/F3)

This is an easy 5.6 km/3.4 mile (2.5 hour) one-way trail leading along the bluffs above Highway 3. The trail connects the Dewdney Trail with the Hope Pass Trail at Cayuse Flats.

Skyline Trails (Maps 6/E7, 7/B7)

Beginning at the Strawberry Flats parking lot, the Skyline Trail leads 12.5 km/7.6 miles (5 hours) one-way to Mowich Camp. Initially, the trail climbs along the ridge with a good view of Manning Park. Continuing on the trail leads through Despair Pass before reaching the camp, at 475 metres (1,544 feet) in elevation. From the camp, it is possible to hike 13 km/7.9 miles (5–6 hours) one-way into the Skagit Valley via the Skyline II Trail. Another option is to start or return to Lightning Lake via the Skyline I Trail. This option is 16.8 km/10.2 miles (6-7 hours) one-way to the camp.

Three Falls / Strawberry Flats Trail (Maps 7/A7-6/G7)

Beginning at the Strawberry Flats parking lot, this is a rather scenic 9km (3 hour) return hike. The trail is wide and well used at the beginning as it leads to the downhill ski area. From there, the trail is less used and continues on to Shadow Lake, Nepopekum Falls and eventually Derek Falls. For the most part, the trail follows Nepopekum Creek gaining 125 metres (406 feet) in elevation along the way.

Windy Joe Mountain (Map 7/B4)

Beginning at the Beaver Pond parking lot, this trail leads 15 km/9.2 miles (5 hours) return along an old fire access road to the summit of Windy Joe Mountain. During the spring, when it is difficult to cross the Similkameen River, an alternative route is to begin at the Canyon parking lot further west. This latter hike is 18km/11 miles (6 hours) return but not recommended for bikers. Either way, the old fire lookout at the summit offers a great view.

**Backroad
Mapbooks**

www.backroadmapbooks.com

North Shore/Howe Sound Trails

Hiking trails on the North Shore range from difficult hikes straight up the side of a mountain to easy forest walks along the valley floor. Due to the possibility of snow, the high elevation trails have a limited season (from July to October). The lower elevation trails, which are open year round, are easier to walk but can be confusing to follow, as they interconnect, and you might not be on the trail you thought.

If you are a biker, the North Shore Mountain Biking Association is the best source of up-to-date information. The advocacy group has lobbied hard to see mountain biking accepted on the North Shore. Check out their website at www.nsmba.com. Unless you are an expert rider you should stick to the easier trails. When a mountain bike trail is marked as a difficult trail, believe it. Although most areas can be ridden year round, some of the trails can get very muddy, and riding these trails in wet weather can cause them to deteriorate rapidly.

Baden Powell Trail (Maps 1, 11)

The main artery to the massive lower elevation trail network of the North Shore Mountains is the Baden Powell Trail. Built in 1971 during BC's Centennial Year, this popular 42 km (25.6 mile) one-way trail leads through the lush second growth forests from Horseshoe Bay all the way to Deep Cove. The trail climbs up and down as it heads east and west. There are several footbridges, wooden stairwells, a number of dramatic canyons as well as some great views of Vancouver and the surrounding area. The route is well maintained and marked and can be accessed from at least 12 different roads as well as numerous trails. It would take at least 18 hours to do the whole route, so most people break the trail up over a series of day hikes, but there are a couple places where backcountry camping is allowed. The hiking season is best from March through November. Most of the route is open to mountain biking but riders should expect a very technical route with lots of ups and downs, tree roots and difficult creek crossings. From west to east, here are the main sections of the trail:

Horseshoe Bay to Cypress Bowl is a 9 km/5.5 mile (3 hour) section gaining 1,140 metres (3,705 feet) as it heads up the steep Black Mountain Trail;

Hollyburn to the British Properties is 10 km/6 miles (4 hours), and loses 470 metres (1,528 feet);

Cleveland Dam to Lynn Creek is one of the easiest sections of the trail, and can be biked by intermediate riders. Over the 12 km/7.3 mile (5 hour) route, the trail loses 30 metres;

Lynn Creek to Deep Cove is the last 12 km/7.3 mile (4-5 hour) section, and you will wind up 120 metres (390 feet) lower than you started.

Brothers Creek Trail (Map 11/C7)

One of the more popular lower elevation trails in the area, it leads 7 km/4.3 miles return along Brothers Creek. The moderate trail combines longer flat sections with some short, steep grades gaining a total of 435 metres (1,414 feet). This is a good year round hike that follows a fire access road through some older second growth timber dotted by large old growth Douglas-fir and Western Red Cedar. The creek cuts through

a scenic canyon that has three sets of waterfalls, while Blue Gentian Lake, which is found on the trail, has picnic tables. Mountain bikers use the road to access some of the steep, difficult trails of the Lower Cypress Area. The trailhead is found on Millstream Road.

Capilano Canyon Trails (Maps 1/D1–11/E7)

Several parking lots off the Capilano Park and the Capilano Roads provide access to this network of trails. The Capilano Canyon is a deep, narrow gorge surrounded by sheer granite cliffs. The trails are all well maintained so it makes for easy travel under the large Douglas-fir. Spawning salmon can be seen in the fall.

The Capilano Pacific Trail is the main trail on the west side of the river and is accessed by either crossing Cleveland Dam or the suspension bridge, which charges a fee. This 7.5 km (4.6 mile) trail heads south to Ambelside Park from Cleveland Dam. Expect to lose 236 metres (773 feet) if you walk to the ocean.

The Chinook Trail meanders through the second growth forest on the east side of the river.

The Coho Loop Trail is a 45 min walk that takes you next to the walls of the canyon over two footbridges and through some old growth cedar, Douglas-fir and hemlock.

Capilano Mountain Trail (Map 11/D3)

Park at Porteau Provincial Park and walk 100 metres (325 feet) north to the end of the concrete wall. From there, a difficult trail leads 26 km/15.9 miles (10 hours+) return gaining 1,600 metres (5,200 metres) to the summit of Capilano Mountain. The trail initially leads steadily uphill through a second growth forest to a gated logging road. This road leads to Phyllis and Marion Lake if you stay right. From the left branch, the trail eventually takes off to the right and leads past Beth Lake to the summit. An alternative route is to follow the logging road from just north of Furry Creek Golf Course. Mountain bikers can use the road to gain access to the lakes, which offer good fishing.

Cypress Park Trails (Map 11/B7)

The Cypress Parkway provides easy access to the sub-alpine area of the provincial park but for the more adventurous, it is possible to hike or bike up. Within the park are a number of trails as well as the Hollyburn Cross-Country Ski Area and Cypress Bowl Ski Area to explore.

The Black Mountain Loop is reached by taking the Baden Powell Trail from the downhill ski area. The trail heads up a series of switchbacks past a few small lakes to the south summit for a view of the ocean and city. This is a 7.5 km/4.6 mile (3 hour) loop, gaining 300 metres (975 feet) to the summit of Black Mountain. This is the easy way up. A more challenging route is to hike up Black Mountain from Highway 99 at the Whistler/Squamish Exit. From the highway, it's a steep 16 km/9.8 mile (6 hour) hike gaining 1,140 metres (3,705 feet).

Hollyburn Cross-Country Trails offer fabulous skiing in the winter or hiking in the summer. Found just before the downhill ski area, this popular trail system offers a wide variety of trails, from fairly level walks to some fairly stiff climbs.

Hollyburn Peak Trail leads from the trailhead sign at the cross-country skiing parking lot some 20 km/12.2 miles (7 hours) return to the top of Hollyburn Mountain. The trail heads east, past the old Hollyburn Lodge next to First Lake before climbing steadily uphill past the powerline and the Fourth and Fifth Lakes. From the summit, there is a great view of the Gulf Islands and Vancouver Island. An alternate and less strenuous option is to follow the Baden Powell Trail from the downhill skiing parking lot.

The Howe Sound Crest Trail is the link between the northern and southern portions of the park. The trail is 29 km (8 hours) one-way and is clearly marked with orange markers. It links a number of North Shore Mountain hikes and is best hiked between mid-July to the first snowfall. This is a difficult but rewarding hike, which offers backcountry camping and shelters. From Cypress Bowl, the trail climbs up to St. Marks Summit, drops a few hundred metres before heading up to Unnecessary Ridge, the highest point on the trail at 1,525 metres (4,956 feet). From here, the trail follows an undulating ridge before dropping down to Deeks Creek. Excellent views of Bowen Island and the Howe Sound as well as The Lions are offered.

Mount Strachan Trail begins at the downhill ski area and leads 10 km/6.1 miles (5 hours) return to the double summit of Mount Strachan (pronounced Strawn) at 1,450 metres (4,713 feet). The trail gains 540 metres (1,755 feet).

Upper & Lower Cypress Biking Trails: Speed demons will enjoy cruising the fire access roads from the upper parking lot down to the first switchback on the Cypress Bowl Road. The route is 7.5 km (4.6 miles) and drops 735 metres (2,389 feet). Others like to ride up the scenic road and explore the numerous trails in the area. The side trails, which eventually bring you back to the parkway, should be left to expert mountain bikers who are prepared for some nifty man-made obstacles. On the other side of the Cypress Bowl Road are the Lower Cypress Trails. The Skyline Trail (see below) provides the main corridor through this challenging biking area.

Yew Lake Trail is a 4 km/2.4 mile (1.5hr) wheelchair accessible trail around Yew Lake. It is a good choice for a family outing as it involves a generally flat walk (145 metres/471 feet in elevation gain) through a sub-alpine forest around a small lake dotted with lily pads. There is some old growth forest in the area as well as a good view of Snug Cove and Deep Bay. The trail becomes accessible in late June with the season ending in October.

Cypress Falls Trail (Map 11/B7) 🚶 👣

Despite it's natural beauty, Cypress Falls Park is not very well known. A shame. The main trail in the park is an easy 6 km (3.7 mile) trail that loops around Cypress Creek's lower and upper falls. The trail starts out steep, but quickly levels out and becomes easier to hike, but there are a number of other interconnected trails in the park as well.

Deeks Lake and Peak Trails (Map 11/B4) 🚶 🐟 👣

From the northern Deeks Creek Trailhead (near Kallahne Creek on Highway 99), there are two difficult trails to explore. Deeks Lake Trail is a 20 km (12.2 mile) route that climbs 1,190 metres (3,868 feet) to the height of land at 1,220 metres (3,900 feet). On the trail, you pass a powerline and then meet an old logging road. Proceed right and follow the road for 40 minutes past a small pond. From there, the trail swings left and rises sharply to the base of the peak, above Deeks Lake. Deeks Peak Trail is a 17.5 km/10.7 mile (8 hour) route that is notorious for it's steep climb. You will climb over 1,500 metres to the height off land at 1,674 metres. From the lake, it is possible to continue on to Brunswick Mountain. The trails are best taken in July through October.

Deeks Bluff Circuit (Map 11/B4) 🚶

Unlike the other trails in the Deeks area, this trail doesn't climb past the 400 metres (1,300 feet) mark, making this a good intermediate trail. Even better, when the higher trails to Deeks Lake and Deeks Peak are snowed under, this trail is still navigable. The trail is 10 km (6 miles) return, and should take about 5 hours to hike. This trail hooks up with the Deeks Lake Trail.

Grouse Mountain Trails (Map 11/E7) 🚶 👣

Starting at the base of Grouse Mountain at the end of Capilano Road are a series of popular trails including the infamous Grouse Grind. Hikers wishing to explore the alpine areas, often prefer to ride the gondola to the top. Those people looking to get a great workout prefer to grunt their way to the top. Either way, the views can be fabulous from the top. Due to snow, hikes up the surrounding mountain are best left until July to early November.

BCMC Trail is nowhere near as popular as the Grouse Grind, but was the original route up to the top of Grouse Mountain. The steep 3.5 km (2.2 mile) trail is only slightly longer than the Grind, and climbs

the same height. A new ski run has forced the last stretch of the trail to be rerouted. This is one of the oldest hiking trails in BC.

Blue Grouse Lake Trail is an easy walking trail at the top of Grouse Mountain that loops around Blue Grouse Lake, which is right near the Chalet. Expect to take about half an hour to make this short circuit.

Crown Mountain Route involves making your way along a difficult, exposed route where one misstep could be disastrous. With this in mind, Crown Mountain is best left to folks who know what they're doing. It is 9.6 km (6 miles) from the top of the gondola to the peak, climbing 695 feet (2,278 feet).

The Grouse Grind isn't a trail, it's a social phenomenon. On evenings after work and on weekends, this trail sees hundreds of walkers, looking for a good burn as the trail climbs just about a kilometre (853 metres/2,772 feet) in 2.9 km (1.8 miles). If you do the math, that's about 1 metre up for every 3.4 metres traveled, which makes this a good cardio-workout. This partially explains the phenomenal traffic the trail sees. Another important element in the Grind's popularity is the fact that there is a bar at the top, and the fact that you don't have to hike back down. Most catch the gondola (for a fee) back down. Besides, who can argue with the chance to hike up a trail with a bunch of young, hard-bodied people wearing really tight clothes? The hike leads straight up the old lift line from the parking lot to the bottom of The Cut. From there, continue up the ski run to the top of the gondola. Although this trail is often hiked all year round, it is not advisable to hike in winter, and people have been killed in avalanches. Save this one for spring.

Goat Mountain Trail is usually accessed from the top of the gondola, which cuts off the first 3 km (1.8 miles) and 1,000 metres or so of elevation. From the gondola, this hike is 8 km/4.9 miles (4.5 hours) return gaining 275 metres (894 feet) to the summit at 1,400 metres (4,550 feet). The hike starts on an old road before the trail heads up Goat Ridge. You can include the Dam Mountain Loop in your hike, and maybe even a side trip to Little Goat Mountain.

The views of the Lower Mainland...on days you can actually see Greater Vancouver.

Peak View Trail is an easy walking trail atop Grouse Mountain. It runs just 500 metres (1,625 feet) from the top of the Peak Chair to a lookout over Vancouver. The trail is longer and more difficult if you chose to walk up from the chalet along the Dam/Goat Mountain Trail. Head right to the peak of Grouse.

Village Chair Trail: One of a series of lesser-known trails up to the top of Grouse Mountain, The Village Chair Trail (or The Cut Trail) is the third trail to leave the Baden Power Trail and head up Grouse Mountain. This 4 km (2.4 mile) trail is a good alternative to avoid the crowd, while still getting that cardio workout. Look for the trail heading up an old chairlift cut-line just before crossing Mosquito Creek, about 30 minutes down the Baden Powell from the parking lot.

Hollyburn Heritage Trails (Map 11/C7) 🚶 ⛺

From the west side of Lawson Creek Bridge on Pinecrest Drive, an extensive trail network leads through the second growth forest typical of the North Shore. The main trail leads 6.7 km/4 miles (3.5 hours) return to the Hollyburn Fir, an 1100-year-old Douglas-fir that is 3 metres (9.7 feet) in diameter. The trail crosses the Crossover and Baden Powell Trails. Within the area, the remains of logging from the 1920s are seen. Another possible access point is at the junction of Eyremount, Crestwell and Millstream Roads.

Lighthouse Park (Map 1/A1) 🏕 🚶 ⛺

From the parking lot at Lighthouse Park, an extensive year round trail network leads through old growth forest to the wave washed rocky shoreline of Point Atkinson. If you hike around the perimeter of the park, the 5 km/3 mile hike should take about 2 hours. But there are many other trails snaking through the forest. Make sure you visit the eponymous lighthouse, which was erected in 1912.

Lions Trail (Map 11/C5) ⛰ 🚶 📷 ⛺

The trailhead to this popular hike is found at Lions Bay by taking the Oceanside Road exit off Highway 99 and driving to the gate at the end of Mountain Drive (parking is limited). The difficult trail follows an old road upward until there is a fork in the road. The right fork leads to the Lions Trail, while the left fork accesses the Brunswick Mountain Trail. You will climb down to Harvey Creek (a depressing prospect, knowing that you'll just have to climb back up again), then heads up through an old growth forest. The last part of the 15 km/9.1 mile (7 hour) hike climbs steeply to a small summit to the south of the West Lion, where it is possible to pitch a tent and enjoy the view of the Howe Sound. You will climb 1,280 metres (4,160 feet). The hike is best done in late summer or early fall.

Found off the Lions Trail are a couple less popular peaks to climb. The Brunswick Mountain Trail is a difficult route that climbs 1,550 metres (5,038 feet) over 15 km/9.1 mile (8 hour) return. The Mount Harvey Trail climbs more steeply; gaining 1,465 metres (4,761 feet) in 12.5 km (7.6 miles). The trail will take most people about 8 hours.

Lower Seymour Conservation Reserve (Map 11/G7) 🚶 🚴 🛶 ⛺

Formerly known as the Seymour Demonstration Forest, this 5,200 ha area was created in 1987 to educate the public about forest ecosystems and logging practices. While these things still happen within the forest, they are no longer the prime emphasis. Within the reserve are several well maintained trails and a few hidden routes to explore. From the parking lot at the end of Lillooet Road, a series of easier routes exist. No dogs are allowed in the reserve.

Seymour Dam Road Path leads 11 km (6.7 miles) one-way to the Seymour Dam and can be walked, biked or even skated by inline skaters. A new paved path has been created to take people off the service road.

The Fisherman Trail is a moderate route, popular with anglers

and mountain bikers, that combines an old road with single-track trail as you skirt along the scenic Seymour River. Follow the Twin Bridges Trail to the bottom of the hill, then head north (left) before the bridge. The trail is 7 km (4.3 miles) long but a side trip to the Seymour Dam can add more distance. Be forewarned that this trail is 'closed' to cyclists.

The Integrated Resource Management Trail is an easy walk through a coniferous forest illustrating different forestry practices.

Poster Child Trail is a new trail built by the North Shore Mountain Biking Association, Poster Child is a brand new bottom half of the old CBC Trail. The trail used to cross into Mount Seymour Park, but after mountain biking trails in Seymour were closed, it had to be rerouted. And so Poster Child, one of the best examples of how mountain biking trails can be built right, was born. It is a difficult trail through a highly sensitive environment, yet the trail has been built to minimize the impact of bikes on the landscape.

The Rice Lake Connector is an easy, short 1.2 km (0.7 mile) gravel road with little elevation gain.

The Twin Bridges Trail is a 2.6 km (1.6 mile) trail that descends 100 m/325 feet (mostly one long hill) to the bridge. Once across the bridge, you can head south along the river to Riverside Drive, or explore the many Lower Seymour Trails in the area.

Lower Seymour Trails (Map 11/G7) 🚶 🚴 🐎

A few years back, the rangers at Mount Seymour Provincial Park closed the Lower Seymour Trails that were inside park boundaries, severely limiting mountain biking in this area. Still, some of the classic rides here (Bridal Path, Severed Dick), located below the park boundaries are still open. Comparatively speaking, this is one of the easier areas to mountain bike on the North Shore. This large network of trails, which are also enjoyed by hikers and horseback riders, extends between Mt Seymour Parkway and Lynn Canyon Park.

Lynn Canyon Park (Map 1/F1) 🚶 ⛺

While it's much bigger brother, Lynn Headwaters, gets all the press, Lynn Canyon is arguably a nicer place to be. Its rewards come early. A suspension bridge, just a few steps from the parking lot, is the main feature of the park, and few people make it much beyond the bridge. Those that do, usually head north, to a rocky beach and waterfall that is surprisingly busy on a hot summer day. What this means is the short loop trail is usually free of foot traffic, even in the middle of summer. A second bridge, below a series of cascades spans the creek, making an easy loop. More energetic hikers can continue straight and connect up with the Baden Powell Trail, which can be used as the second leg in an 8 km (4.8 mile) loop (the third leg is along the Fisherman/Homestead Trails, back to Lynn Canyon).

Lynn Headwaters Regional Park (Map 11/F6) 🚶 ⛺

This popular park offers a wide variety of trails ranging from easy creek side walks to strenuous wilderness treks. The heavily wooded trails make for good wet weather walking. The park is accessed off the Lynn Valley Road past Dempsey Road.

Coliseum Mountain involves a steep 25 km/15.25 mile (11 hour) return hike along a sometimes indistinct route. The route is marked with orange markers as you pass through the steep forested area and enter the Norvan Meadows on your way to Norvan Pass gaining 1,245 metres (4,046 feet). The difficult hike is best left for the drier weather of late summer and early fall. Although there is no camping allowed in the park, the Coliseum is the type of destination that makes a perfect overnight trip.

Hanes Valley Loop brings hikers over to Grouse Mountain along a steep 17 km (10.4 mile) hike along Hanes Creek. The trail gains 900 metres (2,995 feet), most of this as you climb up the steep scree slope out of the valley to Crown Pass. The rough trail leaves the Headwaters Trail at Norvan Creek, and has some difficult creek crossings. Good route finding skills are a must.

Lynn Loop leads over the bridge near the parking lot (as all trails in

Lynn headwaters must) and heads north into the valley along the east bank of Lynn Creek. There is little elevation gain along this trail, and you can return the way you came. However, to complete the loop, you must head up (about 350 metres/1,138 feet) into the woods, and back along a slightly more challenging path. This trail leads through a vast forest of giant stumps and verdant second growth forest. For some, this trail shows the recovery power of nature. For others, it is a reminder of what this forest once was, before the loggers came. Either way, it is an impressive site. This is a 9.5 km (5.8 mile) trip, with a shortcut trail at about the halfway point, creating a shorter loop.

Norvan Falls is a 13.5 km/8.2 mile (5 hour) return hike gaining 375 metres (1,230 feet) in elevation to the scenic falls. The trail follows the same path as the Lynn Loop, but when the loop doubles back on itself, keep heading north for another 3 km (1.8 miles) to the falls. This trail is open year round.

Lynn Lake involves a long trek that few people can manage in a day. You'll really have to leg it to hike the 25 km (15.3 mile) to the lake and back, which means you won't have much time to enjoy your time here. Even better, the trail is ragged and rough and sometimes not even a trail at all. This route is best left for experienced (and fast) hikers.

Lynn Peak at 1,000 metres (3,250 feet), is not referred to as a real mountain. When compared to it's neighbours (Grouse and Fromme to the west; the Mount Seymour peaks to the east), Lynn isn't a standout. But unlike Seymour, which you can drive up, and Grouse, which has its gondola, the only way to the top of Lynn is with your own two feet, and that alone is worth a recommendation. The viewpoint at the top isn't a high alpine clearing, but a rocky outcropping, from which you can see the Seymour River Valley and the Lower Mainland. It'll take about four hours to hike the 7 km/4.3 miles return trip. There are some tough spots, and a few stiff climbs along the way.

The Needles is a recently cleared and marked 8 hour route starting a few hundred metres from Lynn Peak. Do not try bushwhacking down from the top, as there are some steep cliffs between you and Lynn Creek; you'll have to head out the way you came.

Rice Lake is actually outside Lynn Headwaters, and inside the Lower Seymour Conservation Reserve, but a trail runs from the parking lot and around Rice Lake. It is an easy 4 km/2.4 mile (2 hour) loop on an old road gaining 330 metres (1,073 feet). This is the only section of trail inside Lynn Headwaters that is open to mountain biking.

Mosquito Creek Trails (Map 11/E7) 🚶 🚵 🧗

Mosquito Creek Trail is a great choice if you want to sample the North Shore Mountains without the usual elevation gain. This one only gains 320 metres (1,040 feet). From the bottom of the Grouse Mountain Gondola, head east along the Baden Powell Trail, and avoid the steady stream of people climbing the Grouse Grind. The Mosquito Creek Trail departs the Baden Powell only after passing all three (four, if you count the alternate routing of the BCMC Trail) Grouse Mountain Trails. About 25 metres (75 feet) past the Village Chair Trail, the Mosquito Creek Trail finally breaks free of the Baden Powell and heads east to Mosquito Creek. The trail follows the east banks of Mosquito Creek to the Mosquito Creek Cascades (they aren't quite big enough to be called falls). The hike is 8 km/4.8 miles (4 hours) return.

Mount Fromme Trail (Map 11/F7) 🚶 🚵 🧗

A series of trails access Mount Fromme. The main trail is a 15 km (9.1 mile) route that begins off Prospect Road near Mosquito Creek. It is a difficult, steep trail that gains 870 metres (2,828 feet) to the summit. The trail begins on the Baden Powell Trail and shortly turns onto a trail labeled "To the Old Mountain Highway." From there, follow the steep Old Mountain Highway, a popular biking route, past Meech Lake to the summit. Once you reach the top, it is best to descend through Pipeline Pass back to the Old Mountain Highway and walk down the road to

St. George's Trail, an alternate trail up. Eventually, you meet up with the Baden Powell Trail and a return to the start. Another alternative is to follow the Per Gynt Trail to the peak of Mount Fromme. This is one of a collection of trails built by legendary trail builder Halvor Lunden.

Mount Seymour Provincial Park (Maps 1\G1, 11/G7, 12/A6)
🚶 🚵 🐴 🛶 🧗 🎿

The 3,508 ha provincial park is easily reached by way of the Mount Seymour Parkway. The park contains a variety of trails from easy strolls to rough backcountry excursions. All the trails are very popular given their scenic surroundings, views of Vancouver and proximity to the city. The best time to hike in the park is in July through November due to snow accumulations at higher levels. In winter, the hills remain busy with snowshoers and backcountry skiers. Below, we have described the main trails in the park. Please note that the Old Buck Trail is the only trail where horseback riding and mountain biking are allowed:

Mount Seymour Trail is also known as the Three Pumps Trail. This is the main trail leading from the north end of the upper parking lot. The moderate hike is 9 km/5.5 mile (5 hour) return, with an elevation gain to 450 metres (1,463 feet) to the Third (and final) Pump. The popular trail climbs steadily through a fairly open sub-alpine forest before breaking out into the alpine meadows. The trail gets more challenging as you dip and climb to the Second Pump and dip and climb again to the Third Pump, which is the actual 1,450 metre (4,713 foot) summit of Mount Seymour. Since great views of Greater Vancouver are offered from any of the three pumps, most people like to shorten the route do not bother climbing beyond the First Pump. Those that make it to the Third Pump will enjoy even better views and peace and solitude as they look back on the crowds at the First Pump.

Dog Mountain Trail is an easy 6 km/3.6 mile (1.5-2 hour) return hike from the north end of the upper parking lot. Since there is little elevation gain, this trail (along with the Suicide Bluffs Trail) is more popular in winter with snowshoers. It leads through an old growth sub-alpine fir stand to the bluff overlooking the Seymour River and Greater Vancouver. The trail follows the First Lake Trail for 30 minutes, before heading to the west from the lake. On the return trip, complete the First Lake Loop by taking the north branch of the trail at First Lake and connecting with the Mount Seymour Trail. A further option is to hike the short distance (less than a kilometre) to Dinky Peak for another great view.

Elsay Lake Trail is a difficult 20 km/12 mile (12 hour/overnight) hike through Canadian Pass and some rugged alpine country. The total elevation gain is 885 metres (2,876 feet), but there are a couple ups and downs along the way. The hike begins at the north end of the upper parking lot, initially following the Mount Seymour Trail. Take the branch trail just before the First Pump that leads northwest to tiny Gopher Lake. Beyond here, the trail narrows and is occasionally marked. A small backcountry shelter marks the end of the trail at the north end of the lake. Be wary, it is a steeper trek on the return trip.

Goldie Lake / Flower Lake Loops are easy loops found to the east of the upper parking lot and make fine cross-country skiing and snowshoeing routes. The Goldie Lake Loop is a 2 km (1 hour) trail leading past the Goldie Rope Tow area to Goldie Lake, gaining 218 metres (709 feet) along the way. This trail meets with the Flower Lake Loop and the top end of the Perimeter Trail so you can take either of these trails to increase the length of the hike. The Flower Lake Loop is 1.5 km (45 minutes) return with an elevation gain of 150 metres (487 feet). This trail passes through a sub-alpine bog and past a small pond filled with wildlife.

Mount Elsay Trail is little more than a bushwhack from the Elsay Lake Trail. It is 16 km/9.8 miles (9 hours) return from the upper parking lot and involves climbing 1,050 metres (3,413 feet) along a difficult, flagged route with some rock scrambling. From the summit at 1,422 metres (4,665 feet), you are rewarded with an excellent view, and most likely, the peak all to yourself (something that can't be said for most other trails in the park). The hike is best left to experienced backpackers.

Mystery Lake Loop begins at the upper parking lot and follows the Mystery Ski Lift before connecting with the Mount Seymour Trail and the return to the parking lot. It will take about 1.5 hours to complete this 3 km (1.8 mile) loop, with an elevation gain of 180 metres (585 feet). The beautiful sub-alpine lake is a good spot to swim during a hot summer day.

Old Buck Trail starts from the Park Headquarters and climbs steadily uphill connecting with the Baden Powell Trail about 2.3 km/1.4 miles (45 minutes) along the trail. Old Buck also joins the Perimeter Trail near the Deep Cove Lookout about 5.5 km/3.4 miles (2 hours) later. You will climb 670 metre (2,178 feet) along a sometimes washed out, sometimes rocky old road that parallels the Mount Seymour Parkway. Since this trail does not offer the beauty and views of the other trails in the area, the main users of the trail are mountain bikers, who are usually heading downhill.

Perimeter Trail is a 1.5 km/1.2 mile (45 minute) one-way hike gaining 240 metres (780 feet) in elevation. The trail begins at the Deep Cove Lookout and climbs steadily uphill to connect with the Goldie Loop.

Skyline Trail (Map 11/C7) 👤 🚴 🐎 🚻

Not to be confused with the epic hike in Manning Park, this Skyline Trail is actually an old service road for the powerline that gains 375 metres (1,219 feet) over 7 km (4.3 miles). This trail is an easy, surprisingly scenic hike, but a difficult mountain bike ride that forms part of the Trans Canada Trail hiking route. There are several technically demanding and steep mountain bike trails that depart from this trail.

Sunset Trail (Map 11/B7) 👤 🚻

Found opposite the Sunset Marina on Highway 99, the Sunset Trail leads up (up and up) past a gate on the second road (ignore the no trespassing sign), all the way to Yew Lake and Cypress Bowl. You'll have hiked 7 km (14 km/8.5 mile return) and climbed 855 metres (2,779 feet) by the time you're finished. If you still have energy, why not hike to the 1,455 metre (4,728 foot) summit of Mount Strachan. This second alternative is 22 km/13.4 miles (9 hours), climbing 1,400 metres (4,550 feet) along the way.

Three-Chop Trail (Map 1/G1) 👤 🚻

This trail used to be a popular biking destination that is now closed. It is 13 km/7.9 miles (5 hours) return gaining 550 metres (1,788 feet) to a viewpoint overlooking Deep Cove. The route begins at the 3.2 km (2 mile) mark on the Indian River FSR along a hydro access road before the actual trail leads from the road into a second growth forest. From the lookout, you can return to the start via the Old Buck Trail. The hike can be made anytime from May through November.

Unnecessary Mountain Trail (Map 11/D5) 👤 🚻

Unnecessary Mountain gets it's name from the obstacle it forms on the Howe Sound Crest Trail. As a destination, the mountain does offer a rewarding view. Unfortunately, the trail unmaintained is rough, rugged and steep. From the gate on Oceanview Road (right before the Harvey Creek Bridge in Lions Bay), follow the paved and then gravel road to the trailhead marked by orange markers. In all, it is a difficult 9.5 km/5.8 mile (7 hour) return hike gaining 1,310 metres (4,258 feet) to the summit at 1,510 metres (4,908 feet).

Powell River Trails

Appleton Canyon / Marathon Trails (Map 16/G2) 👤 🚻

The trailhead is found only 20 metres (60 feet) north of the Sliammon Lake Trail on the Theodosia FSR. It is a well marked trail that leads along Appleton Creek past some nice waterfalls and through an old growth forest. The Appleton Canyon Trail culminates at the Appleton Creek Recreation Site 2 km/1.2 miles (30 minutes) along the way. The Marathon Trail continues on and eventually leads to the Southview Road. The trail is 4 km/2.4 miles (1.5 hours) one-way and leads past Rieveley's Pond. A side trip leads to the Gibraltar viewpoint, which provides a fantastic view of the Strait of Georgia.

Beartooth Mountain Trail (Map 26/E6) 👤 🚻

This trailhead is accessed by boat on Powell Lake. The difficult trail begins on the north side of Beartooth Creek and extends 8 km 4.8 miles (4 hours) from Powell Lake to the summit of Beartooth Mountain gaining 1,720 metres (5,590 feet) along the way. The trail is generally easy to follow, and is blazed with flagging tape through an old growth forest.

Beta Lake / Knuckleheads Trails (Map 17/G2) 👤 🏕 🚵 🚻

Leading from Branch E-100 off the Stillwater Main, a short, 1.5 km (30 minute) trail leads from the end of the road to a small sub-alpine lake. The trail is not well marked and often has snow into summer. Black bears are common to the area so take precautions. It is possible to continue on to the Knuckleheads, which is an excellent alpine climbing area with views of the surrounding lakes. The Knuckleheads Trail is steep and unmarked and will take 6-8 hours to complete.

Bunster Hills Loop (Map 16/F2–G1) 🚴 🚻

From Wilde Road off Highway 101, this moderate bike ride initially climbs 750 metres (2,438 feet) over 12 km (7.2 miles). Enjoy the views of Okeover Inlet and the Georgia Straight before the descent. The 34 km (20.7 mile) loop is well marked as you follow logging roads back to the highway. Allow 4 hours.

Confederation Lake Trail (Map 17/A1) 👤 🎣 🐟 🚻

The trailhead is found on an old logging road that starts to the east side of Inland Lake. A gate near the Inland Lake Campsite may add an additional 1.5 km (0.9 miles) one-way to the actual trailhead. From the trailhead, a well-marked trail leads past Confederation Lake and eventually to Powell Lake. Along the way you hike through a stand of old growth cedar and Douglas-fir as well as catching glimpses of Inland and Powell Lakes. A forest service log cabin is located on the east side of Confederation Lake and provides a wood stove and accommodation for six individuals. The distance to the log cabin is 8 km/4.8 miles (3.5 hours) one-way. Beyond Confederation Lake, it is possible to continue on to Powell Lake on an old road. The trail from Confederation Lake to Powell Lake is 7.5 km/4.6 miles (3 hours) one-way. The scenic trail descends to Powell Lake ending at the Fiddlehead Farm where there is a bed and breakfast resort complete with showers. The Confederation Lake Trail makes up a portion of the Sunshine Coast Trail.

Diadem Mountain Trail (Map 18/A1) 👤 🚻

This hike is located along a road leading up Lois River Valley. A gate located before the valley may impede travel by vehicle to the trailhead, which is marked by a cairn with flagging tape. The route proceeds through a deep gorge eventually leading up to a ridge. From there, you cross a creek at the end of a box canyon and proceeds up into the sub-alpine past a series of ponds. Eventually, the trail culminates at the summit for a total of 8 km/4.8 miles (6 hours) return.

Duck Lake Area (Map 17/B3) 👤 🚴 🚻

The Duck Lake FSR provides access to several hiking/biking trail systems found just east of Powell River. The variety of activities and proximity of all the trails makes this a good area to explore.

The Blackwater Trail starts about 100 metres (325 feet) south of the Y-fork on the Duck Lake Loop. This 7 km/4.3 mile (2.5 hour) trail begins along an old railgrade for 750 metres (2,400 feet) leading to Blackwater Creek. As the trail leads along the banks of Blackwater Creek, it passes by a series of waterfalls. Eventually, the trail climbs over the divide on an old logging road to Washout Creek. At that location, you will enter a spectacular gorge and continue in a westward direction back to the start.

The Blue Trail is an easy 2 km (45 minute) interpretative trail that follows an old railgrade southwest of Duck Lake. The trail cuts through the woods about 6 km (3.6 miles) along the Duck Lake FSR. It crosses Fred's Trail, which will bring you to Padgett Road outside Powell River, before descending back to the road. A self-guiding brochure is available.

The Cable Trail begins opposite to the Suicide Creek Loop and is an easy 8 km/4.8 miles (3 hour) journey. The trail crosses a footbridge and then meanders through a second growth forest before crossing Sweetwater Creek. From there, the trail follows an old railgrade up a steady incline eventually looping back to Sweetwater Creek and the trailhead. The highlight of the trip is MacGregor Falls.

Duck Lake Loop is a 21 km (12.8 mile) moderate trail, mostly used by mountain bikers. It follows logging roads and the powerlines east of Powell River. The route starts at the 3.5 km mark (2.1 miles) on the Duck Lake FSR. Follow the road north to the intersection at 7.5 km (4.6 miles), and keep right, following the main roads to the powerlines, which will return you to the parking spot.

Hamill Hills Trail requires some bushwhacking and is necessary when walking along the overgrown road that leads to the bluffs of Hamill Hill. The trail starts from the Duck Lake Road near the Maple Springs Ranch, and leads 5 km/3 miles (1.5 hours) through ranch pastures and along an old road eventually culminating at the bluffs. When you reach the bluffs, you will be rewarded with a panoramic view of the coastline.

Lang Creek Loop is an easy, well marked trail that leads south from the 6 km (3.6 mile) mark of the Duck Lake Forest Service Road. The trail is only 3 km/1.8 miles (1 hour) one-way and its gentle grades are well-suited for a family outing. Mountain bikers can expect a moderate route with some of the best single-track riding in the area. Both the Lang Creek and East Lake Recreation Sites provide picnic sites en route. Spawning salmon can be seen in Lang Creek in September and October.

The Mud Lake Trails are a network of generally flat, well marked trails well-suited for a family outing. The total distance of the trail depends on the route you plan to take as there are several interconnecting trails to pick from. Each trail is well signed so you should not get lost. Be forewarned that the area can be muddy during wet weather, especially in the spring. Wildlife viewing and the beautiful wildflowers around Duck Lake are some highlights as is swimming at Haslam Slough. Mountain bikers should be wary of the technical sections around Mud and Deer Lakes.

Suicide Creek Loop is located on the opposite side of the road from the Mud Lake Trails. The trail heads in a southeast direction approximately 8 km/4.8 miles (2 hours). Highlights of the trail include two sets of waterfalls. The Fern Falls has a picnic table and is below the first bridge, while the Mimulus Falls are found between the two footbridges. Mountain bikers should expect a moderate trail with re-routes around the rougher sections.

Sweetwater Creek Loop begins by following an old railgrade leading to Sweetwater Creek. The trail follows the creek draw eventually leading past MacGregor Falls. From there, the trail continues past Donelley Falls before heading south and back to Duck Lake Road. You will cover 7 km/4.2 miles (1.5 hours) along a well marked trail, which is ideal for moderate mountain bikers as well as hikers. The trail also provides access to the Blackwater Trail.

SUNSHINE COAST TRAIL

The Sunshine Coast Trail is located on the Upper Sunshine Coast, and stretches 180 km (109 miles) from Saltery Bay in the south to Sarah Point in Desolation Sound. As a general rule, the closer you get to Sarah Point, the tougher the route gets. In fact, Mount Troutbridge is just a few kilometres before the end of the trail and is the highest point on the trail, at 1,263 metres (4,105 feet). One of the interesting aspects of this trail is the fact that there is a trio of Bed and Breakfasts located en route, including the famous Fiddlehead Farm. Along the trail you can find great ocean views, occasional waterfront access, old growth forests, ocean vistas, an oceanfront campsite, and a lakeside campsite with swimming and freshwater fishing. If you are planning on beginning (or ending) at Sarah Point, you will have to arrange for a water taxi, unless you want to hike in. You will also have to arrange for boat transportation to get across Powell Lake to or from Fiddlehead Farm. To do the whole trail from end to end will take a week to ten days, but most sections are doable as one or two day hikes.

Elephant Lake Loop (Maps 17/G5–18/A5) 🚴 🥾

A long 48 km/29.3 mile (5-6 hour) moderate bike ride that follows the main logging roads north of Saltery Bay. The roads lead past several small lakes and offer views of Jervis Inlet, Lois Lake and the surrounding area. You return along Highway 101. Don't be discouraged by the tough 8 km (4.8 mile) initial climb. The riding does get easier, and the views are spectacular.

Emma Lake Trail (Maps 26/G5–27\A5) 🏕 🥾 🎣 🌲 🐟 🥾

Emma Lake Trail begins off the B-Branch from the Goat Lake Main. The steep trail leads 7 km/4.2 miles (5 hours) to a forest service cabin set on Emma Lake. That cabin provides accommodation for eight individuals but it is usually full. If you are planning on spending the night at this beautiful blue lake, surrounded by sub-alpine meadows containing heather, expect to tent it. If you stay overnight, you can take day trips to Snowy, Thunder Dome and Crossroads Peaks. Also, the South Powell Divide Route leads southward, including a ridge run from Triple Peaks to Center Lakes.

Freda Mountain Trails (Maps 17/G1–18/A1) 🥾 🥾

To reach the summit of Freda Mountain, there are three possibilities. The southernmost route is a long trail leading from the Freda Mountain Main just north of the F-Branch. It involves a day+ hike. A more direct route is found on the J-Branch at the south end of Freda Lake. It is 8 km/4.8 mile (3-4 hour) return trip that leads through an old growth forest to the sub-alpine. The third trail begins on the Jenna Branch Road at the east end of Freda Lake. This involves a 12 hour hike on a well marked (flagged) trail leading through the old growth timber to the sub-alpine.

Frogpond Lake Trail (Map 26/C7) 🥾 🥾

This steep, 5 km/3 mile (2.5 hour) trail leads from Powell Lake up to Frogpond Lake. The trailhead is accessed by taking a boat to Cassiar Falls where the trail begins on the east side of the creek. Half way along the trail you reach a bench, which overlooks Powell Lake with a good view of Fiddlehead Farm and Tin Hat Mountain to the south.

Gallagher Hills Trail (Map 17/A3) 🥾 🥾

The trail begins 100 metres (325 feet) along the Inland Lake Road. The trail leads along an old skid trail up to a rock bluff and then on to a radio tower overlooking Powell Lake and the ocean. The total distance of the hike is 5 km/3 miles (1.5 hours) return. It is possible to take a side trip off the bluff and walk down to Mowat Bay.

Goat II Access Trail (Map 27/A7) 🥾 🥾

At the end of Goat 2 Road is the Goat II Access Trail, a difficult hike to a beautiful alpine area. If you proceed south you will see a trailhead marked by flagging tape. From here, you must do some bushwhacking past two small creeks, across a rockslide before reaching the ridge and ultimately the traverse down to Skwim Lake. If you proceed in a northern direction from the Goat Lake II Road, you will have to walk along the deactivated road to an old trail heading up to the base of Triple Peaks. There are alpine flowers in July and great views of the surrounding mountain peaks. From the alpine area, you can continue on the South Powell Divide Trail leading to Emma Lake and beyond.

Haywire Bay Regional Park Trails (Map 17/A3)
There is a pair of trails here. **The Lost Lake Trail** is 6 km/3.6 miles (2 hours) in length and leads through old growth forest past Lost Lake to Inland Lake. There are several steep sections along the trail. **Tony's Trail** leads along the eastern banks of Powell Lake in a southward direction. This trail is 8 km/4.8 miles (2.5 hours) one-way and culminates at Mowat Bay.

Inland Lake Trail (Map 17/B2)
Inland Lake Trail is a wheelchair accessible area, complete with a cabin, picnic tables and a dock. The trail leads 13 km/7.9 miles (3 hours) around the lake. From the west side of the lake, it is possible to connect with the Lost Lake Trail, which culminates at the Haywire Bay Regional Park. At the north end of Inland Lake, you may wish to hike 700m (one-way) along the portage route to Powell Lake. This is a well marked and popular family trail enjoyed by both hikers and bikers.

Mowat Bay Trail (Map 17/A3)
From the Powell Lake Bridge on Highway 101, a 2.3 km/1.4 mile (1 hour) trail leads to Mowat Bay where you can enjoy a nice swim in Powell Lake. The hike switchbacks (100 metres/325 feet) up the northern side of Valentine Mountain before descending to the bay. From the bay, Tony's Trail (see Haywire Bay above) leads up the eastern shores of Powell Lake.

Myrtle Springs Trail (Map 17/A4)
This 5 km/3 mile (1.5 hour) trail begins approximately 200 metres (650 feet) along the Haslam Lake Road. It follows an old road network eventually leading to Duck Lake Road near the Haslam Slough. You can either return along the logging road or the way you came.

Okeover Trail (Map 16/E1)
This well marked and scenic trail begins at the south end of Okeover Inlet off the Southview Road. It heads 8 km/4.8 miles (3.5 hours) to the Theodosia FSR. Rather than proceeding back the way you came, you can follow the forestry road along the eastern shores of the inlet.

Princess Louisa Park (Maps 27/G4)
The remote access to this hidden inlet discourages most hikers. However, the spectacular fjord-like setting is certainly worth the visit. Once you are at the provincial park, a short, well-used trail leads to the world famous Chatterbox Falls (a ten minute excursion). From there, the trail continues beyond the falls and is called the **Loquita Creek Trail**. The trail passes by Old Henry's Cabin at Snake Falls, gaining 875 metres (2,844 feet) along the way. Eventually, the trail continues on to a gorgeous mountain lake. From there, it is possible to hike in the seemingly endless open alpine country with spectacular views of the inlet and nearby rugged snow-capped peaks.

Saltery Bay Park Trails (Map 17/G6)
Saltery Bay Provincial Park has a network of trails worth exploring. The main trail leads 10 km/6 miles (4 hours) along an overgrown road and then a well-defined trail. There is a steep climb at the beginning of the trail but you get a good view of Nelson and Hardy Islands from the summit. A much easier option is to walk 2 km/1.2 miles one-way from the campsite at the provincial park to the beach.

Sliammon Lakes Trail (Maps16/G2)
The trail begins at the end of Sutherland Street and proceeds northward eventually leading to the Theodosia FSR. The well marked trail leads through second growth timber and up some steep sections. The hike

takes you past Little Sliammon Lake, where there is a nice beach for swimming, and on to Sliammon Lake. The trail connects with Appleton-Marathon Trails so it is possible to walk up to 18 km (11 miles) if you so choose. Other alternatives include a side trail to Three Mile Bay and an old mine site. This trail is 5 km/3 miles (1.5 hours) return. It is also possible to hike up Scout Mountain. This trail offers views of Powell Lake and Wildwood Heights before dropping to the Kinsman Park near the Powell Lake Marina.

South Powell Divide Trail (Maps 26\G5, 27\A6)
This high ridge route extends 20 km/12 miles (two days) from the Goat Access II Trail north to the B Branch Road. Experienced hikers with the appropriate topographic maps and route finding skills should only consider this route. Along the way you can enjoy the splendid views of the surrounding lakes and mountain peaks. The popular Emma Lake Cabin makes for a good overnight destination (if it isn't full).

Tin Hat Mountain Trail (Map 17/C1)
This trail starts just north of Spring Lake, along an old road. While it is possible to drive part of the way, it is best to park your vehicle and walk the old road northward. Eventually, you will pick up a well maintained but difficult trail that leads to the summit some 13 km/7.9 miles (5 hours) return gaining 1,600 metres (5,200 feet) along the way. Alpine flowers, bunchberries and great views of the Powell Lake area are offered. The hike is best left for late summer and early fall.

Toquenatch Trail (Map 16/F2)
This well marked trail begins approximately 3.5 km (2.1 miles) along the Southview Road, from where it leaves Highway 101. The hike extends in a northwest direction 5 km/3 miles (1.5 hours) one-way. It leads past two large Douglas-fir trees, and follows the creek, where salmon spawn in the fall, to the south end of Okeover Inlet.

Walt Lake Ridge Route (Map 18/A2)
A four wheel drive spur road leads to the Walt Lake Ridge trailhead. From there, a difficult and unmarked route leads to the alpine where you can proceed either to the north or south. Either way, you have miles of beautiful alpine meadows to explore. The north branch leads to Beta Lake whereas the south branch leads to Khartoum Lake.

Wednesday Lake Trail (Map 25/D7)
This 8 km/4.8 mile (3 hour) hike leads along an old road from Malaspina FSR to tiny Wednesday Lake, which drains into Trevenen Bay of Okeover Inlet.

Wildwood Hill Trail (Maps 16/G3, 17\A3)
The trail begins on the west side of the Powell Lake Bridge off Highway 101. This trail switchbacks twice before it connects with the powerline to the south. It eventually leads back to the Petro Canada Service Station. The trail is easily followed and is wide enough for both mountain bikers and hikers.

Willingdon Beach Trail (Map 17/A3)
This trail begins at the Willingdon Beach Campsite and follows the shoreline for about 2 km/1.2 miles (30 minutes) one-way. The trail is wide and well marked. Along the way, there is interpretative signs featuring historic logging machinery as well as coastal ecosystems.

Backroad Mapbooks

www.backroadmapbooks.com

Squamish Area Trails

Alice Lake Park (Map 20/D6) 🚶 🚵 🐟

This park offers good access to several trails in and around the area. The most popular year round trail is the **Four Lakes Walk.** This well-developed 6.5 km/4 mile (2-3 hour) trail leads past four woodland lakes providing a leisurely stroll through a second growth forest. The trail also joins with trails leading to Cat Lake, the highway and Garibaldi Estates.

Alice Ridge Trail (Map 20/E3) 🚶 📷 🏕

Take the right fork when the road splits at the Alice Lake Provincial Park Headquarters and drive up the rough 4wd road as far as you can. From the end of the road, hike uphill to the Little Diamond Head and the base of Mount Garibaldi. If you can get to the end of the road, you'll only have to walk 8 km/4.8 miles (5 hour) return hike gaining 700 metres (2,275 feet) along the way. The height of land is at 2,075 metres (6,744 feet) and provides a great view of the Squamish Valley. The route, which is best hiked in July to October, provides an alternative route to the Diamond Head Area.

Brohm Lake Interpretive Trails (Map 20/D5) 🚶 🚵 🐟 🏕

From the parking lot off Highway 99, an easy 5 km/3 mile (1.5 hour) trail with minimal elevation gain circles the lake. The trail provides access to the picnic area next to Brohm Lake and is used for shore fishing as well as wildlife viewing. Around Brohm Lake, you will also find a network of 11 km (6.7 miles) of interconnecting trails used by mountain bikers and hikers. These trails lead away from the lake and through the bluffs and second growth forest typical of the area.

Cat Lake Area (Map 20/E5) 🚶 🚵 🏇 🐟

Around Cat Lake, a series of motorbike trails offer very challenging routes for the mountain biker. These trails can be accessed off of the Cheekeye River FSR at the old gondola base area or the Cat Lake Recreation Site. It is possible to cross the Cheekeye River and follow the trails down to Alice Lake or Garibaldi Highlands.

Cheakamus Canyon Trail (Map 20/C2) 🚶 🚵 🏇 🐟 🏕

The Cheakamus Canyon Route has been absorbed by the Sea to Sky Trail, but it makes an interesting day trip in itself. From the end of Paradise Valley Road, it is 3 km (1.8 miles) to the rather unpleasantly named Starvation Lake. Some people turn around here, but the trip doesn't really get interesting until after the lake, as it skirts the edge of the canyon. While you can walk to where the old cattle trail disappears under the new Highway 99, you probably won't want to walk much farther than 1.5 km (0.9 miles) past the lake before turning around. Near the beginning, if you cut through the bush, you will also find a scenic fisherman's trail that provides a nice riverside walk.

Crumpit Woods (Map 20/E7) 🚶 🚵

This is a mountain biking area for people who want to learn how to ride hardcore. There is some seriously technical stuff, but without the 5-metre spills if you happen to slip up. This network of trails is strung together by an easy loop that circumnavigates Mount Crumpit east of Squamish.

Elaho Loop (Map 37/D7) 🚶 🏕

A 5 km (3.1 mile) loop through the old-growth forests of the Elaho Valley, this trail was designed to showcase the phenomenal beauty of the 1000-year-old cedar trees. This masterpiece of nature is not protected, and is one of the most hotly contested environmental battles in the province.

Garibaldi Provincial Park–Diamond Head (Map 20/D4) ⛰ 🚶 🚵 ⛷ 📷 ⛺ 🏕 🎿

The Diamond Head parking lot is found at the 16 km (9.8 mile) mark of the Mamquam Road. The road to the parking lot is open year round as the road is usually plowed to allow backcountry skiers to access Garibaldi Park. This is one of four main access points into the park. Note that bikes are only allowed on the main trail to the hut at Elfin Lakes.

Elfin Lake Trail is the main trail into the area. To Elfin Lakes it is 11.2km/6.8 miles (3-5 hours) one-way. The trail climbs 600 metres (1,970 feet) up an old road before breaking out into the alpine at Red Heather Day Shelter. Mountain bikers looking for a grueling uphill climb can bike to the hut at Elfin Lake, which sleeps 40 and has a propane heater. Many people set up base camp here, and do day hikes deeper into the park. The trail is open from July to October for hikers and then turns into a popular backcountry skiing/snowshoeing area when the snow falls.

Little Diamond Head continues from Elfin Lakes. It is 7 km/4.3 miles (5 hours) return to the Little Diamond Head. The trail leads through some open sub-alpine meadows gaining 625 metres (2,031 feet) along the way.

Opal Cone is a spectacular volcanic outcrop, located 6.4 km (3.9 miles) from Elfin Lakes. It will take four hours return gaining 250 metres (813 feet).

Mamquam Lake is a popular mountaineering destination. The trail is a strenuous 6.5 km/4 mile (4 hour) scramble from Elfin Lakes gaining 570 metres (1,853 feet) along the way.

Evans Lake Area (Map 20/C5) 🚶 🚵 🐟 🏕

North of Evans Lake Camp, a series of trails/logging roads link up with Levette Lake. The wooded trails provide challenging single-track riding or enjoyable hiking in and around the park reserve and the wilderness lakes. There is even a Skyline Trail here. You can access these trails where the road branches to the camp.

Garibaldi Highlands (Map 20/E6) 🚶 🚵

The Highlands are the most popular mountain biking area in Squamish. You can access the area from Alice Lake Park in the north or Perth Drive and Glacierview Road in Garibaldi Highlands to the south. The moderate trails offer easier, smoother terrain than others in the Squamish area. To really explore the system, try joining the trails to create a long loop ride.

High Falls Creek Trail (Map 20/A2) 🚶 🏕

The High Falls Creek Trail was the first trail that local legend Halvor Lunden built. He still maintains it, even though parts of the trail have recently been clear cut. From the 24 mile mark on the Squamish Main, the steep trail leads 12 km/6.7 miles (6 hours) return to a view of the falls and the Squamish River Valley. Past the falls, the trail continues up, climbing 640 metres (2,080 feet) to the vista at 715 metres (2,324 feet). The trail hooks up with a nearby logging road, and it is possible to head back along the road. You can also find your way up Cloudburst Mountain, or up the road to Tricouni Meadows.

Hut Lake Trail (Map 20/B4) 🚶 🚵 🏇 🐟

With a 4wd vehicle, you can park at the north end of Levette Lake and walk or bike the overgrown, washed out logging road to Hut Lake. It is a 5 km/3 mile (1.5 hour) easy walk gaining 105 metres (341 feet). Without a four wheel drive vehicle, you'll have to hike about another 5 km. The lake offers very good fishing for small rainbow.

Lake Lovely Water (Map 20/B6) ⛰ 🚶 📷 ⛺ 🐟 🏕

The hike into this scenic sub-alpine area, now part of the Tantalus Provincial Park, is difficult but rewarding. It involves crossing an Indian Reserve to the Squamish River and then paddling a canoe across the river. From the west banks of the Squamish River, the trail follows the creek draw leading to the lake set in a large glacial bowl. The trail is 15 km/9.2 miles (12–16 hours) return gaining over 1,200 metres (3,900 feet). While it is a difficult, sometimes impossibly steep climb, the trail is in good condition. The Alpine Club maintains a cabin at the lake, which can be used for a fee ($10–$12). The area also offers good fishing, wilderness camping areas and climbing opportunities.

Marion & Phyllis Lakes Route (Map 11/C3) 🚶 🚵 🐟 🏕

A long bike ride takes you along the gated access road north of the Furry Creek Golf Course past Marion Lake to Phyllis Lake. The 450 metre (1,463 feet) climb over 16 km (9.8 miles) return brings you to some nice vantage points across Howe Sound as well as good fishing holes. The area beyond Phyllis Lake (the Greater Vancouver Watershed) is closed to the public.

Mount Mulligan Trail (Maps 11/F1–20/F7)
From the spur road along Raffuse Creek, a short climb (4 km/2.4 miles) leads to the summit of Mount Mulligan. Great views of the Stawamus River Valley are provided from the top.

Mount Roderick Trail (Map 11/A1–20/A7)
This long day trip requires you to take the ferry to the Woodfibre Pulp Mill before biking or hiking to the trailhead several kilometers up the main logging road. Here you cross a footbridge to join the trail that passes a helipad before narrowing. Continuing north, the trail climbs up the open ridge to the sub-alpine for a great view of Howe Sound. This is a 20 km/12 mile (10 hour) difficult hike gaining 1,475 metres (4,794 feet). The trail is best hiked in June through October.

Petgill Lake Trail (Map 11/C1)
The hike begins on the marked trail north of the parking lot of Murrin Provincial Park (on the opposite side of Highway 99). This 11.5 km/7 mile (6 hour) trail begins by climbing steeply through the bluffs before entering a second growth forest. It soon meets an old logging road and heads south. Eventually, the road becomes completely overgrown at which time the trail departs the road and leads up a ridge to the lake. The trail can be hiked from March through November and gains 640 metres (2,080 feet) in elevation. From the lake, it is possible to access the Goat Ridge Route and several climbing opportunities.

Powersmart Trail (Map 20/E6)
Located near Crumpit Woods, this trio of trails (it is divided into upper, middle and lower section) is one of the most popular in the Squamish area. Mountain bikers should expect a moderately difficult ride.

Ring Creek Rip (Map 20/G7)
This difficult mountain bike trail is found just after the bridge over the Mamquam River on the Mamquam FSR. It begins on an old railbed and heads downhill for about half an hour to the Ring Creek crossing and onto the Diamond Head Road. Using our maps you can make a good loop ride along the various logging roads/trails in the area or even hook up with the Powersmart and Crumpit Woods trail systems.

Ross' Rip/Doris Burma Memorial Trail (Map 20/D2)
The Doris Burma Memorial Trail can be found across from the salt sheds south of Daisy Lake on Highway 99. The trail is marked with orange markers as it follows the river to a unique pine tree bridge. A great 7 km loop trail can be done when combined with Ross' Rip (part of the Sea to Sky Trail), across the highway.

Shannon Falls Trail (Map 11/D1)
From the Shannon Falls Park parking lot, this 5 km/3 mile (2 hour) trail gains 445 metres (1,446 feet) along the creek to a great vantage point overlooking the spectacular 220 metre high (715 foot) waterfall. The trail connects with the Stawamus Chief Trails to the north.

Sigurd Creek Trail (Maps 19/G3, 20/A3)
The trailhead is found at the end of Branch A251 off the Ashlu Road (past the second bridge). The trail climbs 1,322 metres(4,297 feet) over 14 km/8.5 miles (7 hours) return along the creek to Pelion and Ossa Mountains. Along the trail, you will pass by some waterfalls and some nice vistas. The trail is best hiked in mid-July to October.

The Smoke Bluffs Trails (Map 20/D7)
These multi-use trails are located in Squamish around the Smoke Bluffs Climbing Area. From the parking area on Loggers Lane you wind your way through the Smoke Bluffs to the top of Plateau Drive where a good

variety of trails that will suit all levels of mountain bikers can be found. The single-track trails are generally quite technical and twisty.

Squamish Estuary Trails (Map 20/C7)
The sea-level dyke trails found in Squamish offer enjoyable year round hiking or biking. Excellent views of the Stawamus Chief, Shannon Falls and Mount Garibaldi combined with the wide variety of birds (including Bald Eagles in the winter) make this area a nice retreat.

Stawamus Chief Trails (Map 11/D1)
The dramatic 652 metre (2,140 feet) granite wall is the second largest free standing granite outcropping in the world (behind the Rock of Gibraltar). There are a series of very popular trails that head from the parking lot north of Shannon Falls Provincial Park up the back of the Stawamus Chief. To hike to the top of the First Peak is 6 km/3.6 miles (3 hours), to the top of the Second Peak is 9 km/5.5 miles (4 hours) and to the top of the Third Peak is 11 km/6.7 miles (5 hours). Regardless of which hike you choose, you should expect a steep uphill climb that is rewarded with great views from the top. The trails are best hiked in March to November. An alternative is to hike the peak behind the Stawamus Chief (formerly known as the Stawamus Squaw) by way of a 14.5 km/8.8 mile (5.5 hour) trail gaining 500 metres to the summit at 610 metres (1,983 feet). For rock climbers, there is a choice of over 600 routes between The Chief & the Smoke Bluffs.

Stoltmann Wilderness Route (Maps 37\D7–D5)
This wilderness trail was built by the Western Canada Wilderness Committee and is also known as the Elaho-Meager Trail since it joins the two valleys. The 29 km (3–4 days) one-way trail is well marked with orange markers and offers pole and rope bridges. The chance to encounter moose, cougars and Grizzly Bears and the remote nature of the trail makes this an area for experienced, well-equipped backpackers. The route takes you from a gentle valley with rainforest draped canyons, past the Elaho Giant near Sundown Creek and the Grizzly Fir, another large Douglas-fir next to Last Chance Creek. After a day and a half, you will reach the Thousand Lakes Plateau, which offers panoramic views of huge glacier-clad mountains, as you walk among the colourful meadows that connect the crystal clear lakes and ponds. By day three, you will be overlooking the Meager Creek Valley and the half day journey to the hot springs, the perfect end to a difficult trek. The trailhead is found at kilometre 99 on the E1000 Road (off the Elaho Main). It is best to arrange for a second vehicle to pick you up at the Meager Creek Branch Road.

Utopia Lake Route (Map 11/D1)
From Highway 99 at Britannia Beach, it's a 17 km/10.4 mile (8 hour) difficult hike along a gated road then a poorly maintained trail to the lake, gaining 1,390 metres (4,560 ft) along the way. From the alpine, climbers can access Mountain Lake Hut and the surrounding peaks. Along the hike, you will pass by the abandoned mining town site of Mt Sheer. The road crosses private land, and permission to follow the road is required. Call Copper Beach Holdings before setting out.

Sunshine Coast Trails

When hiking or biking in the area, it is well advised to pick up The Trails of The Lower Sunshine Coast guide produced by the Sunshine Coast Forest District. It is available at Visitor Info Centres.

Ambrose Lake Ecological Reserve (Map 18/B7) [hiker] [biker]

To reach the trailhead, follow Timberline Road, which is about 500 metres from the Earl's Cove Ferry Terminal. The trail leads from the end of the road and follows the powerline to the lake. This is an easy 5 km/3 mile (2 hour) return hike. The ecological reserve at the lake is home to an abundance of waterfowl.

Angus Creek Loop (Map 9/G3–10/A4) [biker] [biker]

This mountain bike loop starts on the Sechelt-Crucil FSR, which is found south of the Porpoise Bay Park Campsite. The 22 km (13.4 mile) moderate route follows the main roads in a counter-clockwise direction. The steep initial climb is rewarded with panoramic views and then a downhill ride to the hilly Sechelt Inlet Road and the ride home.

Brodie Trails Loop (Map 10/C6) [biker]

Beginning from the Roberts Creek FSR, you follow the powerline west to the trail. Follow the markings back to the beginning or explore the many difficult side routes. This moderate 7.5km (4.6 mile) route is home to the Brodie Test of Metal Race.

Caren Range Trails (Map 9/F3) [hiker] [biker] [skier] [biker]

The Halfmoon FSR provides access to an excellent area for hikers and mountain bikers in the summer and cross-country skiers during the winter. The best place to start is at kilometre 12 junction, or at kilometre 15, after the road passes though a stand of old-growth timber. The extensive logging road network in the area provides easy backcountry travel with some great views of the ocean and the Sunshine Coast as well as a chance to explore an ancient forest of yellow cedar, hemlock and balsam, believed to be the oldest forest on the coast.

Carlson Lake Loop (Map 9/F3) [biker] [biker]

Found 6 km (3.6 miles) up the Halfmoon Bay FSR (4wd access) this moderate 21 km (12.8 mile) mountain bike loop should take 2.5 hours to ride. The route is marked in a clockwise direction, which begins with a tough initial climb. Most of the route follows old overgrown logging roads as it gains 390 metres (1,268 feet) in elevation. Along the way, you are rewarded with views of Carlson Lake and Sechelt Inlet. The loop eventually brings you back to the Halfmoon Bay FSR.

Chapman Falls Trails (Map 10/A5) [hiker] [biker] [biker]

A series of trails are found along Lower Chapman Creek. Bikers visiting the trails should expect difficult routes. The Chapman Falls Trail is reached by parking at the top of Havies Road and walking along the chain link fence. From there, the trail leads 6 km/3.6 miles (2 hours) return. You start on a wide, muddy trail leading to the powerline before passing through some old growth Douglas-fir on the way to the spectacular falls. The **Hatchery Trail** leads to a viewing platform and a series of spawning channels on Chapman Creek. This is a short (0.5 km), easy trail. The **Lower Chapman Creek Trail** is considered one of the premier short hikes on the Sunshine Coast. The trail leads through a nice second growth forest with large red cedar stumps next to the creek. The 2.8 km/1.7 mile (45 minute) one-way trail also leads to several swimming holes and sandy beaches. The trailhead is located at the parking lot of Brookman Park immediately east of Davis Bay beach on Highway 101.

Clack Creek Loop (Map 10/B6) [biker]

From the junction of Lockyer and Gruman Roads, this 12.3 km (7.5 mile) moderate ride is best done in a counter-clockwise direction. Follow Gruman Road then the Clack Creek FSR to its end. Here an old skid road heads down for a wild 2 km (1.2 mile) descent to the East Wilson FSR and the ride home. Also found at the end of the Clack Creek FSR is the Three Steps Trails which will take you down to Highway 101 along a series of three trails.

Dakota Creek Loop (Map 10/D4) [biker] [biker]

This mountain bike ride is found at the junction of Roberts Creek FSR and the Dakota Creek FSR. It is a moderate 11 km/6.7 mile (1 hour) ride. Following a counter-clockwise direction you will be rewarded with fine panoramic views.

Gray Creek Trail (Map 10/A3–B2) [hiker] [biker]

The Gray Creek Trail takes off just north of where Gray Creek crosses the Sechelt Inlet Road. The trail meanders along the creek leading past two sets of waterfalls and some nice pools and rapids. The trail is approximately 2 km/1.2 miles (1 hour) return and is fairly rough as you have to pass over some windfalls and boulders along the way. Experienced mountain bikers access this trail from the logging roads on the upper (eastern) side of the trail.

Halfmoon Creek Loop (Map 9/D4) [biker] [biker]

Found on an old road on the east side of Homesite Creek just off Highway 101, this easy 8.5 km (5.2 mile) mountain bike loop follows the logging road to the powerline. From the powerline you loop back along the Halfmoon Bay FSR and the highway.

Hillside Demonstration Forest (Map 10/D4) [hiker] [biker]

Located along McNair Creek, this demonstration forest illustrates different silviculture practices of the Sunshine Coast and provides a view of the Port Mellon Mill as well as Howe Sound. The demonstration forest is on the west side of McNair Creek and so it is best to park on the west side of the McNair Creek Bridge and hike up the hill. The demonstration forest trail is 4 km/2.4 miles (1.5 hours) return and has a number of interpretative signs along the way.

Homesite Creek (Gumdrop) Caves (Map 9/D3) [hiker] [biker]

The trailhead is found on the Homesite FSR just north of the powerline and is usually signed as long as vandals have not removed the sign. The trail leads half an hour (one-way) in a southeast direction from the road to a series of twelve limestone caverns, the largest one being 10 metres (33 feet) deep.

Homesite Creek Loop (Map 9/D3) [biker] [biker]

Starting on the Homesite Creek FSR, an 8 km (4.8 mile) moderate bike ride follows the logging roads and power lines to the west of Homesite Creek. This 1 hour loop is best done in a counter-clockwise direction (start left from the FSR and follow the markers). This way you end with a fun 5 km (3 mile) downhill, which takes you back to the highway.

Kinnickinnick Park (Map 9/D5) [hiker] [biker]

This small park is found at the end of Trail Avenue, a short distance from Sechelt. Within the park are a series of easy walking trails, which are clearly marked. These trails are set in a second growth coniferous stand with some larger trees to admire. Mountain bikers often explore the more difficult trails over to and off of the Crowston Lake Road.

Lyon Lake Loop (Map 9/E1) [biker] [biker]

Found on a side road 16 km (9.8 miles) up the Halfmoon Bay FSR (4wd access), this difficult 17 km (10.4 mile) mountain bike loop trail should take 2.5 hours to ride. This well marked route is best cycled in a clockwise direction as you follow a series of logging roads that tend to be steep and rocky in places. The loop takes you through some old growth forests to beautiful, panoramic views.

Mount Daniel Trail (Map 9/B1) [hiker] [biker]

The parking area for this easy, but steep trail is located 3.4 km down the Garden Bay Road north of Pender Harbour. Follow the old road and take the first left, which eventually turns to a trail. Allow 1.5 hours to climb 3.5 km (2 miles) one-way up to the great vantage point. This sacred area also boasts Indian rock formations near the top.

Mount Drew Trail (Map 18/G6) [camp] [hiker] [biker] [biker]

To reach the 1,885 metre high (6,185 foot) summit of Mount Drew is a

difficult trek. Your first obstacle is getting across Sechelt Inlet to the mouth of Earle Creek from Egmont. Boat is the preferred method of travel. From there, hike or mountain bike up the network of logging roads and then scramble to the top of the summit. Given the distance, it is best to make the hike across in two days.

Mount Elphinstone Loop (Map 10/D4–B6)
A long 42 km (25.6 mile) mountain bike route follows the highway and a series of logging roads. Starting from the Langdale Ferry Terminal, you head north, climbing steeply up the Dakota Creek FSR. Turn left on the branch road 2011 and follow the signs back down to the Highway and the ride back to the ferry. This difficult route has a few steep sections but the great views of Howe Sound and the islands are worth it. The Lower Elphinstone Area offers more variety as you cycle old roads and trails through old mining remains.

Mount Hallowell Trail (Map 18/D7)
From the Halfmoon-Carlson FSR, this trail begins at the abandoned red cable spool, about 19.5 km (11.9 miles) from Highway 101. The trail leads through a clearcut and some old growth timber to the summit and a newly restored forest service fire lookout tower. It is about 1 km/0.6 miles (1 hour) to the summit. From the top, you will get an excellent view of the Sechelt Peninsula and the ocean.

Mount Richardson Trail (Map 9/G2)
The best place to access Mount Richardson is from Richardson Lake, which is 4wd vehicle accessable. From the lake, proceed in a southwestern direction by bushwhacking 2 km/1.2 miles (2 hours) one-way to the summit along an old road. From the summit at 986 metres (3,205 feet), you will get a great view of the Sechelt Peninsula and Inlet.

Mount Varley Trail (Map 10/E2)
To reach the summit of Mount Varley, you must bushwhack off the end of Rainy FSR. It is about 3 km/1.8 miles (2 hours) one-way to the summit. In order to reach the end of the Rainy FSR, it is necessary to use a four wheel drive vehicle.

Mount Wrottesey Trail (Map 10/G2–11/A2)
Mount Wrottesey is a prominent land feature overshadowing Howe Sound. To reach the summit, boat to McNab Creek or to Camp Potlatch in Howe Sound. From Camp Potlatch, a well established trail leads along the creek to the Potlatch Road. Continue up the road to where a small creek drains off the southern side of the mountain. From there, bushwhack through the timber to the sub-alpine and then to the summit. From McNab Creek, your must hike/bike up the main haul road and cross over to the Potlatch Road. It is a full day trip (including the boat crossing) involving an elevation gain of 1,625 metres (5,281 feet).

Pender Hill Trail (Map 9/B1)
Allow half an hour to climb the hill, which offers panoramic views of Pender Harbour. The trail begins about 60 metres (200 feet) east of Lee's Road towards Irvine's Landing Road.

Roberts Creek Loop (Map 10/B6–C5)
Starting on the Roberts Creek FSR, this difficult 30 km mountain bike route climbs a stiff 800 metres (2,600 feet) along the B&K logging road. As expected with the elevation gain, the ride has terrific views. It also provides access to a few other trails in the area. For example, the difficult, steep Mexican Jumping Bean Trail heads down to the Brodie Loop Trails. This rough route actually follows an old creek bed.

Ruby Lake–Klein Lake Traverse (Map 18/C7)
This is a fairly new trail, which traverses the saddle between Klein and Ruby lakes, a 4 km (2.4 mile) one-way trip. It is easier to start at Klein Lake (if you start from the south end, you must climb a steep stretch of the trail to the saddle). The highlight of the trail is the excellent views from the rocky bluffs along the route. The southern access is found off an old road 50 metres south of Dan Bosch Park.

Sargeant Bay Park Trails (Map 9/F4)
Beginning 100 metres (325 feet) before the Halfmoon Bay Store along Mintie Road, the Redroofs Loop is a 2 km/1.2 mile (30 minute) circuit alongside the estuary of Halfmoon Creek before returning to Mintie Road via Rutherford Road and Redroofs Road. Along the way, you can watch the waterfowl that frequent the mud flats and the rocky shoreline of the estuary. Another trail leads 4 km/2.4 miles (1.5 hour) one-way from Sargeant Bay Provincial Park to Triangle Lake leading through some old growth timber. Triangle Lake is a shallow boggy lake offering waterfowl viewing. Mountain bikers can enjoy an easy 15 km (9.2 mile) loop starting from Sargeant Bay Park and following Redroofs Road to the logging workshed where you turn right. Follow the signs back to the park. The nature trails that are designated for hikers only.

Skookumchuck Narrows (Map 18/E7)
From Edmont Road, an 8 km/4.8 mile (two hour) easy walk leads along a well maintained trail to the narrows, one of the most popular areas on the coast. You can explore the tidal pools at low tide or watch the tide rip through a narrow, shallow channel during high tide. Consult the tide tables for the best viewing times.

Smugglers Cove Provincial Park (Map 9/C4)
Smugglers Cove has a fascinating 'history' of illegal Chinese labourer smuggling a century ago. Today, tiny Smugglers Cove is a beautiful marine park, and one of the most popular and best summer anchorages on the Sunshine Coast. The park provides easy hiking on a number of short trails totaling about 3.5 km (2 hours). A forested trail leads to the secluded anchorage of Smugglers Cove. A little further on, the main trail ends at a small bay off Welcome Pass, with views across to south Thormanby Island and north to Texada Island. This park is accessed by Brooks Road northwest of Sechelt.

Soames Hill Park (Map 10/E6)
This popular trail network is found to the northeast of Gibsons. The trails can be accessed off Bridgeman or Esperanza Roads, which are side streets off Chamberlin Road. From either trailhead, it takes about half an hour to hike several hundred stairs cut out of fallen logs to the top of the hill. The view from the top (at 240 metres/787 feet) is worth the effort. It is also possible to walk the short wooded trails around the southern slope of the hill.

South Eliphinstone Trails (Map 10/D6)
Mount Eliphinstone has recently been preserved into a provincial park. The southern slopes of the mountain have a long history of logging and many of the access routes have been turned into fine multi-use trails. There are many different access points from side roads north of Gibsons.

Cablevision Trail leads from behind the shed at the top of Gilmour Road. The trail is clearly marked with yellow diamonds for most of its length except towards the top. It takes about 1.5 hours (one-way) to climb to the B&K Logging Road. From there, continue uphill to two abandoned receiver stations which both provide excellent vistas.

From the second receiver, it is possible to continue on to the old ski hut and the summit of Mount Elphinstone.

K2 Summit Traill is marked by pink markers and is accessed by either Stewart Road or Wharf Road. Either way, it is a steady 1.5 hours one-way climb to the K2 summit at 640 metres (2,080 feet) where you get a fantastic view of the ocean and the Sunshine Coast. The trail eventually culminates on a 4wd spur road at the base of the mountain.

Langdale Creek Waterfall Trail takes about 40 minutes one-way to reach the falls. The trail begins 100 m (325 feet) past the powerline off Stewart Road. The trail leads through a second growth stand of Douglas-fir and along an old road next to the creeks. It is fairly steep towards the end but is easily followed because of the blue markers that show the way. An option is to walk down the Waterfall Trail to the Wharf Road trailhead.

Mountain Trail leads about 30 minutes uphill from the south end of the cemetery off Keith Road to the remains of First Camp located next to Chaster Creek. The trail is marked by red markers and a sign. The camp was used by shingle bolt workers in the 1920s. From the First Camp, it is possible to continue uphill to the Second Camp just north of Largo Road or to hike in a northwest direction to the Chinese Camp. In the area, there are remains of an old dam, tramway and wood flume along the trail.

Shaker Trail leads from the powerline off Stewart Road and is clearly marked by orange markers. It leads steadily uphill about 35 minutes one-way to the B&K Logging Road. The highlight of this trail is the wooden flume that used to carry shingle bolts to the First Camp.

Sprockids Mountain Bike Park is a unique community project that created a series of fun, short loops for the young riders of the Sunshine Coast to enjoy. These trails were actually developed as a school project. The trails are accessed off Stewart Road, which is found off of North Road in Langdale.

Tetrahedron Provincial Park Trails (Map 10/C2)

This provincial park is the home of an extensive network of alpine hiking, biking and backcountry ski trails. It also contains a series of small mountain lakes, which provide good fishing opportunities and backcountry huts. The main area is reached off the Sechelt FSR.

Batchelor Lake Cabin is reached by a 1.4 km (0.9 mile) one-way hike through old growth forest to the sub-alpine lake. Blueberries are abundant in July to August but so are the bears.

Chapman Lake is found approximately 3.5 km one-way from Edwards Lake Cabin through some old growth forest and an open meadow. The lake can also be accessed from the McNair Lake Trail (see below) through a lovely sub-alpine meadow.

Five Lake Circuit involves a 10.4 km/6.3 mile (6 hour) hike that passes by five of the larger lakes in the provincial park. The circuit takes you through old growth forest along an old logging road and a series of trails. One of the highlights is Edwards Lake, a beautiful sub-alpine lake in a bowl surrounded by old growth timber. The four other lakes are Tannis, Bachelor, Mayne and Gilbert Lakes. This hike is not accessible until after June when the snow melts, even then it is quite swampy so it is best to bring some good hiking boots. In winter, this area makes a good cross-country ski circuit with cabins on Edwards and Bachelor Lakes.

McNair Lake Trail begins at the end of the McNair FSR (or as far as you can drive). The trail leads 3 km/1.8 miles (2 hours) uphill to the lake and one of the four cabins in the park. The trail parallels McNair Creek on its northeast side and passes through old growth forest and over some rock slides to McNair Cabin. McNair Lake is surrounded by sub-alpine meadows with rugged mountain peaks looming in the background. Wildflowers are a highlight in July and August.

Mount Steele Trail begins by traversing some old growth timber past Edwards and Gilbert Lakes. Eventually, you reach the open sub-alpine terrain and the Mount Steele Cabin. To reach the popular cabin at 1,500 metres, you will climb 540 metre (1,755 feet) across the 9 km/5.5 mile (4 hour) one-way trail. The trail is well marked and is best hiked in July-October. This trail is also very popular with backcountry skiers.

Panther Peak is the prominent southern peak of the park. The best route in begins off the end of the McNair FSR (4wd required). From there, follow the McNair Lake Trail to McNair Cabin, located in the sub-alpine. From the cabin, proceed towards No Name Lake and then climb steadily upward through a snow chute to the summit. It takes a minimum of five hours to reach the summit and another three to climb down. The difficult route is well rewarded with panoramic views and the beautiful sub-alpine terrain.

Tetrahedron Peak is the highest peak on the Sunshine Coast but even the hardcore mountaineers will find it difficult to pick a route up. The easiest route is to travel up the Rainy FSR approximately 6.4 km (3.9 miles) and then take the overgrown spur road that crosses Rainy River. You will have to either ford the roaring currents of the river or use a series of ropes. Once across the river, proceed for an additional 2 km (1.2 miles) up the old road and then take a spur road to the valley between Panther and Tetrahedron Peaks. Eventually, an unmarked route leads northward to the open slopes beneath the peak where you can scramble to the summit, climbing a cool 1,600 metres (5,200 feet). It takes a good day just to reach the summit, where spectacular panoramic views are your reward.

Trout Lake Loop (Map 9/E4)

From the Trout Lake parking lot on Highway 101, this 15 km (9.2 mile) moderate mountain bike loop will take you clockwise along a series of roads back to the highway. Allow 1.5 hours. Between Trout Lake and Redroofs Road a series of moderate trails can be explored. The powerlines above Trout Lake also offer moderate riding that turns quite difficult the further you head west.

Tuwanek Point Beach Trail (Map 9/G3)

The trailhead to this ocean front walk is found off Upland Road just before the gravel pit. The trail leads 2 km/1.2 miles (one hour) to the ocean following the shore of Sechelt Inlet to the point.

Wilson Creek Trail (Map 10/A6)

The trail is found by parking on Jack Road and then crossing Highway 101. The scenic trail leads through a second growth forest along Wilson Creek before crossing a bridge. The trail continues on to the powerlines for a 2 km/1.2 mile (one hour) round trip. This route can be ridden by experienced mountain bikers.

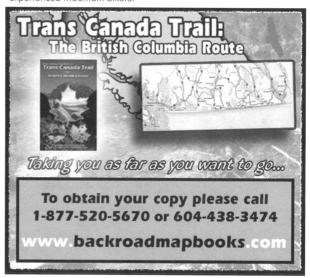

Whistler/Pemberton Area Trails

The Whistler area is quite possibly the most storied recreation area in the province, perhaps the country. Much of its fame is based on the success of Whistler and Blackcomb Mountains, but it is growing into a popular four season destination. Mountain biking is extremely popular, and, much like the North Shore, there are many hardcore trails that remain secret. For the beginner and intermediate rider, there are lots of options and opportunities, many of which are listed below.

A River Runs Through It (Map 29/G5) 🚵

This is a short 2.5 km (1.5 mile) technically challenging single-track that loops back up with the Alta Lake Road. This heavily forested trail leads through the swamp between the road and the Valley Trail south of Rainbow Lake Trail. It is often muddy, has lots of roots and a log bridge to cross. There is no elevation gain, but it makes up for it with some serious technical riding.

Ancient Cedars / Showh Lakes (Map 29/G4) 🥾 🚵 🎣 👫

This trail network is located north of Whistler off the Cougar Mountain Road. The trail is a 4 km/2.4 mile (1.5 hours) loop through some impressive 1000-year-old cedar trees found at the base of Cougar Mountain. This is an easy trail, with 150 metres (488 feet) of elevation gain. However, if you do not have a vehicle that can handle the 4wd access road, you'll have to walk or mountain bike in.

Binty's High Trail (Map 29/G5) 🚵 👫

A Whistler Mountain Biking Classic. This difficult 7.5 km (4.5 mile) trail climbs 510 metres (1,658 feet) from the top of Alpine Meadows (you start on Rick's Roost Trail). Once you reach the top enjoy the view and then hang on. The trail spills you out on Alta Lake Road but not before crossing several side trails, which offer similar thrills.

Birkenhead Lake Loop (Maps 39/E4) 🚵 🎣 👫

This 4 hour loop is a popular, moderate ride along gravel roads through a Lodgepole Pine forest to beautiful Birkenhead Lake. From the D'Arcy Road, you start with a tough 3 km (1.8 mile) climb up the Birkenhead Lake FSR. Look for the gated road on the east that eventually links up with the access road on the north side of the lake. Continue past the main campsite and back to the highway.

Birkenhead River Trail (Maps 30/D1, 39/D4) 🥾 🚵

Starting from the Owl Creek Recreation Site, the Birkenhead River Trail is a scenic 20 km (12.2 mile) trail that makes up part of the Sea to Sky Trail. The easy route follows a rolling road along the powerlines on the west side of the river. From the Birkenhead River crossing, it is a further 15 km (9.2 miles) to Birkenhead Lake.

Blackcomb Mountain (Map 30/B6) 🥾 🚵 🎣 👫

Like Whistler Mountain, the expansive sub-alpine terrain, which is frequented by skiers throughout the winter months, gives way to some great hiking trails in the summer. For a hefty fee, take the Solar Coaster Chair and walk up to the Rendezvous Restaurant and the start of the trails. Be sure to pick up the complimentary map that highlights the short alpine walks available. The longest trail is only 2.5 km/1.5 miles (1 hour) and the elevation gains are minimal (although the Overlord Lookout Trail gains 215 metres/699 feet). Other trails include the **Alpine Forest Trail**, the **Fitzsimmons Meadow Walk**, the **Marmot Trail** and the **Upper and Lower Lakeside Trails**. For mountain bikers, there are guided descents from the top of Solar Coaster, which take about two hours to complete. Adjust your brakes and hang on.

Blowdown Lake Trail (Map 31/G1) ⛺ 🥾 🚵 🎣 👫

To the north of Duffey Lake, the Blowdown Creek Main extends in a southeasterly direction. This is an old mining road, which leads to the alpine and the Stein Valley Provincial Park. The road passes by the old Silver Queen Mine to provide easy access to the Cottonwood Creek Trail and several ridge walks, which in turn connect to the Stein River Trail. The area offers beautiful alpine meadows with great camping and some classic ridge routes.

Brandywine Meadows Trail (Map 29/C6) ⛺ 🥾 🎣 👫

This 6 km/3.7 mile (3 hour) trail is steep and short with an elevation gain of 1,000 metres (3,280 feet). The trail leads sharply upward from the 6.3 km (3.8 mile) mark of the Branch 10 logging road, through the dense old growth forest to the alpine meadow with spectacular views and a rustic camping spot. From the meadows, it is possible to gain access to Brandywine Mountain and the Metal Dome.

Brew Lake Trail (Maps 20/C1–29/C7) 🥾 🎣 🐟 👫

The signed trailhead begins on the BC Rail tracks just south of the Brandywine Falls Provincial Park. It involves a 10 km/6.1 mile (7 hour) return hike gaining 1,200 metres (3,900 feet) along the way. At the end of the steep trail, which is best hiked in July–October, is Brew Lake, where you will find a maintained cabin available on a first come, first serve basis. From the lake, it is possible to explore Mount Brew at 1,740 metres (5,655 feet) in elevation or access the Brew Hut 1,620 metres (5,265 feet). These areas are popular backcountry ski retreats. Brew Lake is at 1,430 metres (4,648 feet) in elevation and is a beautiful mountain lake offering reasonably good fishing.

Cal-Cheak Trail (Map 29/E7) 🥾 🚵 👫

The popular Cal-Cheak, or Brandywine Falls Trails lead 4 km/2.4 miles (one-way) between Brandywine Falls Provincial Park and the Cal-Cheak Rec Site. South of the suspension bridge, the trails split with the western trail (under the powerlines) being the preferred mountain biking route of the Sea to Sky Trail. The trails cut through the second growth forest and require little elevation gain along the way. Once at the park, be sure to take the side route to look at the spectacular Brandywine Falls.

Cerise Creek Trails (Map 31/B1) 🥾 🚵 🎣 📷 🐟 👫

About 41 km east of Mount Currie, turn onto the Cerise Creek Road off Highway 99 and drive approximately 10 minutes to the signed trailhead and the gateway to a popular backcountry hiking and skiing area. From the trailhead, you hike through the forest along Cerise Creek to some alpine meadows where you will find Keith's Hut. It takes about 2–3 hours to reach the hut although it is a fairly easy hike. From the hut, experienced mountaineers can cross over to the Matier Glacier or Joffre Peaks.

Emerald Estates Trails (Map 30/A5) 🚵

There is a network of mountain biking trails in the Emerald Estates area. The most popular trail in this network is the infamous Shit Happens. This 7.5 km (4.6 mile) trail links Emerald Estates to Alpine Meadows to the south.

Emerald Forest (Map 29/G5) 🚵

This area is made up of several short trails around the gravel pit, between Alta Lake Road and the Valley Trail. The Forest is located on private property so please respect your surroundings.

Garibaldi Provincial Park–Black Tusk (Map 20/F2) ⛺ 🥾 🎣 🐟 🛶 🐟 👫

A paved road leads just south of Daisy Lake from Highway 99 to the Rubble Creek parking lot. It is recommended that you either camp at Taylor Meadows or at the Battleship Lakes Camp if you want to explore the surrounding mountains including hiking to the famous Black Tusk. Taylor Meadows is 7.5 km (4.6 mile) from the parking lot.

Garibaldi Lake is 9 km (5.5 miles) from the parking lot along a popular, well maintained trail. The trail is best hiked from July to October and provides fantastic views of surrounding glacier and mountains as you climb 940 metres (3,055 feet).

Black Tusk is an additional 7 km/4.3 mile (5–6 hour) hike from Taylor Campground. The trail leads through a sub-alpine meadow and forest to a rocky slope and eventually onto the prominent volcanic pillar (gaining 820 metre/2,665 feet along the way). In the winter, the area turns to a backcountry skiing haven with an expansive trail network including the Garibaldi Neve Traverse, which extends south from Garibaldi Lake all the way to the Diamond Head Trail near Squamish.

Panorama Ridge is an additional 5 km (3 miles) one-way from Garibaldi Lake, gaining 630 metres (2,048 feet). The ridge is also accessed from Taylor Meadows and Black Tusk Meadows.

Upper Lakes is an additional 4 km (2.4 miles) hike from Taylor Campground. The hike gains little elevation as it passes through an alpine meadow to a series of smaller lakes to the foot of the Helm Glacier.

Garibaldi Provincial Park–Cheakamus Lake (Maps 20/G1, 29/A1)

This popular multi-use trail system begins at the end of the Cheakamus Lake Road, some 8 km (4.8 miles) from Highway 99. Cheakamus Lake is a turquoise coloured lake surrounded by rugged snow-capped peaks that is truly a delight to fish, canoe or just visit. Mountain bikes are allowed on the trail to Singing Creek Camp although hardcore riders may loop back along the south side of the Cheakamus River.

Cheakamus Lake Trail meanders through a boulder field and some slide alders before entering into a forested area following Cheakamus River to the lake. The lake is only 3.2 km (2 mile)

from the parking lot with almost no elevation gain. Don't be surprised to see someone carrying a kayak down the trail, to put in at Cheakamus Lake.

Singing Creek Camp leads along the north shores of Cheakamus Lake, past some large timber, to the Singing Creek Camp. The trail is 14 km/8.5 miles (5 hours) return to the camp with little elevation gain. It is an easy trail and provides a good flavour of the Garibaldi Provincial Park as well as access to a descent fishing lake. Experienced mountaineers can hike up Singing Creek to connect with the Singing Pass Trail and the Musical Bumps Trail to access Whistler Mountain.

Helm Creek Trail used to be accessed by a difficult cable car crossing of the Cheakamus River. A bridge was built a few years back, bringing this once obscure route new found popularity. The trail is 14.5 km/8.8 miles (7 hours) one-way, with an elevation gain of 600 metres (1,950 feet). The trail network connects with the Upper Lakes and the Black Tusk Trail system as it passes through the extensive sub-alpine terrain of the Garibaldi Provincial Park. The hike is best suited for July to October.

Green Lake Route (Map 30/A5)

A moderate mountain bike ride that offers a few tough hills as you head south from the Wedgemont Creek FSR to the Lost Lake Trail system. The route is 11 km (6.7 miles) and climbs 150 m (490 feet) as you alternate from double track to single-track along the powerlines on the eastern shore of Green Lake.

Jane Lake Trails (Map 29/E7)

The main access route to the Jane Lakes, a series of three mountain lakes, is now blocked by a fence built by BC Rail. Therefore, mountain bikers, ATVs and hikers now follow an old washed out road. This is a rugged 18 km (11 mile) return trip along the road to the lakes at 930 metres (3025 feet) in elevation. The lakes provide good fishing throughout the spring and fall as they are stocked regularly.

Joffre Lake Trail (Map 31/A1)

The trailhead is located approximately 23 km (14 miles) east of Mount Currie on Highway 99. The very popular trail is well marked and leads from the parking lot past two smaller lakes on your way to the picturesque Upper Joffre Lake. The upper lake, which offers wilderness camping, is simply spectacular as it lies directly below the icefields of Matier Glacier. The trail is 11 km/6.7 miles (5–6 hours) gaining 400 metres (1,300 feet). Some mountaineers hike to the glacier edge or climb Joffre or Matier Peaks (see Twin Goat Ridge Route below).

Lillooet River Dyke Trails (Map 30/C1)

Starting from Highway 99 on the east side of the Lillooet River Bridge, a gentle trail follows the river in a northwest direction for about 5 km (3 miles). At the end of the dyke road, a moderate single-track loops around MacKenzie Lake. From here, it is possible to return along the steep (1,000 metre/3,280 feet) MacKenzie Basin Road. The Dyke Trail also extends for several kilometers in the

opposite direction. This easy route cuts through the Indian Reserve, marshland and offers fine views of Mount Currie.

Little Spearhead (Map 30/A7)

From the Upper Village, follow the signs to the Singing Pass Parking Lot. Here you cross Fitzsimmons Creek (be careful, there's no bridge) and descend on Blackcomb Mountain. This 13 km (7.9 mile) round trip climbs 325 metres (1,056 feet) and is a moderate ride.

Lizzie Creek (Stein Divide) Trail (Map 31/B5)

After ascending through a narrow gorge on the Lizzie Creek Main using a high clearance 4wd vehicle (or alternately, using your two-leg drive feet), you will reach beautiful Lizzie Lake. From here, it is a steep 5 km/3 mile (3 hour) one-way hike gaining 640 metres (2,080 feet) to the Lizzie Creek Cabin. Initially, you pass by Lizzie Lake and then proceed through the "Gates of Shangri-la" to the alpine meadows where the cabin is located. From the cabin, experienced backpackers can make numerous day trips to explore the many alpine lakes and mountains in the area. To reach the Stein Divide, requires scrambling up a rockslide, hiking past several small alpine lakes to Cherry Pip Pass, and then skirting over to Caltha Lake, which is about a 6–8 hour one-way hike from the cabin. Another two hours or so takes you over the Stein Divide to Tundra Lake. Further along the route are Stein Lake and Elton Lake. This area provides exceptional hiking in the alpine with endless backpacking and backcountry skiing options. The area is quite popular, but is also quite difficult, and should be left to experienced hikers.

Lost Lake Ski Trails (Map 30/A6)

30 km (18.3 miles) of well maintained cross-country ski trails leads from the parking lot adjacent to the municipal hall in Whistler or from the parking lot next to the Chateau Whistler. When the snow is gone, the trail network is heavily used by hikers, joggers and mountain bikers. Periodically, you will find maps and signs to help mark the way. The main trail leads around Lost Lake providing easy access to the north end where you will find a nice wharf and a doggie beach. At the south end of the lake, there is a large sandy beach with an expansive lawn and picnic facilities attracting hundreds of visitors daily. The trail network connects with the Valley Trail network.

Madely Lake Trail (Map 29/D4)

Maintained by the Rotary Club of Whistler, the Madely Lake Trail offers a shorter alternative for hiking to Rainbow Lake...if you can get to the trailhead. The trailhead is found south of Madely Lake along the four-wheel drive/bike access road. From here, the trail leads 6 km/3.6 miles (3 hours) one-way to Rainbow Lake gaining 500 metres (1,625 feet). Along the way, the trail passes over two bridges, one at Madely Creek and one at Beverley Creek before passing Hanging Lake, where there is a campsite together with outhouses. If you're planning on hiking from the Madely Trailhead to the Rainbow Lake Trailhead, it is recommended you do so in that direction, as the Rainbow Trailhead is nearly 1,000 metres (3,250 feet) lower.

Mosquito Lake Area (Map 30/D1)

A challenging network of mountain bike trails that offer fast, undulating single-track trails with extreme descents. The trails are accessed from Ivey Road (at the crest near the sub-station), the recreation site, or along the MacKenzie Basin Road. There are over 80 km (48 miles) of trails here, ranging from intermediate to expert.

Musical Bumps Trail (Maps 29/G7-30/A7)

A fabled 19 km/11.6 mile (5-6 hour) hike starts from the top of the Whistler Village Gondola and leads to Singing Pass. Smart hikers will pay the fee to ride the gondola up. The trail is so named, as it crosses Piccolo, Flute and Oboe summits on its way to Singing Pass and the headwaters of Melody Creek. The trail also leads past Harmony Lake and Burnt Stool Lake over a challenging rockslide and into Garibaldi Park. Along the way, you get great views of Cheakamus Lake and Glacier. An alternative route down is to follow the Singing Pass Trail (see above)

down and out along the Fitzsimmons Creek Valley.

Northwest Passage (Map 29/G6)

Found at the top of Nordic Estates off of Whistler Road, a dirt access road climbs under the Quicksilver Chairlift on the bottom of Whistler Mountain. At the crest of this steep climb (420 metres/1,365 feet), you head left for some downhill, roller coaster thrills. The difficult 7 km (4.3 mile) route will spit you out at Whistler Village.

One Mile Lake Trails (Maps 30/B2)

The popular One Mile Lake picnic area found south of Pemberton offers some enjoyable trails that can be used by mountain bikers or hikers. The One Mile Loop is an easy one km loop around the lake. The most popular trail is the Nairn Falls Trail, which heads 2 km (1.2 miles) south to the provincial campground. This moderate trail has a few sections that require dismounting (if you are on a bike) as you climb over roots and descend along a rocky trail. Side trails also lead to more challenging biking terrain.

Owl Lake Trail (Map 39/B7)

The trailhead to this hike is found off the Owl Lake FSR, which is 4wd accessible. From the trailhead, it is a 7 km/7.4 mile (3 hour) return trip, gaining 140 metres (455 feet) along the way. The trail leads through the Owl Creek Valley to the lake where you will find a recreation site on the western shores.

Place Creek Trail (Map 39/F6)

From Highway 99 just west of Gates Lake, this steep, rugged 21 km/12.8 mile (9 hour) hike gains 1,300 metres (4,225 feet) past several waterfalls to the beautiful Place Glacier. Near the foot of the glacier is an A-frame used for camping by both climbers and mountaineers. The hiking season extends from July to October.

Rainbow Lake Trail (Map 29/E3)

This alpine trail leads from the wooden map located on the west side of Alta Lake Road. The trail follows 21 Mile Creek through a hemlock forest before meeting with an old logging road. The trail then follows the road for a short distance before taking off through a thick second growth forest and eventually past the 21 Mile Creek Waterfalls and over a suspension bridge. Soon, you will enter the alpine meadows of Rainbow Lake at 1,460 metres (4,745 feet) in elevation. The trail to Rainbow Lake is 18 km/11 miles (7 hours) return, gaining 800 metres (2,600 feet). Once in the area, you can try your luck for wild rainbow trout or explore the side trails. **Beverly Lake** is found to the north through a draw at the base of Rainbow Mountain. The route in is more of a bushwhack than a trail. To access **Gin and Tonic Lakes**, look for the undeveloped trail leading south about 200 metres before the suspension bridge. The trail leads to the barren lakes (without fish) at 1,430 metres (4,648 feet) in elevation.

Rainbow Mountain Skywalk Trail (Map 29/E5)

This is a continuation of the Rainbow Lake Trail, or at least, you can't start this trail until you hike the 9 km (5.5 miles) to Rainbow Lake. From there, the trail climbs 850 metres (2,790 feet) to the top of Rainbow in just over 3 km (1.2 miles). That's a wickedly steep climb, but people still somehow drag their bikes to the top.

Rebob Trail (Map 29/G5)

This difficult trail is found 120 metres (390 feet) north of the Rainbow Lake Trailhead. The trail climbs the bank to a series of old roads with lots of obstacles to hop. You can climb to **Binty's High Trail** or exit back out on the road.

Salal Creek/Athelney Pass (Map 37/E1)

Recently the members of the BCMC have opened up a 15 km trail to Athelney Pass (north of our maps), which climbs 800 metres (2,625 feet). Although the trip can be done overnight, allow a few days to explore the surrounding peaks, including Ochre Peak, the "Black Molar", the Icemaker and Guthrum Mountain. The trail leads from the end of the

SEA TO SKY TRAIL

An ambitious trail building project, intended to link Squamish to the tiny hamlet of D'Arcy northeast of Pemberton has seen little progress in the last few years. Still, the off-road route burns brightly in many minds, and there are already some great sections that have been routed/built, including the old Pemberton Trail Section through the Cheakamus Canyon, Ross's Rip, found just north of the Highway 99 salt sheds, and the section near Birkenhead Lake. When (and if) the trail is completed, it will stretch up to 300 km (183 miles), depending on the route taken. Currently, over half that distance (about 180 km) is along paved roads, including many long, dangerous sections along Highway 99.

water barred road past an old mining exploration camp, small lakes, pumice meadows and next to glaciers. Marmots are a common site and bears and wolves are known to frequent the area. If logging does not claim the valley, the BCMC may extend the route to McParlon Creek on the south side of Downton Reservoir. Plans are also in work to restore the old mining cabin at Athelney Pass as part of a backcountry ski route linking the cabins at Pebble (Boulder) and North Creeks. You can find a route description on the bivouac.com web site.

Shadow Lake Trails (Map 30/A4) 🚶 📷 🚴
Shadow Lake Trails are located north of Whistler near the Soo River, right off Highway 99. There are a number of short trails totaling 6 km (3.6 miles) providing examples of the various forest practices. Highlights include a walk around Shadow Lake (1.5 km/0.9 miles) or a stroll through a stand of old growth cedar next to Soo River. This trail network is a good choice if you want to get away from the crowds of Whistler and enjoy an easy stroll through a forested setting.

Singing Pass Trail (Map 30/A7) 🚶 🚵 📷 ⛺ 🚴
The Singing Pass Trail is probably the most popular alpine trail in the Whistler Area. This beautiful hike starts from the end of the well-signed Singing Pass Road. Here you follow Fitzsimmons Creek, and then Melody Creek to the pass. The area offers alpine flowers in late summer along with spectacular glacier and mountain views. Allow 7 hours to travel the moderate 12 km (7.3 mile) hike, which gains 600 metres (1,950 feet). To access the cabin at Russet Lake, is another 2 km (1.2 miles) beyond and 250 metres (813 feet) up. The cabin offers a good base for mountain climbers looking to explore the area's summits. You can also follow a difficult route over the pass to Cheakamus Lake, or return via the Musical Bumps.

Snowcap Lake Route (Maps 21/G4, 22\A4-A1) 🚶 📷 🚴
The east side of Garibaldi is far less traveled than the west side. In fact, this route, accessed off logging roads west of Skookumchuck, is about the only viable entry point into this vast wilderness. Even so, you will probably have to bushwhack your way up from the end of the road to the ridge. Don't despair; it is worth the effort. It's 20 km (12.2 miles) from the end of the road to the lake; more, depending on how far you can drive up the road, which is found at km 24.3 of the West Lillooet Lake FSR.

Tenquille Lake Trail (Maps 38/G4–39/A4)
⛺ 🚶 🚵 🛶 📷 ⛺ 🐟 🚴
Tenquille Lake is a beautiful alpine lake set in meadows surrounded by rugged mountain peaks. At the lake is a cabin together with a recreation site for camping. The area is extremely popular with backpackers, mountaineers, snowmobilers and even extreme mountain bikers. The lake can be accessed four ways. The easiest route (if you have a 4wd vehicle) leads from Branch 12 off the Hurley River Road gaining 450 metres (1,463 feet) over a 12 km/7.3 mile (4 hour) return route. The trail begins in an old cut block and then crosses a creek before joining with the other trail leading from the Lillooet Valley. An alternative and more challenging route is to climb from the Lillooet Valley some 19 km/11.6 miles (7

hours) gaining 1,460 metres (4,745 feet) along the way. Although the hike is extremely strenuous, you will be rewarded with excellent vistas of the valley below as well as the opportunity to walk through beautiful meadows filled with wildflowers. The third route is a recent extension of the Mount Ronayne Trail. It leads from Ogre Lake to Tenquille Lake over 16 km/9.8 miles (5 hours) return gaining 330 metres (1,073 feet) along the way. As this is a rugged mountain route following a series of ridges, it should be left to the experienced backpacker. The final trail is an 11km/6.7 mile (4 hour) hike from the Tenquille Creek Road gaining 427 metres (1,388 feet).

Tour de Soo (Maps 29/B2, 30/G4) 🚵 🚴
30 km (18 miles) of logging roads and 10 km (6 mile) of single-track make up this difficult ride, which will take good riders about three hours including a few mandatory hike-a-bike sections. From the Cougar Mountain (Soo River 03) Road, you climb over to the Soo River Valley and onto Echo Lakes, Rutherford Creek and eventually out to the Highway. From here, make your way north to Pemberton along trails found around and above the railway.

Tower Roads (Maps 21, 29\F7) 🚵 🚴
There are two microwave towers that make for excellent but difficult mountain biking. The Black Tusk Tower requires a 1,270 metre (4,128 foot) climb over 16 km (9.8 miles), while the Whistler Tower is an 8 km return route. The steep roads offer great views and fun descents.

Twin Goat Ridge Route (Map 31/A2) 🚶 📷 🚴
This difficult bit of ridge walking traverses 22 km/13.4 miles (14 hours) one-way from Upper Joffre Lake all the way to Lillooet Lake Road just north of the Twin One Rec Site. Initially, you ascend from Upper Joffre Lake at 1,280 metres all the way to 2,380 metres (7,735 feet) at the foot of the Matier Glacier, then you descend steadily to Lillooet Lake, at 200 metres in elevation. It can only be hiked after the snow melts, which is usually July to September.

Valley Trail System (Map 29/G5) 🚶 🚵 🚵
Within the Whistler Valley is an extensive 20 km (12 mile) network of well-maintained gravel and paved trails. The trail network extends from Alta Lake along the River of Dreams to Green Lake. At most intersections, there are signs marking the various routes. The trail system is heavily used throughout the summer months by mountain bikers, joggers, hikers and in-line skaters and in the winter, by cross-country skiers. The easy trails will take you through the heart of the Whistler Valley past creeks and lakes, forested areas and golf courses.

Wedgemont Lake Trail (Map 30/B5) ⛺ 🚶 📷 ⛺ 🚴
A short but steep trail climbs to a beautiful lake set at the foot of a glacier below cascading peaks. From the end of the Wedgemont Creek FSR, you climb a grueling 1,220 metres (3,965 feet) through the heavy forest, past a rockslide with a view of the falls on Wedgemont Creek, to the rocky sub-alpine meadows around the lake. At the lake, it is possible to camp or use the cabin as a base for further exploration. The 12 km/7.3 mile (5 hour) return trail is best tackled in July to September, after the trail dries.

Whip Me, Snip Me (Map 29/G6) 🚴

This difficult trail is found about 100 metres (325 feet) south of the Rainbow Lake Trailhead. This is another challenging system that climbs north to the Rainbow Lake Trailhead and the cruise down.

Whistler Interpretative Forest (Map 29/F7)
🚶 🚴 ⛷ 🛷 🏇 🐟 ⚕

The Whistler Interpretative Forest is easily accessed by the Westside Main Cheakamus Lake Roads. It is a total of 3,500 ha and ranges from the valley bottom all the way to the sub-alpine at 1,600 metres (5,200 feet). Through the interpretative forest are numerous short trails exploring the various silviculture practices and ecosystems of the Cheakamus Valley. There are stands of old growth timber along the western banks of the Cheakamus River, scenic vistas and access to a good fishing lake. The **Ridge Trail, Lower Riverside Trail, Highline Trail** and the **Logger's Lake Access Trail** are open to everyone, while the **Crater Rim Trail, Riverside Interpretative Trail** and **Whistler West Ridge Trail** are closed to mountain bikes. Several signs within the interpretative forest allow you to decide on which route to travel.

Whistler Mountain Trails (Map 29/G7) 🚶 🚴 ⛷ ⚕

After the ski season and the snow departs, Whistler Mountain becomes a spectacular hiking and biking destination. The glacier covered peaks and the rugged treeless terrain makes the area a gorgeous place to visit. During the off-season, the Whistler Village Gondola runs to the Round-house Lookout for a hearty fee. Be sure to pick up the complimentary map that highlights the routes available. There are four different guided bike routes that lead from the Roundhouse Lookout to the Whistler Village. Regardless of which route you take, adjust your brakes before your descent and hang on. For hikers, the options include the **Glacier Trail**, the **Harmony Lake Trail**, the **Little Whistler Trail, Musical Bumps** (see above) and the **Ridge Lookout Trail**. Outside of the Musical Bumps Trail, the trails are short (up to 3.5 km long) but do require a bit more climbing than the nearby Blackcomb Mountain Trails.

Wilderness Camping

At the time this mapbook is being written, there is a great deal of uncertainty surrounding Wilderness Camping or Forest Recreation Sites. These sites are either camping spots or special use areas, usually situated near a lake or river that backroad explorers have come to depend on. After all recreation sites are a perfect base to explore the surrounding area. But with current government cutbacks, all funding and maintenance is being removed. Further road access is no longer being maintained on many of the forest service roads. This is going to restrict access to many of the sites, and people without access to a four-wheel drive or ATVs may find it more difficult to access the backcountry.

In the past, people could expect to find a rustic area, often with little more than some picnic tables, fire rings, outhouses and garbage containers. In the future, even these amenities will be removed and the sites will no longer be serviced. It is even more important than ever for people to help maintain these sites. Please help keep our province beautiful and pack out any garbage you bring in or is left by the previous inconsiderate visitors.

The more popular sites have been converted to pay-per-use sites that are maintained by campground hosts (similar to a provincial park or private campground). We have marked these enhanced sites.

Chilliwack Forest District

Because these sites are so close to Vancouver, most of these sites see heavy use and abuse. The forest district, which covers the southeastern portion of this book, has put a lot of work into maintaining these sites. Because of this, many sites are now pay-per-night enhanced sites.

Allison Pool Recreation Site (Map 4/G6)

Set in a pretty second growth forest next to the Chilliwack River, 15.5 km (9.5 miles) down the Chilliwack Lake Road. The area is a popular spot for steelhead fishing. There are 5 sites here, and are far enough apart to give people a sense of privacy. There is an overflow parking lot, which is often used by RVs and tent trailers for camping.

Apocynum Recreation Site (Map 24/C1)

This is a small 3-unit site, found along the Nahatlatch River FSR. Whitewater paddling, fishing and hunting are popular pastimes in the area.

Bear Creek Recreation Site (Map 14/G5)

The Bear Creek Recreation Site is tucked in a nook created by the Harrison East FSR, the Bear Creek FSR, and Bear Creek. There are 10 quiet, enhanced, shady camping spots, set into a second growth forest. It is a short hike to nearby Bear Falls.

Cascade Peninsula Recreation Site (Map 14/G6)

This is a small water access site (it is possible, though not easy, to hike in from the Harrison East FSR) on the shores of Harrison Lake. It has several tenting pads tucked away in a secluded cove, and a small pebble beach for sunbathing.

Chehalis Lake Recreation Sites (Map 14/B6)

Chehalis Lake North is an enhanced site with 40 campsites in the forest near the shores of the lake. The busy site also hosts a boat launch and beach. The beach becomes larger by the end of the summer as the water level drops.

Chehalis Lake South is located above the south end of Chehalis Lake (where the lake is narrow and verdant green). This is a popular site, with 25 camping spots and a good concrete boat launch. There is a small beach, and people have been known to swim here, though the lake is high in the mountains, deep, and usually quite cold. The recreation site is 31 km (18.9 miles) down the rough two-wheel drive accessible road.

Skwellepil Creek is another enhanced site on Chehalis Lake. With enhancement comes the fixing up of the steep access road and a busier camping area. The area now offers 48 total sites: 26 single campsites, 7 double campsites, and 7 tent only campsites. It also has a new disabled washroom, and 4 day-use sites.

Chehalis River Recreation Sites (Map 4/D1)

There are actually three separate enhanced sites on the banks of the Chehalis, one on the left side of the road, one on the right before crossing the single lane bridge over the river. The third site is on the far side of the bridge, to your left (to your right is private property). Between the three, there are about 50 campsites, set in an open forest. From the campsite on the north side of the river, a trail runs up the hill, and then follows the edge of a spectacular canyon. There is a nice swimming hole and good access to good river fishing along this trail.

Chipmunk Peninsula Recreation Site (Map 5/A6)

The Chipmunk Peninsula Recreation Site is set in a coniferous forest next to the Chilliwack River, on the Chilliwack Bench FSR. There are 13 units, most of which have picnic tables, and good access to the river and nearby biking trails in the area.

Cogburn Beach Recreation Site (Map 14/G4)

This long, open stretch of beach is a popular weekend getaway with the party crowd. Which is too bad, because this is a really nice spot when not covered in broken glass, half-burned logs and other debris. There are no campsites per se; rather, campers flock here by the dozens, sometimes by the hundreds, park on the side of the Harrison East FSR, and hike on down, pitching their tent on the nearest open plot of beach. This is the northern most recreation site on the east side of Harrison, and the closest one to Clear Creek Hot Springs.

Eaton Creek Recreation Site (Map 5/G2)

A tiny three-unit site found 16.5 km (10 miles) down the Silver Skagit Road. This road is passable by most vehicles. Two of the sites are set in the forest next to the creek, and all three have tables. The site also marks the start of the trail to Eaton Lake, a popular fishing destination.

Francis Lake Recreation Site (Map 14/E7)

Francis Lake is a small lake, and this is an even smaller recreation site. The road up to Francis Lake is four-wheel drive only.

Grace Lake Recreation Site (Map 4/G5)

This is a three-unit recreation site on the rocky outcrops next to Grace Lake and the busy Harrison West FSR. Grace Lake is a good fishing lake with a short trail that skirts the edge of the lake.

Hale Creek Recreation Site (Map 14/D5)

This is a secluded site just above Harrison Lake, used mostly by boaters on the lake. However, it is possible to hike, or even navigate a four-wheel drive down to the site. There is a sandy beach, a cartop boat launch, and a unique barbecue hut.

Hayward Lake Reservoir Recreation Sites (Map 3/C3)

Two different BC Hydro Recreation Sites are found on this popular recreational lake. The Hayward Lake site is found at the north end, while the Ruskin Dam site is found at the south end. Both sites offer day-use areas as well as boat launches. Fishing, hiking, paddling, and wildlife viewing are some of the activities pursued in the area.

Jones Lake Recreational Site (Map 5/C2)

Jones Lake is a BC Hydro maintained site located on the shores of Jones (Wahleach) Lake. There are 15 camping spots, which are big enough for RVs, although it is not recommended that you drive them on the steep, rough road in to the lake. There is also a separate boat launch and picnic area on the popular fishing lake.

Log Creek Recreation Site (Map 24/A1)

A small recreation site is situated at the Log Creek/Nahatlatch River Confluence. The area is popular with anglers and kayakers.

Long Island Bay Recreation Site (Map 14/F4)

A small tenting area on Long Island, this is a popular spot for boaters making their way down Harrison Lake. The sites are secluded, and there is moorage, a beach, a dock, and a barbecue shack.

Nahatlatch River Recreation Site (Map 24/B1)

This is a 6-unit tenting site on the south side of the Nahatlatch. Access is not suitable for RVs or large trailers.

Pierce Creek Recreation Site (Map 5/B7)

Not really a recreation site, Pierce Creek is more a parking lot for folks heading up the Pierce Lake Trail. Found at km 22 of the Chilliwack Lake Road.

Post Creek Recreation Site (Map 5/E5)

A medium sized recreation site with 12 shady camping spots. This is a popular spot, especially on summer weekends. If you are looking for secluded, sedate and uninhabited, you will probably have to look a little further a field than this. In addition to a series of cross-country ski trails, the well traveled, 10 km long Post-Greendrop Trail to Lindeman and Greendrop Lakes starts at this recreation site.

Rainbow Falls Recreation Site (Map 14/G7)

Rainbow Falls Recreation Site is a small boat access site in a protected bay on Harrison Lake formed by Cascade Peninsula. It can also be reached by picking your way down Slollicum Creek. There are several tenting pads, and a nice gravel beach.

Rapids Recreation Site (Map 5/A6)

A small recreation site next to the Chilliwack River that is frequented by kayakers. The site is located just off the Chilliwack Bench FSR, between Eagle's Roost and Chipmunk Peninsula. If there is space here, it is a beautiful spot, but with only three units, your chances of finding space, especially on a summer weekend, are not good.

Ruskin Dam Recreation Site (Map 3/B3)

A picnic site overlooking Hayward Lake, this site is maintained by BC Hydro. There is a hiking/biking route that skirts the reservoir along an old rail bed, leading all the way to Stave Falls Dam. Hayward Lake is also a popular destination for anglers, boaters and canoers.

Scuzzy Creek Recreation Site (Map 24/C5)

This is a small site on the banks of Scuzzy Creek. Most two-wheel drive vehicles with enough clearance can make it to this site. Anglers and hunters are the main visitors to the area.

Sunrise Lake Recreation Site (Map 14/D5)

This isolated site is found at the end of a rough 4wd road off the Harrison West FSR. The BC4WD association has been maintaining the site for years, which may explain why the road has not been upgraded over the years. In addition to having fun bumping their way in, people will find a cartop boat launch and a nice lake to fish.

Tamihi Creek Recreation Site (Map 4/F6)

Set in a large open grassy area ideal for RVs, this is one of the bigger recreation sites in the area. There are 30+ sites (depending on how many people want to squeeze into the open area) including some quaint tenting sites in the deciduous forest next to Tamihi Creek. The site can be overrun with salmon and steelhead anglers in the fall.

Thurston Meadows Recreation Site (Map 5/A6) enhanced

Located 3.5 km (2.1 miles) east of the Tamihi Site (and the bridge over the Chilliwack River), is another large, open enhanced site that is good for RVs. The site also has a number of day-use picnic sites on the bank of the river.

Twenty Mile Bay Recreation Site (Map 14/E3)

The forest service recently put a bunch of work into this lovely enhanced lakeside campsite, one of the nicest in the district. It now features 25 single sites, 9 double sites, 7 tent only sites, plus 16 overflow sites, and a disabled access washroom. The site also has a boat launch for those people willing to bump their way up the often busy logging road.

Weaver Lake Recreation Site (Map 14/E7)

The road to Weaver Lake is accessible by two-wheel drive vehicles. At least, that's what they say, but there is some nasty cross ditching, which will make drivers of smaller vehicles think twice. The lake is 3 km (1.8 miles) off the Harrison West FSR. Weaver Lake is a picturesque lake, and the enhanced campsites are set in a lush forest on the lake's shore. There is a separate day-use/picnic area, a gravel boat launch and a great walking trail that circumnavigates the lake.

Wolf Lake Recreation Site (Map 4/F1)

This is a small three-unit recreation site on the shores of Wolf Lake. Or, at least, one of the campsites is on the shores of this marshy lake; the other two are set back closer to the road.

Wood Lake Recreation Site (Map 14/E5)

A popular, enhanced, pretty site set in an opening next to a small lake. The site has recently been upgraded, and now sports 30 camping spots.

Backroad Mapbooks

www.backroadmapbooks.com

Cascades Forest District

North of the more popular Chilliwack and Squamish Forest Districts, the Lillooet Forest District has a lot of small, pocket sites that see low usage over the summer. This doesn't bode well for these sites, and, chances are, many of them will either be removed or abandoned. Vandalism is less likely in the area so if the sites are closed, there still may be an area to camp in and possibly even a picnic table or two.

BC Hydro Campground (Map 45/B6)

The BC Hydro Campground on Carpenter Lake is on the north shores of the man-made lake, about 19.3 km (11.8 miles) west of Mission Dam. The site is located at the outflow of Bighorn Creek, and has ten campsites, a boat launch, and a picnic area. The lake can be quite beautiful when the water level is up. On the other hand, the endless mud flats and unsightly deadheads make visiting the lake less than appealing when the water level drops.

Beaverdam Creek Recreation Site (Map 45/C1)

Beaverdam Creek is a small, grassy site set in an opening next to the creek. There are 8 spots here, including enough space for RVs to park.

Botanie Lake Recreation Site (Map 33/C1, 42/C7)

The majority of use at this small, 3-unit site next to Botanie Lake comes from fishermen. The site is fairly open (with enough space for RVs), and is located inside the boundaries of the First Nation reserve.

Carol Lake Recreation Site (Map 45/A5)

Carol Lake is a small, popular fishing lake, just above Carpenter Lake. This site is a great place for a picnic, and there are nine camping spots, which have enough room for RVs. There is a cartop boat launch or if you prefer, there is an extensive trail network to the northwest. The trails run north beyond Lac La Mare and Burkholder Lake and eventually hook up with trails that loop back to Carol Lake.

Carpenter Lake Recreation Site (Map 45/E7)

Located along the south shores of Carpenter Lake, this small site has a boat launch. Carpenter Lake is a big man-made lake, in a dry valley, dotted with ponderosa pines.

Cinnamon Creek Recreation Site (Map 41/A2)

There are 11 campsites in this recreation site, located next to the rushing Cayoosh Creek that drowns out the infrequent traffic on the Duffey Lake Road. There are a number of nice spots right on the banks of the creek in this semi-open site.

Cottonwood Recreation Site (Map 41/A3)

This site is located along Cayoosh Creek, and has well-spaced camping spots, seven in total, giving campers a fair degree of privacy.

Donelly Creek Reaction Site(Map 38/F2)

Located just off the summer access only Hurley River Forest Service Road, there are three units at this small, treed site. This site is located in the high country between the Lillooet River and Carpenter Lake.

Friburg Recreation Site (Map 44/C3)

Friburg is found on the western shore of the picturesque Tyaughton Lake. Natives named the lake Tyaughton or 'jumping fish' due to the incredible aerial display the trout in this lake like to perform. The recreation site has room for about five campsites along with a cartop boat launch. This is an open site, with space enough to park an RV or two.

Gott Creek Recreation Site (Map 40/G4)

This is one of the series of easy access recreation sites found next to the Duffey Lake Road. The small site has three picnic tables that appeal more to the day-tripper than campers.

Gun Creek Grassland Recreation Site (Map 43/D2)

A popular destination for horseback riders in the Spruce Lake Trails Area, the grasslands offer a couple of rustic sites, and a corral.

Gun Lake South Recreation Site (Map 44/A4)

Gun Lake is a popular destination lake found just north of Gold Bridge. This site is easily accessible, with eight camping spots, and enough open area to park an RV. There is a boat launch a few kilometres south, near the Lajoie Dam.

Gwyneth Lake Recreation Site (Map 44/A6)

Located at the north end of Gwyneth Lake, just off the infamous Hurley River Road, this site has space for seven groups. There is a cartop boat launch onto the relatively small, marshy lake. This is a good fishing lake, and the site sees a lot of use from anglers.

Hogback Mountain Recreation Site (Map 45/G1)

Despite the remote nature of the area, most two-wheel drive vehicles can access this small three-unit campsite. There in an extensive trail network in the area but the site is used primarily as a staging ground for hunters in the fall.

Hope Creek Recreation Site (Map 38/G1)

A small site, used mostly as a resting stop in summer for backroad enthusiasts as well as hunters in fall. The Hope Creek rec site offers three sites with picnic tables and is located about 1 km off the scenic Hurley River Road.

Hummingbird Recreation Site (Map 43/E1)

Hummingbird Lake is a pretty mountain lake, accessed by foot, horseback or mountain bike. This site is one of a handful of backcountry sites in the Spruce Lake Recreation Area.

Hurley River Recreation Site (Map 44/A7)

A small recreation site on the banks of the Hurley River. The remote nature of the area makes it an ideal spot for hunters.

Jones Creek Recreation Site (Map 45/B5)

Jones Creek is a small site (3 units) on Carpenter Lake, where Jones Creek flows into the man-made lake. The semi-open site has good road access and larger units should have no trouble getting to the area.

Kingdom Lake Recreation Site (Map 44/B6)

Found off the road to Bralorne, this is a nicely treed site, accessible by a short trail. There are 15 camping spots, and a cartop boat launch onto the good fishing lake. There are also trails to nearby Lost Lake and Noel Lake.

Kwotlenemo Lake Recreation Sites (Map 41/F1)

In all there are four different sites to choose from on Kwotlenemo Lake. The popular lake is also known as Fountain Lake and is the northern most lake of the scenic Three Lake Valley. Visitors will find good road access into the area and should note that the lake is only open to boats with electric motors.

Kwotlenemo Lake East Recreation Site is a small, treed site with space for two groups.

Kwotlenemo Lake North Recreation Site is the smaller of the two main recreation sites on the lake. There is space enough for eight groups, and the site is open enough to fit an RV. There is also a cartop boat launch at this site.

Kwotlenemo Lake South Recreation Site offers 21 camping spots in a large open area. The site is the largest of the four recreation sites on the lake.

Kwotlenemo West Recreation Site has three camping spots in a treed area next to the lake There is also a cartop launch at this small site.

Lake La Mare Recreation Site (Map 45/D3)

While it is possible to still access this lake by four-wheel drive vehicle along a road that is slowly deteriorating, it is better to hike in. People who can get their vehicle here can bring along a small boat to launch in the lake. Trail users have the option of continuing on a trail to Buckholder Lake, or along the Hog Creek Trail to Carol Lake. Campers will find room for about three units at Lake La Mare.

Leon Creek Recreation Site (Map 46/B1)
This is a small recreation site, big enough to hold maybe one party. The site appeals mainly to hunters in the fall.

Liza Creek Recreation Site (Map 44/E3)
There is space enough for two groups at this small site on the banks of Liza Creek, just off Marshall Lake Road.

Lost Lake Recreation Site (Map 44/C5)
It's about 500 metres from the road to this small, semi-open tent site on the shores of Lost Lake. There is space for three tenting parties here.

Marshall Creek Recreation Site (Map 44/F3)
Located just below where Marshall Creek flows out of Marshall Lake, this is a small, treed site, with space enough for three groups. There is a cartop boat launch at the site that has good road access.

Marshall Lake North Recreation Site (Map 44/G3)
This is a fairly open site on the northeastern shores of Marshall Lake. There are seven camping spots for anglers and people who are looking for a nice place to camp. Trail enthusiasts will be amazed at the number of trails to choose from in the area.

Mission Dam Recreation Site (Map 45/F6)
This four-unit site is located on the easternmost reaches of Carpenter Lake. The dam is certainly an impressive sight but the busy Carpenter Lake Road detracts from the peaceful nature of the area. The site is open, with lots of space for RVs.

Mowson Pond Recreation Site (Map 44/C3)
Despite the name, Mowson Pond, is actually a scenic lake that offers good fishing. Found just above Carpenter Lake, the recreation site has space for five groups, and is RV accessible. A cartop boat launch is also found at the site.

Murray Creek Recreation Site (Map 42/D6)
There are six camping spots at this recreation site, which is on Murray Creek in the shadow of Murray Peak. Hunters mostly use the site in the fall, although the nearby Onion Lake/Monkey Wrench Riding Area does attract dirt bikers in the summer.

Pearson Pond Recreation Site (Map 44/C4)
Slightly hidden and with a narrow access road, this site is not as busy as other nearby camping areas. Persistent anglers will be happy to find a cartop boat launch and some larger fish in the lake. The open site has enough space for about four groups.

Roger Creek Recreation Site (Map 40/G4)
The Roger Creek Recreation Site is actually a pair of small roadside sites, with nine camping spots in total. The northern site has space for five campers, and is more open, making this a better place for RVs.

Seton Lake Recreation Site (Map 41/A1)
This small tenting site on the shores of Seton Lake is boat access only. There is space for two small groups or one big one.

Seton River Recreation Sites (Map 41/C1)
BC Hydro has created a series of lovely recreational sites just southwest of Lillooet off the Duffey Lake Road.

> Seton River Picnic Site is a new facility complete with ample parking, picnic tables and viewing platform to watch the salmon spawn.

> Seton River Campsite is a popular camping area found near the junction of Cayoosh Creek and the Seton River.

Spruce Lake Recreation Sites (Map 43/G1)
Spruce Lake is a very scenic lake, and the heart of the Spruce Lake Recreation Area. The lake is only accessed by trail or floatplane. As a result the fishing is fabulous and the scenery is unforgettable. It is about 11 km (6.6 miles) from the nearest road to the lake.

> Spruce Lake South Recreation Site offers two tent pads at the south end of the lake.

> Spruce Lake North Recreation Site is a slightly larger (five unit) tenting site that can be accessed by foot and mountain bike. Horses, which are allowed in the area, are not allowed at this site.

Texas Creek Recreation Site (Map 41/E4)
Access to this recreation site, on the Texas Creek FSR, is poor, and, even without recent cutbacks to the Forest Service, this site was probably going to be closed. If you are lucky, you might be able to get a 4wd vehicle up here. The lack of vehicle access and facilities probably suits the visitors to this area just fine. After all most people in the area are hardcore trail users who are prepared for backcountry travel and camping.

Trigger Lake Recreation Site (Map 43/E1)
They don't get much more remote than this. The rustic site is found beside Trigger Lake, far from the nearest road access. The excellent trail system of the Spruce Lake Recreation Area does bring in the odd person on foot or bike but most visitors come via horseback.

Tyaughton Creek Recreation Site (Map 44/C1)
Another small Carpenter Lake site, with 3 camping units. This two-wheel drive accessible site is in the semi-open ponderosa forest that surrounds Carpenter Lake. There is also a rough cartop boat launch.

Yalakom Recreation Site (Map 45/E3)
Located next to the Yalakom River, this small (four-unit) site is open and easily accessed by RV. Fishing, hunting and exploring the endless trail system throughout the area are the popular pastimes in this dry, often hot landscape.

Squamish Forest District

There are lots of recreation sites in the Squamish Forest District, which includes the Sea to Sky (Squamish, Whistler, and Pemberton) Corridor, one of the busiest outdoor recreational areas in the province. This is ground zero for recreation in this province, and, with such a great deal of pressure on these sites, a number of them have been enhanced.

Alexander Falls (Map 29/D6)

This is a small, quiet picnic site overlooking the picturesque Alexander Falls. This site is accessed 8 km (4.8 miles) down the Callaghan FSR, a bumpy road not suitable for RVs. There is space enough for six.

Blackwater Lake Recreation Site (Map 39/G4)

A small site on the road to Birkenhead Lake, this 5-unit site is accessed off of a good gravel road, but RVs are not recommended due to site limitations. The site is located about 15 km (9.2 miles) northeast of Devine, and is a low use site (most people heading this way just go to Birkenhead Park). There is a hand launch for boats.

Brohm Lake Recreation Site (Map 20/D5)

A popular day-use site that is found just off Hwy 99. In addition to the extensive trail system, there is a place to hand launch small boats. It is a short walk to the lake, where you can swim, fish or have a picnic.

Cal-Cheak Confluence Rec Site (Map 29/E7)

An enhanced trio of popular, heavily used recreation sites, near the confluence of Callaghan Creek and the Cheakamus River. The sites are about 7 km (4.3 miles) north of Daisy Lake. There are 36 camping spots divided between the three sites, some of which are walk-in (tenting) only. At the south site, a suspension bridge leads across Callaghan Creek, and down to the Brandywine Falls.

Cat Lake Recreation Site (Map 20/E5)

Cat Lake Road is found down a narrow, winding road north of Alice Lake Provincial Park that isn't recommended for RVs. That's okay, because the 26 camping spots here are all walk-in tenting anyway. The walk is only five minutes from the parking lot to the lake, and like many sites in this area is often busy. As a result it is an enhanced site. There is an extensive network of biking and hiking trails here. There are no powerboats allowed on the lake.

Driftwood Bay Recreation Site (Map 31/A4)

There are five enhanced tent sites on Driftwood Bay, which are often taken up by large parties. The site is found at km 17 on the In-Shuck-Ch FSR, on a beach near the middle of Lillooet Lake.

Lizzie Bay Recreation Site (Map 31/A4)

At km 15.5 on the In-Shuck-Ch FSR, this is probably the nicest site on the lake. The access road is a rough two-wheel drive accessible road so RVs probably want to avoid it. There are 12 enhanced sites here, spread out along next to the beach, but tucked back into the forest enough to create a sense of complete privacy.

Lizzie Lake Recreation Site (Map 31/C6)

High clearance, four-wheel drive vehicles should be able to get to this beautiful mountain lake; the rest of you will have to hike/bike up the 15 km (9.2 miles) to Lizzie Lake along the scenic Lizzie Creek Main. There are five tent pads found a short walk from the parking area. This is also the trailhead for the Lizzie Creek Trail up to Tundra Lake, just inside the boundary of the Stein Valley Niaka'panaux Heritage Provincial Park.

Madely Lake Recreation Site (Map 29/D4)

You will have to walk in about 500 metres to get to this beautiful mountain lake. That is if you can negotiate the 16 km (9.8 mile) of rough road into the lake. The road does deter some, but the site still remains a somewhat popular getaway in summer. In addition to a chance to pitch your tent on the beach, there is good fishing on the lake and a trail leading up to the Rainbow Lake area.

Mosquito Lake Recreation Site (Map 30/D1)

This small, forested day-use only site receives heavy use, especially by anglers. The road is rutted and muddy but water enthusiasts will brave the conditions to enjoy a day at the beach. The lake also makes a refreshing stop over for mountain bikers and hikers enjoying the nearby trail system.

Owl Creek Recreation Site (Map 30/D1)

There are two enhanced sites here, one on Owl Creek, the other on the Birkenhead River. The best spot is the one next to Owl Creek, which has 13 camping spots, and is set deep in the forest. Each spot has a picnic table, and offers some privacy. The other site is just a big roadside pullout, with space for about 11 vehicles. These sites are located a few hundred metres off the road to D'Arcy, but don't see much use.

Spetch Creek Recreation Site (Map 39/F7)

A small, forested site just off the road to D'Arcy, Spetch Creek isn't a busy site, and those who do visit here are usually anglers. There is space for ten vehicles.

Strawberry Point Recreation Site (Map 30/G2)

A small, enhanced, forested site just a few kilometres down the In-Shuck-Ch FSR. It is only a 5-minute walk from the parking lot to the beach on Lillooet Lake, where you can set up your tent. This site receives moderate use, and the number of people you can get here depends on the number of people you can shoehorn onto the beach.

Tenquille Lake Recreation Site (Map 39/A4)

A remote, hike in destination, Tenquille Lake is a spectacular backpacking destination. The lake is situated in an alpine meadow with mountains that tower across the lake. The easiest access into the lake is via the two and a half hour walk from Branch 12, a four-wheel drive road found off the Hurley River Road.

Twin One Creek Recreation Site (Map 31/B3)

This popular enhanced site, located at km 10 on the In-Shuck-Ch FSR, is about 6 km (3.6 miles) south of Strawberry Point. There are eight vehicle/tent units here, a nice beach, and a boat launch. Perhaps not the best getaway spot for a quiet weekend, but a good place for boaters to hang out.

Sunshine Coast Forest District

Including the Howe Sound Islands of Anvil and Gambier and Keats, this large Forest District stretches way, way north, to the Waddington Glacier, well outside this mapbook. But that's okay, because there's not much in the way of recreational sites past Powell Lake. In fact, the majority of this district is a roadless wilderness. But the Forest Service makes up for this in a high concentration of Recreation Sites, especially in the Powell Forest area. Many of these recreation sites are tied into the Powell Forest Canoe Circuit, and some are not accessible other than by foot or by boat.

Appleton Creek Recreation Site (Map 16/G1)

Although noted as a day-use picnic site, there are four tenting sites, along with pit toilets (for the time being) and picnic tables. There is a network of hiking trails leading to Sliammon Lake and Okeover Inlet that can be accessed from here.

Beaver Lake Recreation Sites (Map 17/E1)

Beaver Lake is found along an alternate routing of the Powell Forest Canoe Circuit. The only way here is by boat and as a result these three recreation sites receive few visitors outside of canoe trippers. Beaver Lake is a small, calm and pretty lake that has an abundance of tadpoles during the early summer.

Beaver Lake Recreation Site is only accessible by foot for canoeists willing to venture off the main path of the canoe route. The site is actually located on Dodd Lake, just a short paddle from the start of the portage to Beaver Lake. This is one of the nicest camping spots on the Powell Forest Canoe Route with plenty of space to spread out, and rarely anyone else around.

Lower Beaver Lake Recreation Site is located behind the logjam at the lower end of Beaver Lake. There is just a little clearing, enough for one group to set up.

Upper Beaver Lake Recreation Site offers a lot of space in the clearings around this site for a number of tents. But the site sees even less use than the others because it is located at the far (southeast) end of the small lake that few people carry their canoes up to.

Big Tree Recreation Site (Map 9/D4)

A picnic site found at the end of a short (650 metre) hiking/biking trail. The site is located below a number of large old growth trees just off the Halfmoon/Carlson Forest Service Road. The site is wheelchair accessible.

Bob's Lake Recreation Site (Map 8/E2)

A small, treed site used mainly by hunters and four-wheel drive enthusiasts on Texada Island. The area is also an excellent mountain biking area but please stay on the trail, and try not to damage the flora, especially a rare species of orchid, which can be found in the area. The recreation site is only accessible by foot, mountain bike, or four-wheel drive.

Dinner Rock Recreation Site (Map 16/E1)

Located just off Hwy 101, down a steep, rough, but two-wheel drive vehicle accessible road, the Dinner Rock Recreation Site is a 12-unit, semi-open site located on the ocean. There is good salmon fishing in the area, a cartop boat launch, and even a popular scuba diving area. This area is wheelchair accessible and makes a fine picnic destination.

Dodd Lake Recreation Site (Map 17/E2)

This site is an often busy, sometimes loud site on the shores of Dodd Lake. There are 12 sites, usually full, pit toilets and garbage cans. Powell Forest canoeists might want to give this one a miss in favour of the Beaver Lake Recreation Site (see above). Wise boaters would head for the other site, less than a kilometre away, to get away from the (usually party) crowds here.

East Lake Recreation Site (Map 17/B5)

The East Lake Recreation Site is a picnic site located along the Lang Creek Trail. The site is located on the southern shore of East Lake, and is a short walk from the Duck Lake Road.

Emma Lake Recreation Site (Map 27/A5)

A popular rock climbing site, as well as backcountry skiing and snowshoeing in the winter, Emma Lake is not a recreation site, per se, but a small, semi-alpine cabin, with a maximum capacity of eight. The cabin has restricted access, and is not open from about August to October. Call the Sunshine Forest District (604-485-9831) for more detail.

Goat Lake Recreation Site (Map 26/F7)

Water and foot access only. After carrying your canoe down the long portage from Windsor Lake to the south, the Goat Lake Recreation Site is a sight for sore eyes (and shoulders, and back, and legs...). It is one of the prettier spots on the circuit, while Goat Lake is much calmer and less travelled than Powell Lake itself.

Haywire Bay Campsite (Map 17/A3)

Part of a regional park, Haywire Bay is a big site, that is usually full of drive-in campers. There used to be camping on an island tucked away in this sheltered bay, but it was abused, and ultimately removed. Canoe circuit travellers well schooled in no-trace camping might want to think about staying here, rather than trying to find a place in the main site. The park also offers a good boat launch for visitors to Powell Lake.

Horseshoe Lake Recreation Site (Map 17/E3)

A pretty water and foot access spot, this site is tucked away in a sheltered bay of Horseshoe Lake. The site is very open, on a rocky prominence, with a few big trees, just to keep things interesting. Even if you are not doing the Powell Lake circuit, park your car at Nanton Lake Recreation Site to the north and paddle here. You will be glad you did.

Horseshoe River Recreation Site (Map 17/E3)

Located in the bottom of a narrow valley, this foot-access only recreation site is used mostly by canoeists on the Powell Forest Circuit. It is a pretty area, but it gets dark quickly down here. On a nice day, the more open Horseshoe Lake Recreation Site to the north is much nicer, but, on a windy, raining day, this site offers campers more shelter.

Inland Lake Recreation Site (Map 17/B2)

Located at the south end of Inland Lake, this popular site offers access to 13 km (7.9 miles) worth of wheelchair accessible trails. There are 16 campsites with picnic tables, cabins for disabled people as well as tenting only sites spread around the lake. RVs can access the main campground, while boaters/canoeists will find a beautiful wharf and an island campsite appealing.

Ireland Lake Recreation Site (Map 17/D2)

This is a new, tiny, one-unit site at the north end of Ireland Lake. The site is more functional than pretty; the dock on Ireland Lake itself is an amazing place to watch a sunset, but the actual site is tucked back into the enclosed forest. The site is already infested with mice, no doubt drawn to poorly cached food.

Khartoum Lake Recreation Site (Map 18/A3)

Khartoum Lake Recreation Site is a 16-unit site found down a good two-wheel drive road, although access is controlled. The site is also accessible by canoe from Lois Lake, but few visitors to the Powell Forest Canoe Route venture this far out of the way.

Klein Lake Recreation Site (Map 18/C7)

Accessed off the North Lake FSR, this is a nice, 15 unit site set in the trees on the northern end of Klein Lake. The campsites are spread out, and some are tucked well into forest, so even on a busy summer weekend, you will have at least some privacy. This access is a little rough but this does not deter inconsiderate people with trailers to park their units and leave them for the summer.

Lang Creek Recreation Site (Map 17/C5)

Accessed off the Lang Creek Trail, this picnic area is located across from the salmon hatchery. This is a great place to watch salmon spawning in September and October. Access to this site is along the Lang Creek Trail, either by foot or by mountain bike.

Lewis Lake Recreation Site (Map 17/D2)
A new 2-unit site is available for visitors wishing to explore Lewis Lake or nearby Tin Hat Mountain. The access into the area is rough and best left for high clearance vehicles.

Little Horseshoe Creek Recreation Site (Map 17/E2)
Located on Horseshoe Lake at the outflow of Little Horseshoe Creek, this site doesn't see much use. Most people prefer to follow the canoe circuit to Dodd Lake by canoeing over to Nanton Lake and north past Ireland Lake.

Lois Lake Recreation Site (Map 17/F4)
The starting point of the Powell Forest Canoe Route, this recreation site is used more by cartop campers than by canoeists. No wonder. The site isn't all that pretty, especially compared to other sites, just a short paddle/portage away. There are eight well used campsites here, most of which are in an open area near the shore. There are three tenting pads set back in the forest that are nicer, but these are often inhabited.

Lois Point Recreation Site (Map 17/F4)
Developed to address the issue of canoeists not wanting to share a site with vehicle campers (especially considering that one of the joys of doing the canoe route is the being in touch with the wilderness), this new site has space for three tents. The site is a short (15 minute) paddle along the southeastern shore of Lois Lake, and is water accessible only.

Lower Powell Lake Recreation Site (Map 17/A2)
Accessed by canoe, or by foot from Inland Lake, this isn't one of the prettiest sites on the Powell Forest Canoe Route but it is a good, protected spot when the winds blow up. There are several camping spots here.

Middlepoint Recreation Site (Map 17/D2)
An open site carved out of the forest about halfway along the portage trail between Nanton and Ireland Lakes. Accessed only by foot (usually by people with a canoe on their back), this site is a great place to stop for an evening, with space enough for 2 tents.

Mount Steele Cabins (Map 10/C2)
There are four cabins, (Bachelor Lake, Edward Lake, McNair Lake and Mount Steele) scattered around the sub-alpine lakes of the Mount Steele Trail System of Tetrahedron Provincial Park. Hikers use the trail system extensively in summer and backcountry skiers in winter. The popular Mount Steele Cabin, found in a scenic alpine area, is the largest of them all and sleeps about a dozen people.

Nanton Lake Recreation Site (Map 17/D3)
Found on the western shore of Nanton Lake, this recreation site has 15 sites, 2 of which are right on the lake and 13 of which have picnic tables. Accessed by canoe or by two-wheel drive along the Goat Lake Road.

Nanton-Ireland North Recreation Site (Map 17/D2)
Located on the shores of Ireland Lake at the end of the 2.4 km portage, this site is closed in. The shores of the lake are shrubby, and, although the forest is nice, the other two sites on this portage (Nanton-Ireland South, Middle Point) are nicer. Canoe/foot access only.

Nanton-Ireland South Recreation Site (Map 17/D2)
A nice site located near a marshy area on Nanton Lake. The site is open, with lots of berries in the summer. This is just a short distance from the Nanton Lake Recreation Site, but is a lot more secluded, and not (easily) accessible from the road.

North Dodd Lake Recreation Site (Map 17/E2)
Located at the north end of Dodd Lake, well away from the main recreation site at the south end, this is a pretty, site, enclosed in the forest. The site is accessible by canoe, or by folks willing to do a bit of bushwhacking to get to this remote-feeling recreation site.

Powell Lake Recreation Site (Map 17/A1)
This is a lovely site, tucked into an open forest behind an island on Powell Lake. This site is accessible by foot from inland trails but most people get here by canoe. Because Powell Lake sees more boating traffic, it is not surprising to see other people at this site (which is not always the case at many of the sites on this week long canoe circuit).

Shingle Beach Recreation Site (Map 8/D2)
Located right on the ocean, the site can get hammered fairly hard by winds and storms. There is good road access off the Davie Bay Road as well as good salmon fishing and a popular scuba diving area to attract the people. The site is a small, semi-open site with mooring for boats.

Tony Lake Recreation Site (Map 17/E2)
Located about 1 km off the toe of Horseshoe Lake, this is a new two-unit site for canoeists. The tiny lake offers an even more secluded option for paddlers.

Windsor Lake Recreation Site (Map 17/E1)
This site has one of the most unique pit toilets in the entire province, a hollowed out giant stump of a tree. It's worth the trip just to see it, or, if you like, use it. The portage trail to Goat Lake crosses the Goat Lake Main (at the 36 km mark), so it is possible to hike in from here.

Wildlife Viewing

Some wildlife is easy to spot. Salmon viewing, for instance, is a matter of getting down to the right stream at the right time. On the other hand, many birds and animals tend to flee when they hear, see or smell humans. In order to improve your chances of spotting these more elusive creatures, wear natural colours and unscented lotions. Bring along binoculars or scopes so you can observe from a distance and move slowly but steadily. Keep pets on a leash, or better yet, leave them at home, as they will only decrease your chances to spot wildlife. Early mornings and late evenings are usually the best time to see most birds and animals.

What follows is a list of sites that are designated as official BC Wildlife Watch sites. When combined with the parks section of this book, this list will help you discover one of British Columbia's greatest treasures-wildlife. We would also recommend visiting the BC Wildlife Watch web page at www3.telus.net/driftwood/bcwwhome.htm, where you will also find bird lists for many areas listed below. This site is maintained by some passionate volunteers, including April Mol.

Agassiz Farmlands/Maria Slough (Map 4/G2)

The farmlands around Agassiz are wintering grounds for waterfowl. During the winter months, the area is home to Trumpeter and Tundra Swans, while large flocks of ducks may be seen on flooded fields. Maria Slough, although surrounded by privately owned land, is an excellent place to see spawning salmon and Trumpeter and Tundra Swans from the water.

Alice Lake Provincial Park (Map 20/D6)

This beautiful provincial park is home to one of the most unique spectacles in the region. In mid-summer, a Western Toad Migration occurs at Fawn Lake. Birding is another common pursuit here, with woodpeckers, chickadees, nuthatches and Steller's Jays being among the most common birds spoted.

Alouette River (Map 13/C7)

The Alouette River dyke system is a popular spot for Wildlife Watching. Great Blue Herons and hawks are common throughout the year, while in winter, there are Bald Eagles and occasionally, Trumpeter Swans in the adjacent fields. In addition to birds, the occasional deer or coyote may also be seen. A Great Blue Heronry is located on private property across the Alouette River from a small parking lot off 210 Street, where the road turns right. The best viewing time is from March to late July. Bring binoculars.

Birkenhead Lake Provincial Park (Map 39/D3)

Nestled in the Coast Mountains, Birkenhead Provincial Park is home to Phelix Creek. In September and October, watch for spawning kokanee. Kokanee are an inland bound salmon that create a colourful display when spawning. In addition, snowshoe hare are often seen in the campground, while mountain goats are seen on the cliffs above the lake.

Boundary Bay Regional Park (Map 1/F7)

Boundary Bay is an area of international significance to migrating and wintering birds. There are several trails, a boardwalk and two viewing structures located in the park. Many bird species nest on the ground in the sandy and grassland areas, so please stay on the designated trails. Coyote are often seen in the open grasslands, and Harbour Seals frequent the shoreline waters.

Brackendale Eagles Park (Map 20/F7)

The Squamish River plays host to thousands of bald eagles every winter. These majestic birds can be seen feasting on the spawned out remains of Chum Salmon from late November to January. The area on the west side of the Squamish River has been designated as special eagle habitat by BC Parks. A large information shelter with many interpretive signs provides viewing information and is found on the dykes in Brackendale that run between Government Road and the river.

Burnaby Lake Regional Park (Map 1/G2, 2/A3)

Located in the heart of Burnaby, this park is an oasis for wildlife and humans alike. The marshy edges of the lake are an important feeding and nesting habitat for waterfowl. Common species include Canadian Geese and many varieties of ducks (Wood, Mallard, Canvasback, Northern Pintail, Common Golden Eye and Gadwall). Songbirds, woodpeckers and swallows also frequent the lake edges and forests while Beaver and Muskrat are found in the lake. Trail walkers will often see Douglas' Squirrel and Northern Flying Squirrel in the forests.

Capilano River Hatchery (Map11/D7)

The Capilano River Hatchery is located just below Cleveland Dam in North Vancouver. The hatchery is open every day, but the hours of operation change throughout the year. The best viewing time is October and November to see returning adult salmon, and March to May to see juveniles.

Chapman Creek Hatchery (Map 10/B4)

A number of fish species are reared at Chapman Creek Hatchery, including Coho, Chum, Chinook and Pink Salmon as well as Cutthroat Trout. From August through December adult salmon use Chapman Creek to spawn. Pink Salmon are present in August and September, while Coho and Chum Salmon are present beginning in mid October. A viewing platform provides good views of the creek and a trail leads upstream along Chapman Creek.

Cheam Lake Wetlands Regional Park (Map 4/G4)

Located in Popkum, about 15 km east of Chilliwack, Cheam Lake is a fine example of habitat restoration. The original lake was drained in the 1950s to mine marl from the bottom sediments but a water control structure with a fish ladder was installed in 1992 to allow the lake to flood. Changes are occurring as the lake reestablishes, and new wildlife species are beginning to visit the park. A wide variety of birds are already present, including many species of waterfowl, songbirds and woodpeckers. There are beaver and muskrats, and from late March through August, the park is a good place to look for butterflies. The park entrance is at the end of Egley Road, off Yale Road.

Chehalis River Hatchery (Map 4/D1)

The Chehalis River Hatchery is responsible for rearing and for releasing a wide range of fish species, including Coho, Chinook and Chum Salmon as well as Steelhead and Cutthroat Trout. The hatchery compound is open to visitors year round, and there are self-guiding interpretive signs on site. Within the hatchery, fish of various ages are visible in the troughs and tanks throughout the year, but the best viewing time is November, when salmon spawn in the hatchery outflow channel and in the small stream near the parking lot.

Chilliwack Lake Provincial Park (Map 5/E5)

There are good salmon viewing opportunities near where the Chilliwack River flows out of the northern end of Chilliwack Lake. October to mid November is the best time to view Pink (odd years only), Sockeye and Coho Salmon. In April look for Steelhead Trout spawning.

Chilliwack River Hatchery (Map 5/A6)

The Chilliwack River Hatchery is situated just upstream of the junction of Slesse Creek and the Chilliwack River. It is open daily from 8 am to 3:30 pm, and is involved in the rearing of Chinook, Coho, Pink and Chum Salmon as well as Steelhead Trout. A summer run of chinook begins to arrive at the hatchery in August, and the hatchery is busy through to December with other species of salmon returning. Steelhead Trout return in March and April. In addition to fish, watch for birds, including Belted Kingfisher and Bald Eagles.

Colony Farm Regional Park (Map 2/C2)

Located along the Coquitlam River, this park provides nesting and feeding habitats for a wide range of birds, especially raptors and songbirds. The wooded areas are good places to look for woodpeckers and chickadees, while the old fields are frequented by Short Eared Owls. Many waterfowl species are also seen in the river and main ditches. From Highway 7, turn south onto Colony Farm Road and continue to the parking area at the end of the road.

Copeland Islands Marine Park (Map 16/C1–25/C7)
The Copeland Islands are a small chain of islands, islets and rocks off the northern corner of the Sunshine Coast. It is an excellent place to explore by kayak or canoe, and is home to marine mammals like seals and sea lions as well as numerous species of waterfowl.

Cultus Lake Provincial Park (Map 4/B7)
A popular destination for sun worshippers, Cultus Lake is also home to a wide variety of bird species, such as Osprey, Steller's Jay and Winter Wrens. In summer months, bats feed in forest clearings and along the edge of the forest. In fall, the Sweltzer River at the north end of Cultus Lake is home to spawning salmon. A short trail provides access to the river.

Cypress Provincial Park (Map 11/B4)
Established in 1975, this 2,996 ha park is made up of several types of old growth forests, some mixed second growth forests, sub-alpine wetlands, rocky bluffs and mountaintop plateaus. Black bears and cougars frequent the park and may be encountered on hiking trails and in open areas. More common mammals include Douglas Squirrels, Yellow-pine Chipmunks and Common Pikas. The park is home to many woodpeckers, chickadees, nuthatches, Brown Creepers and songbirds. In addition, hawks can often be seen during migration periods.

Fee Creek Spawning Channel (Map 30/D1)
Located about 11 km (6.6 miles) from Mount Currie along Highway 99, Fee Creek runs into the Birkenhead River. The man-made channels in this area provide important, year-round habitat to young salmon. Watch for fry darting about the channels.

Garibaldi Provincial Park (Maps 20, 21, 22, 29, 30)
Garibaldi is a big, spectacular park, containing all kinds of animals and birds. In particular, watch for Hoary Marmots and pika in or near the alpine meadows, or in talus slopes. Access into Garibaldi is mainly on foot.

Gates River Spawning Channel (Map 40/A5)
The spawning channel at Gates River is an excellent place to observe spawning sockeye salmon in late summer and early fall. Amazingly, the fish come up the Fraser River, through the Fraser Canyon, Hell's Gate and finally through Seton and Anderson Lakes into Gates River. There is a large fish ladder that provides fish with access from Gates River into the channel. The spawning channel is located in Devine, just south of D'Arcy.

George C. Reifel Migratory Bird Sanctuary (Map 1/B5)
Over the course of the year, this sanctuary is ground zero for Lower Mainland birders. The sanctuary is part of the Alaksan National Wildlife Area, and is located on Westham Island in Delta. It contains habitats important for migrating birds, including tidal saltwater mudflats, freshwater, brackish and salt marshes and upland fields. All types of birds, including raptors, shorebirds, woodpeckers are found here year round. But during the late fall and early winter months the island comes alive with over 25,000 Lesser Snow Geese visiting the area.

Golden Ears Provincial Park (Map 13/A7-B7)
Golden Ears is another big, spectacular park that is home to all sorts of birds and mammals. From chipmunks to black bears and cougars to cowbirds and ospreys you never know what you may encounter next. In the high country, you may even see mountain goats on the rocky mountain cliffs. One of the best viewing areas is tiny Mike Lake, which is home to a small population of beaver, as well as numerous species of birds, both water and song. Another good viewing spot is along the Spirea Nature Trail, a loop around and through a boggy area. In the summer, expect to see Cedar Waxwing, MacGillivray's Warbler, woodpeckers, chickadees and several species of swallows. In addition

to birds, the bog is home to many interesting plants, including the insect eating Sundew Plant.

Great Blue Heron Nature Reserve (Map 4/B6)
Located in the Wet Bridge training area of the old Chilliwack Armed Forces Base, the Great Blue Heron Nature Reserve is one of the few nesting sites for herons in the Lower Mainland. Look for the colony nests west of the parking area, and along the dyke off Sinclair Road. Things start to happen here in March, when adults begin claiming nests. They are most visible before the leaves are on the trees, although viewing will continue to late July. To get to the viewing area, follow Yale Road West to Sumas Prairie Road and turn right. Continue to the end at Sinclair Road and up onto the dyke.

Harrison Bay/Chehalis Flats (Map 4/D2)
In winter, Bald Eagles hang out around the Chehalis Flats in great numbers (some years, there are over 1,000 eagles here). The eagles arrive in November, and stay until January, attracted by dead and dying spawning salmon. As an added bonus, this is also a winter feeding ground for Trumpeter Swans. Two good viewing areas include; Kilby Provincial Park and the Chehalis Flats, which are located upstream of the Highway 7 (Lougheed Hwy) Bridge over the Harrison River.

Hayward Lake Reservoir (Map 3/C3)
While wildlife can be seen throughout the Hayward Lake area, the Pond Trail is where you will see more action. Birds (waterfowl, woodpeckers and assorted songbirds) and beavers…or at least, signs of beavers (lodges, felled trees, etc.) are seen from the trail. Nearby Ruskin Dam features a spawning channel where Chum Salmon may be observed from early October through late November. The presence of spawning fish attracts many bird species, including bald eagles that are visible along the river during the winter months.

Hope and Camp Sloughs (Map 4/D3)
Hope Slough and Camp Slough are also known as Hope River and Camp River. Whatever they are, they meander through the farmlands north of Chilliwack, along the Fraser River. The sloughs run primarily through private property, but there is road access in some places, as well a canoe route (see paddling). The wetlands are home to all sorts of waterfowl from widgeons to herons.

Inch Creek Hatchery (Map 3/G4)
Throughout the year, you can see and learn about young salmon in various stages of development in the tanks and troughs. On site, there is a large pond, which is home to several large white sturgeons, the largest of which weighs over 91 kg (200 lb). The hatchery compound is open to visitors every day (except Christmas Day) from 9 am to 3 pm.

Indian Arm Provincial Park (Maps 2/A1, 12/A6)
Indian Arm Provincial Park plays host to a number of large mammals, including black bear, blacktail deer, cougar, coyote and red fox. But most visitors are interested in the marine life. The sandy isthmus connecting Twin Islands is home to a variety of clams and other shellfish, while tidal pools along the rocky shoreline abound with sea life. Further north, the Indian River supports the five species of West Coast salmon, sea-run cutthroat, and small steelhead populations. The river estuary is also vital

habitat for prawns, crab, and many species of over-wintering waterfowl. Harbour seals are a common sight in the arm.

Iona Beach Regional Park (Map 1/B3)

This island has long been recognized across North America as one of the best places to study shorebirds. The riverbank, Fraser River tidal flat, marsh, grassland and beach habitats attract a wide range of birds, including many rare and vagrant species. There are over 280 species of birds to be seen here throughout the year, including: loons, cormorants, herons, geese, ducks, Red-tailed Hawks, Rufous-necked Stint, Curlew Sandpiper and many, many others.

John Daly Regional Park (Map 9/C1)

John Daly Regional Park is located on Anderson Creek, an important salmon spawning creek. Chum and coho spawn here in October and November. From Highway 101, just north of the community of Madeira Park, turn west onto Garden Bay Road. At Roosen Road turn left and continue a short distance to the park entrance. If the gate is closed, park and walk in.

Jones Creek Spawning Channel (Map 5/B1)

This spawning channel is located west of Hope near Laidlaw. Chum, coho and, on odd-numbered years, pink salmon spawn here during October. Access is from Jones Creek Road east off Highway 1.

Kanaka Creek Regional Park (Maps 2/G3, 3/B3)

This park stretches along Kanaka Creek, and has two primary viewing areas. Upstream, just off 256 Street, a fish fence was built in conjunction with the **Bell-Irving Hatchery**. Every October, this location plays host to the annual Return of the Salmon event, during the heart of the chum and coho spawn. Throughout the year the site is also a popular place for Great Blue Heron, ducks and belted kingfishers. The hatchery is open to visitors year round. The Chum Salmon release in late April is another event worth catching.

A second viewing area is found along the estuary portion of the creek, south of the Lougheed Highway (Hwy 7). A trail runs along the creek to the Fraser River, then loops back through several habitat types. Great Blue Heron, belted kingfisher, and Canadian Geese are common throughout the year, while ducks such as Bufflehead, and the Common Merganser are seen in the winter months. Spring and summer are the best times to watch for woodpeckers, swallows and other songbird species.

Lang Creek (Map 17/C5)

Where the fresh water of Lang Creek enters the salt water of Malaspina Strait attracts many different waterfowl and shorebirds. In the fall salmon migration into Lang Creek attracts many bald eagles that feed on the fish carcasses. November to January is the best time to see the eagles. The estuary is found south of Highway 101 on Brew Bay Road. Also in the area, the Lang Creek Hatchery offers a chance to watch salmon in a spawning channel from mid August to late November. The nearby forest service rec site located at Creek Falls, is a also a great place to watch spawning salmon as they attempt to jump up the falls.

Mamquam Spawning Channel (Map 20/D7)

This series of spawning channels is located on the north side of the Mamquam River just east of the bridge over the river on Highway 99. Coho and Chum Salmon can be seen in November and December.

Manning Provincial Park (Maps 6 & 7)

Manning Park is a big, beautiful park, and more than 200 species of bird have been seen here. In addition to birds the park is a wonderful place to view a wide range of small mammals, and, perhaps some larger mammals, including black bears and Mule Deer. Some popular viewing areas include the Manning Park Lodge, the Beaver Pond about 1 km (0.6 miles) east of the lodge, Lightning Lakes, the Cascade Lookout, and the alpine around Blackwall Peak.

Maplewood Flats (Map 1/F1)

Maplewood Flats is located on the north shore of Burrard Inlet about 2 km (1.2 miles) east of the Second Narrows Bridge. This 96 ha area is made up of mudflats and some salt marsh, which make ideal waterfowl and bird habitat. In addition, several disused log pilings provide perching and nesting habitat for Osprey. This site teams with waterfowl during winter and both migration periods. Loons, grebes, Canadian Geese, and other birds are present in large numbers in the flats, while songbirds can be viewed in the small upland section of the area. Access to Maplewood Flats is through the parking area of the Pacific Environmental Science Centre off Dollarton Highway.

Millar Creek (Maps 29/F7, 28/G7-F7)

Located in the southwestern portion of Whistler, the creek is home to rainbow trout, which can be observed spawning in May and June.

Nanton Lake Recreation Site (Map 17/E2)

There is a small herd of Roosevelt Elk, which have been transplanted to this area. The best viewing times are in the early morning and before dusk. The site is located off Dixon Road on the Weldwood Main. The rough road is usually closed during weekdays.

Nicomen Slough (Maps 3/G5-4/A4)

Nicomen Slough contains habitat that is important to many species, including bald eagles and spawning salmon. Most notably, the slough provides important wintering habitat for between 100 and 200 Trumpeter Swans, from late November through January.

Noons Creek Hatchery (Map 2/B1)

Started by a handful of area residents who wanted to see salmon reintroduced to Noon Creek, the Noon Creek Hatchery now releases thousands of Coho and Chum Salmon every year. The best viewing times are in May, when fingerlings are released, and in fall, when salmon return to spawn. The hatchery is located on the west side of the Port Moody Recreation Centre on Ioco Road.

Pitt-Addington Marsh Wildlife Area (Maps 2, 12/C7)

The Pitt-Addington Marsh Wildlife Management Area encompasses 2,972 hectares (7,344 acres) south of Pitt Lake that includes Grant Narrows Regional Park, Addington Marsh, Pitt Polder, and MacIntyre Creek. The tidal freshwater mudflats, marshes, and wetlands are viewable along a network of dykes, as well as a number of viewing platforms and towers. Viewing highlights include Great Blue Herons, Trumpeter Swans, Ospreys and other raptors, Sandhill Cranes and a wide variety of songbirds. While in the area, be sure to visit the many dykes and surrounding farmlands to see many species of waterfowls in winter, and hawks and other raptors during summer.

Porpoise Bay Provincial Park (Map 9/G4)

Porpoise Bay Provincial Park is located on the east side of Sechelt Inlet, 4 km north of Sechelt. The park offers excellent year round birding. In winter, watch for loons, grebes, cormorants, ducks and gulls. In spring there are migrant warblers and vireos in the woods, while in July and August the intertidal mudflat of the Angus Creek estuary is very good for shorebirds. Bald Eagles can be seen throughout the year and Chum and Coho Salmon spawn in Angus Creek in fall.

Ruby Creek (Map 18/C7)

Ruby Creek is a short creek that connects Ruby Lake to Sakinaw Lake. Through habitat enhancement projects, new gravel beds and covers over portions of the creek have been added. These features will help protect the spawning habitat for a rare population of Coastal Cutthroat Trout and for Kokanee Salmon in fall.

Sargeant Bay Provincial Park (Map 9/E4)

This park contains a shingle beach, a small lake with a cattail marsh, and an upland area of second growth forest. The park is noted for its beautiful bay and excellent bird watching. In winter there are many birds on the bay, including loons, grebes, cormorants and alcids. In spring there are migrant warblers and vireos. The upland forest is good in summer for flycatchers and Western Tanagers, and in the fall the lake is visited by a variety of ducks. Bald eagles and other raptors are quite common in all seasons.

Sasquatch Provincial Park (Maps 4, 5, 14, 15)

There are three main wildlife viewing areas in Sasquatch Provincial Park. The most active site is the Beaver Pond area where beavers, or tell tale signs of beaver activity can be seen. The best times to observe one of Canada's icons is at dawn or just before sunset. Bird life also abounds in this area, including Downy and Hairy Woodpeckers, Red-breasted Sapsuckers and many others. In late July and early August you will find thousands of young Western Toads. Another place to watch wildlife is at the outlet of Hicks Lake, which features a small dam and fish ladder. A trail leads along the creek and across the dam. In March and April, look for spawning Cutthroat Trout. They are best seen early in the morning or at sunset. Finally, watch for spawning Chum Salmon in October and November in the lower reaches of the Trout Lake Creek.

Sechelt Marsh (Map 9/G5)

This marsh is located across the street from the head of Sechelt Inlet. Together the freshwater marsh and the saltwater inlet provide important wildlife habitat, mostly for waterfowl and shorebirds. You will also see woodpeckers and songbirds in the upland areas.

Serpentine Wildlife Area (Map 2/C6)

The Serpentine Wildlife Area contains 71.3 hectares (176 acres) of extensive marshes, which can be accessed along the many trails in the area. There are three covered viewing towers but please note that many of the dykes are closed to public access. While birds are the big things to see here (from herons to raptors to waterfowls), you will also find small mammals (like muskrats), coyotes and harbour seals in the Serpentine River.

Shoreline Park (Map 2/B1)

There is little natural habitat left on Burrard Inlet, so this small park located at the head of Port Moody is a treasure. It is home to a wide variety of habitats and species. There is a 3 km (1.8 mile) trail from Rocky Point Park to Old Orchard Park, passing through woodlands, past berry bushes and over two salmon-bearing streams. Boardwalk and trail openings provide excellent views of the extensive tidal flats. Viewing highlights include waterfowl during the winter, including loons, ducks, geese and mergansers. Woodpeckers and chickadees are common year round, and in spring and summer, songbirds. The main access to the Shoreline Park area is from St. Johns Street in Port Moody.

Skagit Valley Recreation Area (Map 6/D6)

The Skagit Valley is home to a diversity of wildlife habitat, and, not surprisingly, a diversity of wildlife. Nearly 200 species of bird have been recorded in the area, and commonly seen mammals include Columbian Black-tailed Deer, Mule Deer, Snowshoe Hare, beaver and Common Pika. More secretive and less abundant are elk and moose and even Black Bears and cougars. The open meadows near Ross Lake play home to many butterfly species.

Skookumchuk Narrows Provincial Park (Map 18/D7)

Chickadees, nuthatches and woodpeckers are common along the forest trail to the viewpoint over the narrows. At the viewpoint, many diving ducks are visible, including mergansers and grebes. Harbour Seals are also common along the inlet.

Sliammon Creek Hatchery (Map 16/G3)

Located alongside Sliammon Creek, the best time to watch spawning Chum Salmon is during October and November. The hatchery is north of Powell River along Highway 101.

South Arm Marshes Wildlife Area (Map 1/D6)

The Fraser River estuary is the single most important area of aquatic bird and raptor migration and wintering habitat in British Columbia. The 937 hectare (2,316 acre) South Arm Marshes Wildlife Management Area provides critical wintering, migration and breeding habitats for waterfowl, shorebirds, raptors and many passerine species. The management area contains a series of islands surrounded by both freshwater and intertidal marshes, including Ladner Marsh, Ladner Lagoon and seven main islands—Woodward, Barber, Duck, Kirkland, Rose, Gunn and Williamson. There are more species of birds here than you could shake a spotting scope at, plus seals, sea lions, beavers, mink and other species of mammals.

Squamish Estuary (Map 11/C1)

The Squamish Estuary is located at the head of a steep wall fjord that is Howe Sound. The estuary features a range of habitats, including marine, intertidal mudflat, saltwater marsh, mixed forest, freshwater wetland, riparian and modified. The late fall salmon runs of the Squamish River and its tributaries attract British Columbia's largest congregation of wintering bald eagles. Throughout the year there is a wide range of birds that may be seen. Harbour seals also frequent the estuary.

Stanley Park (Map 1/D1)

Stanley Park is a well groomed showcase of the natural wonders that surrounds Vancouver. It is the green heart that beats in a city of concrete and steel. Lost Lagoon teams with waterfowl and small critters, while the rest of the park is home to a wide variety of birds and small mammals that have thrived because of their interaction with humans.

Tenderfoot Creek Hatchery (Map 20/G4)

Located off Paradise Valley Road, the hatchery contains tanks and troughs holding young fish most of the year. During November and December spawning Coho and Chum Salmon may be observed next to the hatchery.

Texada Island (Maps 8, 9, 16, 17)

With no natural predators, Texada Island is home to a large population of Mule Deer. They are visible during most times of the year, especially during dawn and dusk periods. If you get away from the more populated areas, sit along a road or well worn trail and wait. The island is also home to birds, smaller mammals, and harbour seals down on the beach. But the biggest highlight here is the deer.

Weaver Creek Spawning Channel (Map 4/E1)

Weaver Creek spawning channel is one of the biggest in the area. An average of 32,000 Sockeye Salmon and 2,500 Chum Salmon use the channel, depositing an estimated 76 million eggs. Next to the Adams River, this is the best site in British Columbia to see sockeye spawning in September. In winter, the channel and surrounding streams are terrific places to look for American Dippers, a small slate-grey songbird that walks under water.

Winter Recreation

(Skiing, Snowshoeing and Snowmobiling)

Skiing and Snowshoeing

Snowshoeing is a sport that has been rapidly gaining popularity. Part of its newfound appeal can be attributed to backcountry snowboarders. But most of the rise in popularity should be attributed to the radical design innovations that have taken place over the last few years. Snowshoes have gone from unwieldy racquets attached to the feet, to devices that are only slightly larger than a pair of boots, and are just as easy to walk in.

Whatever the reason, you will now find people snowshoeing all sorts of snow-covered trails in winter. They also tie in well with the few cross-country areas that exist in Southwestern BC.

The Coast Mountains are also a paradise for people who like to do ski touring. Routes range from easy (cross-country skiers will find that they don't need special touring skis to do some of these routes), with little avalanche hazard, to the extremely precipitous.

We are not going to list the really hardcore routes, or even all the places you can go on a pair of skis (which is just about anywhere above the snowline), but you will find a good selection of the most popular routes in this section. Remember, that these are only a fraction of the places the intrepid explorer can get to in winter with a good pair of touring skis. If you're looking for more adventurous trips, there are groups out there, like the Federation of Mountain Clubs, who can help.

Winter storms that bring endless rain to Vancouver in January bring inches, feet, even yards of snow. While never ending snow might sound like a good thing, it can make touring the mountains dangerous; not just for avalanche hazards, but simply for navigation purposes. Mid-winter trips tend to contain extended periods of time stuck in a tent.

But, come April, the sun comes out, and there are a few weeks—and in higher elevation snowfields, months—of perfect touring weather. Sunny, warm, and snow everywhere.

It is important to remember that backcountry travel comes with a degree of risk that, while manageable, is never non-existent. If you don't know what you're doing, don't do it! Travel with someone who has more experience, take a lesson, and always carry an avalanche transceiver.

Black Tusk/Garibaldi Lake (Map 20/E2) 🎿 🏕 🥾 🏂

This area is an advanced backcountry ski touring area. There are huts on the east side of Garibaldi Lake, and people ski across Garibaldi Lake during January and February to spend the night. The day-use shelters at Garibaldi Lake can be used for sleeping in during the winter months only. The road to the parking lot is not plowed during the winter. Parking is along Highway 99.

Brandywine & Metal Dome (Map 29/C6) 🎿 🚡 🏕 🥾 🏂

This is a popular summer destination that loses none of its beauty and appeal in winter. The only complaint could be its popularity, both with snowmobilers and heli-skiers. It is still possible to find some areas that are not tracked out. A ridge connects Brandywine Mtn and Metal Dome, although there is a bit of scrambling required to make the traverse. There is a snowmobile warming hut near Metal Dome.

Brohm Ridge (Map 20/F4) 🎿 🚡 🏕 🥾 🏂

Because it is located outside of Garibaldi Park, anything goes on Brohm Ridge. Depending on when you show up and where you go, you might see ski tourists, snowmobilers, and even snowboarders building the biggest darn half pipe you'll ever see. There is a warming hut and lots of great skiing. Easily done in a day.

Cambie Creek Trails (Map 7/B5) 🎿 🥾 🏂

Located in Manning Provincial Park, this series of cross-country ski trails

(Cambie Loop, Big Ben and Fat Dog) range from easy to expert (Fat Dog is the toughest, heading all the way up into the sub-alpine). These trails are not groomed, but are usually well tracked.

Cayoosh Range (Map 40) 🎿 🥾 🏂

This is a phenomenal ski area. It's so good, in fact, that plans have been underway for about a decade to turn this area into a ski hill. It may take even longer than that to see these plans come to fruition. In fact, the hill may never happen, but that doesn't mean that you can't ski it currently. Without the lifts, plan on spending at least two days here, more if you want to explore the Northern part of this range. Most of the skiing happens on Mount Rohr and Cayoosh Mountain, which are more easily accessed of the Duffey Lake Road (Hwy 99).

Cypress Bowl (Map 11/B7) 🎿 🏕 🏂

The closest place to Vancouver for cross-country skiers to get their fix, Cypress Bowl has 19 km (11.6 miles) of trails groomed for skate and classic. 4 km (2.4 miles) of the trails are lit for night skiing. There are some challenging up and down hill sections, but novices will be able to find some interesting loops, too. Cypress is also home to several kilometres of snowshoeing trails.

Dakota Ridge Area (Map 10/D4) 🎿 🥾 🏂

This is a newly developed area, earmarked for cross-country skiing, but with options for snowshoeing and backcountry skiing. In the summer, this area is far too boggy to support recreation, but in winter, the place freezes up, and there are a number of natural and man made routes that can be followed. With an elevation above 1,000 metres (3,500 feet), there is usually snow. At the time of this writing, there are still no formal trails in the 620 ha (1,200 acre) site behind Mount Elphinstone, but plans are underway for three trails, ranging from 5 km (3 miles) to 20 km (12.2 miles) in length. Access is 13 km (7.9 miles) along the Wilson East Forest Service Road, which leaves Highway 101 about 20 minutes north of the Langdale Ferry Terminal.

Dam Mountain (Map 11/E7) 🥾 🏂

A popular hiking route in the summer, Dam Mountain is gaining popularity as a winter snowshoeing route. The 3 km (1.5 mile) trail is groomed and patrolled, making it a great place for beginners to practice their snowshoeing chops. The route heads to the left of the lifts from the lodge, and climbs stiffly up to the peak of Dam Mountain. On a clear day, stop here and admire the view; on a stormy, foggy, nasty day, continue on the trail, which loops around Dam Mountain, then back to the Grouse Mountain Lodge for a little après-snowshoe.

Diamond Head (Map 20/G6) 🎿 🏕 🥾

Diamond Head is an intermediate backcountry ski touring area that follows the main trail to Elfin Lakes and beyond. In summer, the alpine area is a fragile environment, and hikers are bound to the main trail. In winter, the whole area is a playground, and some great skiing can be found right near Red Heather Shelter. The Rangers mark the route past the shelter with orange snow poles (below the shelter the trail is fairly obvious through the forest). Snow removal is periodic on the road to the Diamond Head parking lot, and you may require a four-wheel drive. This touring area is the most popular ski touring destination in Southwestern BC, with the exception of Hollyburn in Cypress.

Garibaldi Neve Traverse (Map 20/G4) 🎿 🏕 🥾

This moderate route is one of the most popular multi-day skiing trips in the area. The climbs are gentle, and there is little in the way of avalanche hazards. The trip crosses a number of glaciers, and in times of low snow there are some dangerous crevasses near the Sharkfin. From The Black Tusk Trailhead to the Diamond Head Trailhead is just over 30 km. The trip takes most groups take two or three days.

Helm Creek Trail (Map 20/G1–29/G7)
This trail is used to access the alpine meadows east of Black Tusk. Although it is longer than the Black Tusk Trail, it is less crowded. Expect to take at least two days to do a return trip, though a day trip to the Black Tusk Trailhead is possible if you can arrange a shuttle pick-up.

Hemlock Mountain (Map 14/D7)
Better known for it's small but interesting downhill area, there are cross-country and snowshoe trails in the area. The ski trails are not groomed or track-set, but there still is a trail fee. The trails wander around and sometimes through the village at the base of the ski hill. There are also old logging roads in the area for folks looking to do some easy backcountry exploration.

Hollyburn Mountain (Map 11/C7)
In the winter, this popular hiking area becomes a popular ski destination for all types of skiers. Cypress maintains a popular ski area (see above), but for folks wanting to learn the basics of ski touring, this is also a popular destination. Trips in this area don't usually last more than a day, and there are many routes to choose from.

Knucklenead Recreation Area (Map 17/G3)
This is a popular winter recreation area, accessed beyond the Stillwater Mainline. The area can be accessed in the summer for hiking and bicycling, but has become an extremely popular winter destination in the past few years. It is possible to do this as a day trip, but why not spend the night at the warming hut? From here, you can do a number of day trips into the area.

Lost Lake Cross-Country Area (Map 30/A6)
Nestled amongst the trees at the base of Blackcomb Mountain, this 32 km (19.5 mile) series of trails are some of the best cross-country skiing in the province. The amenities are pure Whistler—water stations, a warming hut, lessons and of course, rentals—the views of the surrounding mountains (at times, the trails break out into flat, wide, open areas, which in summer are golf courses) are breathtaking, and the (daily) grooming impeccable. The trails are well signed, and rated from novice to expert. There's even 2.5 km (1.5 miles) of trail around Lost Lake lit for night skiing. There are also snowshoe trails located in the same area.

Mad River Nordic Centre (Map 29/C5)
Located 13 km (8 miles) west of Whistler, the Mad River Ski Area is often used as a staging area for trips to the Callaghan Lake Lodge, 12.5 km (13.4 miles) up trail from Alexander Falls. There are a total of 32 km (19.5 miles) of groomed trails in the area, plus lost of great backcountry skiing, especially around the lodge found at an elevation of 1,370 metres/4,500 feet. Most people who travel this way stay at the 5-room backcountry lodge, but this is by no means a requirement of using this area. You do have to pay the trail fees, though. In addition to cross-country and backcountry skiing, there is also backcountry snowshoeing. Explore the old growth forests and sub-alpine meadows of the Upper Callaghan Valley by snowshoe.

Magnesia Meadows (Map 11/B3)
One of the few open alpine meadows this close to the highway, the route to Magnesia Meadows is mostly along old logging roads. The meadows are tucked in behind Mount Harvey. There is a shelter at the head of Magnesia Creek.

Manning Park Resort (Map 7/C5)
Located between the Manning Park Lodge and the downhill area, the Manning Park Cross-Country Ski Trails are a favourite getaway for many Vancouver cross-country skiers. The trails weave in and out and up and down the rolling forested hills around Lightening Lake. The 30 km (18.3 miles) of groomed trails include 17 km (10.4 miles) groomed for skating. There are also many backcountry routes in the area, from skiing the 3 km (1.8 miles) to the end of Lightening Lake,

to some serious climbs up to the ridge of the Three Brothers (to the north of the highway).

Meslillooet Mountain (Map 12/B3)
The Meslillooet Icefield is the closest glacier to Vancouver, just north of Indian Arm. However, getting to the Icefield is a bit of an adventure, as there is no easy road access. Rather, it is off a long trip north up Hwy 99, then backtracking southeast along the Mamquam and Stawamus-Indian Forest Service Roads. An alternate approach would be via boat up Indian Arm, then hike/ski in along the Hixon Creek FSR. Give yourselves at least three days for either option.

Mount Bishop (Maps 11/G7-12/A6)
Mount Elsay and Mount Bishop are the two big summits in behind Mount Seymour. These mountains are accessed from the Mount Seymour Trail at Brocton Point. Many people just stay in the Mount Elsay area, but it is possible, in good snow conditions to make it to Mount Bishop beyond. There is a cabin near Elsay Lake, but this intermediate trip can be done in a day.

Mount Brew (Map 29/C3)
Access to the Mount Brew area is from the Brandywine FSR. The low, gentle summit is perfect for ski touring, and there is a large cabin near the summit for people spending the night. It is possible to do this moderately difficult area as a day trip, but most people stay a few days to explore the terrain of the Squamish/Cheakamus Divide (see below).

Mount Cheam (Map 5/A4)
Mount Cheam is one of the most prominent peaks in the Fraser Valley. How far you have to ski depends on how high you can get a vehicle up the Chipmunk Creek FSR to the south. At the base of Cheam is a lovely open meadow, and the ascent, while stiff, isn't too difficult. Nearby Knight Peak is another popular ski destination.

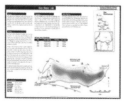

Mount Sedgewick (Map 20/A7)

Mount Sedgewick is located on the west side of Howe Sound, past Mount Roderick on the Mount Roderick Trail. Give yourselves at least two days to explore this moderately difficult area. Access to the area is via the Woodfibre Ferry, just south of Squamish.

Pemberton Icefield (Maps 28, 29, 37, 38)

This huge icefield north of Whistler and east of Pemberton is a backcountry winter sport mecca. The ascents and descents are gentle, and a backcountry ski trip here dovetails nicely into the Squamish-Cheakamus Divide (see below), making a good weeklong trip. To ski from the north trailhead to the south trailhead can take as little as three days, but most people take a few more days to explore.

Post Creek Cross-Country Trails (Map 5/E5)

A 7.3km (4.5 mile) cross-country ski trail system with easy and moderate trails. It is recommended to ski these trails in a counter clockwise direction, as this is the way the trails are signed. The trails are found adjacent to the Post Creek Recreation Site across from the Chilliwack Lake Road.

Seymour Mountain (Map 11/G7)

The official Seymour snowshoeing trails lay to the east of the parking lot, between the Mystery Peak Chairlift and the Goldie Rope Tow. There are ten short trails, ranging from 0.1 km to 1 km (.05 to .5 mile). These add up to 5.5 km (3.4 miles) of trails, mostly in the beginner to intermediate range. But there are other, more challenging, places you can go on snowshoes and backcountry skis. For instance, you can follow a trail from the parking lot along the left-hand edge of the ski area boundary, all the way to the top of the mountain. It is a 10 km (6.1 mile) return trek with a fairly stiff uphill climb all the way to the top. Expect to take about four hours to the top; another two if you want to follow the ridge along the three pump routes. On a clear day, the views are worth the effort. An easier trail runs up the mountain to the right of the ski lifts. This route is also popular with backcountry skiers.

Singing Pass (Maps 30/A7–21/A1)

Access to Singing Pass is via Fitzsimmons Creek, which flows between Whistler and Blackcomb Mountains. This is a moderate route, with a good cabin at the north end of Russet Lake, maintained by the BCMC. This trip can easily be done in a day, but the whole joy of this area is exploring the slopes behind Whistler Mountain. Avid skiers spend days on end up here enjoying the wide variety of terrain.

Sky Pilot (Map 11/E2)

At the base of Sky Pilot Mountain (the highest summit in the area) is an area of rolling basins and fine sub alpine skiing. This area is well suited for easy day trips, although the BCMC maintain a locked cabin near Mountain Lake for overnight excursions. This area is reached fairly easily off the Stawamus-Indian FSR.

Snowcap Lake Route (Maps 21/G4, 22/A4-A1)

Most of the terrain in Garibaldi Park is accessed from the west side, which means that those people willing to take the extra effort will find more peace and solitude on the east side of the big park. Snowcap Lake is one such location. Allow about three days from logging roads off the Lillooet Lake Road to access the lake. The route isn't as high as some, and so it must be done in late winter/early spring. The route does cross over the Icemantle Glacier, and the 2,370 metre (7,702 foot) Greenmantle Mountain. From here, longer, more difficult trips can be made to Thunderclap Glacier, Misty Glacier, and Stave Glacier, deep in the untrammeled heart of Garibaldi Park.

Snowspider Mountain (Map 31/C2)

Located in the high mountains above Lillooet Lake, Snowspider Mountain is a great weekend trip. Although the trip can be done in two or three days from the Van Horlick Creek Road, arguably the best approach is to ski up Cerise Creek from the Duffy Lake Road.

Squamish-Ashlu Divide (Maps 28/E7-19/G1)

Also known as the Ashlu-Elaho Divide, this area is heavily glaciated, and is a great ski touring terrain. The divide is best accessed from the southwest, along an unnamed creek west and slightly south of Porterhouse Peak, though the road is not usually passable until early May. Expect to take about three days to reach the south trailhead on logging roads just off Branch A-700.

Squamish-Cheakamus Divide (Maps 29/A3–20/B1)

One of the most popular multi-day trips in the area, the Squamish-Cheakamus Divide was built for ski touring with easy climbs and some great descents. The moderate trip is generally best done from Callaghan Lake south to Tricouni Meadows. The four day route hooks up with other trails, including the Brandywine and Metal Dome Route as well as Brew Mountain and Roe Creek. These other access points allow people to shorten the trip.

Spearhead Traverse (Maps 39/B7-21/C1)

This route follows the string of glaciers behind Blackcomb Mountain deep into the heart of Garibaldi Provincial Park. The area is a popular heli-skiing destination, and you may even see snowshoers in the area. The traverse is best done clockwise, starting at the Blackcomb Ski Area, along the Blackcomb, Decker, Trorey, Tremor, Platform and Fitzsimmons Glaciers, then south to Overlord Mountain. The loop takes you back to Whistler Mountain, either via the Singing Pass Trail or over the Musical Bumps. This moderate route will take most parties three days, although bad weather can extend the length of this trip.

Stein Divide (Maps 31/A4-24/A1)

Give yourself at least a week to ski this route that is as challenging as it is rewarding. The route starts from Lizzie Creek FSR, most likely where it meets the In-Shuck-Ch FSR. The route follows the road and then the hiking route to Cherry Pip Pass. Once in the alpine, experienced route finders can head farther south, past Figure Eight Lake and onto Mount Skook Jim. From here, the route heads east onto the Rutledge Glacier, past Longslog Mountain, eventually meeting logging roads that head up Log Creek.

Tantalus Range (Maps 20/A5)

The Tantalus Range are not good winter ski routes, as the mostly up and down construction makes this a place for mountaineers, not ski touring. However, from the ACC hut at Lake Lovely Water, there are a couple of good destinations, including Mount Pelops and Mount Niobe. These trips are fairly strenuous, and shouldn't be undertaken by the inexperienced.

Tetrahedron Plateau/Mt Steele (Map 10/C2)

At 1,738 metres (5,699 feet), Tetrahedron Peak is the highest on the Sunshine Coast. The surrounding area makes for an easy to moderate ski touring destination with lots of gentle, rolling terrain and some good downhill skiing from either Mount Steele or Panther Peak. The popular area has a well established trail system and four cabins from which to base camp.

Wedge Mountain (Map 30/B5)

Wedge Mountain is the highest peak in Garibaldi rising some 2,905 metres (9,441 feet) above sea level. Although the mountain can be scrambled up, the real appeal of this trip is the series of glaciers (Weart, Needle, Chaos) north and east of the peak. Give yourself at least two days to explore. The BCMC maintains a cabin at Wedgemount Lake. It is also possible to access this area from Blackcomb Mountain to the south via Wedge Pass.

Wedge-Currie Traverse (Map 30/B5–C3)

This difficult route follows the Weart Glacier north onto the Hibachi Ridge, which straddles the Garibaldi Park border. From here, experienced route finders can make their way to Mount Currie, and out along Gravell Creek.

Snowmobiling

Finding places near the Lower Mainland to ride a sled is a challenge, as the lower valleys usually have no snow, and the higher mountains are mostly protected behind park boundaries, all of which are snowmobile-free zones. But, while it might seem a foreign concept in temperate Vancouver, snowmobiling is actually quite popular once you start to head a bit farther out of the city. Even around Chilliwack, you will start to find areas that are good snowmobiling territory.

The heartland of snowmobiling, at least in this mapbook, is the region around Pemberton, Bralorne and Gold Bridge. There are dozens of places to snowmobile that are accessed off the Hurley River FSR and the Lillooet FSR. As always, this is not a complete list, but an introduction to some of the most popular snowmobiling areas.

Black Tusk Microwave Tower (Map 29/F7-20/E2)
This is a very limited riding area along the Black Tusk Microwave Tower Road, just south of Whistler at Function Junction. Riding is not permitted in Garibaldi Park so stick to the trail area when in the alpine.

Brohm Ridge (Map 20/F4)
Snowmobilers are not allowed into Garibaldi Provincial Park, but this ridge just outside the park is a good approximation of the terrain and scenery inside the boundaries. This is also a busy area for ski touring, and in spring, this is a popular backcountry destination for snowboarders, who like to build big half pipes here. A local snowmobile club leases two chalets in the area, and provides a trail maintenance service at a small cost.

Burke Mountain (Map 2/C1-12/D7)
When and if snow is available, riding in the Burke Mountain area starts from the first gate on Harper Road. The area consists of various old logging roads that lead up to Dennett and Munro Lakes.

Cypress Bowl (Map 11/B7)
Although Cypress bowl is best known as a ski area in winter, there are a trio of trails, totaling over 15 km (9.2 miles) for snowmobilers. The riding area is below the ski area, but when ski conditions are good on top, it doesn't necessarily mean good riding below.

Lone Goat Snowmobile Area (Map 43/G7-38/E1)
A sprawling area, known for alpine bowls, snow caves and light, fluffy powder, there are about 115 km (70 miles) of trails to explore in this area. The trails are best left to intermediate and expert riders. The Bridge River Snowmobile Club maintains an emergency shelter in the area.

Noel Snowmobile Area (Map 44/A7-39/A1)
In Upper Noel Creek you will find a rolling alpine country with a beautiful 46 metre (150 foot) high glacier. This terrain is recommended for intermediate and advanced riders. In all, there are about 80 km (50 miles) worth of trails to explore.

Pemberton Icefield (Maps 28, 29, 37, 38)
The Pemberton Icefield is a winter mecca, a seemingly endless area of ice and snow that is popular with snowmobilers and backcountry skiers. A new winter trail up the Rutherford Valley, developed by a local snowmobile club, is the best access to the icefield. Alternatively, riders like to access the area from Meager Creek. Excellent conditions exist between December to April.

Slim Creek (Map 43/D4)
The vast, open expanses of the Slim Creek area can be accessed from the north end of Gun Lake. Climbing as high as 2,700 metres (9,000 feet), you can ride all day here without crossing your tracks. You can cover up to 200 km or more in a day, so bring extra gas. Be wary, this is an area for experienced riders only. It is also a terrible place to be in a snowstorm. It is easy to get lost in the wide open terrain, especially if you can't follow your tracks back.

Taylor Basin (Map 44/B2)
Taylor Basin is an excellent alpine area to play in. In addition to a warming cabin at the 2,000 metre (6,600 foot) level, there are two mountain slopes that climbing up to 2,460 metres (8,000 feet) in elevation. This area is open to all skill levels, but the higher slopes are best left to intermediate and expert riders. Expect to put on up to 100 km (60 miles) as you play around on these open slopes.

Upper Lillooet Area (Maps 37, 38, 39)
When the snow falls and the roads remain unploughed, there are seemingly endless places for sledders. In particular, the 45 km (27.5 mile) trip along Upper Lillooet and Meager Creek Forest Service Roads north of Pemberton is a popular route for beginners. There are a number of alternate routes in this area for snowmobilers to explore. Avalanche Hazards exist in some areas, especially along Meager Creek.

Southwestern B.C. Mapkey

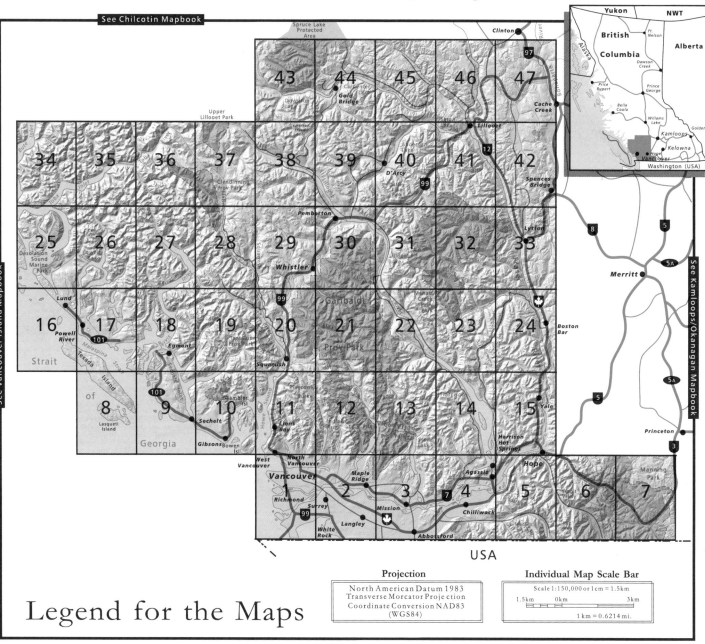

See Chilcotin Mapbook

See Vancouver Island Mapbook

See Kamloops/Okanagan Mapbook

SWBC Maps

Legend for the Maps

Projection

North American Datum 1983
Transverse Mercator Projection
Coordinate Conversion NAD83
(WGS84)

Individual Map Scale Bar

Scale 1:150,000 or 1cm = 1.5km

1.5km   0km   3km

1 km = 0.6214 mi.

Recreational Activities:

Anchorage ....
Boat Launch ....
Beach ....
Campsite / Limited Facilities ....
Campsite / Trailer Park..................
Campsite (trail / water access only).......
Canoe Access Put-in / Take-out ....
Cross Country Skiing ....
Diving...................................
Downhill Skiing.........................
Fishing.................................
Golf Course ....
Hang-gliding ....
Hiking ....
Horseback Riding ....
Mountain Biking ....
Motorbiking / ATV.......................
Paddling (canoe-kayak)..................
Picnic Site..............................
Portage.................................
Rock Climbing ....
Snowmobiling...........................
Snowshoeing............................

Miscellaneous:

Airport / Airstrip ....
Beacon ....
Cabin / Lodge / Resort ....
Deactivated Road ....
Fishing BC Lake ....
Float Plane Landing.....................
Forestry Lookout (abandoned) ....
Gate ....
Highways ....
  Trans-Canada ....
  Secondary Highway ....
Interchange ....
Lighthouse ....
Marsh ....
Microwave Tower ....
Mine Site (abandoned) ....
Parking ....
Point of Interest ....
Portage (metres) ....
Ranger Station ....
Town Village, etc ....
Travel Information ....
Viewpoint ....
Waterfalls ....

Line Definition:

Highways...............................
Paved Secondary Roads ....
Forest Service / Main Roads ....
Active Logging Roads (2wd) ....
Logging Roads (2wd / 4wd) ....
Long Distance Trail ....
Unclassified / 4wd Roads ....
Deactivated Roads......................
Trail / Old Roads ....
Routes (Undeveloped Trails) ....
Snowmobile Trails ....
Skytrain Route ....
Paddling Routes ....
Powerlines ....
Pipelines ....
Railways ....
Wildlife Management Units ....

Provincial Park

Recreation Area/
Ecological Area

City

Restricted Area /
Private Property

Swamps

Indian Reserve

SWBC Maps

See Vancouver Island Mapbook

N

West Vancouver

North Vancouver

Deep Cove

Burrard

Ship Lanes

2-8

Lighthouse Park
Grebe Islets
Passage Isl
Point Atkinson
Point Grey
Sandy Cove
Dundarave Park
Ambleside Park
Jack Pt
Lions Gate Bridge
Prospect Pt
Third Beach
Ferguson Pt
Second Beach
First Beach
Stanley Park
Brockton Pt
Coal Harbour
Seawall Walk
Lost Lagoon
Vanier Park
Kitsilano Beach Park
English Bay
Waterfront Park
Lonsdale Quay Market
Seabus
Vancouver Harbour
Gastown
Ballantyne Pier
New Brighton Park
Burrard View Park
McGill
PNE
Hastings Park
Confederation Park
Montrose Park
Berry
Second Narrows Bridge
Maplewood Flats
Seymour Golf Club
Seymour Prov Park
Mt Seymour Pkwy
Cates Park
Roche Pt
Burnaby Mtn Park
refinery
SFU

Inlet

Indian Arm

Burnaby

LOUGHEED
Burnaby Mtn Golf Course
SPERLING
CURTIS
PARKER
HASTINGS
GILMORE
WILLINGDON
BOUNDARY
DEER
OAK
CANADA
Deer Lake Park
Burnaby Lake Park
WINSTON
ROYAL OAK
IMPERIAL
RUMBLE
MARINE
Mussio Ventures

2-8

New Westminster

Point Grey Beach
Spanish Banks
Jericho Beach Park
University of British Columbia
Wreck Beach
Bell Buoy
Point No Point
QA Marker
Douglas Fir Trail
Pacific Spirit Park
SW MARINE Dr
NW MARINE Dr
WESTBROOK
DUNBAR
ALMA
4th Ave
10th Ave
16th Ave
33rd Ave
41st
49th
ARBUTUS
GRANVILLE
OAK
CAMBIE
MAIN
FRASER
KNIGHT
VICTORIA
NANAIMO
KINGSWAY
Queen Elizabeth Park
Langara Golf Course
54th Ave
Everett Crowley Park
KERR
SW MARINE

Vancouver

BROADWAY
12th
KING
EDWARD
TERMINAL
CLARKE
1st Ave
RENFREW
RUPERT
Rupert Park
HASTINGS
GRANDVIEW Hwy
Trout Lake
22nd Ave
29th Ave
Skytrain
JOYCE
Central Park
OAKLAND St
DEER Lk
WAY
Burnaby Lake

Strait

Of

Georgia

Sturgeon

Bank

Iona Beach Reg Park
Iona Isl
McDonald Rd
Point Grey Golf Course
McCleary Golf Course
Marine Dr Golf Course
Arthur Laing Bridge
GRAUER Rd
GRANT McCONACHIE
Sea Island
Vancouver International Airport
South Terminal
Swishwash Island
No.2 Rd Bridge
Middle Arm
West Arm
North Arm
Oak St Bridge
Mitchell
BRIDGEPORT
CAMBIE
King George Park
GARDEN CITY
SHELL Rd
Richmond Nature Park
DND
RICHMOND -ANNACIS Hwy
WESTMINSTER Hwy
Mayfair Lakes Golf Course
Fraser
Fraser Foreshore Park
BRYNE
MARINE
10th
8th
6th
Queensborough Bridge

T10 Marker

Richmond

GRANVILLE Ave
Terra Nova Park
Quilchena Golf & Country Club
BLUNDELL
FRANCIS
WILLIAMS
STEVESTON Hwy
RAILWAY
GILBERT
No 1 Rd
No 2 Rd
No 3 Rd
No 4 Rd
No 5 Rd
No 6 Rd
No 7 Rd
Country Meadows Golf Course
SIDAWAY
NELSON Rd
Annacis Island
Fraser River
City
Alex Fraser Bridge
NORDEL
Burns Bog Trails
Delta Nature Park
Sunshine Hills Golf Course

Lulu Island

2-4

Bank

Steveston
Steveston Jetty Trail
MONCTON
Garry Point Park
George C Reifel Migratory Bird Sanctuary
Steveston Isl
FINN Rd
Richmond Golf & Country Club
DYKE
Gilbert Beach
Pelly Isl
Reifel Isl
Woodward's Isl
South Dyke Trail
Kirkland Island
Deas Island Park
Delta Millennium Trail
George Massey Tunnel
Vancouver- Delta Disposal Site
FERRY
628 St
64 St
68 St
80 St
96 St
104 St
10
17
99
BURNS Dr

Sand Heads

Alaksen National Wildlife Area & Bird Sanctuary
Westham Island
Duck Isl
South Arm Marshes Wildlife Area
Barber Isl
Ladner Harbour Park
48 Ave
LADNER TRUNK Rd
HORNBY Dr
Delta Air Park
Boundary Bay Airport
72 St
88 St

Ladner

Port Guichon
TAMBOLINE
WESTHAM ISL Rd
Canoe Passage
ARTHUR
WEST Rd
46A Ave
36 Ave
34B Ave
Musqueam IR
DELTAPORT WAY
Cohilukthan Slough
TSAWWASSEN Rd
28
52 St
53
57
56
BLUFF
30 Ave
64 St
72 St
88 St
96 St
Boundary Bay Regional Park
Beach Grove Spit
Centennial Beach

Roberts

Bank

Tsawwassen

Roberts Bank Superport
English Bluff
Tsawwassen Ferry Terminal
Tsawwassen Beach
Can-USA border
Pt ROBERTS, WA

Boundary

Bay

Grauer Beach

Greater Vancouver

See Map 11

See Map 2

1.5 km   0 km   3 km

1

© Mussio Ventures Ltd.

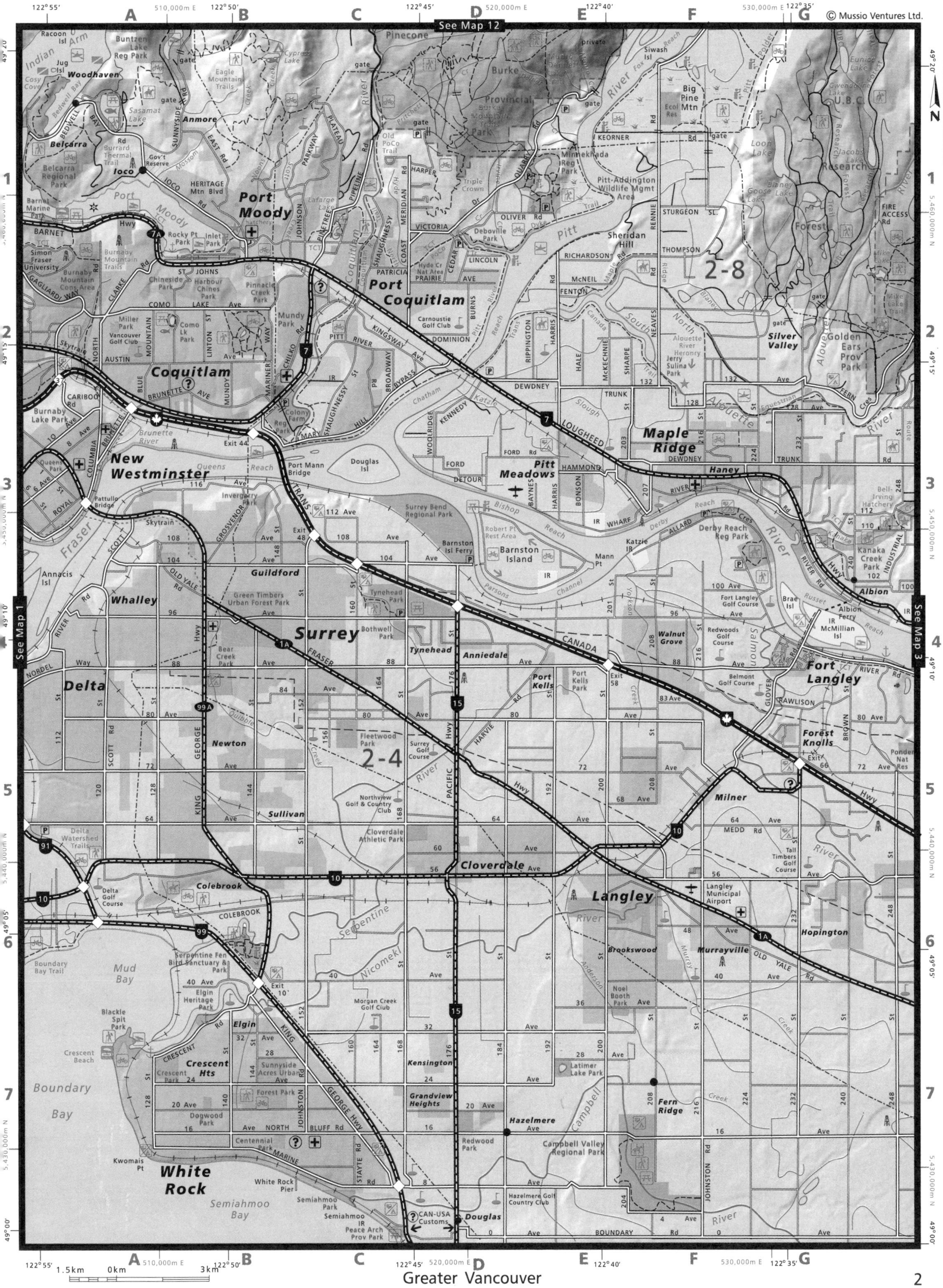

SWBC Maps

N

See Map 12

2-8

Port Moody

Port Coquitlam

Coquitlam

New Westminster

Maple Ridge

Pitt Meadows

Barnston Island

Fort Langley

Surrey

Whalley

Guildford

Delta

Newton

2-4

Sullivan

Port Kells

Walnut Grove

Forest Knolls

Milner

Cloverdale

Langley

Colebrook

Hopington

Murrayville

Brookswood

Crescent Hts

Elgin

Kensington

Grandview Heights

Hazelmere

Fern Ridge

White Rock

Boundary Bay

Mud Bay

Semiahmoo Bay

CAN-USA Customs

Douglas

Greater Vancouver

2

1.5km 0km 3km

122°55' 122°50' 122°45' 122°40' 122°35'

510,000m E 520,000m E 530,000m E

SWBC Maps

See Map 2

See Map 4

Abbotsford

2-8

2-4

Golden Ears Prov Park

Alouette Peak
Evans Peak
Alouette Mtn 1371m
North Beach
Gold Creek Campground
Alouette Campground
Scout Bay Trails

Mt Crickmer 1360m
Mt Crickmer Trail

Stave Lake

Sayres Lake
Sayers Point
old sawmill

Davis Lake Prov Park
McKay Lake
MUNDRO Mt St Benedict 1280m
Lost Lake
Sonny Lake

Cascade Falls Regional Park
gate end pavement

Miracle Valley
HARTLEY RD
Allan Lake

Durieu
Pattison

Blue Mtn
Blue Mtn Trails
gates
BLUE MTN FSR
ROCKWELL Rd
Devils Lake
Devils Lake Rec Site
Hoover Lake
Mt Cannell
Cannell Lake

Rolley Lake Prov Park
Rolley Lake
Rolley Falls Trail
Kanaka Creek Park

Stave Lake Campsite
Hoover Lake Trail
Stave Dam Trail

Webster's Corners
DEWDNEY
Iron Mtn
Whonnock Lake
Ruskin
Ruskin Rec Site
Langley IR

Stave Falls
Steelhead
Steelhead Hayward Lake Reservoir Rec Site
Red Mtn
Silver Creek Park
Bear Mtn
Pioneer Trail

Steelhead Lookout Trail
CAMPBELL ST
Carral Loop
Hatzic
Prairie
Dewdney Peak 920m
FARMS

Nicomen Mtn

Grant Hill
Spawning channel
Silvermere Lake
Caswell Trail

Silverhill
Silverdale
Fraser River

Whonnock
Glen Valley Reg Park
Crescent Isl

Glen Valley
Pemberton Hills
McCormick

West Heights
Hatzic Lake
Neilson Reg Park
Hatzic
Dewdney Nature Park
Strawberry Isl
Dewdney

Nicomen Island

Mission
Mission Bridge
Three Islands Park
Matsqui Island
Matsqui IR

Page Road Trailhead
Page Lake
Ridgedale

Sumas Mtn Park
Chadsey Lake
Sumas Mtn Trail

Mount Lehman
Matsqui Main IR
Glenmore Rd Trailhead
Matsqui

Sumas Mtn Park Taggart Peak 795m

Bradner
TOWNSHIPLINE
Gifford
Clayburn
Willband Creek Park
Straiton
Sumas Mountain

TRANS-CANADA
Exit 73
Exit 83
Clearbrook Park
Ledgeview Golf Course
TCT Cycle Route
Bateman
Sahhacum IR
McKee Peak
Kilgard

Aldergrove
Aberdeen
Simpson
Clearbrook
Exit 87
Exit 90
Fraser Centennial Park
Mill Lake
Abbotsford
Hougen Park
CAMPBELL
Rest Area

Abbotsford Airport
Albert Dyck Park
North Poplar
South Poplar
Laxton Lake
Judson Lake

Vye
Norton
Arnold

Aldergrove Lake Regional Park
Huntingdon

1.5km   0km   3km

Abbotsford

© Mussio Ventures Ltd.

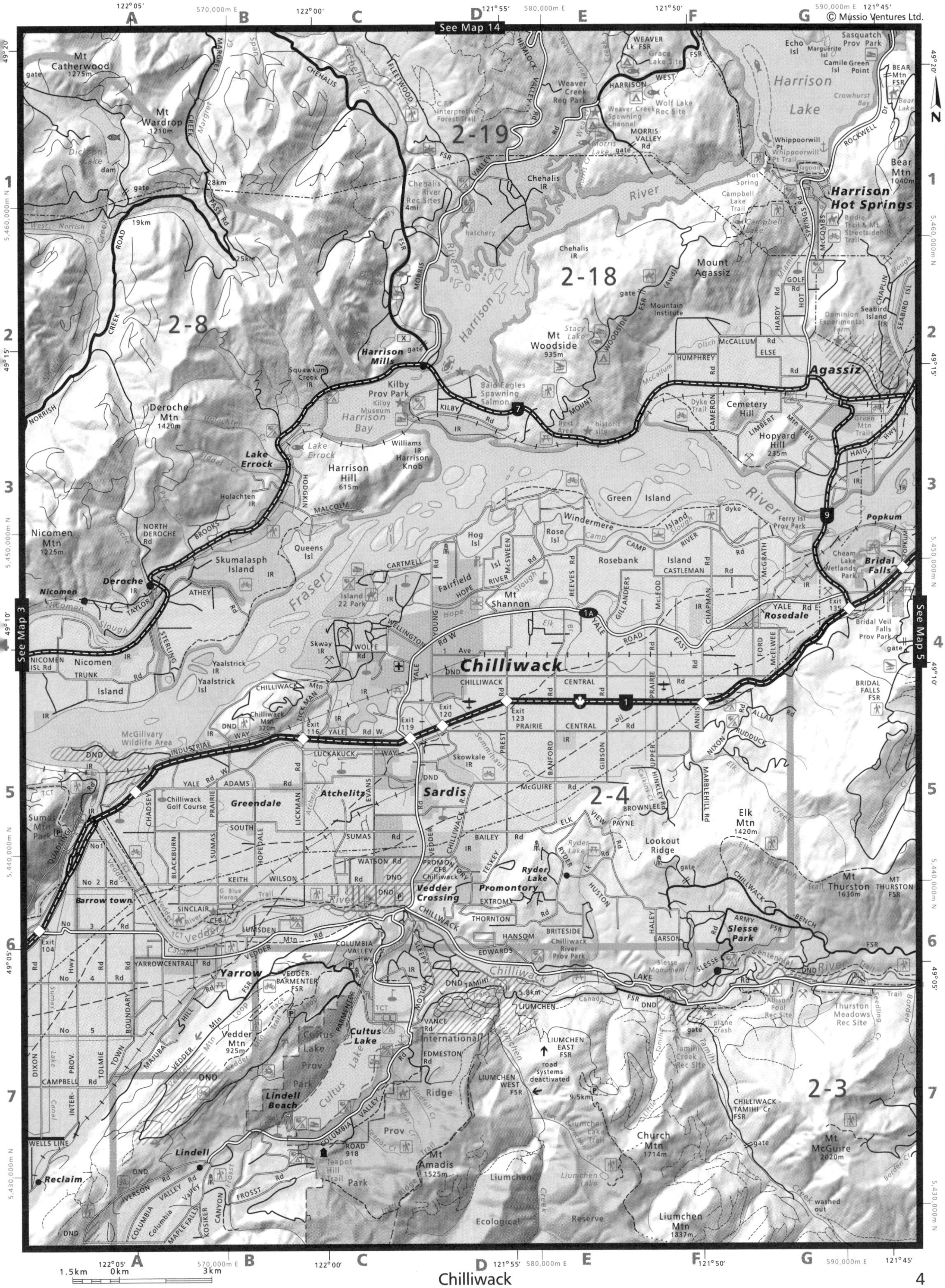

N

See Map 14

Harrison Lake

Harrison Hot Springs

Agassiz

Bridal Falls

Rosedale

Popkum

Chilliwack

Sardis

Vedder Crossing

Yarrow

Cultus Lake

Lindell

Reclaim

Barrowtown

Deroche

Nicomen

Harrison Mills

Lake Errock

2-8

2-19

2-18

2-4

2-3

Mt Catherwood 1275m

Mt Wardrop 1210m

Deroche Mtn 1420m

Nicomen Mtn 1225m

Harrison Hill 615m

Mt Woodside 935m

Mount Agassiz

Hopyard Hill 235m

Bear Mtn 1040m

Cheam Lake Wetlands Park

Bridal Veil Falls Prov Park

Elk Mtn 1420m

Mt Thurston 1630m

Slesse Park

Mt Amadis 1525m

Church Mtn 1714m

Liumchen Mtn 1837m

Mt McGuire 2020m

Cultus Lake Prov Park

Chilliwack

4

1.5km 0km 3km

SWBC Maps

N

See Map 4

See Map 6

2-18

Hicks Lake Trail
Hicks Lake
Sasquatch Prov Park
Mt Hicks 815m
Laidlaw
Seabird Overlook Trail
Bear Mtn 1040m
F.H. Barber Prov Park
Exit 151
Sea Bird Island IR
Sea Bird Isl
Cheam View
Mt Ludwig 1396m
Fraser River
Herrling Isl
Popkum IR
Mt Devoy 1422m
Skagit Ridge
Mt Barr 1910m
Jones Lake Rec Area
dam
Jones (Wahleach) Lake
Four Brothers Mtn 1525m
Mt Ling 1990m
Ling Lake
Lucky Mine Trail
Conway Peak
2-3
Cheam Peak 2107m
Cheam Ridge
Cheam Peak Trail
Mt Cheam Trail
Knight Peak 2235m
Stewart Peak
Baby Munday Peak 2190m
The Welch Peak 2357m
Still
Foley Peak
Wahleach Glacier
Lucky Four Glacier
Goetz Peak 2035m
Mt Archibald 1730m
Spoon Lake
SPOON Cr Rd
Mt Laughington 1770m
Williamson Lake
Williamson Lake Trail
Airplane
Williams Peak 2123m
Three Creeks Trail
Mt Mercer 1705m
Mt Thurston
CHIPMUNK FSR
gate
Chipmunk Creek Motorcycle Area
Chipmunk Peninsula Rec Site
FOLEY
Foley Lake
Ford Mtn 1421m
FORD Mtn FSR
Ford Mtn Trail
CHILLIWACK
28.5km
Williams Peak Trail
Chilliwack Bench
Centennial Trail
BENCH FSR
CHILLIWACK
Pierce Creek Rec Site
Pierce Lake Trail
Pierce Lake
falls
Mt Pierce 1959m
Thurston Meadows Rec Site
BORDEN
Mt MacFarlane 2025m
Crossover Peak
Department of
Defense
National
Mt Parkes
Slesse Mtn 2440m
Nesakwatch Creek
Plane Crash Monument
Illusion Peaks
Illusion/Rexford Group
Mt Rexford 2320m
Mt Rexford Trail
Spencer Peak
Canadian Border Peak 2290m
11km
Mt Cope
2-2
Eureka Mine Rd
gate
Silver Lake Prov Park
Wells Peak 1830m
WRAY Cr FSR
Isolillock Peak 2076m
National Second Century Fund Cons Area
Mt Stoneman
Sowerby Creek
Silverhope Creek
Skagit
16.5km
Eaton Lake Rec Site
Swanee Lake Trail
Swanee Lake
Eaton Lake
Eaton Peak
Mt Hansen
Jeffrey Peak 2050m
Cantidon Creek
Mt Nowell
gate
Centennial Trail
Mt Northgraves 2100m
Yola
HICKS
SPUR
Mt Holden
gate
Chilliwack
SILVERHOPE
UPPER Silverhope
Greendrop Lake
falls
Mt Wittenberg 1952m
Flora Lake
Klesilkwa Mtn 2072m
Lindeman Lake
Flora Lake Trail
Post Creek Rec Site & X-C Trails
Chilliwack Lake
CHILLIWACK LAKE ROAD
bridge out
P
Chilliwack River
Camp Foley
Centre Creek FSR
Mt Corriveau
Radium Lake
old cabin
Mt Webb 2163m
MacDonald Peak 2244m
Mt Lindeman 2310m
Chilliwack Provincial Park
Custer Ridge Trail
Balancing Rock
Paleface Mtn
Mt Meroniuk
NORTH Br
PALEFACE Canada Cr FSR
Paleface Cr
DEPOT
gates
Mt Edgar
Depot Cr FSR
Upper Chilliwack River Trail
Chilliwack River Ecological Reserve
Hanging Lk

Chilliwack Lake

1.5km   0km   3km

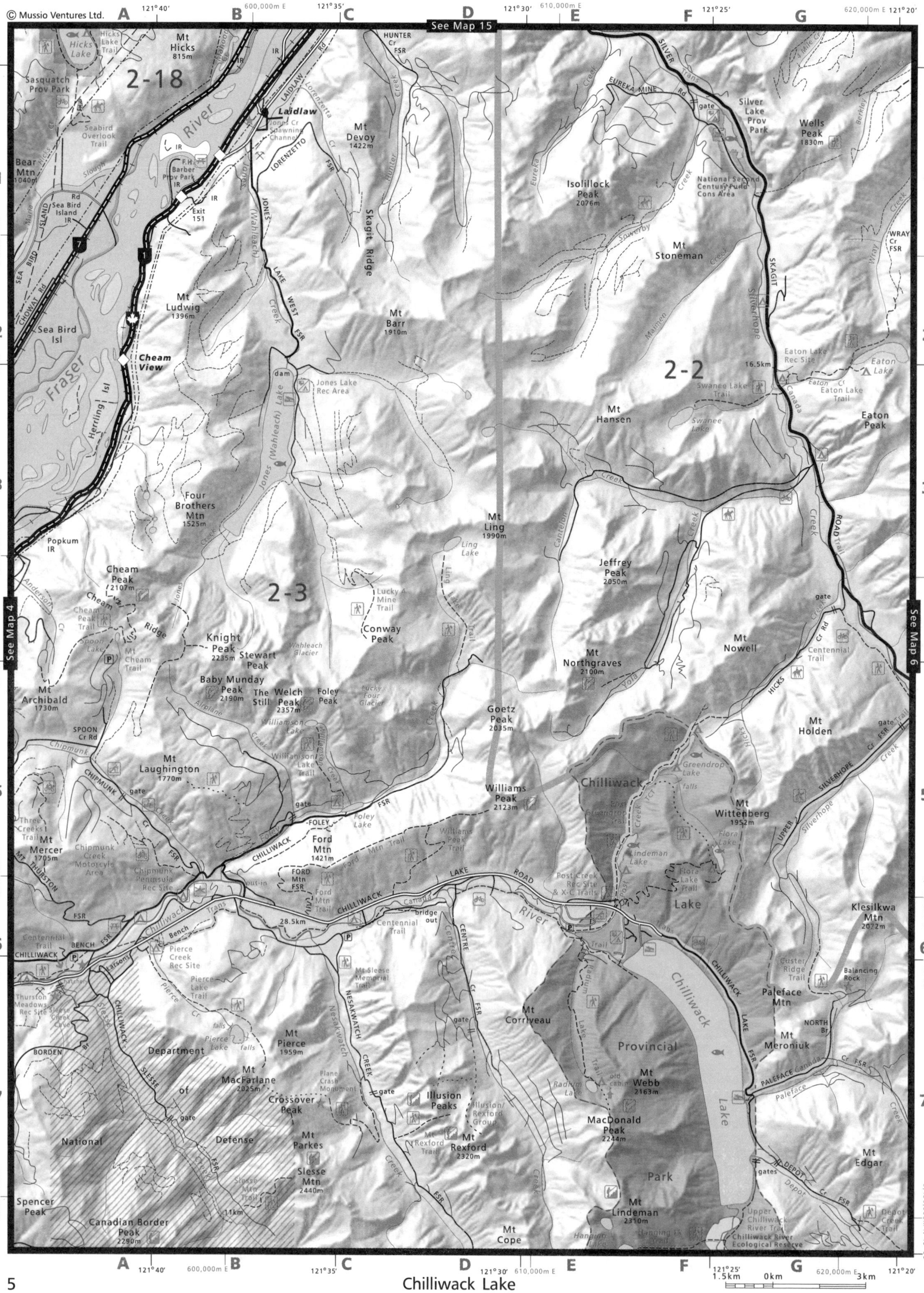

© Mussio Ventures Ltd.

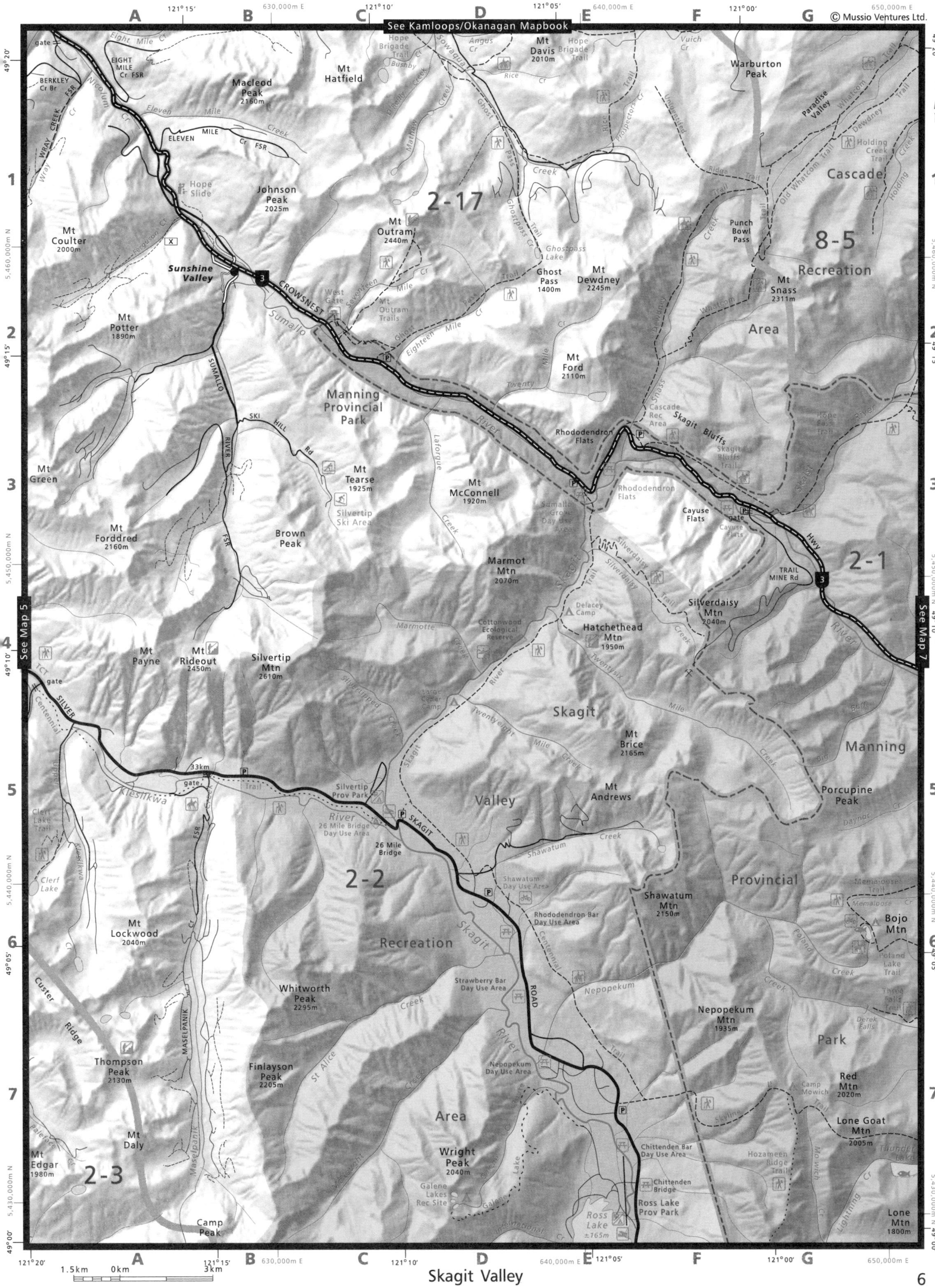

SWBC Maps

N

8-5

2-17

2-1

2-2

2-3

Grid references (top): A | B | C | D | E | F | G
121°15' | 630,000m E | 121°10' | 121°05' | 640,000m E | 121°00' | 650,000m E

Left edge: 49°20' | 5,460,000m N | 49°15' | 5,450,000m N | 49°10' | 5,440,000m N | 49°05' | 5,430,000m N | 49°00'

See Map 5

See Map 7

Gate, BERKLEY Cr Br, WRAY CREEK, EIGHT MILE Cr FSR, Eight Mile Cr, Nicolum Cr, Eleven Mile Creek, ELEVEN MILE Cr FSR

Macleod Peak 2160m, Mt Hatfield, Mt Davis 2010m, Warburton Peak

Hope Brigade Trail, Angus Cr, Sowaqua Cr, Rice Cr, Vuich Cr, Paradise Valley, Whatcom, Holding Creek Trail, Cascade

Johnson Peak 2025m, Hope Slide, Mt Outram 2440m, Mt Coulter 2000m, Sunshine Valley, West Gate, CROWSNEST Hwy 3, Sumallo

Ghostpass Lake, Ghost Pass 1400m, Mt Dewdney 2245m, Punch Bowl Pass, Mt Snass 2311m, Recreation Area

Mt Potter 1890m, SUMALLO RIVER, SKI HILL Rd, Manning Provincial Park, Eighteen Mile Cr, Mt Ford 2110m, Skagit Bluffs Trail, Cascade Rec Area, Skagit Bluffs

Mt Green, Mt Tearse 1925m, Silvertip Ski Area, Mt McConnell 1920m, Laforgue Cr, Rhododendron Flats, Cayuse Flats, Silverdaisy, gate

Mt Forddred 2160m, Brown Peak, FSR, Marmot Mtn 2070m, Silverdaisy Mtn 2040m, TRAIL MINE Rd, Hwy 3

Mt Payne, Mt Rideout 2450m, Silvertip Mtn 2610m, Marmotte Cr, Cottonwood Ecological Reserve, Delacey Camp, Hatchethead Mtn 1950m, Silverdaisy Mtn 2040m, Manning

TCT, gate, SILVER Centennial, Skagit River, Skagit Valley, Mt Brice 2165m, Porcupine Peak

Clerf Lake Trail, Klesilkwa, 33km, gate, Silvertip Trail, Silvertip Prov Park, Mt Andrews, Provincial

26 Mile Bridge Day Use Area, 26 Mile Bridge, Shawatum Cr, Shawatum Day Use Area, Memaloose Cr, Bojo Mtn

Mt Lockwood 2040m, MASELPANIK FSR, SKAGIT, Recreation, Shawatum Mtn 2150m, Roland Lake Trail, Park

Custer Ridge, Palefy, Whitworth Peak 2295m, St Alice Cr, Strawberry Bar Day Use Area, Rhododendron Bar Day Use Area, ROAD, Nepopekum, Nepopekum Mtn 1935m, Three Falls, Derek Falls

Thompson Peak 2130m, Finlayson Peak 2205m, Camp Mowich, Red Mtn 2020m

Mt Daly, Skagit River, Nepopekum Day Use Area, Skyline Trail, Hozameen Ridge Trail, Lone Goat Mtn 2005m

Mt Edgar 1980m, Wright Peak 2040m, Area, Galena Lakes Rec Site, Chittenden Bar Day Use Area, Chittenden Bridge, Ross Lake Prov Park

Camp Peak, Ross Lake ±765m, Lightning, Thunder, Lone Mtn 1800m

Scale: 1.5km | 0km | 3km

A B C D E F G

120° 55' 120° 50' 120° 45' 120° 40' 120° 35'

660,000 m E 670,000 m E 680,000 m E

5,465,000 m N

49° 20'

1

Wells Lake Trail

Granite Mtn

Cascade

Recreation

Kettle Mtn

Hudson Bay Meadows

Paddy Pond

Fifteen Mile

Fourteen Mile Creek

Whipsaw Creek

FRIDAY

MAIN

Kennedy Lake

Gulch

Deep Creek

River

5,460,000 m N

49° 20'

2

Area

Skaist Mtn

The Zigzags

Nicomen Lake (Three Brothers) Trail

8-5

Forty-seven Mile

Garrison FSR

Whipsaw

Friday Mtn

SUNDAY

Sunday Summit 1280m

SUMMIT

FSR

MAIN

3

49° 15'

3

Grainger Creek Trail

Nicomen Lake Camp

Nicomen

Ridge

Heather Trail

BR 09

Garrison Lake Rec Site & Trails

Garrison Lakes

Copper

SUNDAY

Copper Creek Ct FSR

2km

PLACER Mtn

Copper Creek Rec Site

Placer Cr

5,450,000 m N

49° 15'

4

See Map 6

Fourth Brother Mtn 2155m

Three Brothers Mtn 2245m

First Brothers Mtn 2270m

Second Brothers Mtn 2250m

BR 06

Bonnevier

Ridge

Bonnevier

Bell Creek

EASTGATE Rd

CROWLEY CREEK FSR

Mt Angus

Similkameen Falls

See Volume III Kamloops/Okanagan

49° 10'

5

Manning

Big Buck Mtn 2145m

Buckhorn Camp

2-1

Blackwall Sub-Alpine Meadow Area

Bonnevier

Old Yellow Creek

Eastgate

PASAYTEN

Trail

Pasayten Lake

5,440,000 m N

49° 10'

6

Skagit River

CROWSNEST

Allison Pass 1340m

Cambie Creek X-C Trails

Provincial

Paintbrush Nature Trail

Blackwall Peak 2065m

Nellie Ridge

Spotted

Sandstone

Mule Deer Campsite

Similkameen

HWY

RIVER

Calcite Creek

49° 05'

7

Poland Lake Trail

Gibson Pass Ski Area

Gibson

Coldspring Campsite

Manning Park Lodge

Dry Ridge

Manning Visitor Center

Cascade Lookout & Dry Ridge

Hampton Campsite

Boyd's Meadow

Park

Chuwanten Mtn 2150m

8-4

RIVER

PASAYTEN

5,430,000 m N

49° 05'

Three Shadow Falls Trail

South Gibson Trail

Lightning Lake Campsite

GIBSON PASS Rd

gate

Lightning Lake

Similkameen West Trail

Windy Joe Trail

Windy Joe Mtn 1825m

Chuwanten Creek

McAlmon Creek

Monument

Skyline

Centennial

Lightning

Strike Lake Camp

Flash Lake

Frosty Mtn Trail

Frosty Creek

Castle Creek

Windy Joe Trail

Chuwanten

Trail

Monument

Monument 83

UPPEBYE Cr

Thunder Lake

Passpe

Frosty Mtn 2410m

To USA & Mexico

Monument 78

Castle Creek

Centennial Trail

River

49° 0'

120° 55' 120° 50' 120° 45' 120° 40' 120° 35'

660,000 m E 670,000 m E 680,000 m E

1.5km 0km 3km

390,000m E 124°30' A 124°25' B C 400,000m E 124°20' D E 124°15' F 410,000m E G 124°10' © Mussio Ventures Ltd.

N

Gillies Bay
GILLIES BAY Rd
CENTRAL Rd
Creek
SHELTER POINT Rd
Shelter Point Park
BELL
Texada
Cape Cockburn
Nelson Island

Dick Island
TEXADA
Rd
Mouat Creek
FSR
BC HYDRO EAST
Acland Rock

DAVIE
Shelter Point Trail
Mouat Bay
gate
THOMPSON Rd
BC HYDRO REACTOR Rd
LONG BEACH Rd
East Hydro Substation
Malaspina

BAY
Island
Rd
Reactor Station
Mt Grant
Bob's Lake Rec Site
2-16

Mouat Islets

Davie Bay
gate
Loop
BREAK YOUR ASS HILL Rd
Island
Mt Davies 760m
COOK

Strait

West Hydro Substation
Shingle Beach Rec Site
BAY
Rd
ANDERSON
BAY

Cook Bay
Mt Shepherd 891m
South
pHings Rd

Spring Bay
Boot Pt
Marine Isl
Scottie Bay
Lindbergh Islet
Jelina Isl
West Pt
Bunny Isl
Jervis Island
Partington Point
Sabine
Texada Island
Anderson Bay Prov Park

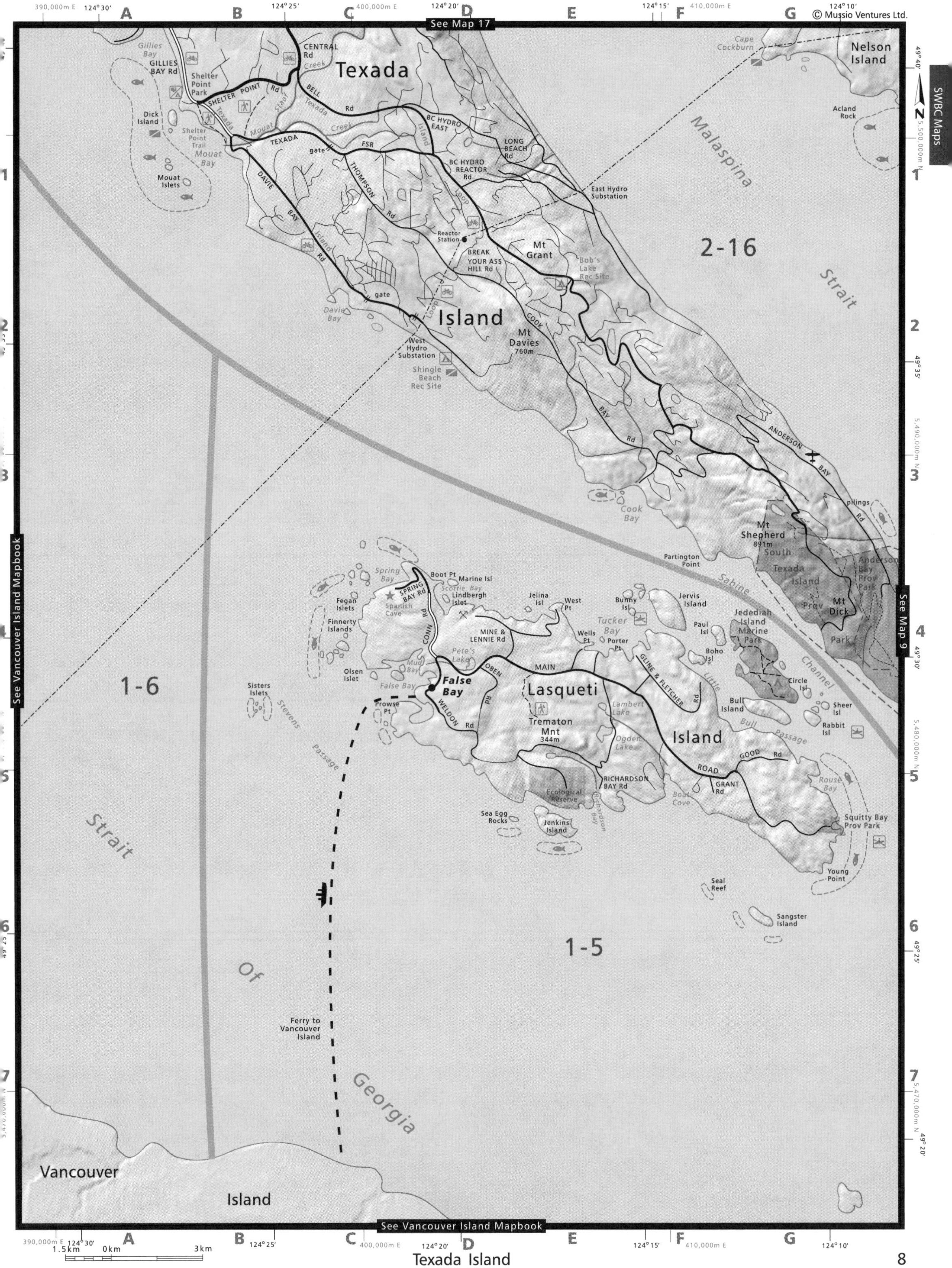

See Vancouver Island Mapbook

Fegan Islets
Spanish Cave
SPRING BAY Rd
MINE & LENNIE Rd
Wells Pt
Tucker Bay
Paul Isl
Porter Pt.
Boho Isl
Jedediah Island Marine Park
Prov
Mt Dick
Park

Finnerty Islands
UNION Rd
Pete's Lake
MAIN
Lambert Lake
GLINE & FLETCHER Rd
Circle Isl
See Map 9

1-6
Sisters Islets
Olsen Islet
Mud Bay
OBEN Rd
False Bay
False Bay
Lasqueti
Trematon Mnt 344m
Ogden Lake
Island
Bull Island
Little
Bull Passage
Sheer Isl
Rabbit Isl

Prowse Pt
WELDON Rd
Rd
RICHARDSON BAY Rd
Richardson Bay
Boat Cove
ROAD
GOOD Rd
GRANT Rd
Rouse Bay
Squitty Bay Prov Park

Strait
Stevens Passage
Ecological Reserve
Sea Egg Rocks
Jenkins Island
Young Point

Of
Seal Reef
Sangster Island

Ferry to Vancouver Island

Georgia
1-5

Vancouver
Island

390,000m E 124°30' A 0 km 1.5 km 3 km B 124°25' C 400,000m E D 124°20' E 124°15' F 410,000m E G 124°10'

Texada Island

8

© Mussio Ventures Ltd.

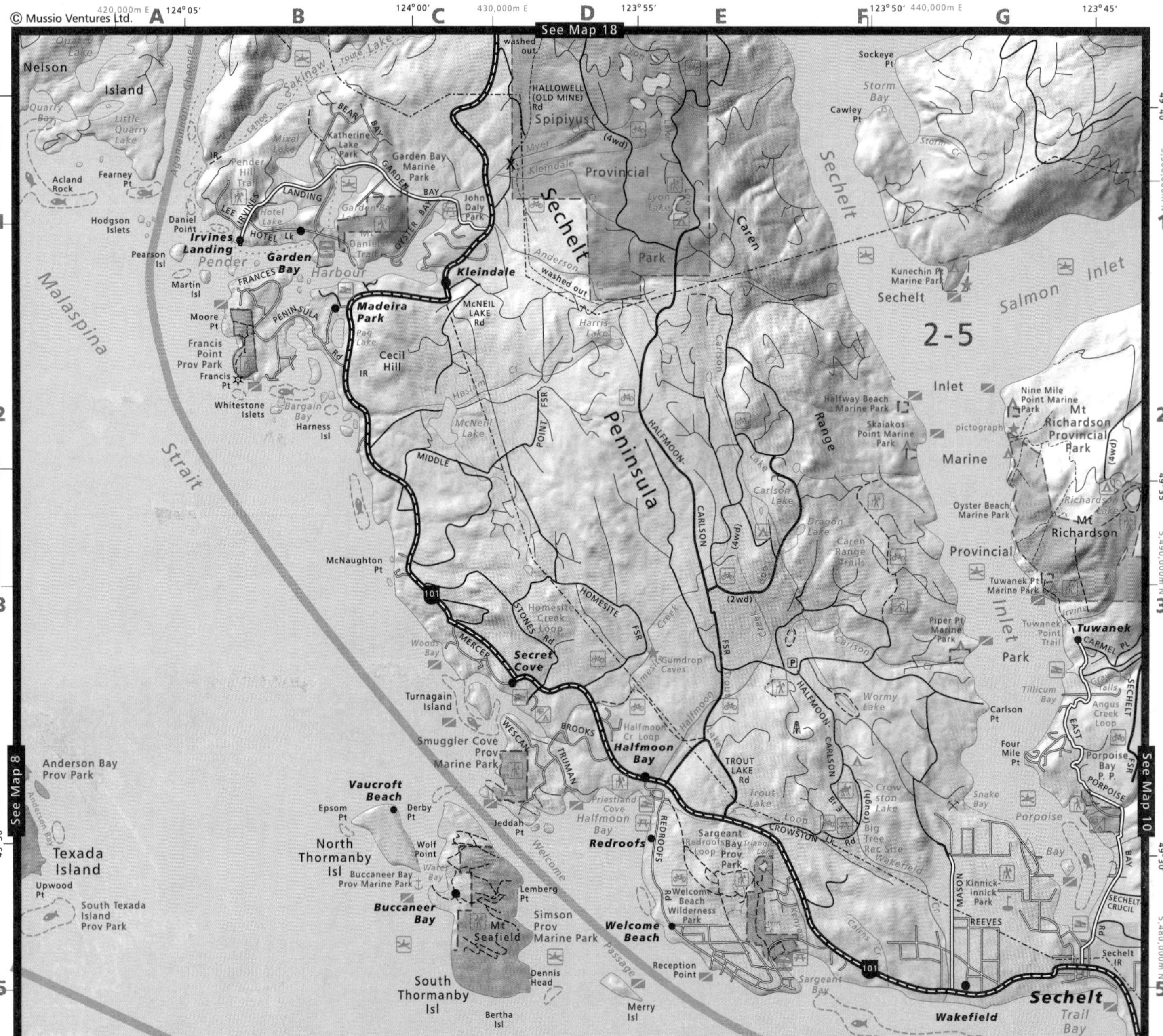

SWBC Maps

N

420,000 m E 124° 05' A 124° 00' B C 430,000m E D 123° 55' E F 123° 50' 440,000 m E G 123° 45'

49° 40'

Nelson

Island

Quarry Bay

Little Quarry Lake

Acland Rock

Fearney Pt

Hodgson Islets

Daniel Point

Pearson Isl

Irvines Landing

Garden Bay

Pender Harbour

Martin Isl

Moore Pt

Francis Point Prov Park

Francis

Whitestone Islets

Bargain Bay

Harness Isl

Madeira Park

McNeil LAKE Rd

Kleindale

Cecil Hill

McNeil Lake

McNaughton Pt

Woods Bay

Secret Cove

Turnagain Island

Smuggler Cove Prov Marine Park

Anderson Bay Prov Park

Vaucroft Beach

Epsom Pt

Derby Pt

North Thormanby Isl

Buccaneer Bay Prov Marine Park

Wolf Point

Jeddah Pt

Buccaneer Bay

Mt Seafield

Lemberg Pt

Simson Prov Marine Park

South Thormanby Isl

Dennis Head

Bertha Isl

Texada Island

Upwood Pt

South Texada Island Prov Park

Malaspina

Strait

1-5

Strait

Of

Georgia

2-16

Halfmoon Bay

Redroofs

Welcome Beach

Reception Point

Merry Isl

Sargeant Bay

Wakefield

Sechelt

Trail Bay

Trail Islands

Sechelt Peninsula

Spipiyus

Provincial Park

Sechelt

2-5

Sechelt Inlet

Salmon Inlet

Kunechin Pt Marine Park

Nine Mile Point Marine Park

Mt Richardson Provincial Park

Mt Richardson

Marine

Provincial

Park

Tuwanek

Caren Range

Halfmoon Range

Carlson

Tuwanek Pt Marine Park

Piper Pt Marine Park

Carlson Pt

Four Mile Pt

Porpoise Bay P. P.

Snake Bay

Porpoise

Kinnickinnick Park

REEVES

SECHELT CRUCIL

Sechelt IR

9

1.5 km 0km 3 km

Sechelt

© Mussio Ventures Ltd.

SWBC Maps

Grid references / coordinates (top): 450,000m E · 123°40' · 123°35' · 460,000m E · 123°30' · 123°25' · 470,000m E · 49°40' · 49°35' · 5,500,000m N

Column letters: A B C D E F G

Salmon Inlet

New Comb Point
Mid Point
Black Bear Bluff
Gustafson Bay
Steelhead Point
Chum Point
Thornhill Point
Thornhill Creek Marine Park
Misery Bay
Sechelt Creek
Sechelt Lake
Sechelt Ridge

Tetrahedron Provincial Park
Tetrahedron Peak 1737m
Mt Steele Cabin
Edwards Gilbert Lake Cabin
Mount Steele Backcountry Trail System
Tetrahedron Peak Trail
Chapman Lake
No Name Lake
McNair Lake Cabin
Panther Peak 1690 m
Upper McNair Lake
Mt Crucil
Tannis Lake
Bachelor Lake Cabin
Margie Lake
Mayne Lake
Edwards Lake
Four Lake Circuit
gate
Mt Richardson Prov Park
Gray Creek
Sechelt FSR

Mt Varley 1639m
Mt Varley Trail
Rainy Creek
Rainy River
Box Canyon
McNab Creek
Mt Wrottesley 1625 m
Mt Wrottesley Trail
POTLATCH
McNab Creek

Thornbrough Channel
Ramillies Channel
Ekins Point
Ekins Pt
Linfoot Lake
Gambier Lake
GAMBIER FSR
Gambier Creek

2-5

Angus Creek Loop
Chapman Rd
Burnett Cr
WEST
EAST
Chapman Falls Trails
C.F.P. Demonstration Forest Trails
FSR
Mexican Jumping Bean
CLACK Cr FSR
Clack Creek Loop
Gough Creek
DAKOTA
Roberts Cr
SECHELT
ROBERTS
B & K Rd
Wilson Creek Trail
Wilson
Roberts Creek Prov Park
CRYSTAL
FIELD
HANBURY
LOCKYER
Camp Olave
Mission Point
Wilson Creek
White Islets
Roberts Creek
Rock Point
BEACH
LOWER Rd
Camp Byng
Hwy 101
PIXTON
REED
Gibsons Cr
Gower Point
CHASTER
GOWER POINT RD
Gibsons

Dakota Creek Loop
bridge out
SOUTH
DAKOTA LOOP
Elphinstone Creek
Mt Elphinstone 1280m
Mt Elphinstone Prov Park
South Elphinstone Heritage & Rec Trails
QUILLET Cr FSR
Ouil Cr
PORT MELLON HWY
Twin Creeks
Fish Hatchery
Mariners Rest
Williamsons Landing
New Brighton
Gambier Harbour
Thornbrough Bay
Burgess Cove
Hutchinson
K 2 Summit Trail
Langdale Cr
WHARF
BYPASS
Langdale
NORTH
Soames Hill Park
Sprockids Mtn Bike Park
Hopkins Landing
Granthams Landing
Plumper Cove Prov Marine Park
Keats Island
Keats Island
Home Isl
Preston Isl
Barfleur Passage
Shoal Channel
Seaside Park
Port Mellon
Woolridge Isl
Latona Pass
Andys Bay
Witherby Point
West Bay

Gambier Island
Mt Liddell 903m
Mt Killam 844m
Gambier Mannion Creek
Whispering Cr
McDonald Cr
Centre Bay
Camp Artaban
Mt Artaban 610m
Halkett Bay Prov Park
Gambier Point
Carmelo Point
Port Graves
Hope Point

2-16

Howe Sound

Hutt Isl
Grafton Bay
Honeymoon Lake
Killarney Lake
Crippen Regional Park
Mt Collins
Miller's Landing
Cotton Pt
Eastbourne
Mount Gardner Park
Mt Gardner 719m
Mount Gardner
BOWEN PIT Rd
Killarney Trail
Mt Gardner Trails
Bowen Island
Snug Cove
Grafton Lake
Bowen Bay
Arbutus Pt
WINDJAMMER
BOWEN BAY
COWAN
GRAFTON
ADAMS
TUNSTALL
Tunstall Bay
Josephine Lake
Cape Roger Curtis
Seymour Landing
Cowans Pt
Apodaca Marine Prov Park
Ecological Reserve

Ragged Isl
Mickey Isl
Pasley Island
Hermit Isl
Little Popham Isl
Popham Isl
Worlcombe Isl
Collingwood Channel

Strait Of Georgia

See Map 9 · See Map 11 · See Vancouver Island Mapbook

Bottom scale/coordinates: 450,000m E · 123°40' · 123°35' · 460,000m E · 123°30' · 123°25' · 470,000m E · 123°20' · 49°30' · 49°25' · 5,490,000m N · 5,480,000m N · 5,470,000m N

1.5 km 0km 3km

Gibsons

10

SWBC Maps

N

49°40'
49°35'
49°30'
49°25'

See Map 10
See Map 12

123°20' | 480,000m E | 123°15' | 123°10' | 490,000m E | 123°05' | 500,000m E | 123°00'

See Map 20

2-6

2-7

2-5

2-16

Henriette Lake
Mount Roderick Trail
Mount Squamish
Brennan Lakes
Mt Ellesmere 1402m
Camp Potlatch
Defence Islands
Domett Point
Leading Peak
Anvil Island
Irby Point
Christie Islet
Pam Rock
Gambier
Island
Halkett Bay Prov Park
Halkett Point
Bowyer Island
Langdale
Hood Pt
Snugglers Cove
Finisterre Isl
Cates Bay
Bowen Island
Eagle Cliff
Millers Landing
Dorman Point
Whyte Cliff
Horseshoe Bay
Eagle Isl
Passage Isl

Woodfibre Mill
Squamish Harbour
Squamish Estuary
Darrell Bay
Shannon Falls Prov Park
Stawamus Chief Prov Park
Watts Point
Murrin Prov Park
Petgill Lake
Petgill Lake Trail
Old Brittania Mine
Britannia Beach
Britannia
gate
Minaty Bay
Mineral Cr
Daisy Creek
Furry
gate
washout
Porteau Cove Provincial Marine Park
Kallahne
Marion Lake
Phyllis Lake
gate
Deeks Lake & Peak Trails
Deeks Peak 1675m
Brunswick Point
Mt Windsor 1680m
Cypress Prov Park
Mt Hanover 1747m
Brunswick Mtn 1785m
Magnesia Meadows Shelter
Brunswick Beach
Mt Harvey 1705m
Lion's Bay
The Lions Trail
Unnecessary Mtn Trail
The Lions 1646m
Mt Unnecessary
St Marks Summit 1371m
Strachan Creek
Cypress
Mt Strachan 1455m
Cypress Mtn Ski Hill
Hollyburn Mtn 1325m
Hollyburn Trails
Sunset Beach
Black Mtn Trail
Black Mtn 1217m
Provincial Park
Yew Lake
Sunset Beach Trail
Lower Cypress Trails
Dick (Eagle) Lake
dam
Cypress Falls Park
gate
West Vancouver
CYPRESS Exit
Nelson Canyon Park
Tyee Pt

Mt Mulligan 1820m
Alpen Mtn 1705m
Mt Baldwin
Mt Habrich 1700m
Goat Ridge
Sky Pilot Mtn 2025m
Ledge Mtn
Utopia Lake
Route Lake
Park Lane Lake
Mt Lake Hut
Mt Sheer
Omer Lake
Red Mtn
Binghorn Lake
Ben Lomond
Mineral Claims
Mineral Claims
Loch Lomond
Clarion Lake
Delta Lake
Stawamus Lake
Seymour
Mt Jukes
Fannin
Bivouac Mtn
Range
Mt Eldee
Capilano Mtn 1685m
Capilano
Appian Mtn
Dickie Lake
Orchid
2-8
Watershed
Watershed
Cathedral Mtn 1730m
Palisade Lake
Lynn Lake
Burwell Lake
dam
Seymour Falls Dam
Encichantment Lake
Little Capilano Lake
(Restricted Access)
Mt Burwell 1545m
Coliseum Mtn 1445m
Coliseum Route
fish hatchery
Lynn
Headwaters
Lower Seymour
Mount Seymour
Crown Mtn
Goat Mtn 1400m
Regional
Kennedy Lake Watershed
The Needles 1250m
Mt Elsay 1422m
Little Goat Mtn
Goat Mtn Dam
Crown Mtn
Lynn Peak 1000m
Park
Headwaters Trail
Rolf Lake
Crown Mtn Ski Hill
Grouse Mtn (gondola)
Grouse Grind
Mt Fromme 1175m
Lynn Mill Trail
Mt Seymour Ski Hill
Conservation
Mt Seymour
Dog Mtn 1050m
Dog Mtn Trail
Cleveland Dam
Capilano Dam
North Vancouver
Rice Lake
Reserve
Lower Seymour
Seymour Pkwy

Howe Sound
Montagu Channel
Ramillies Channel
Queen Charlotte Channel

99
2
4
7

123°15' | 480,000m E | 123°10' | 490,000m E | 123°05' | 500,000m E | 123°00'

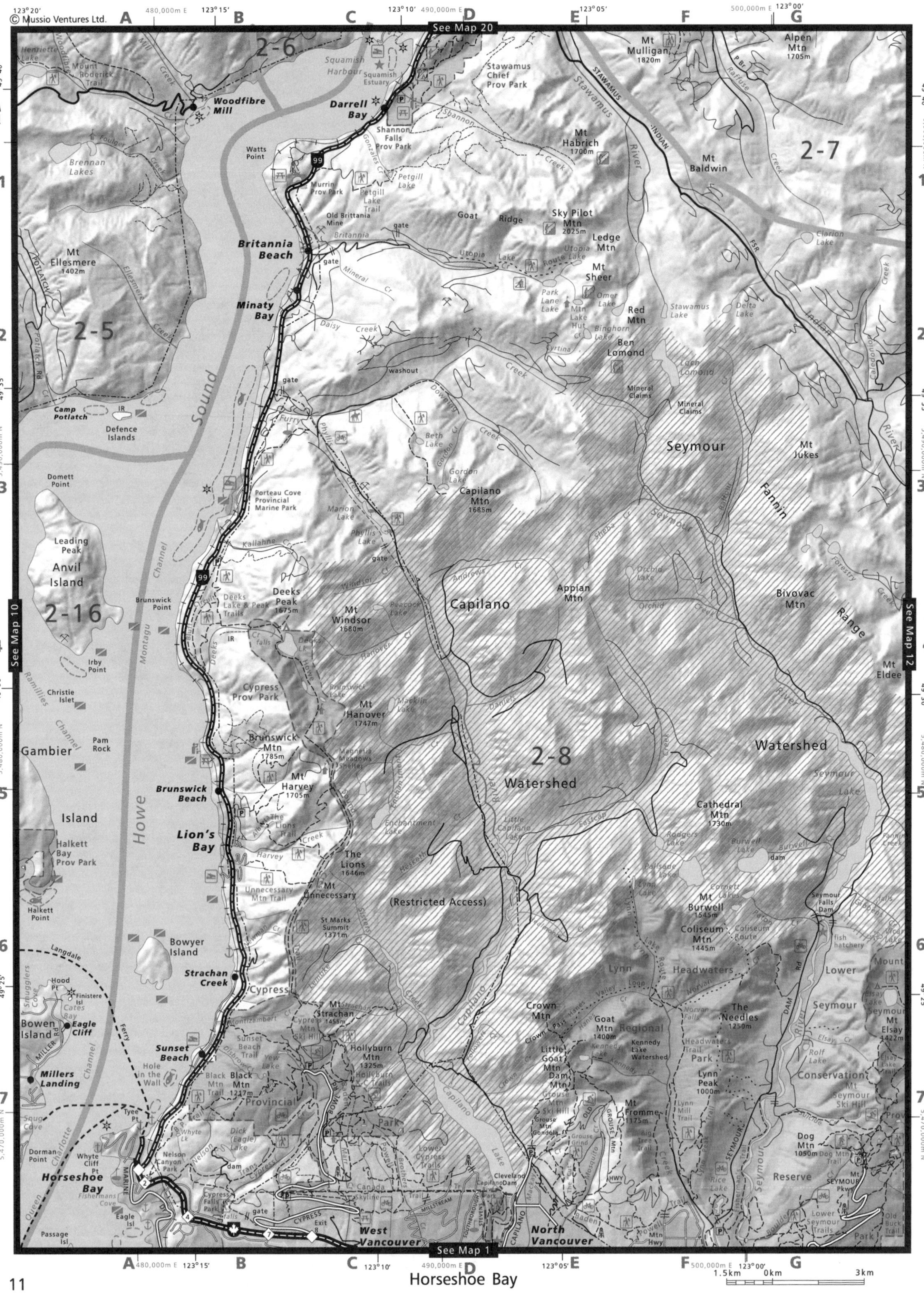

Horseshoe Bay

1.5km | 0km | 3km

© Mussio Ventures Ltd.

2-7

122°55' · 122°50' · 122°45' · 520,000m E · 122°40' · 122°35' · 530,000m E

A · B · C · D · E · F · G

Golden
Piluk Peak
Piluk Glacier
Remote Peak 2100m
Ears

MAMQUAM RIVER FSR
21km
26km

Mamquam River
W Br
Crawford

Knothole Lake
Pinecone Lake
Bigga Route
trailhead

See Map 21

STEVE Cr Br
PITT RIVER

FOREST

BOISE
Cougar Lakes
Fish Hatchery
Alvin

Provincial

Mamquam Pass 1360m
Gold Route
Pinecone
Scary Crossing Grove 760m
Cedar Spirit Grove 560m
Homer Creek
Boise
trailhead
Bull Creek

Bull Canyon 680m

SERVICE
Park

Mestilloet
Meslilloet Mtn 2000m
Mislilloet Icefield

Young Lake
Joseph Lake
Anne Lake
Little

Bull Pass 1060m

400
MAIN ROAD (2nd boat access)

2-8

North End Dock

Indian
STAWAMUS
Don Lake

Mt Bonnycastle 1740m
Disappointment
Benson Lake
Norton Lake
Brandt
gate
Rd
HIXON CREEK
Hixon

Five Fingers Spires 1990m

Consolation Lakes
Mid Valley Camp
Disc Creek Canyon 480m
Obelisk Peak
Obelisk Lake

Burke

See Map 13
Isabel Lake
Cacus Point
Deer Point

Fannin Range
Seymour
Mt Dickens
Wigwam Inn
Watershed

Mt Felix 1320m
Indian

Coquitlam
Coquitlam Lake
Peneplain

Provincial
Peneplain Peak 1700m
±771m
Spindle Lake
Widgeon Valley Camp

Cozen Point

Pitt Pass 720m

Mt Bishop 1510m
Mount Seymour
Iron Bay
Croker Isl
Granite Falls
Arm
Falls
Johnson
Crocker Lookout
Dilly Dally Pass

Watershed
Coquitlam Mtn 1583m

Widgeon Falls
Gold
bridge out
Widgeon
Falls

Goose Isl

Pitt Lake

Elsay Lake Trail
Coldwell Beach
Prov Park
Best Pt
Buntzen Bay
Hydro Plant
Dilly Loop
Dilly Dally Peak
Provincial Park
Eagle Trail
Swan Falls

Coquitlam Private Road
Coquitlam Isl
(Restricted Access)

Widgeon Peak 1433m
Widgeon Bowl Trail
Widgeon Lake Rec Site

Golden Ears Prov Park

Brighton Beach
Indian Arm Provincial Marine Park
Racoon Isl
Twin Islands
Buntzen Lk
Buntzen Lake Regional Park
South Beach
Eagle Mtn 1060m

See Map 2

Widgeon Valley National Wildlife Area
Siwash Isl
Grant Narrows Park
Pitt Polder Trails
U.B.C. Research Forest

See Map 11

1.5km 0km 3km

Pinecone Burke Park

12

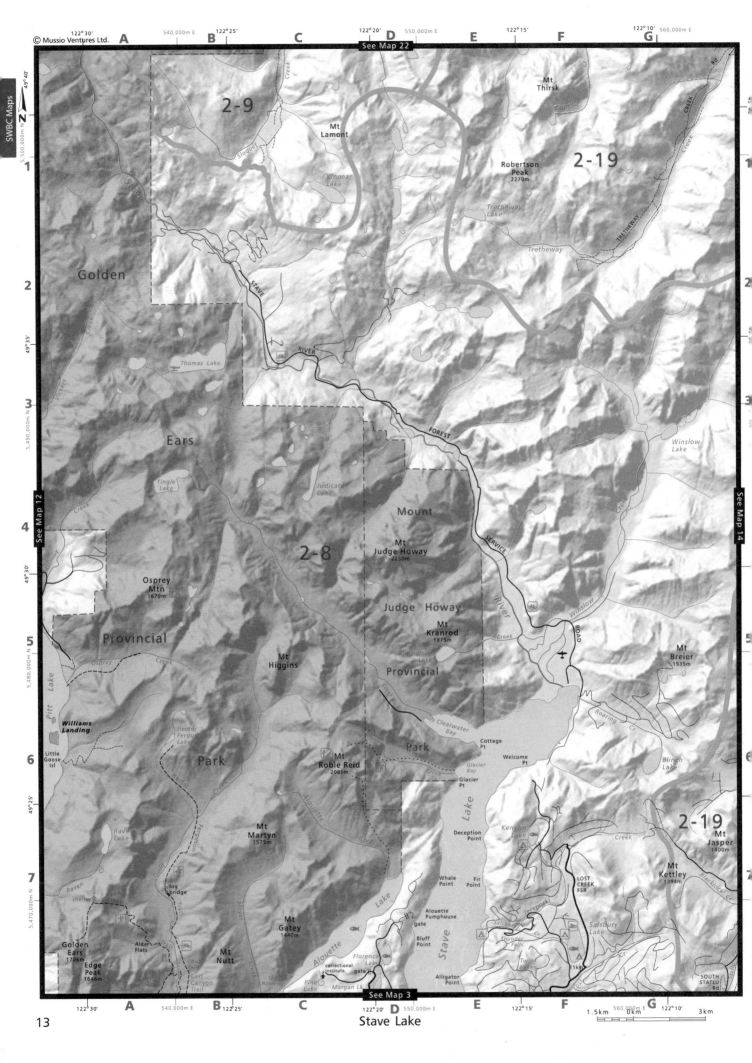

© Musso Ventures Ltd.

See Map 23

See Map 13

See Map 15

2-18
2-8
2-19

Clear Creek Hot Springs Access
7.6km

CLEAR
CREEK
HARRISON
Silver
HORNET CREEK
HORNET MAIN
MAIN
Cook Creek
Bremner Creek
Cool Creek
4wd road
Kaiyama Petroglyphs
Doctors Pt
Westwood Bay
HARRISON WEST
Doctors Creek
Harrison Creek
Trio
Grainger Peak 2200m
Grainger Group
Mt Grainger Trail
Nursery Peak
Davidson Creek
Kirkland Creek
49km
6km put-in
gate
gate
gate
put-in
gate
Silver River
Silver Creek Camp
East Bay
COGBURN Cr FSR
put-in
Cogburn Creek
Bear Creek
Nursery Pass
Viennese Peak
Mt Clarke 2170m
Clarke Group
Brotherhood Trail
Statlu Lake Trail
falls
falls
Statlu Lake
40km
bridge out
Eagle Cr
EAGLE
Twenty Mile Creek
Mile Cr
Twenty Mile Bay Rec Site
Harrison Lake
FOREST
gate
41.5km
gate
FSR
MYSTERY
Mystery Creek
Lookout Lake
HALE Cr
Sunrise Lake Rec Site
Harrison Lookout Trail
Towboat
Long Island
Deer Island
Long Island Bay Rec Site
Cogburn Beach Rec Site
Bear Creek Rec Site
EAST
FOREST
Stonerabbit Peak
Chehalis River
Mt Orrock 1555m
33.5km
Chehalis Lake North Rec Site
Mt McRae 1527m
Hale Creek
Hale Creek Rec Site
20km
Wood Lake Rec Site
SERVICE
Strait
BEAR Cr FSR
Bear Cr
22km
Field Peak 1565m
Skwellepil Creek
bridge out
Olive Lake
Skwellepil Creek Rec Site
30km
Wilson Lake
Middle Cr
Mt Downing 1505m
CREEK
Eagle Falls
WALION
Walion Creek
Simms Creek
Ten Mile Bay
Sheers Isl
Cascade Peninsula Rec Site
Cooks Cove
Lookout Lake
Lookout Peak 1529m
Beach Bay
Mt Fletcher 1405m
Third Cr
Chehalis Lake South Rec Site
CHEHALIS FSR
Mt Davis 1240m
20km
Malsal Cr
SIMMS Cr FSR
Cartmell Creek
Limbert Rock
ROAD
Rainbow Falls Rec Site
Cascade Peninsula
Cascade Bay
Klollicum
SERVICE ROAD
Bentley Canyon
14.5km
Bentley Cr
Chehalis Cr
FLEETWOOD River
Vaughan Creek
Sakwi Creek
Mt Keenan 1400m
Hemlock Valley Ski Resort
Mt Klaudt 1370m
Mt Klaudt Trail
Denham Trail
HEMLOCK VALLEY Rd
Brett Creek
Weaver Lake Rec Site
FRANCIS LAKE FSR
Francis Lake Rec Site
19km
Camp Cove
Echo Island
Lone Tree Isl
Sasquatch Prov Park
7.3km
Trout L
N STATLU Rd
STATLU Creek
gate
Statlu Rd
Paradise Cr

1.5km 0km 3km
122°05' A 570,000m E B 122°00' C 121°55' D 580,000m E E 121°50' F 590,000m E G 121°45'

49°40' N
49°35'
5,500,000m N
5,490,000m N
49°30'
5,480,000m N
49°25'
5,470,000m N

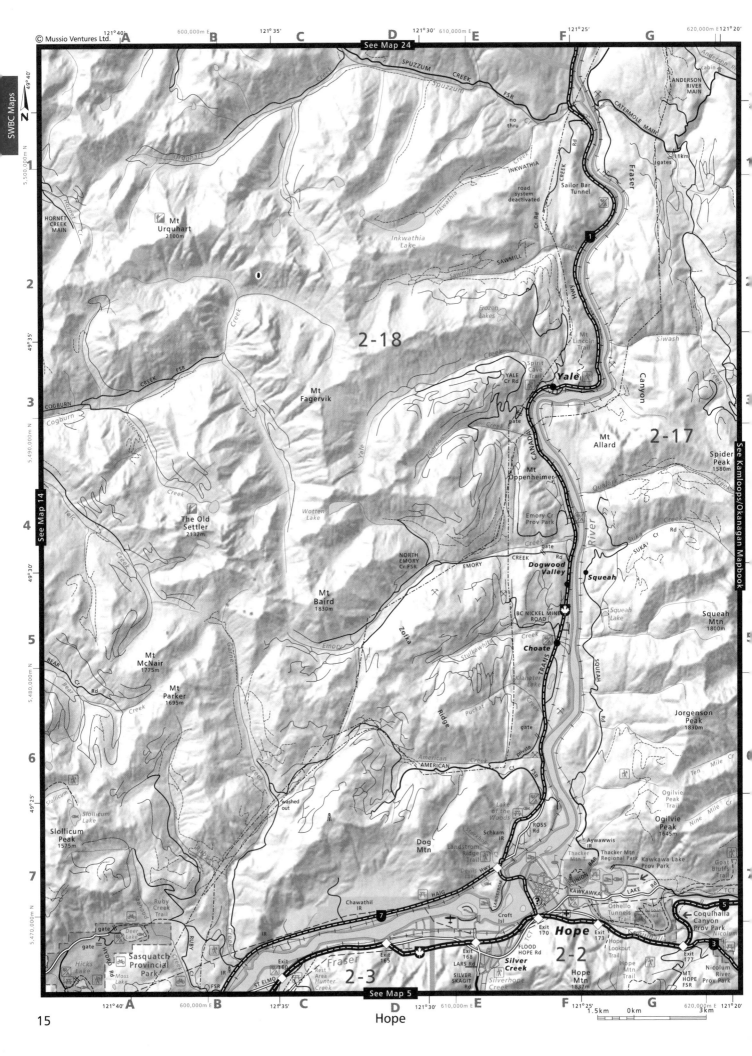

See Map 24

See Map 14

See Kamloops/Okanagan Mapbook

121°40'   600,000 E   121°35'   121°30'   610,000 E   121°25'   620,000 E   121°20'

49°40'N
49°35'
49°30'N
49°25'
5,500,000 N
5,490,000 N
5,480,000 N
5,470,000 N

HORNET
CREEK
MAIN

Mt
Urquhart
2100m

Urquhart Creek

Mt
Fagervik

Cogburn

COGBURN

Settler FSR

The Old
Settler
2132m

Wotten
Lake

Mt
McNair
1775m

Mt
Parker
1695m

BEAR

Bear Cr Rd

Slollicum
Lake

Slollicum
Peak
1575m

Telc Creek

Gamel Creek

Ruby Creek Trail

Sasquatch
Provincial
Park

Deer
Lake

Hicks
Lake

Moss
Lake

HYDRO

RUBY

IR

ST ELMO

FSR

Chawathil IR

7

Fraser

Exit
160

Hunter Creek

2-3

Rest
Area

Exit
165

Exit
168

LARS Rd

SILVER
SKAGIT Rd

Silverhope Creek

SILVER
CREEK Rd

Silver
Creek

FLOOD
HOPE Rd

2-18

2-17

SPUZZUM   CREEK

Spuzzum Cr

SPUZZUM FSR

no thru

INKWATHIA
CREEK

road system
deactivated

Inkwathia
Lake

Inkwathia Creek

SAWMILL

Sawmill Creek

Frozen
Lakes

Mt
Lincoln
Trail

Sailor Bar
Tunnel

Rd

1
Hwy

Fraser

CATERMOLE MAIN

Anderson Rd

ANDERSON
RIVER
MAIN

cabin

11km
gates

Siwash Creek

Canyon

2-17

Spider
Peak
1580m

Mt
Allard

Quaiek Creek

STIKA Cr Rd

SUKA Cr Rd

Squeah
Mtn
1800m

Squeah
Lake

Jorgenson
Peak
1830m

Ten Mile Cr

Nine Mile Cr

Ogilvie
Peak
Trail

Ogilvie
Peak
1645m

Goat
Bluffs
Trail

TCT

5

Coquihalla
Canyon
Prov Park

Exit
177

3

Nicolum
River
Prov Park

MT HOPE
FSR

Hope
Mtn Trail

Hope
Lookout
Trail

Exit
173

Hope

Exit
170

2-2

Hope
Mtn
1827m

Othello
Tunnels
Trail

KAWKAWA LAKE Rd

Kawkawa Lake
Prov Park

Thacker Mtn
Regional Park

Aywawwis
IR

Thacker Mtn T

Landstrom
Ridge
Trail

Schkam
IR

ROSS
Rd

Lake
of the
Woods

Schkam.
IR

Landstrom IR

Croft
Isl

HAIG

Devils Lake

UNION BAR

KAWKAWA

Stulkawhits Creek

Squeah

Dogwood
Valley

Squeah

SQUEAH Rd

Emory Cr
Prov Park

NORTH
EMORY
Cr FSR

EMORY   CREEK

Emory Creek

YALE
Cr Rd

Spirit Cave
Trail

Yale

Mt
Oppenheimer

Gordon Creek

Yale Creek

CANADA

Mt
Baird
1830m

Zofka Creek

Ridge

Klaneter
Lake

Puckat Creek

American Creek

AMERICAN

washed
out

Dog
Mtn

TRANS

Choate

Creek

BC NICKEL MINE
ROAD

Rd

gate

gate

gate

private

Cr

15   Hope   1.5km   0km   3km

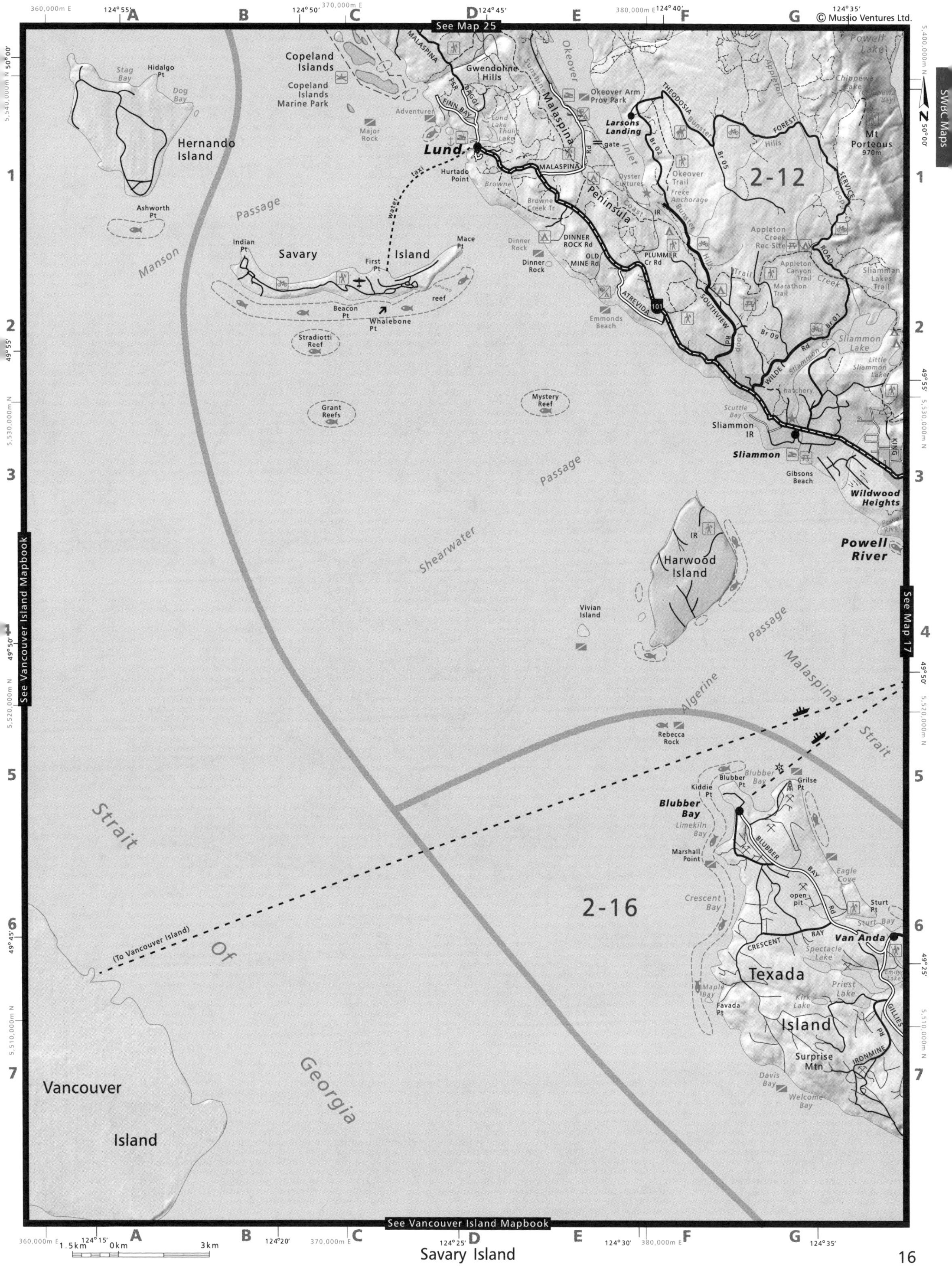

© Mussio Ventures Ltd.

360,000m E 124°55' A B 124°50' 370,000m E C D 124°45' E 380,000m 124°40' F G 124°35'

See Map 25

Stag Bay
Hidalgo Pt
Dog Bay
Hernando Island
Ashworth Pt

Copeland Islands
Copeland Islands Marine Park
Major Rock

MALASPINA
Gwendoline Hills
Adventurer
FINN BAY
Lund
Hurtado Point
Browne Cr
Browne Creek Tr
Lund Lake
Thulin Lake
MALASPINA

Okeover Arm Prov Park
gate
Okeover Trail
Oyster Cultures
Freke Anchorage
Larsons Landing
THEODOSIA (Dunster)
FOREST
Mt Porteous 970m
Chippewa Lake
Powell Lake
Appleton

2-12

Okeover Inlet
Malaspina Peninsula
Coast
IR
Br 02
Br 05
Appleton Creek Rec Site
Appleton Canyon Trail
Sliammon Lakes Trail
Marathon Trail
SERVICE ROAD

DINNER ROCK Rd
Dinner Rock
OLD MINE Rd
PLUMMER Cr Rd
SOUTHVIEW Rd
ATREVIDO 101
Emmonds Beach
Hill
Br 09
Br 01
WILDE Loop
Sliammon Cr
hatchery
Scuttle Bay
Sliammon IR
Sliammon Lake
Little Sliammon Lake

Savary Island
Indian Pt
Mace Pt
First Pt
reef
Beacon Pt
Whalebone Pt
Water taxi

Stradiotti Reef
Grant Reefs
Mystery Reef

Manson Passage
Passage

Shearwater Passage

Harwood Island
IR
Vivian Island

Gibsons Beach
Wildwood Heights
Powell River

See Vancouver Island Mapbook

Algerine Passage
Rebecca Rock
Malaspina Strait

See Map 17

Blubber Bay
Kiddie Pt
Blubber Pt
Grilse Pt
Limekiln Bay
BLUBBER BAY Rd
Marshall Point
Eagle Cove
Crescent Bay
open pit
Sturt Pt
Sturt Bay

2-16

CRESCENT BAY Rd
Spectacle Lake
Van Anda
Texada Island
Maple Bay
Kirk Lake
Priest Lake
Emily Lake
GILLIES Pt
Favada Pt
Surprise Mtn
Davis Bay
Welcome Bay
IRONMINE

Strait
Of
Georgia

Vancouver Island

(To Vancouver Island)

1.5km 0km 3km

360,000m E 124°15' A B 124°20' 370,000m E C 124°25' D E 124°30' F 380,000m G 124°35'

See Vancouver Island Mapbook

Savary Island

16

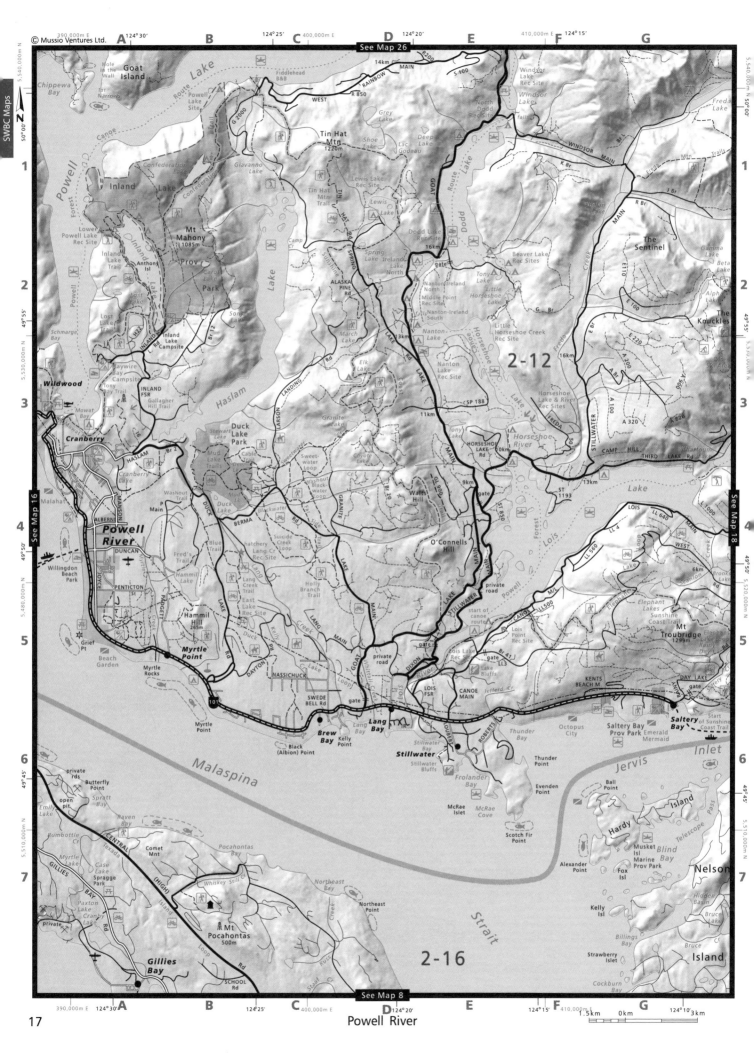

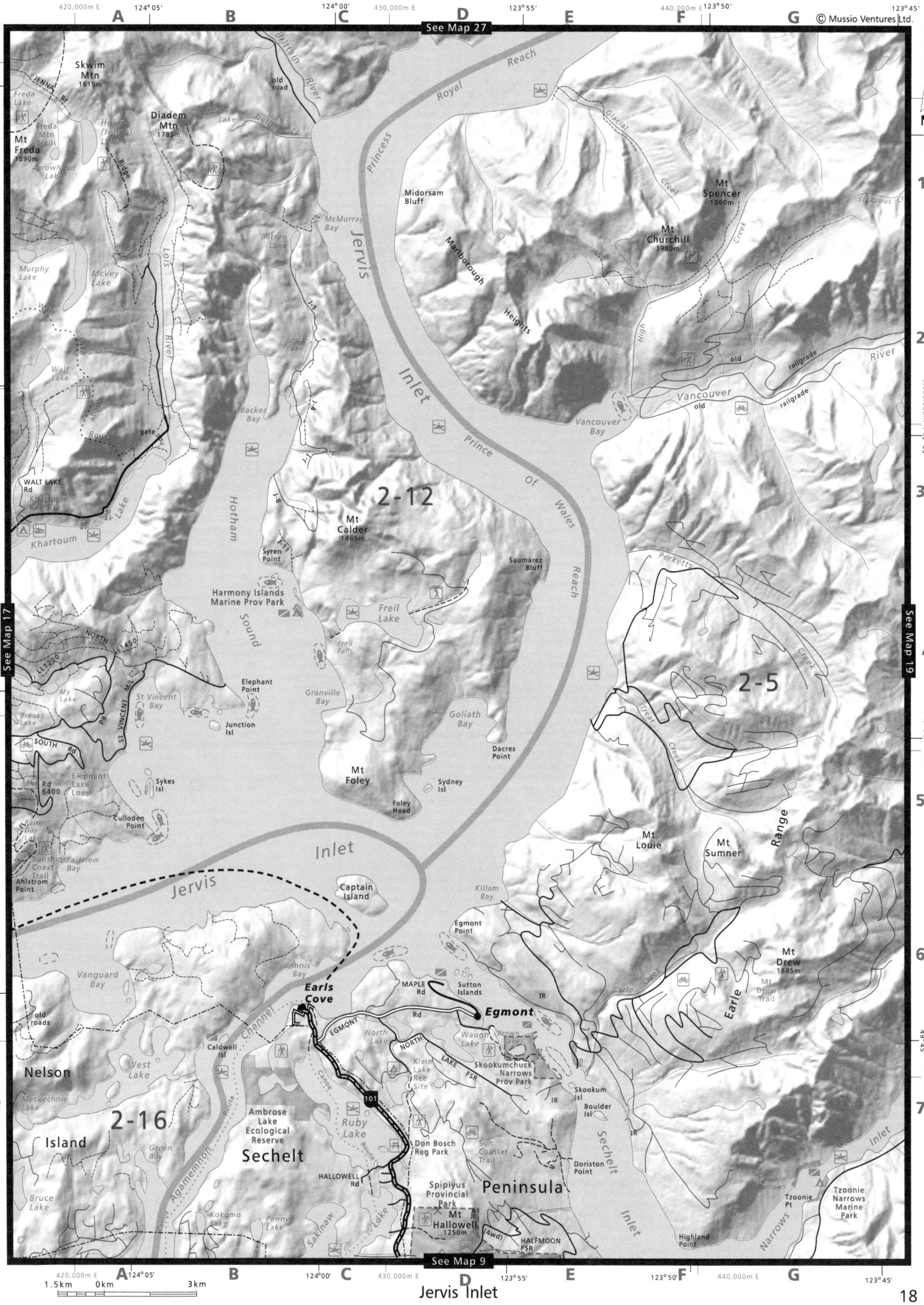

© Mussio Ventures Ltd.

N

420,000m E 124°05' 124°00' 430,000m E 123°55' 440,000m E 123°50' 123°45'

A B C D E F G

50°00'

Skwim Mtn 1615m

Freda Lake
Freda Mtn Trails
Helena (Jenna) Lake
Mt Freda 1890m
Arrowhead Lake
Ridge
Diadem Mtn 1785m
Diadem Lake
old road
Brittain River
Trettle Cr
McMurray Bay

Mt Spencer 1860m
Glacial Creek
Mt Churchill 1980m

1

Midorsam Bluff

Murphy Lake
McVey Lake
Walt River Route
Lois River
Barren Lake
Lena Lake
Marlborough Heights

High Creek

Vancouver River

2

49°55'

5,530,000m N

Walt Lake
gate
Backed Bay
Vancouver Bay
old railgrade
old railgrade

WALT LAKE Rd
Khartoum Rec Site
Khartoum Lake

2-12

Mt Calder 1465m

Saumarez Bluff

Prince Of Wales Reach

3

5,530,000m N

Syren Point
Harmony Islands Marine Prov Park

Hotham Sound
Freil Lake
Perketts

NORTH LL1430
LL1200

Freil Falls
Granville Bay

2-5

4

49°50'

5,520,000m N

My Lake
Brooks Lake
St Vincent Bay
ST VINCENT MT Rd
SOUTH Rd
Elephant Lake Loop
Rd 6400
Elephant Point
Junction Isl
Sykes Isl
Culloden Point

Goliath Bay
Dacres Point
Mt Foley
Sydney Isl
Foley Head

Jervis Inlet

Treat Creek
Mt Louie
Mt Sumner
Range

5

5,520,000m N

Rainy Day Lake
Sunshine Coast Trail
Fairview Bay
Ahlstrom Point

Captain Island

Killam Bay
Earle Creek
Mt Drew 1885m
Mt Drew Trail

6

49°45'

5,510,000m N

Vanguard Bay
old roads
Annis Bay
Earls Cove
MAPLE Rd
Sutton Islands
Egmont
Egmont Point
Earle Creek

Nelson
West Lake
Caldwell Isl
Channel
EGMONT Rd
North Lake
NORTH LAKE FSR
Waugh Lake
Brown Lake
Skookumchuck Narrows Prov Park
Skookum Isl
Boulder Isl
IR

Sechelt Inlet

7

5,510,000m N

Mackechnie Lake
2-16
Island
Bruce Lake
Green Bay
Ambrose Lake Ecological Reserve
Sechelt
Ruby Lake
101
Klein Lake Rec Site
Don Bosch Reg Park
Sun Coaster Trail
Doriston Point
IR
Narrows
Highland Point
Tzoonie Narrows
Tzoonie Pt
Tzoonie Narrows Marine Park

Peninsula
HALLOWELL Rd
Spipiyus Provincial Park
Mt Hallowell 1250m
(4wd)
HALFMOON FSR

Kokomo Lake
Penny Lake
Sakinaw Lake
Canoe Route

420,000m E 124°05' 124°00' 430,000m E 123°55' 440,000m E 123°50' 123°45'

1.5 km 0 km 3 km

Jervis Inlet

18

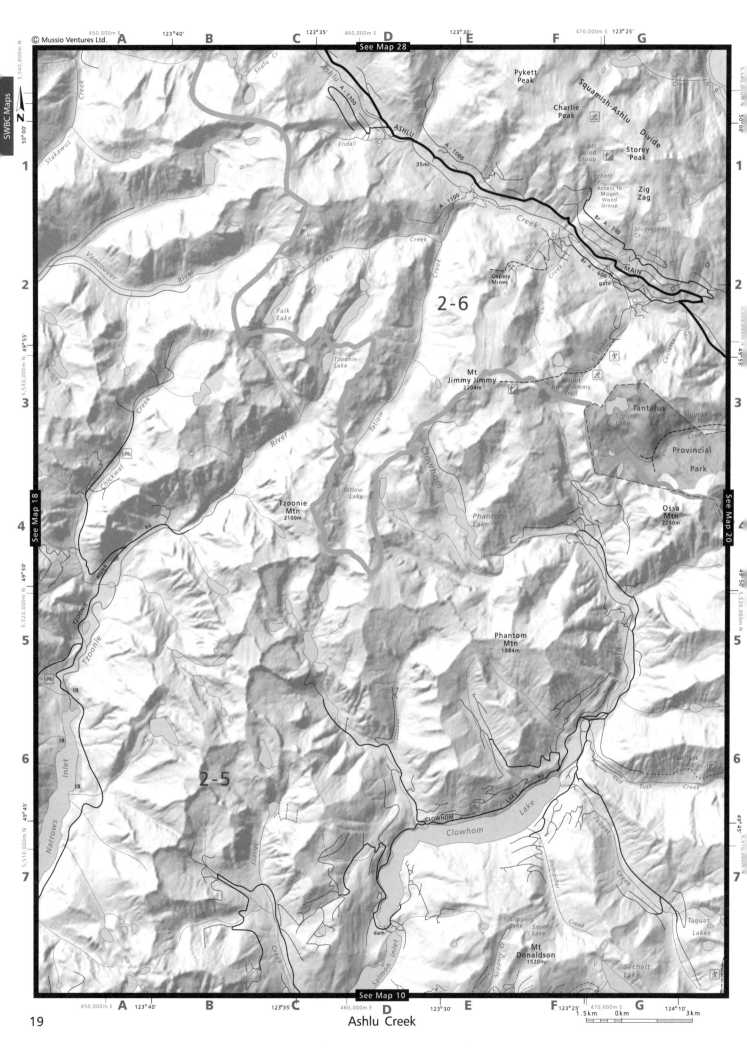

See Map 18

See Map 20

A 450,000m E 123°40' **B** 123°35' **C** 460,000m E **D** 123°30' **E** **F** 470,000m E 123°25' **G**

5,540,000m N 50°00'

SWBC Maps

N

49°55'

49°50'

49°45'

5,530,000m N

5,520,000m N

5,510,000m N

Stakawus Creek

Vancouver River

Snafu Cr

Ashlu

ASHLU A - 1300

35ml

A - 1000

A - 1100

Endall Cr

Creek

Creek

Falk

Falk Lake

Tzoonie Lake

Chickwat Creek

River

Tatlow

Tzoonie Mtn
2100m

Tatlow Lake

Clowhom

Pykett Peak

Squamish-Ashlu Divide

Charlie Peak

Mt Wood Group

Storey Peak

Pykett

Access to Mount Wood Group

Zig Zag

Stuyvesedt Cr

Br A - 700

Marion Cr

Creek

Coin Creek

Br A - 600 gate

MAIN

Cassetta Cr

Squamish R.

Spam Creek

Ospery Mines

2-6

Mt Jimmy Jimmy
2204m

Mount Jimmy Jimmy Trail

Tantalus

Sigurd Lake

Sigurd Creek Trail

Provincial Park

Ossa Mtn
2260m

Phantom Lake

Narrows Inlet

IR

IR

IR

TZOONIE RIVER Rd

Tzoonie

2-5

Misery Creek

Phantom Mtn
1884m

River

Red Tusk Route

Red Tusk Creek

CLOWHOM

LAKE Rd

Clowhom Lake

Taquat Creek

Dempster

dam

Salmon Inlet

Slippery Cr

Slippery Lake

Smithe Lake

Creek

Mt Donaldson
1520m

Taquat Lakes

Sechelt Lake

A 450,000m E 123°40' **B** 123°35' **C** 460,000m E **D** 123°30' **E** **F** 123°25' 470,000m E **G** 124°10'

19

Ashlu Creek

1.5 km   0 km   3 km

See Map 29

See Map 19

See Map 21

See Map 11

Squamish

Squamish

20

Garibaldi

Provincial

Park

Tantalus

Provincial

Park

Nature

Conservancy

Area

Whistler Interpretive Forest

BLACK TUSK TOWER Rd (4wd)

Brandywine Falls Prov Park

Black Tusk Village

Empetrum Ridge

Empetrum Peak 1990m

Helm Peak 2145m

Corrie Peak

Corrie Lake

Cheakamus Lake

Cinder Cone

The Black Tusk 2315m

Gentian Peak 2145m

Castle Towers Mtn

Phyllis Engine

Garibaldi Lake

Sphinx Glacier

Sphinx Bay

Burton Hut

Price Bay

Mt Price 2050m

Clinker Peak

Table Meadow

The Table 2020m

Sentinel Glacier

Glacier Pikes

Warren Glacier

Tusk Ridge

Lava Flow

Clinker

Mt Garibaldi 2678m

Atwell Peak

Opal Cone

Diamond Head 2620m

The Gargoyles 1830m

Columnar Peak

Elfin Lakes Shelter

Round Mtn

Paul Ridge

Brohm Ridge Route

Packer Meadows

Taylor Meadows

Black Tusk Trail

Mimulus Lake

Helm Glacier

Upper Lake

Panorama Ridge

Barrier Lake

Battleship Lakes

Garibaldi Lake Camp

Cloudburst Mtn

Tricouni Peak 2130m

Tricouni Meadows

Tricouni Meadows Trail

High Falls

High Falls Cr Trail

Squamish Cheakamus Divide Route

Brew Lake

Brew Lake Trail

Pinecrest Lakes

Shadow Lake

Lake Lucille

Daisy Lake

Rubble Cr (Black Tusk) Trailhead

Rubble Cr

Cheakamus Canyon (Sea to Sky) Trail

Butterfly Lake

Starvation Lake

Logan Lake

Conroy Cr

Conroy FSR

Jack Webster Bridge

Cheakamus Canyon

Pelion Mtn 2290m

Zenith Mtn 1980m

Zenith Lake

Mt Tantalus 2605m

Mt Dione

Cheakamus

Hut Lake

Island Put-in

hatchery

Levette Lake Rec Site

Levette Lake

Paradise Valley

Evans Lake Camp

Brohm Lake Rec Site

Brohm Lake

Brohm Lake Interpretive Trails

Cheekye

Alpha Mtn 2305m

Serratus Mtn 2325m

Red Tusk 2100m

Mt Pandareus

Omega Mtn

Lake Lovely Water

Brackendale

Eagles

Baynes Isl

Mt Niobe 2010m

Mt Thyestes

Brackendale

Garibaldi Estates

Alice Lake Prov Park

Garibaldi Highlands Trails

Watershed Reserve

Mt Sedgewick 2075m

Mt Conybeare

Mt Murchison

Echo Lake

Alec Lake

Scott Lake

Mt Roderick

Woodfibre Lake

Mount Roderick Trail

Tantalus Lakes

Powersmart Trails

Red Heather Day Shelter

RING Cr N. Rd

Mamquam River

Crumpit Woods

Smoke Bluffs

Spawning Channels

Stawamus Chief Prov Park

STAWAMUS INDIAN FSR

Watershed Reserve

Mt Mulligan Trail

SQUAMISH VALLEY Rd

Cat Lake Rec Site

CHEEKEYE R. FSR

Brohm Line Rd

Alice Ridge Route

Stump Lake

2-5

2-6

2-7

2-8

Br 400

Br 300

Br 220

Br 200

25mi

21mi

MAIN IR

Ashlu Canyon

Ashlu Rd

Sigurd Cr Trail

Crooked Falls

Madden Falls

SQUAMISH

PARADISE VALLEY RD

CHEAKAMUS RIVER

99

GOVT Rd

LOGGERS

12.7km

16km

1.5km 0km 3km

SWBC Maps

122°55' 122°50' 122°45' 122°40' 122°35'
510,000m E 520,000m E 530,000m E

A B C D E F G

N

Cheakamus Lake Trail
Singing Pass
Adit Lakes
Himmelsbach Hut
Russet Lake
Overlord Glacier
Spearhead Traverse
Naden Pass
Carcajou Peak
Outlier Peak

Cheakamus Lake
Fitzsimmons
Fissile Peak 2420m
Overlord Mtn 2625m
Mt Fitzsimmons 2650m
±835m
Whirlwind Peak 2420m
Range
Diavolo Peak 2588m
Cheakamus Mtn 2590m
Cheakamus
River

Nivalis Mtn
Talon Peak

Castle Towers
Cheakamus

McBride Glacier
Range

Garibaldi
Mt Davidson 2500m

Veeocee Mtn
Ubyssey Glacier
Mt Sir Richard 2710m

Adieu Mtn

Provincial

2-7

Cheakamus Glacier

Snow Bowl

Isosceles

Mt Carr 2590m

McBride

Tuwasus
Creek

2-9

Graymantle Mtn

Icemantle Glacier

Gray Pass

Forger Glacier

South Tuwasus Cr

Hellbore Creek

Tuwasus Mtn 2515m

Greenmantle Mtn 2370m

Isosceles Peak 2530m
Isosceles Glacier

Raindrop Pass
Icefield

Three Bears Mtn

Mt Luxor 2320m
Tutankhamen Peak 2530m

Icefield
Mt Pitt 2500m
Roller Coster Ridge

Snowcap Lakes
Lower Snowcap Lake
Rainbow Pass
Cutoff Lake
Snowcap Lake Ski Route

Pitt

Park

Hourglass Lake

Viking

Rain God Mtn 2425m
Thundercap Glacier

Nip & Tuck Peaks
Perce-neige

Mamquam Lake
Spire Ridge
Glacier

Snowcap

Snowcap Peak 2410m
Icefield

Misty Lake

Pyramid Mtn 2130m
Eanastick Meadows

Mamquam
Icefield

River

2-8

Misty Icefield

Terra Alba Glacier

Mamquam Mtn 2595m
Delusion Peak

Stave Peak 2350m
Glacier

Stave

2-7

Bucklin

Nimbus Glacier
Nimbus Peak

Nebula Peak

Katzie Mtn

Watersprite Lake

Pinecone
Burke
PINECONE

Golden
Ears

Martin Cr
Falls

Prov
Creek
Shale Creek

Prov
Pukulkul Peak 2100m

MAMQUAM FSR
Crawford Cr
Steve

Pit River Hot Springs
21km
PITT RIVER FSR

Park

Park

See Map 20
See Map 22

21

Garibaldi Provincial Park

1.5 km 0 km 3 km

122°50' 122°45' 122°40' 122°35'
510,000m E 520,000m E 530,000m E

50°00' 49°55' 49°50' 49°45'
5,540,000m N 5,530,000m N 5,520,000m N 5,510,000m N

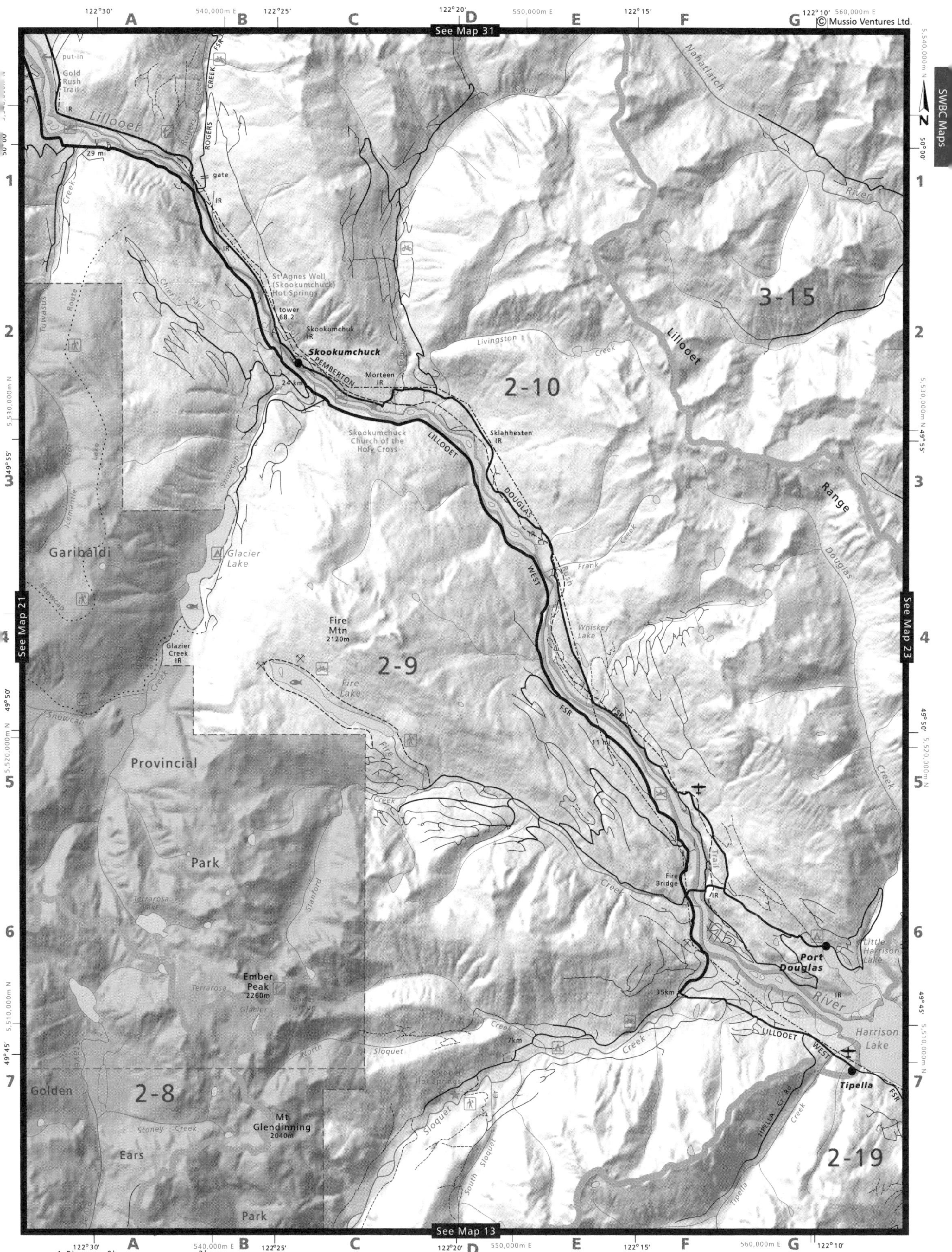

See Map 31

N

122°30'   A   122°25'   B   122°25'   C   122°20'   D   550,000m E   E   122°15'   F   122°10' 560,000m E   G

3-15

2-10

Lillooet

Creek

Nahatlatch

River

put-in
Gold Rush
Trail

IR

Lillooet

29 mi

Rogers

Creek

ROGERS CREEK FSR

gate

IR

IR

St Agnes Well
(Skookumchuck)
Hot Springs

tower
68.2

Skookumchuck
IR

Skookumchuck

PEMBERTON

24 km

Morteen
IR

Sklahhesten
IR

Livingston

Creek

Garibaldi

Cheer

Snowcap

Paul

Skookumchuck
Church of the
Holy Cross

LILLOOET

DOUGLAS

WEST

IR

Frank

Bush

Whiskey
Lake

Range

Douglas

Glacier
Lake

Fire
Mtn
2120m

2-9

FSR

FSR

Tuwasus

Route

Icemantle

Lake

Creek

Snowcap

Glazier
Creek
IR

Fire
Lake

Fire

Creek

11 mi

Provincial

Park

Terrarosa
Lake

Stanford

Creek

Trail

Fire
Bridge

IR

Port
Douglas

Little
Harrison
Lake

IR

River

35km

Terrarosa

Ember
Peak
2260m

Glacier

North

Creek

Sloquet

7km

Creek

Harrison

Lake

Golden

2-8

Stoney Creek

Mt
Glendinning
2040m

Sloquet
Hot Springs

Sloquet

South Sloquet

Creek

LILLOOET

WEST

Tipella

FSR

TIPELLA GR Rd

Creek

Tipella

2-19

Ears

Park

See Map 21
See Map 23
See Map 13

122°30'   A   122°25'   B   122°25'   C   122°20'   D   550,000m E   E   122°15'   F   560,000m E   G   122°10'

1.5 km   0km   3km

Lillooet River

22

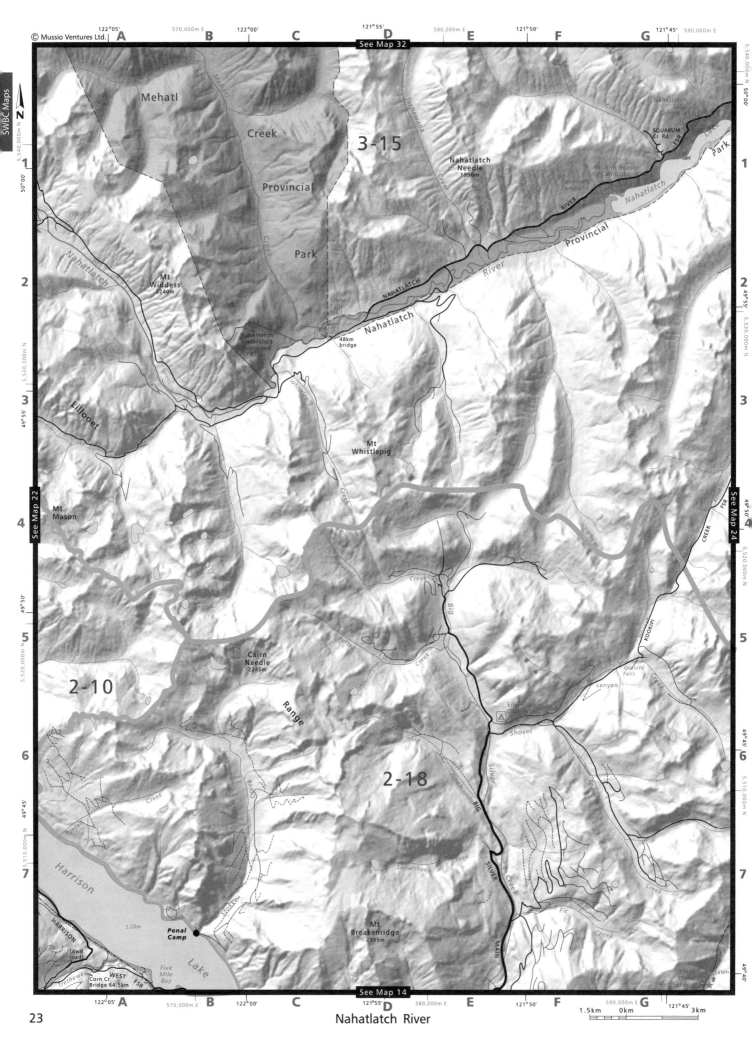

SWBC Maps

© Mussio Ventures Ltd.

A 122°05'   B 570,000m E   122°00'   C   D 121°55'   E 580,000m E   121°50' F   G 121°45'   590,000m E

Mehatl

Creek

Provincial

3-15

Park

Nahatlatch
Needle
1950m

Nahatlatch Lake
Campsite

SQUAKUM
Cr Rd

Salmon Beach
Campsite

Squakum
Campsite

Mt
Widdess
2240m

Nahatlatch
Watershed
Protected
Area

48km
bridge

Nahatlatch

NAHATLATCH

River

Provincial

Park

Nahatlatch

Lillooet

Mt
Whistlepig

Mt
Mason

KOOKIPI FSR

Hipper Creek

Big

Cairn
Needle
2245m

Butter Creek

Granite
Falls

canyon

Range

2-10

Silver River
Campsite

Shovel

KOOKIPI

Silver

Creek

2-18

Gold Creek

BIG

Creek

Snowshoe Creek

SILVER

Purcell Creek

Stokke Creek

Harrison

Mt
Breakenridge
2385m

Fir Creek

±20m

Penal
Camp

HARRISON

(4wd road)

Trethewey FSR

Corn Cr
Bridge 64.5km

WEST
FSR

Five
Mile
Bay

Lake

MAIN

Clear
Creek
Hot Springs

A 122°05'   B 570,000m E   122°00'   C   D 121°55'   E 580,000m E   121°50' F   G 590,000m E 121°45'   49°40'

23

Nahatlatch River

1.5km   0km   3km

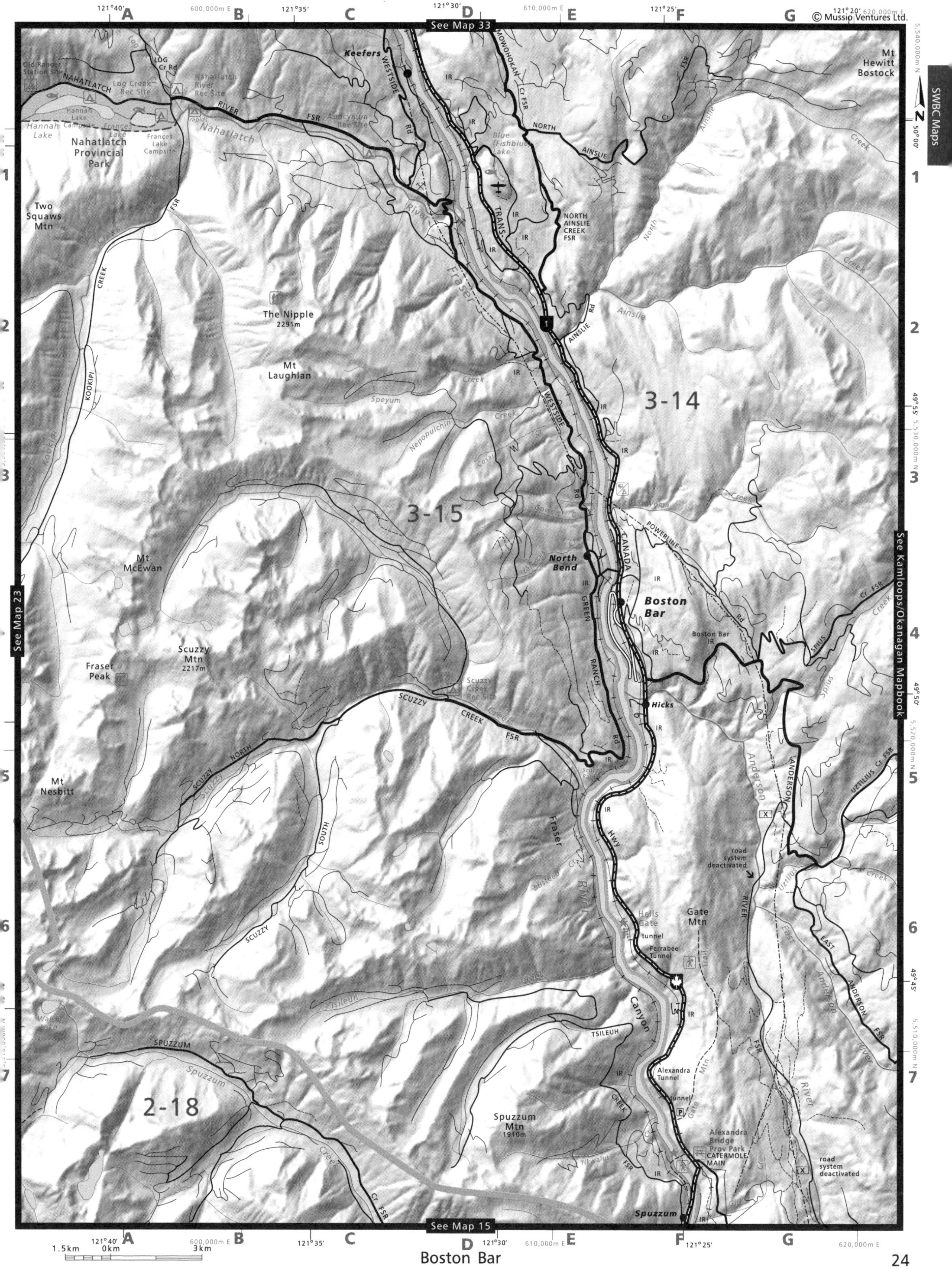

See Map 33

See Map 23

See Kamloops/Okanagan Mapbook

A · B · 600,000m E · B · 121°35' · C · 121°30' · D · 610,000m E · E · 121°25' · F · G · 121°20' 620,000m E

121°40'
50°00'
N

Old Range
Station Site
NAHATLATCH
LOG
Cr Rd
Log Creek
Rec Site
Nahatlatch
River Rec Site
Keefers
Mt Hewitt
Bostock

Hannah
Lake
Hannah
Lake
Campsite
Frances
Lake
Frances Lake
Campsite
Nahatlatch
Provincial
Park
RIVER
Nahatlatch
FSR
Apoynum
Rec Site
WESTSIDE Rd
MOWHOKAN Cr FSR
NORTH
AINSLIE

1

Two
Squaws
Mtn
CREEK
River
rapids
Blue
(Fishblue)
Lake
TRANS-
NORTH
AINSLIE
CREEK
FSR
Ainslie

KOOKIPI
The Nipple
2291m
River
Fraser
AINSLIE
Ainslie
Cr

2

KOOKIPI CREEK
Mt
Laughlan
Speyum
Creek
WESTSIDE
Ainslie Rd
3-14

3

Nepopulchin
Creek
Coza Creek
3-15
Rd
Creek

Mt
McEwan
Haskell
Creek
North
Bend
POWERLINE
CANADA
Rd
Creek

4

Fraser
Peak
Scuzzy
Mtn
2217m
Scuzzy
Creek
Rec Site
SCUZZY
CREEK
FSR
GREEN
Boston
Bar
Boston Bar
IR
Spius Cr FSR
UZTILIUS Cr FSR

Mt
Nesbitt
NORTH SCUZZY
SCUZZY
RANCH Rd
Hicks
Rd
Spius
Creek
ANDERSON
road
system
deactivated

5

SCUZZY
Fraser
Busteak Cr
River
Uztilius
Creek
EAST ANDERSON

6

Tsileuh
Creek
Hells
Gate
tunnel
Ferrabee
Tunnel
Gate
Mtn
Anderson
FSR

2-18
SPUZZUM
Spuzzum
TSILEUH
Canyon
Alexandra
Tunnel
tunnel
Gate Mtn
Anderson
RIVER

7

Walsh
Lake
Spuzzum
Mtn
1910m
Tikwalus
CREEK
Alexandra
Bridge
Prov Park
CATERMOLE
MAIN
road
system
deactivated

Creek
FSR
Spuzzum

See Map 15

1.5km
0km
3km
A · 121°40' · B · 600,000m E · C · 121°35' · D · 121°30' · E · 610,000m E · F · 121°25' · G · 620,000m E

Boston Bar

24

© Mussio Ventures Ltd.

SWBC Maps

N

360,000m E 124°55' 124°50' 370,000m E 124°45' 124°40' 380,000m E 124°35'

A **B** **C** **D** **E** **F** **G**

50°20'

George Head
Mt Hayes
Mainland
Raza Island
Tibbs Point
Connis Point
Elizabeth Isl
Double Isl
Channel Isl
Hepburn Point
Brettell Point
Mt Grazebrooke
Mt Whieldon

Pryce Channel
Toba Inlet
Attwood Bay
Homfray Creek

1

Deer Passage
Redonda Bay
Mt Perritt
Gloucester Point
Dean Point
Walsh Cove Prov Marine Park
Walsh Cove
East
Mt Bunsen
Homfray Channel
Foster Point

2

50°15'
5,570,000m N
Redonda Bay
Tom Lake
Baile Lake
Bishop Point
Docto Bay
Cloud Lake
Shirley Point
Redonda
Mt Addenbroke 1500m
Ecological Reserve
Pictographs
IR
Forber Cr
Forbes Bay

West
Lewis Channel
Ellis Lake
Redonda
Allies Isl
Waddington Channel
Walter Point
Pendrell Sound
Island
Durham Point
Booker Point
Bohn Point

3

50°15'

Teakerne Arm Marine Prov Park
Cassel Lake
Church Point
Lloyd Point
Lloyd Creek
Dudley Cone

Robertson Lake
Cliff Peak
Willey Lake
Von Donop Inlet
Teakerne Arm
Talbot Cove
2-13 Island
Teakerne Arm
Llanover Mtn
Roscoe Bay Prov Marine Park
Black Lake
Marylebone Point
Horace Point
Sound
Price Point
Unwin Range

4

5,560,000m N
50°10'
Ha'thayim (Von Donop) Marine Park
Refuge Lagoon
Squirrel Cove
Junction Point
Desolation
Melville Isl
Scebelt Isl
Cobblestone Isl
Prideaux Heaven
2-12
Desolation Sound

5

IR
Boulder Point
Refuge Cove
Morgan/Otter Isl
Curme Isl
Tenedos Bay
Unwin Lake
private
River MAIN

Cortes
Squirrel Cove
Channel
Martin Islands
Mink Island
Bold Head
Mt Spooner 460m
private

6

5,550,000m N
Seaford
GORGE HARBOUR Rd
SEAFORD Rd
1-15 Island
WHALETOWN Rd
Gunflint Lake
Kw'as Park
CORTES BAY Rd
Station Island
Kinghorn Isl
Call Bight
Portage Cove
Marine
Mt Weaver 705m
Provincial
Toquana IR
THEODOSIA
HEATHER
Theodosia Inlet
H 5

50°05'
Cedar Ridge Trail
Hague Lake
Tiber Bay
Cortes Bay
BARTHOLOMEW
Cortes Bay
Mary Point
Zephine Head
private
Galley Bay
Gifford Peninsula
Park
Wootten Bay
Lancelot Inlet
private
Bunster Range
MAIN
H S

7

Sarah Point
Sunshine Coast Trailhead
Malaspina
Bliss Landing
Malaspina!
Hinds Lake
Parker Harbour
IR
Isabel Bay
Stopford Pt
Scott Pt
Oyster Cultures
Edith Isl
Bunster Pt
Theodosia Arm
Hillingdon Ptt
Theodosia
Pat Lake
Aillee Lake
H300

Twin Islands
Powell Islets
Townley Islands
Copeland Islands Provincial Marine Park
MALASPINA FSR
Wednesday Lakes
Turner Bay
Coast Trail
Prov Park
Wednesday Lake Trail
Tidakoor Bay
Kerda Peninsula
Okeover Inlet

Strait Of Georgia
Baker Passage

See Map 26

© Mussio Ventures Ltd.

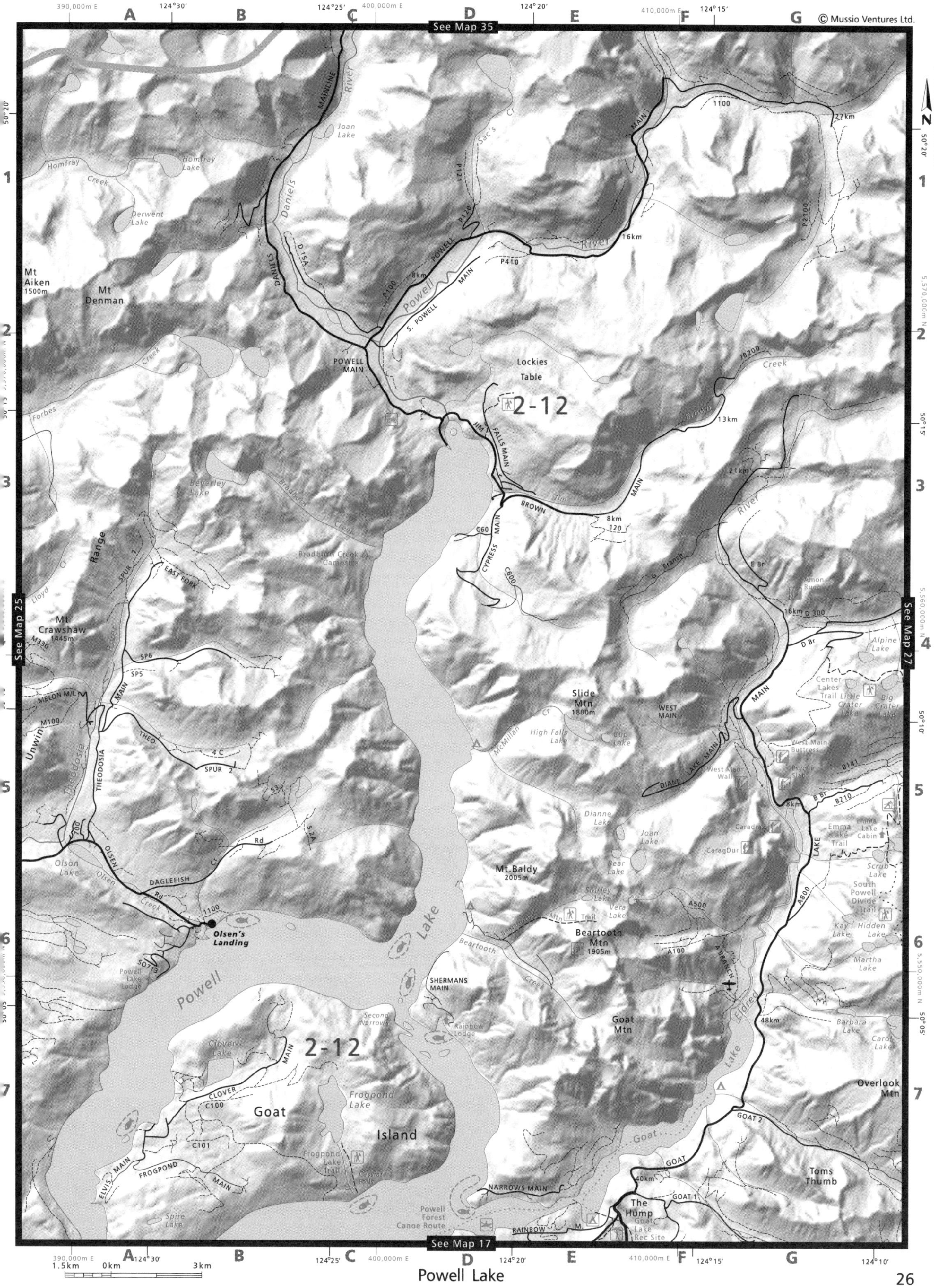

SWBC Maps

N

See Map 25

See Map 27

Mt Aiken 1500m

Mt Denman

Homfray Creek

Homfray Lake

Derwent Lake

Joan Lake

Daniels River

MAINLINE

DANIELS

D 15A

P100

P150

POWELL MAIN

S. POWELL

8km

POWELL MAIN

P120

P410

Sac's Cr

River

16km

1100

27km

P2100

Forbes Cr

Creek

Lockies Table

2-12

JIM FALLS MAIN

BROWN MAIN

CYPRESS MAIN

C60

C600

Brown Creek

13km

21km

8km

120

R8200

Jim River

8km

Beverley Lake

Bradshaw Creek

Bradshaw Creek Campsite

Range

SPUR 1

EAST FORK

SPUR

SP6

SP5

Mt Crawshaw 1445m

M330

MELON M/L

M100

THEODOSIA

THEO

THEO MAIN

4 C

SPUR 2

Unwim

Theodosia River

Olsen

OLSEN

700

Olson Lake

DAGLEFISH

Rd

1100

SO713

Olsen Creek

Olsen's Landing

Powell Lake Lodge

Powell Lake

53

S 2A

Rd

E Br

16km D 300

D Br

Alpine Lake

Center Lakes Trail

Little Crater Lake

Big Crater Lake

B141

West Main Buttress

Psyche Slab

B Br

B210

Slide Mtn 1800m

McMillan Cr

High Falls Lake

Cup Lake

WEST MAIN

DIANE LAKE MAIN

West Main Wall

8km

DIANE

Dianne Lake

Joan Lake

Bear Lake

Caradras

CaragDur

West Main

LAKE

A800

Emma Lake Cabin

Emma Lake Trail

Scrub Lake

South Powell Divide Trail

Kay Lake

Hidden Lake

Mt.Baldy 2005m

Shirley Lake

Vera Lake

Mtn Trail

Beartooth Mtn 1905m

A500

A100

Beartooth Creek

Eldred Lake

48km

Martha Lake

Barbara Lake

Carol Lake

Clover Lake

2-12

Goat Island

CLOVER MAIN

C100

C101

Goat

Frogpond Lake

Frogpond Lake Trail

Cassier Falls

FROGPOND MAIN

ELVIS MAIN

Spire Lake

Second Narrows

SHERMANS MAIN

Rainbow Lodge

Goat Mtn

Overlook Mtn

GOAT MAIN

GOAT 2

40km

GOAT

GOAT 1

Toms Thumb

The Hump

Goat Lake Rec Site

NARROWS MAIN

RAINBOW

M

Powell Forest Canoe Route

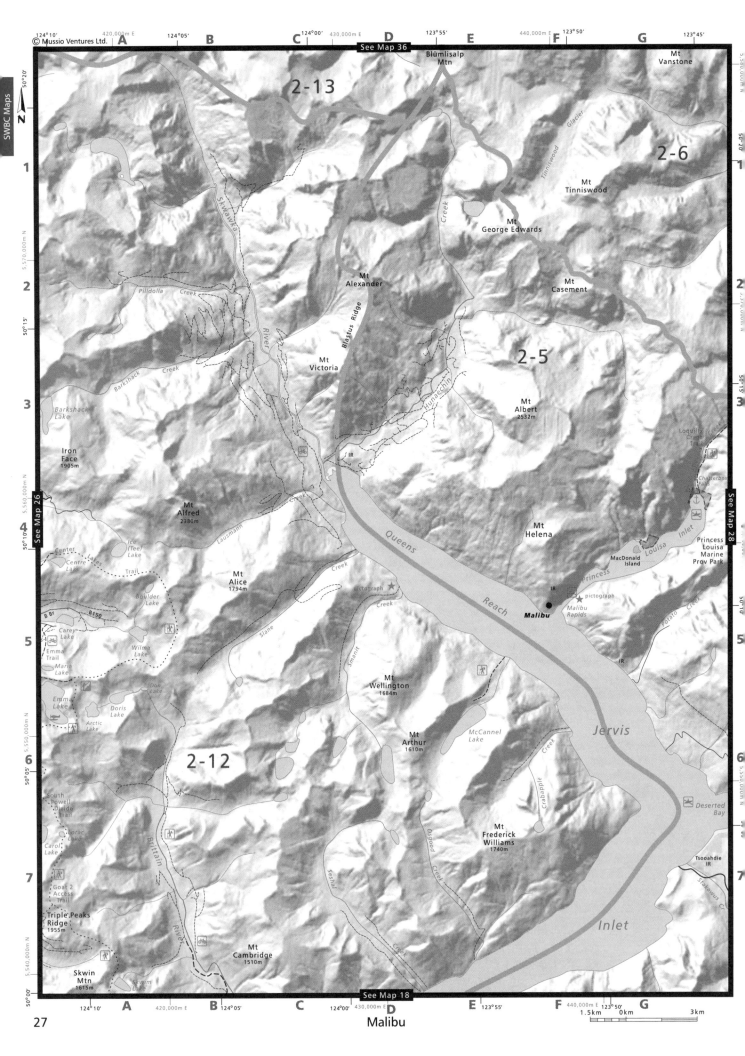

124°10' 420,000m E   124°05'   124°00' 430,000m E   123°55'   440,000m E 123°50'   123°45'

N

See Map 36

A   B   C   D   E   F   G

2-13

Blümlisalp
Mtn

Mt
Vanstone

2-6

Mt
Tinniswood

Tinniswood Glacier

Creek

Mt
George Edwards

1

Skwawka

Pilldolla Creek

Mt
Alexander

Mt
Casement

2

River

Blastus Ridge

Mt
Victoria

2-5

Barkshack Creek

Hunaechin

Mt
Albert
2532m

3

Barkshack
Lake

Iron
Face
1905m

IR

Loquilts Creek Trail

See Map 26

Creek

Mt
Alfred
2380m

Mt
Helena

Chatterbox
Falls

Inlet

4

Lausmann

Queens

Princess Louisa

MacDonald
Island

Princess
Louisa
Marine
Prov Park

Center
Lakes

Ice
(Tee)
Lake

Creek

Mt
Alice
1794m

pictograph ★

IR

See Map 28

Centre
Lake

Trail

Boulder
Lake

Reach

Malibu
Rapids

pictograph ★

5

B Br
B150

Slane

Creek

Malibu

Emma
Trail

Carey
Lake

Wilma
Lake

Smanit

Mt
Wellington
1684m

IR

Maria
Lake

Don
Lake

Emma
Lake

Doris
Lake

Arctic
Lake

Mt
Arthur
1610m

McCannel
Lake

Jervis

6

2-12

Crabapple Creek

South
Powell
Divide
Trail

Osgood Creek

Deserted
Bay

Corat
Lake

Carol
Lake

Brittain

Mt
Frederick
Williams
1740m

Tsooahdie
IR

7

Goat 2
Access
Trail

Seshal

Stakawus Cr

Triple Peaks
Ridge
1955m

River

Inlet

Skwin
Mtn
1615m

Skwim
Lake

Mt
Cambridge
1510m

Creek

See Map 18

124°10'   124°05'   124°00' 430,000m E   123°55'   440,000m E 123°50'   123°45'

A   B   C   D   E   F   G

Malibu

1.5 km   0 km   3 km

© Mussio Ventures Ltd.

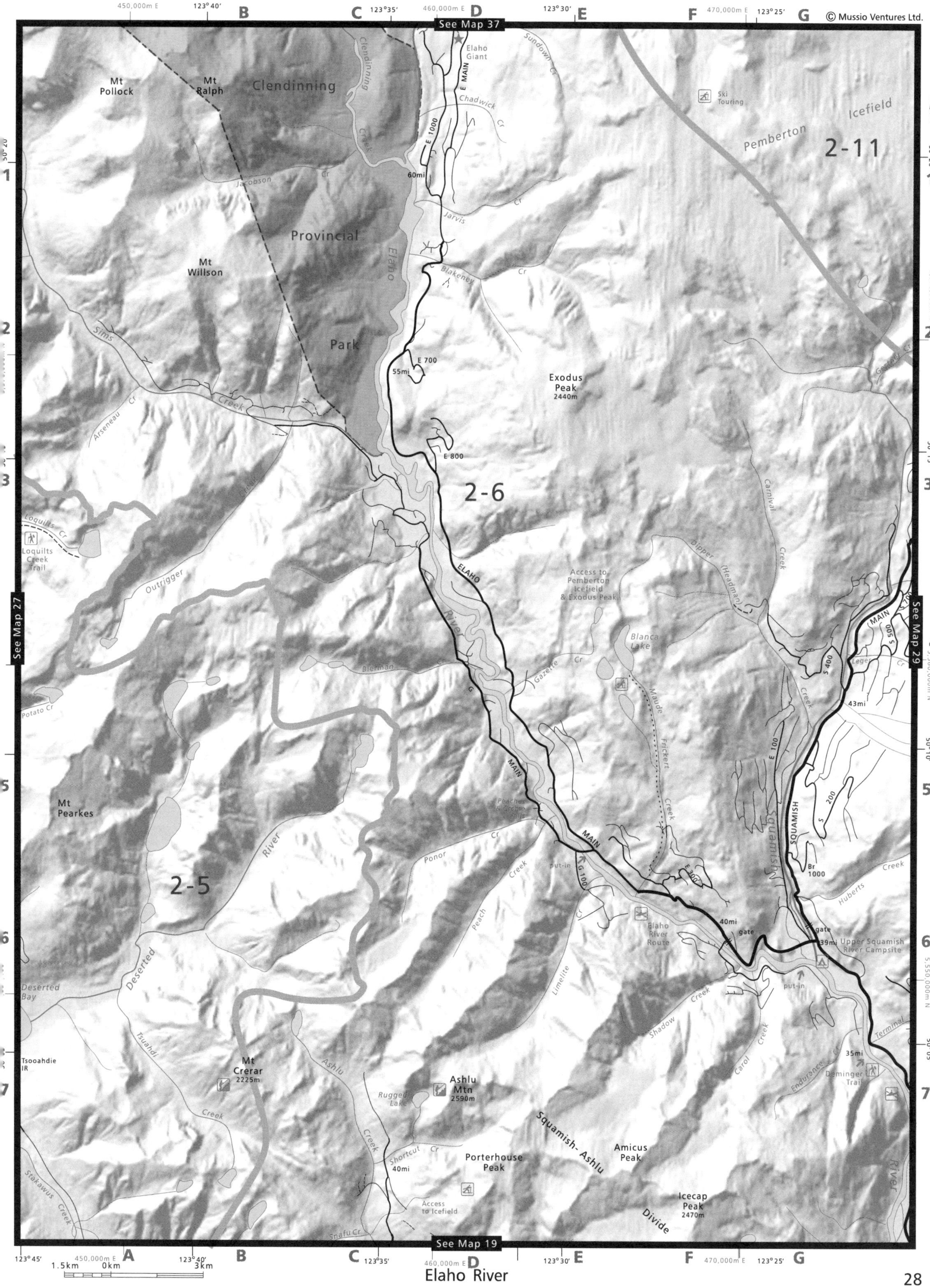

450,000m E   123°40'   123°35'   460,000m E   123°30'   470,000m E   123°25'

See Map 37

N

2-11

Pemberton Icefield

Mt Pollock
Mt Ralph
Clendinning
Elaho Giant
Chadwick Cr
Sundown Cr
Ski Touring

E MAIN
E 1000

Mt Willson
Provincial
Jacobson Cr
Jarvis Cr
Blakeney Cr
60mi

Park
Elaho
Sims Cr
Arseneau Cr
Creek
E 700
55mi
Exodus Peak
2440m

Carnival Creek

See Map 27

Loquilts Cr
Loquilts Creek Trail
E 800
2-6
ELAHO
Access to Pemberton Icefield & Exodus Peak
Blanca Lake

Sipper Cr
Headman Cr

See Map 29

S 500
S MAIN
43mi
Outrigger

River
G MAIN
Blobman Cr
Gazette Cr
Maude Frickert Creek

S 400
Legend Cr

Potato Cr

Mt Pearkes

River
2-5
Peaches Group
Ponor Creek
Peach Cr
put-in
G MAIN
put-in
G 100
Elaho River Route

Deserted
Deserted Bay
Tsuahdi Creek
Ashlu Creek
Limelite Cr
40mi
gate
gate
39mi
Upper Squamish River Campsite

Squamish River
SQUAMISH
E 100
S 200
Br 1000
Huberts Creek
5,550,000m N
50°05'

Tsooahdie IR
Mt Crerar
2225m
Rugged Lake
Ashlu Mtn
2590m
Shadow Creek
Carol Creek
35mi
Deminger Trail
Enduro Creek

Starsawus Creek
Shortcut Cr
40mi
Porterhouse Peak
Squamish-Ashlu
Amicus Peak
Icecap Peak
2470m
Divide
Terminal Cr
River

Snafu Cr
Access to Icefield

See Map 19

1.5 km   0 km   3 km

123°45' 450,000m E 123°40'   123°35'   460,000m E   123°30'   470,000m E 123°25'

Elaho River

28

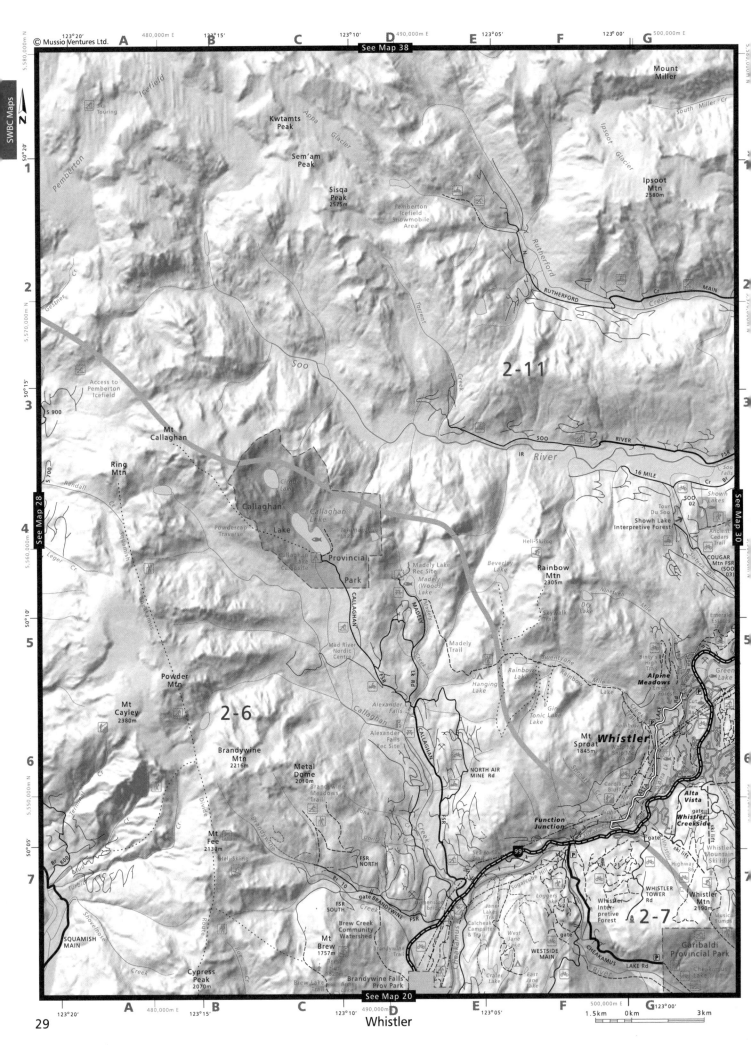

SWBC Maps

N

See Map 28

See Map 30

A · B · C · D · E · F · G

123°20' 123°15' 123°10' 123°05' 123°00'

480,000m E 490,000m E 500,000m E

5,580,000m N
5,570,000m N
5,560,000m N
5,550,000m N

50°20'
50°15'
50°10'
50°05'

Mount
Miller

South Miller Cr

Ipsoot Glacier

Ipsoot
Mtn
2580m

Rutherford

RUTHERFORD
Creek
MAIN

2-11

Pemberton
Icefield

Kwtamts
Peak

Sem'am
Peak

Sisqa
Peak
2575m

Appa Glacier

Pemberton Icefield
snowmobile
Area

Torrent
Creek

Soo

Creek

SOO RIVER
IR River
16 MILE

Soo
Falls
Br

FSR

Showh
Lakes

SOO
02

Tour
Du Soo

Showh Lake
Interpretive Forest

Ancient
Cedars
Trail

COUGAR
Mtn FSR
(SOO
03)

Access to
Pemberton
Icefield

Mt
Callaghan

Ring
Mtn

Gestner Cr

Rendall Cr

Leger Cr

Sockeye Minus

S 900
S 700

Cirque
Lake

Callaghan
Lake

Callaghan
Lake

Tehtamijii
Lake

Powdercap
Traverse

Callaghan
Lake
Campsite

Provincial

Park

Madely Lake
Rec Site

Madely
(Woods)
Lake

Heli-Skiing

Beverley
Lake

Rainbow
Mtn
2305m

Dry
Lake

Ninete Mile

Emerald
Estates

Powder
Mtn

Mt
Cayley
2380m

2-6

CALLAGHAN

FSR

Madely Lk Rd

MADELY Creek

Mad River
Nordic
Centre

Alexander
Falls

Callaghan

Madely
Trail

Hanging
Lake

Rainbow
Lake

Gin &
Tonic Lake
Lake

Skywalk Trail

TwentyOne
Mile

Rainbow Mile

Binty's
High
Trail

Alpine
Meadows

Green
Lake

Emerald
Forest

Rainbow

Mt
Sproat
1845m

Whistler

Brandywine
Mtn
2216m

Metal
Dome
2010m

Brandywine
Meadows
Trail

Edna
Cr

Dario Cr

Squamish

Brandywine

Divide

FSR

North Air
Mine Rd

NORTH AIR
MINE Rd

Function
Junction

Snowy

Cardinal
Bluff

Alta
Vista

gate
Whistler
Creekside

ski lift

Mt Fee
2130m

Heli-Skiing

FSR
NORTH

Br. 10

FSR
SOUTH

gate BRANDYWINE
Creek

Brandywine
Trail

99

Sugarcube Hill

Loggers
Lake

Janel
Lakes

Sea to Sky

Callaghan

Whistler
Inter-
pretive
Forest

WHISTLER
TOWER
Rd

2-7

Whistler
Mtn
2190m

Musical
Bumps

Whistler
Mountain
Ski Hill

ski lift

Br. 800

Mud Cr

Shovelnose Cr

Turbid

SQUAMISH
MAIN

Route

Cypress
Peak
2070m

Mt
Brew
1757m

Brew Lake Trail

Brew Creek
Community
Watershed

Brandywine Falls
Prov Park

Brandywine

Calcheak
Campsite
& Trail

West
Jane
Lake

East
Jane
Lake

Crater
Lake

WESTSIDE
MAIN

Cheakamus

CHEAKAMUS
LAKE Rd

River

gate

P

Garibaldi
Provincial Park

Whistler

29

1.5km 0km 3km

© Mussio Ventures Ltd.

122° 55'   510,000m E   122° 50'   122° 45'   D   520,000m E   E   122° 40'   F   122° 35'   530,000m E   G

See Map 39

N

2-10

2-11

Goat Meadows Hut

Ryan River

Lillooet

MacKenzie Lake

Cassiope Peak 2290m

South Miller Cr

Miller River

gate

MILLER Cr Rd

PEMBERTON MEADOWS Rd

Dyke Trail

MacKenzie BASIN Trail

OWL Cr FSR

OWL Cr

Owl Creek

Birkenhead River Trail

Owl Creek Rec Site

REID Rd

Ivey Lake

Owl Creek

Fish Hatchery

IR

IR

Pemberton

Watershed Reserve

Pemberton Creek

Pemberton Park

Mosquito Lake Rec Site & Trails

Private Campground

IR

Mount Currie

IR

Indian Reserve

XIT'OLACW Rd

Xit'olacw Lake

Duffy Lake

Joffre Creek

Duffy Lake Rd

Watershed Reserve

One Mile Lake

IR

Big Sky

Mount Currie

River

IN-SHUCK-CH

99

Ure Creek

Joffre Creek

HAUL Rd

Lillooet Lake

Marlatt Cr

Strawberry Point Rec Site

RUTHERFORD

Rutherford Cr MAIN

RUTHERFORD SOUTH

Nairn Falls

River Nairn Falls Prov Park

GREEN

RIVER

gate

FSR

GRAVELL Cr MAIN

Gravell Creek

Lil' Wat Pictograph

Echo Lakes

Tour

99

Green River

Mt Currie 2536m

Ure Creek schist

Cr

Shadow Lake Trails

Hibachi Ridge

2-9

Bastion

Bastion Peak 2545m

Halberds Edge Ridge

16 MILE Cr Br

Soo Bluffs

SOO RIVER FSR

Soo River

Mystery Creek

Garibaldi

Mystery Glacier

Kakila

Rampart Mtn Range

See Map 29

See Map 31

Cougar Mtn

Mt Moe

Tour Du Soo

COUGAR Mtn FSR (SOO-03)

Trill Me Kill Me Trail

Emerald Estates

WEDGE Cr FSR

Wedgemount Lake Trail

Wedgemount Lake Rec Site

The Owls

Mt Weart 2870m

Weart Glacier

Eureka Mtn

Carter Glacier

Mt Neal 2530m

Ure Creek

30 km

Green Lake Loop Route

Wedgemount Lake Bluff

Wedgemount Glacier

Rethel Mtn 2400m

Parkhurst Mtn 2480m

Needle Glacier

Provincial

Lost Lake X-C Ski Trails

Green Lake

Rethel Creek

Wedge Creek

Wedge Mtn 2891m

Fingerpost

Peggy Lake

Chaos Glacier

Chaos Lake

Gunsight Peak

Upper Village

ski lift

Blackcomb

Horstman Cr

Blackcomb Mountain Ski Hill

Glacier

Blackcomb Mountain Ski Hill

Seago Lake

Fingerpost Ridge

Berna Lake

Mt James Turner 2685m

Chaos Ridge

Chaos Creek

Little

Tenas Lake Bridge

36 km

50°05'

Blackcomb Mountain Ski Hill

Horstman Glacier

Phalanx Mtn

Spearhead Glacier

Wedge Pass

PEMBERTON-DOUGLAS FSR

bridge out

Little Spearhead

Blackcomb Peak 2420m

Spearhead

Decker Mtn 2410m

Tremor Glacier

Budder Glacier

Shatter Glacier

Tremor Mtn 2650m

Billygoat Creek

Lillooet (Tenas)

Comming

IR

Fitzsimmons

Singing Pass Trail

Melody Cr

Mt Trorey

Mt Pattison

Traverse Glacier

Range

Park

LILLOOET TENAS NARROWS FSR

Flute

Musical Bumps Trail

Singing Pass

Fitzsimmons Range

Fitzsimmons Glacier

See Map 21

122° 55'   A   0km   510,000m E   B   122° 50'   C   122° 45'   D   520,000m E   E   122° 40'   F   122° 35'   G   530,000m E

1.5 km   3 km

SWBC Maps

N

A | B | C | D | E | F | G

122°30'   540,000m E   122°25'   122°20'   550,000m E   122°15'   122°10'   560,000m E

See Map 40

Hwy 99

JOFFRE Cr MAIN

Lower Joffre Lake

Joffre Lakes Provincial Park

Mt Chief Pascall 2190m

Middle Joffre Lake

Upper Joffre Lake

Joffre Peak 2701m

Stonecrop Glacier

Matier Glacier

Cerise Creek Trail

Keith's Hut

Ski Touring

Cerise Creek

Caspar Cr Rd

Caspar Creek

Mt Caspar

Gott Peak

MINE Rd

Blowdown Cr

Blowdown Lake Trail

S. Cottonwood Cr

Blowdown Lake

Mt Taylor 2318 m

Tszil Mtn 2377m

Slalok Mtn 2650m

Mt Matier 2770m

Vantage Peak 2230m

Twin One Glacier

Twin One Lake

Mt Duke 2380m

VAN Cr

HORLICK

HORLICK CREEK

North Seudamore Cr

Stein Valley

Duffey Peak 2230m

Tszil Ridge

Twin Goat Mtn 2130m

Br 30

Snowspider Mtn

Twin One Creek

3-16

Van Horlick Pass

North Horlick Ridge

Nlaka'pamux Heritage

McCulloch Cr

Lillooet Lake

Br 10

TWIN ONE CR MAIN

gate

Twin One Creek Rec Site

12km

Twin Two Cr

Twin Two Peak 2351m

Storm Peak 2460m

Brimstone Mtn 2220m

North Stein River

Stein Trail

Provincial Park

See Map 30

private resort & campground

+/-200m

Lizzie Bay Rec Site

16km

Meadow Dome 2250m

Battleship Lake

Meditation Mtn 2520m

Brimstone Lake

Lindisfarne Mtn 2490m

Auroa Peak 2400m

Stein River

See Map 32

Driftwood Bay Rec Site

Br 2

FSR

LIZZIE Cr

4wd access only

Priory Peaks

2-10

Stein River

Snake Falls

Stein Lake

Elton Lake Route

Bella Vista Ridge

No Camp Lake

Siamese Twins

EAST FORK

Tundra Lake

Pyramidal Peak 2115m

Elton Lake

Elton Falls

IN-SHUCK-IN

Lizzie Peak

Onion Ridge

Lizzie Falls

Whisky Peak 2000m

Anemone Peak 2255m

Stein Divide Trail

Cherry Pip Pass

Calthar Lake

Iceberg Lake

Figure Eight Lake

Lizzie Creek Rec Site & Trail

cabin

Arrowhead Mtn 2165m

Tao Peak

Wild

Dragonfly Lake

Tarn Peak

Doctor's Ridge

Arrowhead Lake

Long Lake

Snake Lake

Tynemouth Mtn 2195m

Long Peak

Rainbow Lake

Mt Skook Jim 2605m

Mt Klackarpun 2605m

Salamander Mtn

Tao Lake

falls

Shields Peak 2100m

Crystal Lakes

Diversion Peak

Vanguard Peak 2190m

Crevasse Crag 2485m

Little Lillooet Lake

Hanging Mist Peak

Cloudraker Mtn 2390m

Ridge

Famine

Mehatl Creek

Dewdrop Lake

Salamander Lake

Allenby Cr

Rogers Creek

ROGERS CREEK FSR

Nahatlatch Creek

Mehatl River

3-15

Provincial Park

SOUTH TENAS Rd

Lillooet River

See Map 22

Lillooet Lake

122°30'   540,000m E   122°25'   122°20'   550,000m E   122°15'   122°10'   560,000m E

1.5km   0km   3km

31

SWBC Maps

N

See Map 41

See Map 31

See Map 33

122° 05'
122° 00'
121° 55'
121° 50'
121° 45'

570,000m E
580,000m E
590,000m E

5,580,000m N
50° 20'
5,570,000m N
50° 15'
5,560,000m N
50° 10'
5,550,000m N
50° 05'

Three Summits Campsite

MINE
Rd

South Fork Cottonwood

Silver Queen Mine

Silver Queen Mine Campsite

Cottonwood Creek

Cottonwood Creek

Cattle Valley Trail

Blueberry/ Blackberry Hollow

Siwhe Mtn 2855m

Inkoiko Creek

Stein Mtn 2625m

Mesomy Lake Campsite

Evenglow Mtn

Stein

North

Seudamoil Creek

Ponderosa Shelter

River

Ponderosa Shelter

suspension bridge

Stl. Canoe Landing Kltlal Cabin

Valley

Rowat Crossing Campsite

Unnessary Knob

Kent

Petlushkwohä Creek

pictograph Trail

Earl's Cabin

Devil's Staircase

Nlaka'pamux

Kent Lake

Ponlem Cabin site

Stein

Doss

Nesbitt Creek

Heritage

Petlushkwohap Mtn 2957m

Earl Creek

Stryen Cr Trail

Akasik Mtn 2455m

Grizzly Creek

Raven Flats

Doss Peak Lakes

3-16

Cantilever

Provincial

Mt Roach 2643m

Avalanche Cr Camp

Look-out Camp

Upper Canyon

Island Camp

Skihist Mtn 2965m

Range

Park

Stryen Creek East Br

Nikaia Mtn 2560m

Rutledge Creek

Claimpost Peak

Antimony Mtn 2650m

Antimony Lake

Eagle

North Kwoiek

NORTH

KWOIEK

Br

Doss Peak 2590m

Vesuvianite Lake

Antimony Creek

Ridge

Eagle Ridge

Kwoiek Creek

The Woodpile 2560m

Mt Nielsen

Kha Lake

KWOIEK

Kwoiek

Kfept Lake

John George Lake

CREEK

Kwoie Valley Trail

Kwoiek Creek

Kwoiek Lake

FSR

Mehatl

Rutledge Glacier

Stukolait Lake

Curd Mtn

Kokwaskey Lake

3-15

Kwoiek Peak 2690m

Kwoiek Glacier

Hanyon Peak

Chochiwa Lake

Mehatl Peak

Kumkan Peak

Kwoiek Needle 2650m

Tiara Tower

N Mehatl Creek

Tzequa Lakes

Chochiwa

Creek

Creek

Prov

Mehatl Creek

Chochiwa Glacier

Longslog Mtn

Park

Tachewana Peak

Log Creek

See Map 23

Stein River

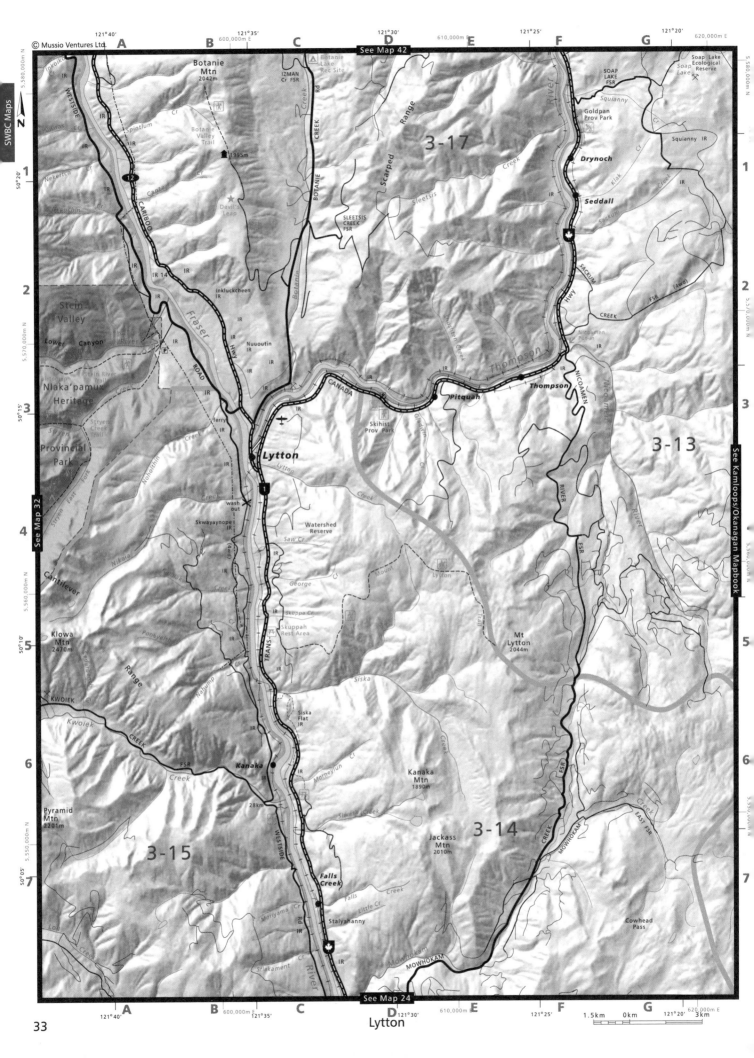

SWBC Maps

N

121°40'
121°35'
600,000m E
121°30'
610,000m E
121°25'
121°20'
620,000m E

5,580,000m N

A B C D E F G

Soap Lake
Ecological
Reserve

SOAP
LAKE
FSR

Soap
Lake

Botanie
Mtn
2042m

Squianny
Cr

Botanie
Lake
Rec Site

IZMAN
Cr FSR

Goldpan
Prov Park

Squianny IR

Scarped

River

Range

3-17

Drynoch

Sleetsis
Creek

Seddall

SLEETSIS
CREEK
FSR

SACKUM

Klak
Cr

IR

Hwy

1

50°20'

12

CARIBOO

Spintlum

IR

Devil's
Leap

1995m

Botanie Valley Trail

inkluckcheen
IR

Botanie

CREEK

Rd

5,570,000m N

2

Stein
Valley

Lower Canyon

Fraser

River

ROAD

Nuuoutin
IR

Hwy

IR

IR

IR

Shasten Creek

Thompson

Nicoamen Pot-ah

Nicoamen

SACKUM
CREEK

FSR
(4wd)

5,570,000m N

2

50°15'

3

Nlaka'pamux
Heritage

Stein River
Trail

P

ferry

IR

CANADA

IR

Gladwin
Cr

Pitquah

Thompson

Nicoamen

River

3-13

3

Provincial
Park

Stryen
Creek
Trail

Skihist
Prov Park

Lytton
Creek

Lytton

50°10'

4

Cantilever

Noholthin
Creek

Skwayaynope IR

wash out

IR

(4wd)

Watershed
Reserve

Saw Cr

Mount

Lytton

Mt
Lytton
2044m

FSR

5,560,000m N

4

5

Klowa
Mtn
2470m

Range

Poneyelhum

Nahump

TRANS.

IR

George

Skuppa Cr

Skuppah
Rest Area

Siska

Lytton
Trail

5

50°10'

KWOIEK

Kwoiek

CREEK

Cr
FSR

IR

Siska
Flat
IR

Siska
Creek

Kanaka
Mtn
1890m

Creek

3-14

MOWHOKAM

FSR

5,550,000m N

6

Pyramid
Mtn
2201m

Creek

Kanaka

Morneyiun
Cr

Siwash Creek

Jackass
Mtn
2010m

MOWHOKAM

CREEK

EAST FSR

6

7

3-15

WESTSIDE

28km

Falls
Creek

Meriyama
Cr

Falls
Creek

Little Cr

Stalyahanny

IR

Cowhead
Pass

50°05'

Loh
Creek

Siakament

Rd

IR

River

MOWHOKAM

7

A B C D E F G

121°40'
600,000m E
121°35'
121°30'
610,000m E
121°25'
121°20'
620,000m E

Lytton

1.5km 0km 3km

33

50° 40'

A **B** **C** **D** **E** **F** **G**

1

2-15

Paradise

Alpha
Bluff

Inlet

Hovel
Bay

Orford

River

5,610,000m N

2

Bute

Orford
Bay

Orford
Bay IR

Dupont

Algard

Creek

50° 35'

3

Clipper
Point

Amor
Point

2-14

Creek

See Map 35

5,600,000m N

4

Clipper

Creek

Hillis

2-13

Brem

Tosan

River

50° 30'

5

Mt
Eliza

Mt
Powell

Mt
Doogie
Dowler

Creek

Creek

Ramsay

River

Face
Mtn

Salmon Bay
IR 3

Brem
River

Mt
Barner

5,590,000m N

6

Brem
Bay

50° 25'

7

Arm

Quatam
Bay

Deep Valley
IR 5

Quatam

Range

Izela

Creek

Toba

Snout
Point

Inlet

5,580,000m N

Gastineau

See Map 25

Brem River

2-14

Mamook
Peak

Tahumming   Glacier

Headwall

Creek

Filer

Portal
Peak

Creek

Tahumming

Klite

2-13

River

River

Toba

River

Klahoose
IR 1

Little

Boyle

Toba

Boyle
Lake

Chusan

Inlet

Julian
Peak

Cr

River

Toba

Creek

Daniel's Lake

Well
Lake

Racine

River

Powell

River

Raindrop
Lake

Creek

Hat
Mnt

Alpine

Creek

2-12

Daniels

D 80

Marika
Lake

See Map 34

See Map 36

See Map 26

Toba Inlet

390,000m E

124° 30'

124° 25'
400,000m E

124° 20'

410,000m E

124° 15'

50° 40'

50° 35'

50° 30'

50° 25'

5,610,000m N

5,600,000m N

5,590,000m N

5,580,000m N

1.5 km   0 km   3 km

Mt
Argyll

Dalgleish

Creek

Mt
Dalgleish

Daldleish
Glacier

River

East

Toba

Jenni

Creek

Montrose

Marlin
Peak

Sirenia
Glacier

Sirenia
Mtn

2-13

River

Filer
Creek

Toba

Jimmie

Toba

Creek

Exit
Glacier

Albino
Glacier

Elaho

Raccoon

See Map 35

Swede Saw
Mtn

Belinda
Mtn

Plateau

Mittelberg
Mtn

See Map 37

Perin
Lake

Belinda
Lake

Raccoon
Mtn

Range

Creek

Procyon
Lake

Racoon
Lakes

Icefield

Havoc

Glacier

Elaho
Mtn

Flipper
Glacier

Wave

Teeter
Peak

Clendinning

Provincial

Blacklin
Glacier

Glacier

Beach
Mtn

Limpt
Ridge

Clendinning

Cr

Creek

Clendinning

Clendinning
Lake

Frontline
Mtn

Little

Lunar

Creek

Lunar
Pass

Doolittle

Doolittle
Glacier

2-6

Park

Toba

Terrific
Glacier

Glacier

Howitzer
Peak

Boardman
Glacier

Windiger
Mtn

Clendinning

Range

Glacier

Mt
Thomas

Whiting

Mt
Perkins

River

Ross

Arm

Pivotal
Mtn

Swiss

Arm

1.5 km
0 km
3 km

123°45'   450,000m E   123°40'   B   C   123°35'   460,000m E   D   123°30'   E   F   470,000m E   123°25'   G

A 450,000m E **A**   123°40' **B**   **C** 123°35'   460,000m E **D**   123°30' **E**   **F** 470,000m E 123°25' **G**

N

50°40'

Upper

Lillooet

Salal Creek/
Anthelney Pass
Trail

Mt
Athelstan
2770m

Obelia
Peak

Manatee

Ridge

Polychrome

Mosaic
Creek

Provincial

Keyhole
Falls

Lillooet

Keyhole Falls
(Pebble Creek)
Hot Springs

put-in

Pebble

UPPER

5,610,000m N

Plinth
Peak
2680m

Job Glacier

Mt Job

Mt
Meager
2650m

39km

Upper Lillooet
Rec Site

LILLOOET

River

FSR

Dolphin
Peak

Dolphin
Glacier

Mosaic Glacier

2-11

Capricorn
Mtn
2570m

Devastation
Glacier

Capricorn   Cr

MEAGER

Creek

50°35'

Remora
Peak

Manatee
Group

Manatee
Glacier

Park

Devastation Creek

Pylon
Peak
2470m

Devastator
Peak

Boundary Cr

Canyon Cr

Angel Creek

Pika
Peak
2530m

Dugong
Peak

2-13

Meager

Meager
Glacier

Meager
Creek

Hot Springs

Meager Creek
Hot Springs
& Rec Site

Hot Springs   Cr

Spidery
Peak
2650m

5,600,000m N

See Map 36

Meager

Meager
(Fish)
Lake

Access to
Pemberton
Icefield

Overseer
Mtn
2745m

See Map 38

50°30'

Elaho
Glacier

Elaho

Moose Pasture Cr

Meager
Trailhead

Meager Creek
Snowmobile
Area

Harrison
Hut

Ski Touring

50°30'

5,590,000m N

Thousand
Lakes
Plateau

Mist Lake
Camp

Route

Marlow   Cr

Ryan

River

Clendinning

Jackson Cr

(Elaho-
Meager
Trail)

Pierra Cr

Last Chance
Camp

Pemberton

50°25'

Provincial

2-6

Elaho

River

Wilderness

Canyon Camp

Cosna

Creek

Ski Touring

50°25'

5,580,000m N

Mt
Oswald

Park

Stoltman

Rocky
Camp

Douglas Fir
Loop

Lava
Camp

Elaho
Trailhead

Lava   Creek

Icefield

Sundown Cr

See Map 28

450,000m E   123°40' **B**   **C** 123°35'   460,000m E **D**   123°30' **E**   **F** 470,000m E 123°25' **G**

37

Meager Creek

1.5 km   0 km   3 km

123°20'

© Mussio Ventures Ltd.

See Map 43

SWBC Maps

N

HURLEY RIVER – LONE GOAT CREEK FSR (deactivated)

summer travel only

Goat   Creek

Lone

SERVICE

RIVER

50°40'

1

5,610,000m N

Pebble   (boulder)   Creek

McParlon Glacier

Pebble   Glacier

3-33

HURLEY   WEST

HURLEY   RIVER

Hurley

Hope Creek Rec Site

HOPE   CREEK

HOPE

Sugus Mtn

Sessel Mtn 2710m

HURLEY   RIVER

Donnelly Creek Rec Site

31km

FOREST

Grouty Peak 2375m

EAST HOPE CREEK NORTH FSR

2

5,610,000m N

Spindrift Mtn

Boomerang Glacier

Mt Delilah

Mt Samson 2800m

Freight   Cr

Creek

RIVER

50°35'

Blockhead Mtn

North   Creek

Delilah   Creek

Face Mtn 2490m

Rainbow Pass 1400m

Chipmunk Mtn 2330m

3

Hemionus Mtn 2260m

UPPER

LILLOOET

alpine

Train Glacier

Handcar Peak

Locomotive Mtn

3

50°35'

Pemberton

Lillooet

NORTH CREEK MAIN

NORTH CREEK MAIN EAST

Samson   Creek

Buck   Cr

HURLEY

See Map 37

Valley

FOREST

EAST

Twentyfive Mile Cr

SAMPSON   MAIN

Br 12

Goat Peak 2470m

4

5,600,000m N

See Map 39

SERVICE

Railroad

20km

Tenquille Lake Trail

Copper Mound 2165m

Creek

Mt Pauline

Mowich

50°30'

South   Creek

Mt Morrison

2-11

River

ROAD

Coast Mtn Outdoor School

Wolverine   Cr

Johnny Bend Cr

5

Lillooet

23km

50°30'

The Camels Back

6

5,590,000m N

Ryan   River

Creek

Wasp   Creek

Mt Ross

50°25'

Access to Pemberton Icefield

Petersen   Creek

Sugarloaf Mtn

7

5,580,000m N

Pemberton

Icefield

Longspur Peak

Rhododendron Mtn

Miller   Creek

50°25'

See Map 29

A 510,000m E B 122°50' C 122°45' D 520,000m E E 122°40' F G 122°35' 530,000m E

122°55'

N

Waterfalls Cr

Mt
Noel
2530m

Noel
Snowmobile
Area

NORTH
Br.

NOEL Cr

WEST NOEL Cr

NOEL Cr FSR

Chism Creek

Old
Mine

Royal
Peak

High
Trail

Mt
Piebiter

Cadwallader

Chism
Pass
Trail

3-33

Mt
Weinhold

Copp Creek

Cadwallader Creek

KINGDOM LAKE

Standard
Cr

Standard

Mt
McGillivray

McGillivray
Pass

McGillivray

McGillivray Pass FSR

High
Trail

Star
Mtn

Ridge

1

Mt
Aragorn

Mt
Shadowfax
2285m

Mt
Taillefer
2410m

Prospector
Peaks
2500m

Range

2

Mt
Gandalf

Sockeye Creek

Phelix Creek

3

Birkenhead

Lake

Mt
John Decker

Copp Creek

BLACKWATER
LAKE Rd

EAST
HOPE
CREEK
NORTH
FSR

gate

Kokanee
Spawning

Birkenhead
Lake
Loop

Anderson
IR

See Map 40

Grizzly Pass

Tenquille
Mtn
2400m

Conservation

Headquarters

Birkenhead

Tenquille
Lake Rec Site
& Cabin

Tenquille
Pass

Wilderness
Trail

Goat Lookout
Trail

Blackwater
Lake Rec
Site

Blackwater Cr

4

Tenquille Creek

Tenquille Lake

Area
Mt
McLeod

Tenquille Creek

foot
bridge

Bear
Trail

Park

1920m

TENQUILLE
CREEK Rd

Birkenhead

Lake

(Proposed
Trail)

Mt
Barbour
2285m

Gingerbread
Lake

Sun God
Mtn
2410m

Cerulean
Lake

Provincial

Birkenhead
Peak
2525m

Gates

Gates River

5

Seven O'Clock
Mtn

Tenas Creek

Taillefer Creek

Lindsborough
Whistering
Falls
resort &
campground

gate

3-16

2-11

Ogre
Lake

Fowl Creek

Birkenhead

Birkenhead
Lake
Loop
(Sea to Sky
Trail)

LAKE

Birken

Gates Lake

Mt
Ronayne

Mount Ronayne Trail

River

FSR

Place
Falls

Place Creek

6

Fowl
Lake

Gates
Peak
2380m

Pemberton Rd

Lillooet

Owl
Lake

Watershed

Owl Lake Trail

Place Creek
Trail

A-Frame

Mt
Gardiner
2380m

Place
Glacier

PEMBERTON MEADOWS Rd

Owl Lake
Rec Site

Reserve

Owl
Lake
Chain

Spetch
Creek
Rec Site

Mt
Olds
2468m

Place Glacier
Ridge Route

Cirque
Peak
2500m

7

Pemberton
Meadows

Owl Creek

Salmon
Spawning

Creekside

Spetch Creek

Eight Mile Creek

Mt
Fraser

OWL Cr

Birkenhead River

Saxifrage
Peak
2500m

39

122°55' A 510,000m E B 122°50' C 122°45' D 520,000m E E 122°40' F 122°35' G 530,000m E

1.5km 0km 3km

Birkenhead Lake

SWBC Maps

N

See Map 45

Seton Lake IR

Seton Lake

Seton Portage

Whitecap Mtn 2911m

3-33

Whitecap R.

Seton R.

Spider Cr

Machute Creek

Seton Ridge Trail

Copper Creek

Cinnamon Creek

Anderson Lake

Valley Creek

Range

CREEK Rd

DOWNTON

Creek

McGillivray Pass Trail

McGillivray Creek

bridge out

private

McGillivray Pt ★ pictographs

★ pictographs

★ pictographs

Wade Cr

Lost Creek

3-16

Downton Creek

See Map 41

See Map 39

D'Arcy

Anderson IR

Nequatque IR

Pinney Cr

Young Cr

John Cr

Gott Creek Rec Site

Gott Creek

Roger Creek Rec Site

one lane bridges

GOTT Rd

gravel quarry

Devine

Gates River Spawning Channel

Gates R.

Blackwater Cr

Spruce Creek

Haylmore Creek

Cayoosh

Twin Lakes

Melvin Lake

Melvin Creek

Melvin Creek

99

ROAD

Nequatque Lake

Nequatque Mtn 2650m

Mt Marriott 2748m

Elliot Creek

Blackwater Trail

Common Johnny Cr

Cayoosh Channel Creek

Gott Creek

deactivated road

P

Duffey Lake Pass Trailhead

Blowdown Creek Trail

BLOWDOWN

Seven Mile Cr

Marriott Basin Trail

Rohr Lake

Rohr Lake Trail

Mt Rohr 2440m

Duffey Lake Prov Park

Duffey Lake

STEEP Cr Rd

G. MAIN

Stein Valley Nlaka'pamux Heritage Prov Park

Cayoosh Mtn 2590m

alpine

Cayoosh Pass

99 DUFFEY

JOFFRE

Cayoosh Cr M

CERISE

VAN HORLICK MAIN

Blowdown Pass

See Map 31

1.5 km 0km 3 km

Anderson Lake

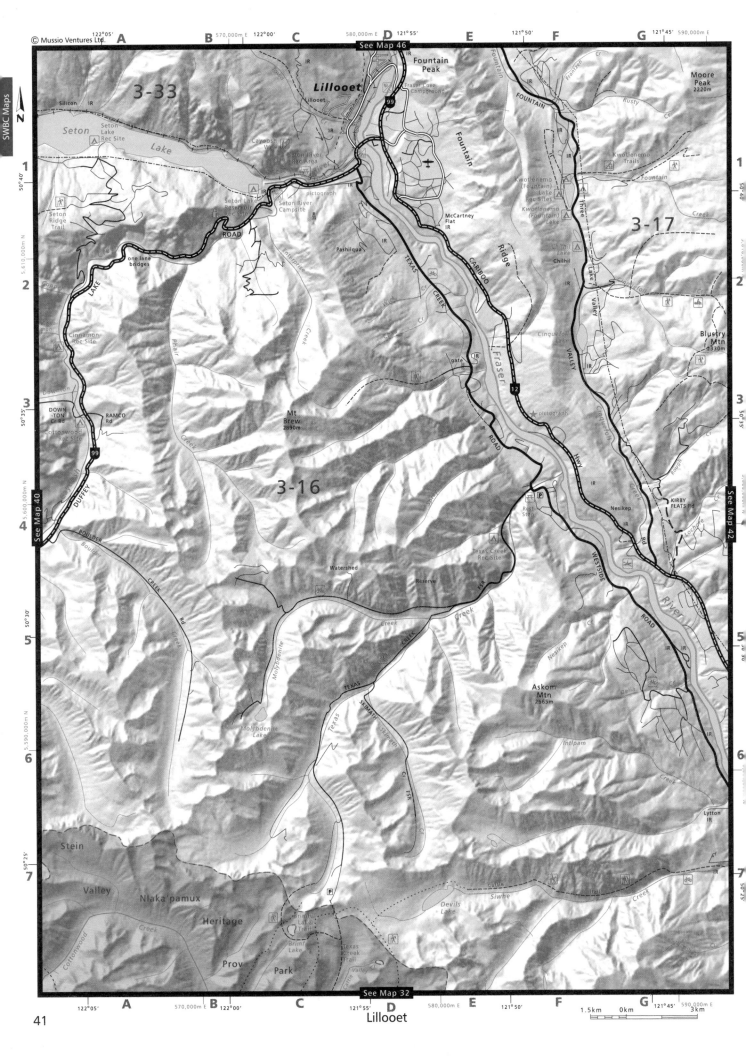

N

A   570,000m E   122°00'   C   580,000m E   D   121°55'   E   121°50'   F   G   121°45'   590,000m E

122°05'

See Map 46

3-33

Lillooet

Fountain Peak

Moore Peak
2220m

Silicon IR

Seton Lake Rec Site

Seton
Lake

Lillooet

Fraser Cove Campground

99

FOUNTAIN

Rusty Cr

Kwotlenemo Trails

Seton Ridge Trail

Cayoosh
Seton River Rec Area

pictograph

Fountain

Kwotlenemo (Fountain) Lake Rec Sites

Kwotlenemo (Fountain) Lake

3-17

Seton Lake Reservoir Rec Site

Seton River Campsite

McCartney Flat IR

Chilhil Lake

Chilhil

ROAD

Pashilqua

3-17

LAKE

Cinnamon Rec Site

Mt Brew
2890m

gate

Fraser

12

CARIBOO

Ridge

Cinquefoil Lake

VALLEY

Blustry Mtn
2330m

DOWN-TON Rd

RAMCO Rd

Cottonwood Rec Site

99

3-16

ROAD

IR

pictograph

Cinquefoil Creek

Hwy

KIRBY FLATS Rd

See Map 40

DUFFEY

Rest Stop

P

Nesikep

Lochore

See Map 42

BOULDER

Boulder

Texas Creek Rec Site

WESTSIDE

CREEK

Watershed

Reserve

Nesikep Creek

Rd

Rd

Creek

River

ROAD

Molybdenite

Askom Mtn
2565m

Pella

Molybdenite Lake

TEXAS

SKIMATH Skimath Cr

Intlpam Creek

Texas

Texas FSR

Lytton IR

Stein

Valley

Nlaka'pamux

Heritage

Devils Lake

Siwhe Creek

Cattle

P

Brimful Lake Trail

Prov

Park

Brimful Lake

Texas Creek Trail

Cattle Valley

See Map 32

122°05'   A   570,000m E   B   122°00'   C   121°55'   D   580,000m E   E   121°50'   F   G   121°45'   590,000m E

Lillooet

1.5 km   0 km   3 km

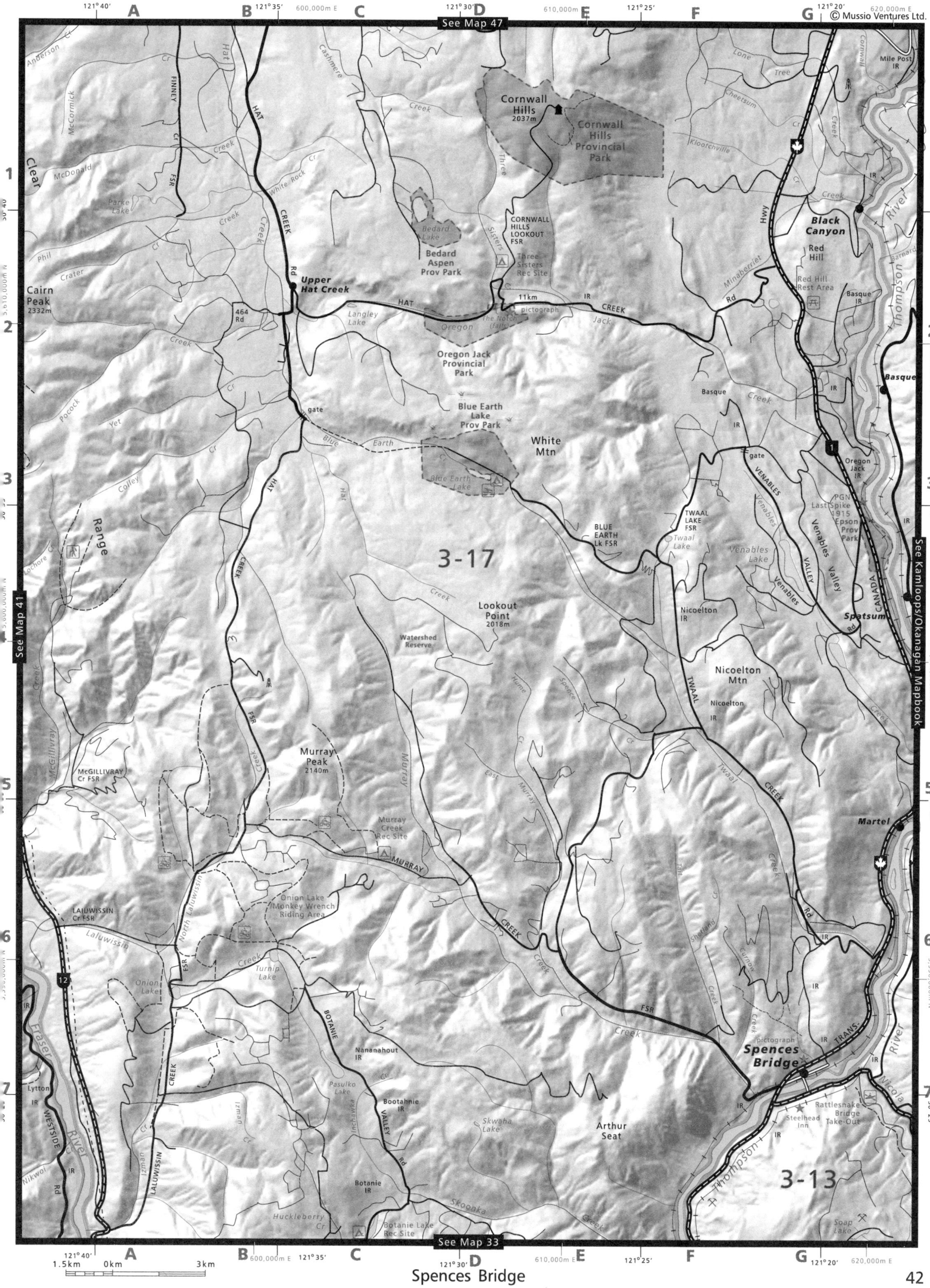

© Mussio Ventures Ltd.

SWBC Maps

N

A 121°40' **B** 121°35' 600,000m E **C** **D** 121°30' **E** 610,000m **F** 121°25' **G** 121°20' 620,000m E

Anderson Cr

Clear

McCormick

FINNEY

McDonald

HAT

Cr

Parke Lake

White Rock

CREEK

Cashmere Creek

Creek

Cornwall Hills 2037m

Cornwall Hills Provincial Park

Phil

Crater

Cairn Peak 2332m

Three

Sisters

Cr

Bedard Lake

Bedard Aspen Prov Park

CORNWALL HILLS LOOKOUT FSR

Three Sisters Rec Site

Lone

Tree

Cheetsum

Kloorchville

Creek

Black Canyon

Red Hill

Red Hill Rest Area

Basque

Thompson

River

Barnard

Hwy

IR

464 Rd

Upper Hat Creek

HAT

Rd

Langley Lake

Oregon

11km pictograph

Jack

CREEK

The Notch (falls)

Minaberriet Rd

Basque

IR

Basque Creek

Pocock

Yet

Cr

gate

Blue Earth

Oregon Jack Provincial Park

Blue Earth Lake Prov Park

White Mtn

IR

gate

VENABLES

Oregon Jack IR

Last Spike 915 Epson Prov Park

Colley

Cr

HAT

Range

Blue Earth Lake

BLUE EARTH Lk FSR

TWAAL LAKE FSR

Twaal Lake

Venables

Venables VALLEY

Venables Lake

CANADA

Spatsum Rd

See Kamloops/Okanagan Mapbook

3-17

Creek

Lookout Point 2018m

Watershed Reserve

Nicoelton IR

Nicoelton Mtn

Nicoelton IR

CREEK

McGilivray

McGILLIVRAY Cr FSR

Murray Peak 2140m

CREEK

FSR

Murray

Hume

East

Spence

Murray

TWAAL

Twaal

CREEK

Martel

Murray Creek Rec Site

MURRAY

LAIUWISSIN Cr FSR

North Laiuwissin

Onion Lake Monkey Wrench Riding Area

Laiuwissin

Creek

CREEK

FSR

Spatsum

Creek

IR

12

Fraser

River

Onion Lake

Turnip Lake

BOTANIE

Izman

Cr

Nananahout IR

CREEK

Pasulko Lake

FSR

Creek

pictograph

IR

Spences Bridge

TRANS-

Lytton IR

WESTSIDE

River

LALUWISSIN

Nikwoi Rd

Bootahnie IR

Skwaha Lake

Arthur Seat

Steelhead Inn

Rattlesnake Bridge Take-Out

Thompson

Nicola

3-13

Botanie IR

BOTANIE VALLEY

Inchawaa

Skookana

Creek

Botanie Lake Rec Site

Huckleberry Cr

Soap Lake

A 121°40' **B** 600,000m E 121°35' **C** **D** 121°30' **E** 610,000m **F** 121°25' **G** 121°20' 620,000m E

1.5km 0km 3km

N

5-4

3-32

3-33

See Chilcotin Mapbook

See Map 44

See Map 38

Porteau
Mtn
2741m

Warner
Glacier

Warner
Lake

Wilson

Gun

Ridge

Taylor
Pass

Gun Creek

Dear
Pass
Trail

Mt
Sheba
2665m

Sheba

WD
Trail

Greasy Hill
Trail

Spruce
Lake Cr
Trail

Spruce
Lake North
Rec Site

Spruce
Lake East

Trigger
Lake Rec Site

Spruce

Lake

Hummingbird
Lake Rec Site

Lower
Grasslands
Trail

Cowboy
Camp

Tyax
Camp

Upper
Grasslands Trail

Copper
Mtn
2606m

Wolverine
Pass

Leckie
Lake

Leckie

Leckie
Peak

Range

Leckie Creek

CREEK

Slim Creek
Snowmobile
Area

Rd

Socerer
Glacier

Upper

Slim

Creek

Slim

Slim
Mtn

Pequet

Recreation

SLIM

Nichols

Creek

Dickson

Area

Range

Dickson
Peak
2811m

Roxey

Roxey
Creek
Trail

Mt
Penrose
2627m

Penrose

Ipoo
Mtn

Scherle
Peak

Porcupine
Mtn

(closed to
motor vehicles)

Bridge

River

±747m

Lake

Downton

RIVER

BRIDGE

FSR

gate
bridge
out

McParlon

Creek

3-33

Mt
Ethelweard
2743m

Mt
Vayu
2723m

Mt
Vayu
Trail

The Frost
Fiend

The
Frost
Fiend
Trail

Mt
Sloan
2723m

Ault

Creek

Ault Creek
Trail

Fasp
Mtn

Thiassi
Glacier

Surfusion
Glacier

Mount
Thiassi
Trail

Mt
Thiassi

Lone
Goat

Lone
Goat
Snowmobile
Area

Creek

HURLEY RIVER
-LONE GOAT FSR

Lone Goat

43

Spruce Lake

1.5km   0km   3km

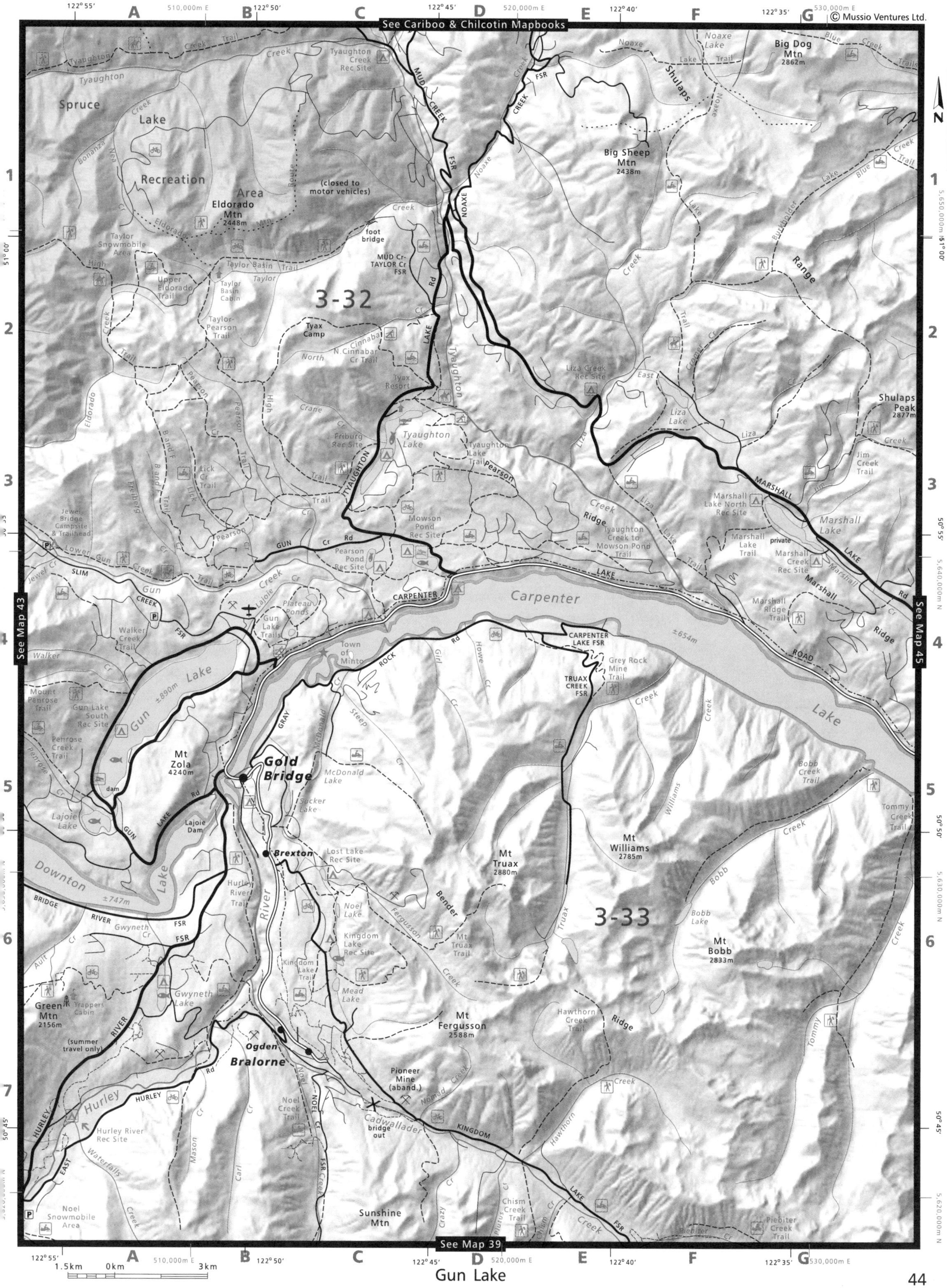

© Mussio Ventures Ltd.

See Cariboo & Chilcotin Mapbooks

N

122° 55'   A   510,000m E   B   122° 50'   C   122° 45'   D   520,000m E   E   122° 40'   F   122° 35'   G   530,000m E

Spruce Lake Recreation Area

Tyaughton Creek

Tyaughton

Bonanza Cr

Nea Cr

Eldorado Mtn 2448m

Taylor Snowmobile Area

High

Upper Eldorado Trail

Taylor Basin Cabin

Taylor Basin Trail

Taylor

Taylor-Pearson Trail

Eldorado

Pearson

B and E

Freiburg

Tick Cr Trail

Jewel Bridge Campsite & Trailhead

Lower Gun

SLIM

Gun CREEK

Walker Creek Trail

Walker

Mount Penrose Trail

Penrose Creek Trail

Lajoie Lake

Downton

BRIDGE

RIVER

FSR

Gwyneth Cr

Aurl

Green Mtn 2156m

Trappers Cabin

(summer travel only)

Gwyneth Lake

HURLEY

Hurley River Rec Site

Waterfalls

EAST

Noel Snowmobile Area

122° 55'   A   510,000m E   B   122° 50'   C

3-32

Tyax Camp

North

N. Cinnabar Cr Trail

Crane

Tyax Resort

Friburg Rec Site

Tyaughton Lake

Mowson Pond Rec Site

Tyaughton Lake Trail

Pearson

GUN

Cr Rd

Pearson Pond Rec Site

CARPENTER

Gun Lake Trails

Plateau Ponds

Gun Lake

Town of Minto

McDonald Lake

Gold Bridge

Mt Zola 4240m

dam

Lajoie Dam

Brexton

Tucker

Lost Lake Rec Site

Hurley River Trail

Noel Lake

Kingdom Lake Rec Site

Kingdom Lake

Mead Lake

Ogden

Bralorne

Rd

Pioneer Mine (aband.)

Cadwallader bridge out

Noel Creek Trail

NOEL

KINGDOM

Sunshine Mtn

foot bridge

MUD Cr-TAYLOR Cr FSR

(closed to motor vehicles)

MUD CREEK

NOAXE

FSR

Tyaughton

LAKE

Rd

Liza Creek Rec Site

East

Liza Lake

MARSHALL

Creek Ridge

Tyaughton Creek to Mowson Pond Trail

Carpenter

Carpenter Lake

CARPENTER LAKE FSR

Grey Rock Mine Trail

TRUAX CREEK FSR

ROCK

GRAY

Cr

McDonald

Steep

Girl

Howe

Rd

Bender

Mt Truax 2880m

Mt Truax Trail

Fergusson

Mt Fergusson 2588m

Crazy

3-33

Truax

Williams

Mt Williams 2785m

Bobb

Bobb Creek Trail

Bobb Lake

Mt Bobb 2833m

Hawthorn Creek Trail

Ridge

Hawthorn

Noaxe Lake

Big Dog Mtn 2862m

Shulaps

Blue Cr

Big Sheep Mtn 2438m

Burkholder

Range

Shulaps Peak 2877m

Jim Creek Trail

Marshall Lake North Rec Site

private

Marshall Lake

Marshall Lake Trail

Marshall Creek Rec Site

Marshall Ridge Trail

ROAD

Marshall

Ridge

Lake

Williams Creek

Bobb

Tommy Creek Trail

Tommy

Kingdom Creek

Chism Creek Trail

Plecius Cr

Piebiter Creek Trail

± 890m   Gun Lake

± 747m

± 654m

See Map 43

See Map 45

See Map 39

Gun Lake

1.5km   0km   3km

122° 55'   A   510,000m E   B   122° 50'   C   122° 45'   D   520,000m E   E   122° 40'   F   122° 35'   G   530,000m E

5,650,000m N   51° 00'

50° 55'   5,640,000m N

5,630,000m N   50° 50'

50° 45'   5,620,000m N

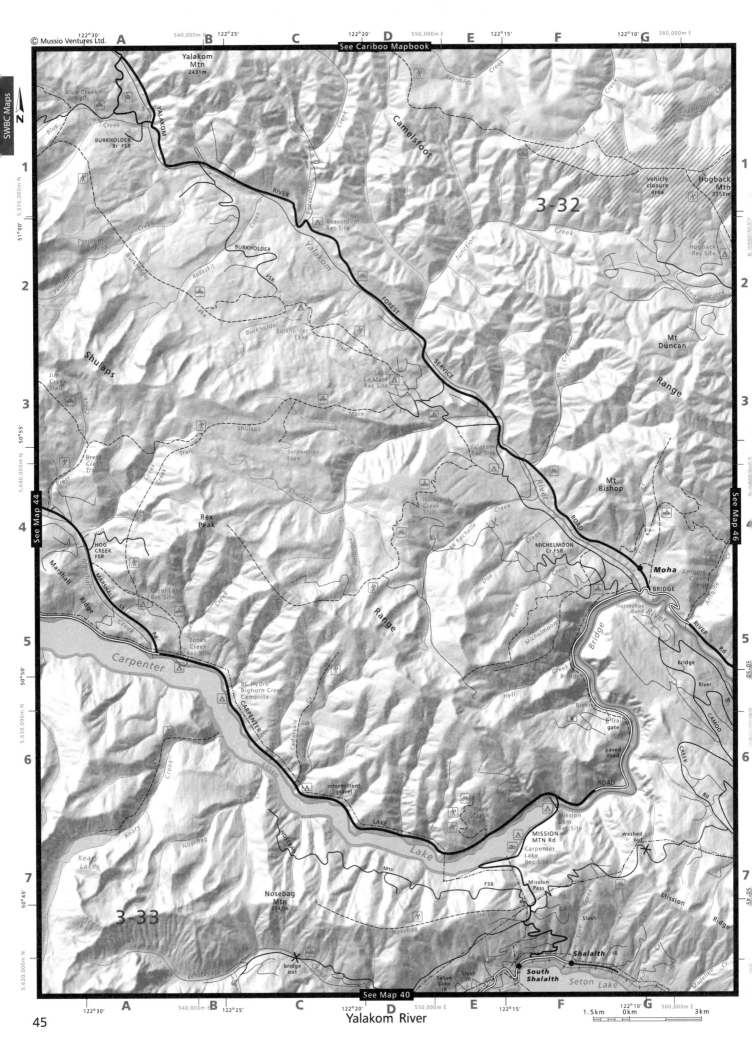

© Mussio Ventures Ltd.

SWBC Maps

N

3-32

3-33

Yalakom
Mtn
2431m

Hogback
Mtn
2155m

Mt
Duncan

Camelsfoot

Shulaps
Range

Mt
Bishop

BURKHOLDER
Br FSR

Beaverdam
Rec Site

BURKHOLDER

Jim
Creek
Trail

Brett
Creek
Trail

Peridotite
Lake

Burkholder
Lake

Lake
La Mare
Rec Site

Yalakom
Rec Site

Serpentine
Lake

Shulaps
Trail

Rex
Peak

Holbrook
Creek
Trail

MICHELMOON
Cr FSR

Moha

BRIDGE

HOG
CREEK
FSR

Marshall
Ridge

Carol Lake
Rec Site

Horseshoe
Bend

Jones
Creek
Rec Site

Carpenter

BC Hydro
Bighorn Creek
Campsite

Keary
Lake

Kwoiek
Creek

Nosebag
Mtn
2242m

intermittent
gravel

Viera
Creek
Site

Mission Dam
Rec Site

MISSION
MTN Rd

Carpenter
Lake
Rec Site

paved
road

washed
out

Lake

ROAD

FSR

Mission
Pass

Shalalth

South
Shalalth

Seton Lake

See Map 44

See Map 46

bridge
out

Whitecap

45

Yalakom River

1.5km   0km   3km

SWBC Maps

N

A **B** 570,000m E **C** **D** 580,000m E **E** **F** **G** 590,000m E

122°05' 122°00' 121°55' 121°50' 121°45'

Edge

Hills

3-31

Marble Range
Prov Park

Clinton

Kelly Lake

Provincial

Park

KELLY LAKE Rd

51°00'

5,650,000m N

vehicle
closure
area

FSR

Leon
Creek
IR

Downing
Provincial
Park

Pearl
Lake

Hambrook

Harman
Lake

Marble

CREEK

Camelsfoot

LEON CREEK

Leon Creek

Fraser

Rail

Mt
Carson

Range

50°55'

5,640,000m N

3-32

Slok
Hill

Moran

BC

PAVILION

Gillon Rd

Milkranch Cr

Clark Cr

Antoine Creek Trail

See Map 45

Range

Slok

FSR

IR

Pavilion
IR

CLINTON

Hwy

Pavilion

Pavilion

TOM

Marble
Canyon
Demo Forest

Maria Cr

Felix

See Map 47

5,630,000m N

50°50'

24.5km

BRIDGE

intermittent
gravel

Applespring

Backhill

Creek

River

99

CARIBOO

Tiffin

Mt
Cole

COLE

MTN

TOM COLE
COLE Cr FSR

FSR

Marble
Canyon
Prov Park

pictograph

Lake

CAMOO
Cr Rd

Bridge

RIVER

Bridge

River

Camoo Cr

IR

SLOK-CAMEL FSR

FSR

PAVILION

IR

TIFFIN

Keatley Cr

Sallus

Creek

FSR

Mt
Martley

3-17

Moon
Lake Trail

Moon
Lake

3-33

Chilcotin

ROAD

WEST

IR

IR

Fountain

Bridge
River
Rapids

Lillooet

Dickey

Ranges

pictograph

IR

IR

Fountain
IR

Kettle

Fountain
IR

Gibbs Cr

Finney Cr

Chipuin Mtn
2168m

Chipuin Brook

Mission

Mt
McLean
2435m

Ridge

Moon

Creek

IR

IR

FOUNTAIN
VALLEY Rd

50°45'

5,620,000m N

A **B** 570,000m **C** **D** 580,000m E **E** **F** **G** 590,000m E

122°05' 122°00' 121°55' 121°50' 121°45'

1.5km 0km   3km

Pavilion

46

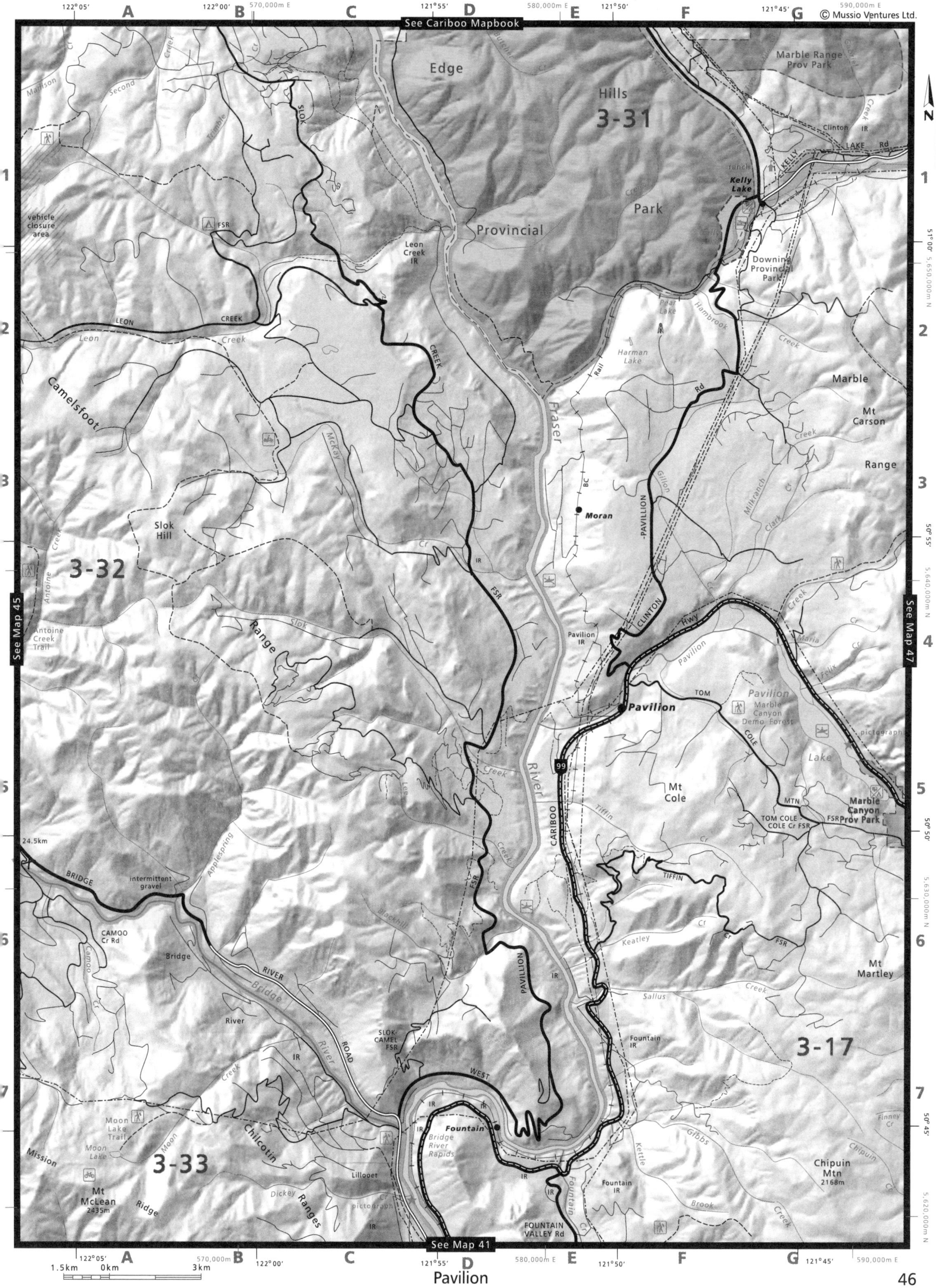

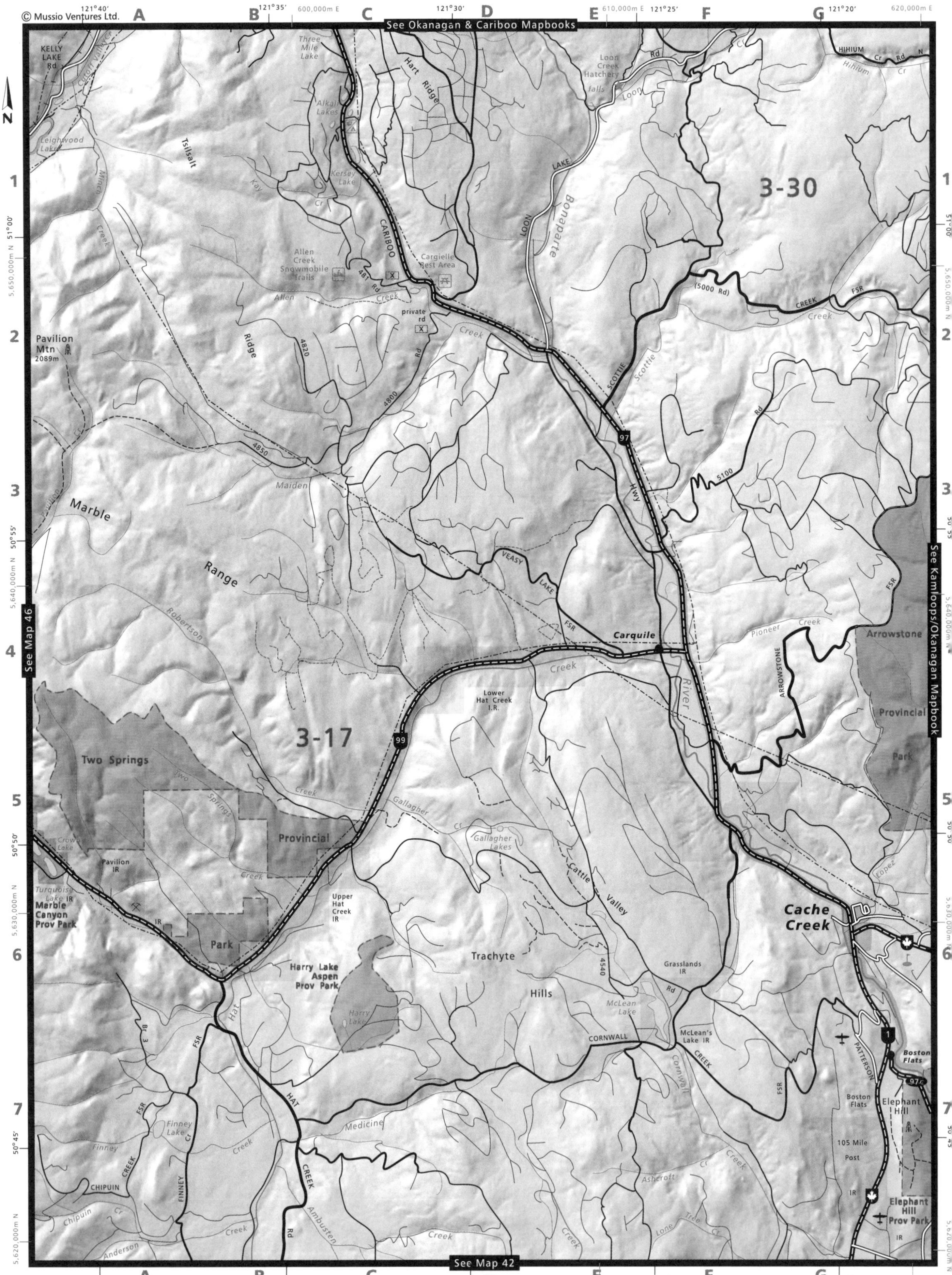

121°40'
121°35'
600,000m E
121°30'
610,000m E
121°25'
121°20'
620,000m E

A   **B**   **C**   **D**   **E**   **F**   **G**

KELLY LAKE Rd

Three Mile Lake

Loon Creek Hatchery falls

HIHIUM Cr Rd

Hihium Cr

3-30

Leighwood Lake

Tsilsalt

Kay Cr

Alkali Lakes

Hart Ridge

LOON LAKE Rd

Bonaparte

51°00'

5,650,000m N

CARIBOO

Kersey Lake

Cargielle Rest Area

CREEK FSR

(5000 Rd)

SCOTTIE

Pavilion Mtn
2089m

Ridge

Allen Creek Snowmobile Trails

4820

4870 Rd

private rd

Creek

97 Hwy

Scottie Rd

Allen Creek

X

X

Creek

50°55'

5,640,000m N

4800

Maiden

VEASY LAKE

5100

Marble

4850

FSR

Arrowstone

Pioneer Creek

ARROWSTONE FSR

See Map 46

Range

Robertson

Carquile

Creek

River

Provincial Park

See Kamloops/Okanagan Mapbook

Two Springs

Lower Hat Creek I.R.

99

Creek

3-17

Creek

50°50'

5,630,000m N

Crown Lake

Pavilion IR

Two Springs Creek

Provincial

Gallagher

Cr

Gallagher Lakes

Cattle

Valley

Cache Creek

Turquoise Lake IR

Marble Canyon Prov Park

IR

Park

Upper Hat Creek IR

Harry Lake Aspen Prov Park

Harry Lake

Trachyte

Hills

4540

McLean Lake

Grasslands IR Rd

McLean's Lake IR

1

PATTERSON

Boston Flats

Hat

FSR

CORNWALL

Cornwall

Cr

Boston Flats

97

50°45'

5,620,000m N

E&B

FSR

FSR

Finney Lake

Medicine

Hat

CREEK

Ambusten Rd

Creek

Asheroft

Cr

Lone Tree Cr

FSR

105 Mile Post

Elephant Hill

Chipuin

CHIPUIN

FINNEY CREEK Cr

Finney Cr

Creek

Anderson

Chipuin Cr

Creek

IR

Elephant Hill Prov Park

IR

121°40'
121°35'
600,000m E
121°30'
610,000m E
121°25'
121°20'
620,000m E

A   **B**   **C**   **D**   **E**   **F**   **G**

1.5km   0km   3km

Service Providers

Accommodations

Buck Mountain Campground

Beautiful river side campground. 50 sites, small swimming lake, portable water, fire rings, picnic tables, outhouses, dog run. Showers & washroom facilities available for group bookings.

Mile 20, Upper Squamish Valley Road
Squamish, BC
604-898-4633

www.elahoadventures.com

Fraser Cove Campground

Full hook-up sites, Waterfront, Hot showers, Scooter rental, Cabin rental, and more.
David Rd (off Hwy 99)
Lillooet, BC

250-256-0142
www.frasercove.com

Small campground, BIG fish

Gold Bridge Hotel

Our scenic mountainous valley offers goldpanning, fishing, hunting, snowmobiling, hiking, biking and horseback riding. Rooms, home cooked meals and a Big Screen in the bar. All major credit cards. Reservations recommended.
General Delivery
Gold Bridge, BC V0K 1P0
Phone/Fax: **250-238-2343**

Heritage Valley Resort & R.V. Park
On Sumas Mountain, Abbotsford

30 acres of wilderness, gardens & ponds with rustic heritage buildings make this the perfect setting for any occasion. Weddings & banquets, retreats, reunions & camping. Serviced sites, indoor tennis, pool, jacuzzi, showers, laundry, dormitory & 1911 C.P.R Station.

4709 Willet Rd, Abbotsford, B.C, V3G 2E8
Toll free 1-866-864-8887
www.heritagevalley.com

Lillooet Lake Lodge

Charming, comfortable cabins on the lake, breathtaking views, Joffre & Lizzie lakes and hotsprings nearby.

PO Box 75
Pemberton, BC V0N 2L0
1-604-905-9246
http://lillooetlakelodge.cottagelink.com/

Othello Tunnels Campground & RV Park

Open all year. Full, Partial H/ups & Tent Sites

67851 Othello Rd
Hope, BC V0X 1L1

1-877-869-0543
www.othellotunnels.com

Tours & Guides

Awesome Wilderness Adventures
Premier wilderness expeditions in BC:

Sea kayaking, multi-activity adventures, 4X4 eco-safaris, whitewater rafting and mountain biking. 1-7 day scheduled and custom trips. Open year round. Novices & families welcome.

Vancouver, BC
Toll Free 1-877-736-2147
www.awesomekayak.com
www.canadian-expeditions.com

Bridge River Fishing Adventures

Come and experience one of B.C.'s best kept secrets!
Fly- in guided fishing trips, gear rentals & adventure packages. Spring and fall specials.

General Delivery
Gold Bridge, BC V0K 1P0
250-238-2346
www.fishing.bc.ca

Canadian Snowmobile and Canadian All Terrain Adventures

Year Round Snowmobile and ATV Adventures. Guided and Private Adventures to Whistler/ Blackcomb, Callaghan Valley and Bralorne.

4282 Mountain Square
Whistler, BC V0N 1B4
1-877-938-1616
www.canadiansnowmobile.com

Cross Country Connection
Whistler

Skiing & Biking
Snowshoeing-Naturewalks
Instruction-Rentals-Tours-Service
Find us on the trails in Lost Lake Park

604-905-0071

www.crosscountryconnection.bc.ca

Elaho Adventures

Only an hour away from both Vancouver and Whistler, our pristine river side location in the Upper Squamish Valley allows guests to raft various classes of river and experience spectacular west coast backcountry.

For more information call

1-800-713-7238 or visit

www.elahoadventures.com

Gravity Fed Adventures Ltd

Mountain bike tours, Helicopter Bike descent (7000 ft), Cabin to Cabin all singletrack high mountain bicycle extravaganza.

Lillooet and Goldbridge

250-238-0170

www.gravityfedadventures.com

Kumsheen Rafting Resort

An upscale whitewater rafting company and adventure resort on the Thompson River near Lytton, BC.

Highway #1 6km East of Lytton
Lytton, BC V0K 1Z0

1-800-663-6667

www.kumsheen.com

Questlinks Outdoor Traveler

From local parks, attractions & activities, to adventure businesses, accommodations and more.
Search, Find, Plan, Share, Add
-Create your own customized QuestGuide
-GPS data exchange

www.QUESTLINKS.com

REO Rafting Resort

World Class III-V Rafting
Hot Tub, Sauna, Massage
Cabins and Camping

604-461-7238
1-800-736-7238

www.reorafting.com

Slipstream Rock & Ice Guides

Specializing in first time rock climbing for groups & families at our private cliffs. Instruction and guiding for all abilities.

Box 219 Paradise Valley Road
Squamish, BC, V0N 1H0

1-800-616-1325
WWW.GETCLIMBING.COM

Takaya Tours

First Nation interpretive ocean-going canoe adventures. Kayaking rentals, lessons and tours. All fitness levels welcome. Fun for everyone. May to October.

3093 Ghum-Lye Drive
North Vancouver, BC V7H 2V6
604-904-7410
www.takayatours.com

Tube-it Flyfishing Adventures

Flyfish the Sunshine Coast for Coho salmon or Cutthroat trout. All inclusive trip to Cariboo, Chilcotin for trophy rainbow. Also flyfishing lessons.

RR #6 1517 Langdale Rd
Gibsons, BC V0N 1V6

1-604-886-1409

Important Numbers

General
BC Ferries 1-888-223-3779
Highways Report 1-800-550-4997
Sea to Sky Corridor .... (604) 893-2411
To Report Forest Fires 1-800-663-5555
....*5555 (cellular phones)
Tourism BC 1-800-435-5622
....www.hellobc.com
Updates... http://www.backroadmapbooks.com/bmupdates.htm
Weather Conditions ....
....................http://www.weatheroffice.ec.gc.ca/canada_e.html

BC Forest Service (Road & Trail Conditions)
Ministry of Forests.............................http://www.gov.bc.ca/for/
Chilliwack Forest District............................. (604) 702-5700
Cascades Forest District .... (250) 256-1200
Squamish Forest District .... (604) 898-2100
Sunshine Coast Forest District .... (604) 485-0700

Fish & Wildlife
Fish and Wildlife Conservation
Observe, Record and Report 1-800-663-9453
Sport Fishing Information .... http://www.sportfishing.bc.ca
Conservation Officers
Chilliwack..(604) 795-8422
Lillooet ....(250) 256-4636
Maple Ridge ....(604) 465-4011
Squamish..(604) 892-5971
Surrey...(604) 582-5200

Parks
BC Parks.............. http://wlapwww.gov.bc.ca/bcparks/index.htm
Garibaldi/Sunshine Coast District ....(604) 898-3678
Lower Mainland District ....(604) 582-5200
Park Reservations......................................(604) 689-9025
1-800-689-9025
www.discovercamping.ca
Thompson River District..............................250) 851-3000
Regional Parks
GVRD Parks ....(604) 432-6350
FVRD Parks .... (604) 702-5000 or 1-800-528-0061

Other Numbers
BC Hydro ....www.bchydro.bc.ca/environment
Canada West Mountain School ....(604) 737-3053

Backroad Mapbooks
www.backroadmapbooks.com

Index